POSTMODERNISM AND
POPULAR CULTURE

POSTMODERNISM AND POPULAR CULTURE

A Cultural History

JOHN DOCKER

CAMBRIDGE
UNIVERSITY PRESS

Published by the Press Syndicate of the University of Cambridge
The Pitt Building, Trumpington Street, Cambridge CB2 IRP, UK
40 West 20th Street, New York, NY 10011–4211, USA
10 Stamford Road, Oakleigh, Melbourne 3166, Australia

First published 1994

Printed in Australia by Brown Prior Anderson

National Library of Australia cataloguing-in-publication data
Docker, John, 1945-
Postmodernism and popular culture.
Includes index.
1. Popular culture. 2. Postmodernism. 3. Postmodernism –
Australia. 4. Popular culture – Australia. I. Title.
306.40994

Library of Congress cataloguing-in-publication data
Docker, John.
Postmodernism and popular culture: a cultural history/John Docker.
Includes bibliographical references and index.
1. Modernism (Art) 2. Postmodernism. 3. Arts, Modern –
20th century. 4. Popular culture. I. Title.
NX456.5.M64D63 1994   94–11552
700'.9'045–dc20   CIP

A catalogue record for this book is available from the British Library.
ISBN 0 521 46045 X Hardback
ISBN 0 521 46598 2 Paperback

For Ned Curthoys

Contents

Plates

Preface

This book has seen at least two false starts. I had long been intrigued by the thought that modern popular culture, especially television, wasn't what it was usually thought to be. I knew that in my sub-culture, the 'left' intelligentsia, 'radical' and 'oppositional', largely though not completely composed of university teachers, mainly of history, philosophy, literature, media and cultural studies, the amount of popular TV watching I did was considered more a matter for joking reference at dinner parties than intellectual discussion. If I were suspected of being serious, I was usually told rather roughly that mass culture was the major means by which in this century the mass of people were secured for and dominated by capitalist values.

In the late 1970s and early 1980s 'dominant' was a key word, a required notation; various forces were always dominating. If you didn't see various things as dominating, not least, mass culture produced by media barons for 'the market', that source of evil in the world, then you were naive, slightly ridiculous, and uncaring about how people were the victims of the media and mass culture and how mass culture kept social and ideological change, disruption, transformation from happening. You were perhaps in danger of withdrawing from the proper fight, which was to limit, by critique and by assisting the regulatory powers of the state (something I thought was strange for a 'left' that had emerged from the anarchist and libertarian New Left of the 1960s), the dominating power of the media barons. Also, how could I possibly like the American programs I kept saying I so much liked, when it was clear 'American cultural imperialism' was a major terrible force in the world and in any case it was axiomatic that British television, to be watched on the Australian Broadcasting Commission, the heir of Britain's BBC, was the world's superior mode of broadcasting?

But I had my doubts, and I had looked at a great deal of popular TV –
unlike my mentors, whom I quickly realised had seen very little of the
culture they denounced. I'd watched a great deal of TV since our son
had been born in late 1974, first out of exhaustion, later out of
childminding, to keep him company, to enjoy what he was enjoying, to
try and see why he liked what he liked and why certain programs
obviously fascinated him, from the cartoons (mostly American, some
Japanese) when he was little to comedies like *I Dream of Jeannie* or
Bewitched. Why was a boy so absorbed in watching young women
characters as heroines of fantastical stories where they use magical
powers to quickly do this or that? Why did he like American shows so
much?

Occasional Australia Council grants, and some part-time teaching,
supported my writing, principally in the fields of cultural and
intellectual history, and literary theory and criticism. In the early 1980s,
I wanted also to teach and write about popular culture and especially
television, and in 1983 snared a position at the then Canberra College
of Advanced Education, now the University of Canberra. The job was
actually, or at least initially, to teach public relations. It quickly took in
media and cultural studies more generally. I could now try my hand
teaching with concepts and readings that questioned the usual critical
theory, which had every appearance of being a solid orthodoxy.

I would like to thank my students of those years, 1983–1985, for
listening so politely to one of their lecturers telling them how much he
enjoyed soaps ranging from *Dallas* to *Days of Our Lives* to *Prisoner*. I
would also like at this point to thank the then dean, Bill Mandle, for
having me on staff and encouraging my teaching in whatever curious
directions I wanted to take it. As anyone would know in this strange
world, some people want nothing to do with you, other people go out of
their way to extend kindnesses and give opportunities. So I would also
here like to thank those who invited me in subsequent years to teach
courses in popular culture, TV study, modernism and postmodernism:
Jan Bruck in General Studies at the University of New South Wales, and,
at the University of Technology, Sydney (formerly NSWIT), Liz Jacka in
Humanities and Craig McGregor in Design. Jan Bruck and I also
collaborated in a critique of John Berger's *Ways of Seeing*.[1] I also taught a
continuing education course at UTS in 1990 on modernism and
postmodernism. I would like to thank the students in all these courses
for years of lively discussion, frequently including sharp disagreement
with what I was saying.

As a research scholar, for a few short months in the summer of
1983–84 at the Humanities Research Centre, Australian National
University, I took the chance to begin reading in the history of carnival

in early modern Europe. Frequently on television I was seeing what I took to be not a reflection or inscribing of 'dominant' capitalist values, but the reverse of such, images and dramas overturning usual social relations, in terms of power, gender, status, age, authority. I was at the HRC at a fortunate time. Its then director was Ian Donaldson, author of *The World Upside-Down*, on inversion in seventeenth- and eighteenth-century English comedy. I learned a great deal from this book and enjoyed my conversations with Ian, though he was visibly doubtful of my main proposition – or hope – that continuities could be perceived between television and pre-industrial popular traditions. Didn't carnival, he gently queried, take place in the streets, while television . . . and wasn't the society of early modern Europe stable and hierarchical, enabling inversion because people knew what they were inverting, whereas modern societies are so fluid. . .? I said I'd have to shelve such questions for a while, while I explored the writings on carnival and inversion of Mikhail Bakhtin, whom I'd *just* discovered, and others I soon came to hear of and read, Natalie Davis, David Kunzle, Emmanuel Le Roy Ladurie, Peter Burke.

Also at the HRC in those months was the Bakhtin scholar Michael Holquist, who listened kindly if also quizzically to my attempts to relate Bakhtin to contemporary mass culture. I recall venturing that melodrama might somehow be seen as continuing a carnivalesque cosmology. I'd been struck by the way in *Dallas* a major inversion appeared glaringly to be happening: embodied in the evil figure of JR, the desire for wealth and power, supposedly central to American society, was created as destructive, of family, love, friendship, kinship, community. Holquist then told me I should read Peter Brooks' *The Melodramatic Imagination*. He also showed me material he'd written (this was before I could acquire the biography of Bakhtin, which he co-authored with Katerina Clark) relating Bakhtin to specific political situations in Soviet history.

By 1985 Ann Curthoys and I felt ready to write a book-length essay on popular culture, and made a proposal to a university press. They had, however, to let it go when the reader's report came in; it was too hostile to ignore. They were probably right: the project was as yet in too early a form, undeveloped, inchoate, though the hostility was interesting, even encouraging. We left it for a while, and busied ourselves writing other things. But the idea nagged, and when I received a two-year fellowship from the Literature Board of the Australia Council (for 1991–2), I determined to try again, though now looking more broadly at contemporary mass culture, not only television. But, again, there was a false start. I sketched a first chapter, but Ann said hold on, you're going too fast, you haven't really explained to an interested general reader what modernism is. You got to postmodernism too quickly without explaining what it was post to.

Derrida has argued that we are always inside the concepts and philosophies we wish to critique. I am sure that my own debt to modernism, to its great literature and its critical theories, concepts, and methods, will be more than I know myself. I suspect too that while I have tried to present cultural history as replete with heterogeneity, fragmentation, discontinuity, multiple and conflicting and contesting meanings and values, history as finally undecidable textuality, my argument probably keeps reintroducing the very notions I'm trying to oppose. While I'm suspicious of psychoanalysis, particularly in cultural studies, where it frequently operates in terms of categories that unify and universalise, I know I keep returning to its terms and modes of explanation, even if ironically.

I don't of course claim my critique of modernism as unique. As Roland Barthes notes in his 'The Death of the Author' essay, writing, textuality, is a 'multidimensional space in which a variety of writings, none of them original, blend and clash', and the writer's 'only power is to mix writings, to counter the ones with the others, in such a way as never to rest on any one of them'.[2] I have tried to 'stage' my narrative as a scene of many writings coming together, as a conversation with many other critics. In this method I acknowledge the influence not only of Bakhtin but also Walter Benjamin, particularly in his writings on Baudelaire. My debt to recent critics of modernism like Andreas Huyssen will be clear.

Barthes' phrase about never resting on any one writing or position is important. I cannot envisage any 'movement', modernism or post-structuralism or postmodernism, any single aesthetic, philosophy, cosmology, discourse, as ever adequate to humanity and the world's infinitely variegated differences, conflicting values, argumentativeness, and lunacy.

My own speaking position is as a scholar with only loose and intermittent connections with the academy, working in cultural theory and history in Australia. In a necessarily nebulous sense I feel *Postmodernism and Popular Culture: A Cultural History* has benefited from the vigorous life of theoretical argument and debate in Australia in the last couple of decades. Antipodean cultural studies and history have been fortunate in the mix and variety of influences they have been eager to attend to, enjoy, adapt and transform. Such can be clearly observed in the history of broadcasting this century, with state-funded media, in the Australian Broadcasting Commission (or Corporation), looking largely to British examples and exemplars, while commercial radio and then television would look largely to United States forms and genres. Similarly, antipodean intellectual life has been attentive to a variety of influences and schools, British, French, German and Central European, North American. I hope the present work speaks to this distinctiveness. Australian intellectual life of course has never been and isn't now an homogeneous scene, particularly in differences between its main centres, Sydney and Melbourne. Sydney intellectual traditions have been hospitable to pluralism, libertarianism, anarchism, nihilism, with intellectuals feeling ever at the margins of society and power. In Melbourne, intellectuals have seen themselves as important even central to Australian society and history. [3]

There are many people to thank for this book, not least the Literature Board of the Australia Council for a Senior Fellowship for 1991–2. For the stimulus of agreement and disagreement, knowledge and advice, over the years, I'd like to thank: Veronica Kelly, John Kavanagh, Jenna Price, Keith Windschuttle, Brian Stoddart, Kalpana Ram, Albert Moran, Di Powell, Camille Guy, Clive Kessler, Noel King, Tony Branigan, Tony Mitchell, Paula Hamilton, Heather Goodall, John Castles, Jane Connors, Emma Graham, Martin Barker, Lesley Johnson, Stephen Muecke. In the very early 1980s I was kindly invited into a popular culture discussion group which also included Pauline Johnson, Richard Osborne, Lorraine Mortimer, Kathy Robinson. I would like to thank the Melbourne journal *Arena* for its eclectic hospitality in publishing a paper that came out of that group, 'In Defence of Popular Culture', my first substantial contribution to the field, along with replies to the replies that came in. Other journals I would like to thank here for their hospitality are *Australasian Drama Studies, Overland, Continuum, Social Alternatives, Media Information Australia, Theory Culture and Society.* In 1984 I was part of a 'theory' discussion group that included Pauline Johnson, Guther Kress, Liz Jacka, Drusilla Modjeska, Susan Dermody. Another discussion group, in 1987, the 'Shibboleths of the Left' group, John Bern, Baiba Berzins, Peter Bryant, Ann Curthoys, Carol Johnston, Jan Larbalestier, Jeannie Martin, assisted with my attempts to relate postmodernism to social and political theory; Peter Bryant in particular urged me to read Alec Nove. I would also like to acknowledge the stimulation of more recent discussion with Helen Irving and Stephen Gaukroger.

The late Henry Mayer once invaluably advised me, when I told him I was embarking on a book on mass culture, to focus on genres rather than particular programs, which can be ephemeral. Professor Mayer was also a pluralist, hospitable editor of *Media Information Australia.*

I sent a draft of the chapter on fools to the Australian comedian Graham Kennedy, and the King kindly sent back to one of his admiring subjects an encouraging thank you card.

Mike Chesterman and Colleen Chesterman lent me a copy of poems and songs lampooning the Sydney monorail.

Bob Perry gave me useful information about Darling Harbour and the Harbourside Festival Marketplace. Ann Curthoys and I wrote together the chapter on *Prisoner* (or *Cell Block H*). Our *Prisoner* project had a long and odd history in the 1980s. It was developed while we participated in a discussion group including the late Bill Bonney, Helen Wilson, and Di Powell, which was preparing ideas for the Australian Communication Conference to be held in Sydney in 1983. We presented it as a paper to this conference, but couldn't get the subsequent article published until 1989, when it was included in a collection of essays compiled by John Tulloch and Graeme Turner on Australian TV.[4]

I would also like to acknowledge, for their encouragement and support, my literary agent, Lyn Tranter, and my editor at Cambridge University Press, Phillipa McGuinness; and for thankfully astringent final editing, Carla Taines. My special thanks to Meaghan Morris and Iain Wright for thorough and helpful readings of the manuscript.

This book was assisted by a writer's fellowship from the Australia Council, the federal government's arts funding and advisory body.

Introduction

In this book I question the way a century of modernist critical theory has understood twentieth-century mass culture, and suggest that postmodernism promises more illuminating approaches. Modernist critical theory has demonised mass culture by apocalyptically condemning it as the chief danger to civilisation, leading to mass acceptance of, lack of resistance to, all that is bad and wrong in the world. There are an infinite number of things wrong with the contemporary world, but mass culture and the media are not the chief culprits. Rather might we think of racism, colonialism, lack of democracy and human rights, state censorship, political repression, torture, sexual violence, history as threat, fear, destruction and cruelty. Western mass culture and the media have neither univocally supported such forces nor unilaterally reconciled the mass of people to them. In many many cases, and very often, it's been the reverse.

Postmodernism – or at least the strands I like – does not ascribe to popular culture phenomena any single commanding meaning or purpose. It does not assume any easily explicable relationship between popular culture and its audiences, and it does not see audiences as transparent in their desires and consciousness (or their unconscious). It does not wish to install and police a hierarchy of genres in culture in general. It does not prescribe innovation and experiment as cultural absolutes by which to judge all aesthetic expression. Rather it is interested in a plurality of forms and genres, a pluralising of aesthetic criteria, where such forms and genres may have long and fascinating histories, not as static and separate but entwined, interacting, conflicting, contesting, playing off against each other, mixing in unpredictable combinations, protean in energy, moving quickly between extremes, from pathos to farce, intensity to burlesque, endlessly fertile as narrative, theatricality, and performance. Postmodernism defends the 'lower female genres' and their readers and audiences so excoriated by modernism this century. It sees popular culture as a frequent site of flamboyance, extravagance, excess, parody, self-parody, a self-parody that has philosophical implications for popular culture as a worldview, a cosmology, a poetics.

While my sympathies are clearly with postmodernism rather than modernism, I do not pose them as alternatives in any simple way. I have tried to present postmodernism as varied, heterogeneous, contradictory, as was, is, modernism. 'Post' means coming after as well as critical of, in tension with. The history of their relations is inevitably messy and confused.

To explore postmodernism, then, we have first to evoke modernism, that movement that gathered momentum in another Nineties period, the 1890s, and was at its most powerful and striking and new in the early part of the twentieth century and especially in the 1920s. In architecture and design there was the Bauhaus movement and the key manifestos and exhibitions of Le Corbusier. In poetry there were Ezra Pound's *Hugh Selwyn Mauberley* (1920) and T.S. Eliot's *The Waste Land* (1922). In the novel D.H. Lawrence's *Women in Love* was published in 1920, Joyce's *Ulysses* appeared in 1922, and Virginia Woolf's *To the Lighthouse* in 1927. The various avant-garde movements, German Expressionism, French Dada and Surrealism, Italian and Russian Futurism, shocked audiences by paying scant respect to previous boundaries between cultural forms and were indeed exhilaratingly iconoclastic, experimental and daring. Modernism flowered into a great aesthetic movement, challenging and transforming every received art form, from literature and music to painting and architecture.

But modernism was also deeply divided, bewilderingly diverse, often highly contradictory. It was international, yet different in different continents and different cities. It was always more than a cultural phenomenon; it always involved philosophical, sociological and economic contexts and arguments as well. Like any influential aesthetic, its political implications and affiliations varied enormously, from, at various times and places, the nihilist, the socialist, to the conservative, even the fascist.

I start with Le Corbusier because much postmodernist theory has focused on postmodern architecture as the defining break from modernism. But I also wish to show just how varied twentieth-century modernism is by contrasting Le Corbusier's 1920s conceptions of modernity to those of high literary modernism, beginning with the writings in the 1930s of F.R. Leavis, in his *Mass Civilisation and Minority Culture*, and Q.D. Leavis, in her *Fiction and the Reading Public*. These early essays of the Leavises now appear as uncannily foundational, prefiguring – though not necessarily by direct connection or influence – major modernist mass culture theories and movements to come. From there I move on a decade, to the cultural theories of the Frankfurt School, especially Adorno and Horkheimer's essay 'The Culture Industry: Enlightenment as mass deception' in *Dialectic of Enlightenment* (1944), as well as Adorno's postwar essay 'Television and the Patterns of Mass Culture' (1954).

Postwar cultural studies began to grow and institutionally take grip as mass culture, media, and advertising themselves began in a recovering and recovered world a new efflorescence. I continue tracing the lineage of 'high literary modernism' in Roland Barthes' *Mythologies* (1957), before turning to a book, published just across the English Channel in the same year, that perhaps more than any other launched postwar British cultural studies. Richard Hoggart's *The Uses of Literacy* inaugurated the left turn in British mass-culture theory that would continue in the Marxism of Hoggart's successors at the Birmingham Centre for Contemporary Cultural Studies, in particular the commanding figure of Stuart Hall. An important feature of the work of Barthes, Hall, and the Birmingham Centre at this time was structuralism, an approach which sought a central identifying feature to a mass culture text, or to mass culture itself. In the 1970s another critical movement, Screen Theory, became a persuasive force. While also structuralist in method, Screen Theory effected a shift in geocultural focus from Birmingham to London, and from ethnographic research into various youth sub-cultures to analysis of film and television texts, in terms of literary history and psychoanalysis. Accordingly this part of the book looks at and picks over the implications of two influential essays, Colin McCabe's 'Realism and the Cinema: Notes on Some Brechtian Theses' and Laura Mulvey's 'Visual Pleasure and Narrative Cinema'. So ends Part One, with modernism at its most institutionally and discursively powerful.

Part Two charts modernism's strange decline, in the coming of postmodern architecture and its challenge to the International Style. Here I focus on Robert Venturi, Denise Scott Brown and Steven Izenour's *Learning from Las Vegas* (1972), and in a continental change of location, the application of postmodern ideas and ideals of building and design to Sydney – yes, I can't but add, home of the Olympics in the year 2000. In mass-culture theory, modernism encountered the rise of poststructuralism (I focus on Derrida) and its challenge to decades of structuralism. There were also new conceptions abroad of the age as postmodern, in the work of Baudrillard, Lyotard, and Jameson. Yet this cannot be a simple narrative. In cultural studies as a specific field, I trace the difficult disintegration of the certainties of high literary modernism, not least in Raymond Williams' *Television: Technology and Cultural Form* (1974). These uncertainties had been evident earlier, notably in Walter Benjamin's differences with mainstream Frankfurt School theory in the 1930s.[1] But now they began to increase and multiply, as shown in the work in the late 1970s and early 1980s of Tania Modleski and Dorothy Hobson, exploring strengths in TV soap opera and defending their audiences, and John Fiske in the later 1980s evoking the various pleasures of popular culture. I also ponder here the dangers of a new orthodoxy developing around the notion of pleasure.

Part Three is devoted to those theorists who offer a positive account of popular culture, especially Mikhail Bakhtin's theories of carnival and carnivalesque, of monologic and dialogic and heteroglossia, and differing fictional notions of time, space, and character. This journey from early modern Europe to the present takes in festivity and theatre, fools and tricksters, vaudeville and television, melodrama and the detective novel. I test Bakhtin's theories across a range of cultural material, and discuss other theorists of trickster figures, festive inversion, and world upside-down, like Enid Welsford, Natalie Davis, David Kunzle, Emmanuel Le Roy Ladurie, Peter Burke, Peter Stallybrass and Allon White.

In his introduction to the memorial volume of Allon White's writings, *Carnival, Hysteria, and Writing*, Stuart Hall discusses the major transition that occurred in cultural theory from the 1970s to the 1980s. Hall argues that the work White wrote with Peter Stallybrass, *The Politics and Poetics of Transgression* (1986), was a landmark text in cultural studies because it helped shape and define this transition. As Hall sees it, the 1970s 'moment' in cultural studies was characteristically Marxist. Key metaphors were of social, cultural and political transformation where a dominant order and class could possibly be overthrown by subordinate, oppositional forces. The dominant and the subordinate were in constant relations of negotiation, resistance and struggle. The 1980s 'moment' disturbed such clear binary oppositions, drawing on Bakhtin's notions of carnivalesque to point to cultural life, particularly in its relations of 'high' and 'low', as historically ever hybrid and ambiguous. An imperative to order, regulate, and exclude is confused by powerful unpredictable desires for the 'low', the other. The dialectic, enshrining a notion of history, theory, culture as moving forward through the resolution of conflicts and contradictions, had now to compete with the notion of the dialogic, of language and culture as ceaseless unpredictable heterogeneity, history as reversible. Where the dialectic assumes history as meta-narrative, as governed by logic and laws, the dialogic refers to forces and meanings which endlessly shift and slip. The dialectic looks to a transcendence of that which is opposed; the dialogic suggests spatial metaphors, the dispersal of conflicts and antagonisms into repetition and ambivalence.[2]

The transition Stuart Hall talks of, from binary metaphors of cultural and symbolic transformation to tropes of dispersal, is intensifying to the point where the very project of cultural theory, the attempt to comprehend the relations between 'the social' and 'the symbolic',[3] has become deeply problematic. The key figure in this movement is, perhaps, Meaghan Morris, her cultural theory writing a kind of mimesis of post-marxist epistemological vertigo, a poetics of witty self-reflexivity and self-disturbance returning again and again to the enigmatic status of cultural studies itself, facing the impossibility of its project, its unthinkable death. In this sense, *Postmodernism and Popular Culture: A Cultural History* is the charting of a century's passage in cultural theory towards the vertiginous uncertainty of the 1990s, its Janus face, foreboding and hope, opportunity or end, new futures or disaster, dream and nightmare.

PART ONE

Modernism in Conflict

CHAPTER ONE

Architectural Modernism:
Le Corbusier

Architecture is the masterly, correct and magnificent play of masses brought together in light. Our eyes are made to see forms in light; light and shade reveal these forms; cubes, cones, spheres, cylinders or pyramids are the great primary forms which light reveals to advantage; the image of these is distinct and tangible within us and without ambiguity. It is for that reason that these are *beautiful forms, the most beautiful forms.* Everybody is agreed as to that, the child, the savage and the metaphysician. It is of the very nature of the plastic arts.

A house is a machine for living in. Baths, sun, hot-water, cold-water, warmth at will, conservation of food, hygiene, beauty in the sense of good proportion. An armchair is a machine for sitting in and so on.

Our modern life, when we are active and about (leaving out the moments when we fly to gruel and aspirin) has created its own objects: its costume, its fountain pen, its eversharp pencil, its typewriter, its telephone, its admirable office furniture, its plate-glass and its 'Innovation' trunks, the safety razor and the briar pipe, the bowler hat and the limousine, the steamship and the airplane.

Our epoch is fixing its own style day by day. It is there under our eyes.

Eyes which do not see.

Le Corbusier, Towards a New Architecture, *1923*[1]

Wyndham Lewis was much in Paris [in the spring of 1921] and would often join Joyce at the Gipsy Bar near the Pantheon or at a small cafe. Alcohol helped to make them companionable, though they often disagreed. So, when Lewis objected to the cathedral at Rouen because of its heavily encumbered façade, which he described as a 'fussy multi-plication of accents, demonstrating a belief in the virtue of

2

quantity', and argued against Gothic . . . Joyce remarked that
he liked this multiplication of detail and added, 'As a matter
of fact, I do something of that sort in words.'[2]

Le Corbusier was the pen-name, or *nom de guerre*, of Charles-Edouard
Jeanneret (1887–1965), the dominant figure in the modern movement
in architecture from the 1920s to the 1960s. Born in Switzerland, widely
travelled, he established himself in Paris as a city planner, architect,
designer, painter, sculptor. He felt his face resembled a raven (*corbeau*),
and indeed he was throughout his life a fierce polemicist, not least
against his fellow architects. His manifesto *Vers une architecture* was
published in Paris in 1923 and was translated into English in 1927 by
Frederick Etchells as *Towards a New Architecture*.

In *Towards a New Architecture* Le Corbusier scorns conventional architects for still insisting on the suffocatingly dead styles of the nineteenth
century. Present architecture, he felt, was in a state of 'retrogression',
stifled by 'custom', by an obsession with inherited 'styles', a term Le
Corbusier can only bring himself to mention with repeated lashings of
contempt.[3]

The present architecture and interior design of our houses are
ruining our health and our morale. The architects of today keep
designing houses that are too crowded with features, with decorated
façade, pilasters, 'foliage', lead roofs. Surfaces have become parasitical,
obscuring what is beneath. Inside, such houses are gloomy, secretive,
with rooms that are too small, and with a conglomeration of useless
disparate objects, of absurd bric-à-brac. People can barely navigate the
labyrinth of their heavy furniture: chandeliers ('these horrors' that fill
up the middle of a room and are bad for the eyes at night), mantel-
pieces, thick carpets, washstands, commodes, elaborate bookcases,
consoles, china cabinets, dressers, sideboards, draped curtains,
cushions, canopies, damasked wallpapers thick with colour and motley
design, carved and gilt furniture, faded or arty colours, mirrored
wardrobes. It's like a bazaar, a Western bazaar. No wonder, Le Corbusier
feels, people fly from their homes to frequent restaurants and night
clubs. People should rise up and demand the resignation of all the
professors in the architectural schools.[4]

Towards a New Architecture particularly dislikes the reliance of
conventional architecture on surface effects, on the decorative, the
ornamental, the symbolic. Such effects promote the sensation, 'so
insupportable to man', of shapelessness, disorder, wilfulness. They
promote heterogeneity, ambiguity, capriciousness, riot, stitching together elements which have nothing to do with each other. Le
Corbusier was not impressed by the contemporary arts decoration

movement which was supposedly regenerating French art and interior
design. On the contrary, such a movement, he averred, was at the
dangerous height that goes before a fall. The tail pieces and garlands,
exquisite ovals where triangular doves preen themselves, boudoirs
embellished with poufs in gold and black velvet, all such stifling
elegancies, as well as the follies of Peasant Art, are intolerable witnesses
to a dead spirit. The decorative arts are not part of the new modern
architecture to be.[5]

The sense of 'plan', of overall structure, clarity, and ease, inside and
out, has been lost for the last hundred years. Conventional architecture
was indeed contributing to the almost apocalyptic crisis history and
society were now facing. The various classes of workers of today, from
artisan to intellectual, no longer have dwellings adapted to their needs.
In Le Corbusier's view, the question of building was at the root of contemporary social unrest. We should repudiate the existing layouts of our
towns and quarters where the congestion of buildings grows ever
greater, interlaced by narrow streets full of noise, petrol fumes and dust,
and where on each storey the windows open on to the foul confusion
below.[6]

Society, Le Corbusier feels, is threatened by a violent desire for
change. People are conscious that there is a new world coming into
being, yet feel hindered from enjoying it by their living environment, of
town, street, house, flat. The symptoms are alarming, but revolution can
be avoided by a new architecture that clears away the stifling accumulation of age-long detritus, an architecture that is in tune with the
emerging modern world. It is 'Architecture or Revolution'.[7]

Architects have to catch up to other arts and sciences. They could, for
example, look to cubism, which has taken the aesthetic lead in attuning
itself to the modern epoch; it is not distracted by realism, and it has
purged painting of 'wall decoration, tapestry and the ornamental urn'.
Above all, however, we should look to the engineer's aesthetic as the key
to the new architecture. Like the cubists, engineers employ forms which
satisfy our eyes by their geometry, our understanding by their
mathematics.[8]

Towards a New Architecture presents a paean of praise to the engineer
as heroic modern figure. Engineers are healthy and virile, active and
useful, balanced and happy in their work. Architects have forgotten
what engineers know, that our eyes are constructed to perceive simple
primary geometrical forms. Engineers are governed by the mathematical calculation which puts us in accord with universal natural law,
thereby achieving harmony. Engineers conceive of what they create as
a living organism. The engineer of today knows the best way to
construct, to heat, to ventilate, to light. While architects have been

asleep, engineers having been busy creating bridges, Atlantic liners, mines, railways.[9]

Building too should be in accord with universal natural law generated by primary forms and masses. Architecture then will become 'plastic', will achieve order, economy, rationality. It will be not only utilitarian but 'poetic'. Here is architectural emotion, where the 'work of man' rings in unison with 'universal order', where architecture moves us as a pure creation of spirit. We have to strip decoration and ornament away, to bring out the geometry that is the primal 'language of man'. Architecture, says *Towards a New Architecture* in a saying that became almost a byword of the modern movement, is the masterly, correct and magnificent play of masses brought together in light, and the great primary forms which light reveals to advantage are prisms, cubes, cones, spheres, cylinders, pyramids. How such forms are arranged creates an appreciable rhythm, a unity of idea. It is the regulating lines which create beauty and grandeur. In the great epochs of architecture, an astonishing diversity is created, not from the play of decoration, but from different combinations of primary forms.[10]

Throughout *Towards a New Architecture* Le Corbusier constructs a cultural history of architecture and design guided by the standard of the geometric. As we might expect, he vigorously dislikes examples from the past not based on the mathematical, on axes, the square, the circle. Italy does not come off well. Le Corbusier admires Michelangelo's creations as a 'gigantic geometry of harmonious relationships', Michelangelo having learnt from the 'rare proportions' of the coliseum of old. But foolish and thoughtless Popes dismissed Michelangelo and destroyed his work by extensions and additions. After Michelangelo's cupolas, there is nothing. Rome, Rome in particular, is and has been for the last four centuries a disaster, a merely picturesque 'bazaar'. In Rome the uglinesses are legion, for everything is too huddled together. To send architectural students to Rome is to cripple them for life, and indeed emulating Rome has become the cancer of French architecture.[11]

Wrong stones

The Gothic cathedral, so beloved of nineteenth-century English romantics like John Ruskin in his essay 'The Nature of Gothic' in *The Stones of Venice* (1853), also scores badly in *Towards a New Architecture*. In Ruskin's view, influenced by nineteenth-century race theories about the supposed differences between northern and southern Europeans, medieval Gothic architecture derives from the tribes of northern Europe. It is to be distinguished from the art originating from south of the Alps, in particular from the Greek and Roman styles of architecture.

Ruskin is opposed to Greek and Roman art because, like the aesthetic attitudes which came in with the Renaissance, it demands perfection. In insisting on art as finished and complete, Greek and Roman architecture becomes 'artificial', divorced from nature, for in nature nothing is ever complete, nature is always in a state of becoming, of change, growth, and decay, and then new growth.

Like the changeability and unpredictable richness of vegetation and foliage, Gothic follows 'natural forms'. Ruskin argues that a key element of Gothic is its quality of redundance, and he describes a cathedral front which was like a study of the 'minute and various work of Nature' so that the façade was 'at last lost in the tapestry of its traceries, like a rock among the thickets and herbage of spring'.

The very imperfection of Gothic art allowed the participation and inventiveness of the workmen involved. As in the freedom of nature, they are permitted to 'imagine, to think, to try to do anything worth doing'. The element of the grotesque in Gothic reflects not the supposed barbarism of the Middle Ages, but the imagination of the workmen, a 'delight in fantastic and ludicrous, as well as sublime, imagery'. Against the alienating division of labour of the industrial age, the Gothic style enables the creation of wholeness, the romantic ideal of unity of humanity and nature, art and daily life, mind and sense, intellect and feeling. It is the very 'rude and wild' quality of Gothic that deserves the most reverence.[12]

Ruskin's 'The Nature of Gothic' was greatly admired by William Morris, who had the essay reprinted by itself at his Kelmscott Press in 1892, with a preface hailing Ruskin for possessing the key to the problem of human happiness in his concept of pleasurable work.[13] Morris argued that art, as craft, as the design and making of household items and features, from pottery to chairs to wallpaper, should be seen as useful in daily life. Pre-Raphaelite, poet, novelist, pamphleteer, designer, libertarian socialist, utopian, Morris was important in the late nineteenth- and early twentieth-century period in trying to counter the astonishing crowdedness and clutter of high Victorian interiors and design, and restore principles of rationality and usefulness. In Australia as in Britain and Europe, Morris proved influential in the Aesthetic Movement, Arts and Crafts, and to some extent Art Nouveau, movements which helped prepare the way for the modernist surge in architecture and interior design.[14] Morris also was influential in the early Bauhaus in Germany, however severe and functionalist it later became.[15]

Towards a New Architecture is, nonetheless, vastly unimpressed by the Gothic cathedral. (Le Corbusier doesn't mention Ruskin by name, though he does at one point enigmatically tell us that relating architecture to mathematical order is of greater value than 'many dissertations on the soul of stones'.) Gothic architecture is not based on spheres, cones, and cylinders; it does not proceed from the great primary forms; it even fights against the force of gravity, and so is not an example of plastic art. It is, therefore, not very beautiful.[16]

Gothic also suffers in terms of being of a female orientation. It can, says Le Corbusier, arouse sensation only of a sentimental kind. Like other decorative styles, it is to architecture what a feather is on a woman's head, sometimes pretty, though not always, and never anything more. Further, Le Corbusier is opposed to Ruskin's conception of architecture growing like nature. He dislikes decorative 'foliage'. He is highly approving of the way the industrial age replaces heterogeneous natural materials with artificial products.[17]

The architecture of the past that *Towards a New Architecture* admires, in Europe and the East, includes the Pyramids, the Temple of Luxor, the Towers of Babylon, the Parthenon, the Colosseum, Hadrian's Villa, Constantinople's Santa Sophia, the Mosques of Stamboul, the Tower of Pisa, the cupolas of Michelangelo. Above all, it is the classical Greek, in particular, the Parthenon, that again and again stirs *Towards a New Architecture* to eulogy. Of a photo of a section of the Parthenon, Le Corbusier writes: 'Brutality, intensity, the utmost sweetness, delicacy and great strength'. Where Ruskin dislikes the idea of perfection in classical architecture (as preventing participation by craftspeople, as permitting only an admiring gaze), Le Corbusier hails the Parthenon as raising the possibility precisely of perfection. The Parthenon is the 'apogee' of the development of profile and contour in an architecture of geometric forms: 'The sum of its inevitable elements gives the measure of the degree of perfection to which man can attain when he is absorbed in a problem definitely stated.' We are ravished by its 'pure forms in precise relationships'.[18]

The Parthenon gives us sure truths and emotion of a 'superior, mathematical order'. It is a triumph of ancient mathematics, and the ancient mathematicians would, Le Corbusier feels sure, have loved to live in the twentieth century, because it represents a new age of standardisation. If Ruskin and William Morris disliked the standardisation that was part of the industrial age, Le Corbusier gratefully welcomes the 'spirit of mass-production and industrial organization', as in the way the car is produced. He also welcomes something Morris, like other socialists, excoriated: capitalist competition. For in competing with each other, manufacturers search for harmony and beauty in the cars they make, attaining a 'state of perfection universally felt'.[19]

Towards a New Architecture celebrates modernity, modernity as technological 'progress'. Part of the reason the Parthenon is so admired is that its marble gives the impression of 'naked polished steel'. The new architecture and design, using modern materials like steel and reinforced concrete, and based on the engineer's aesthetic and geometric forms, can already be observed in factories ('the reassuring first fruits of the new age'), the steamship, the airplane, and the automobile.[20]

Look at these photos of steamships, ocean-going liners, built not by architects but by engineers, like the Cunard *Aquitania*. Unlike the small hole-like windows in our present dismal houses, the ship's saloon, for example, is a wall all windows, full of light. Architects, says Le Corbusier, please think how a seaside villa would be like if designed like the stern of the *Aquitania*, whereas such villas now are spoilt by their heavy tiled roofs. (This exhortation certainly rings true for Sydney; its harbourside hills feature many a ship-like house.) Liners are free of the 'styles' that afflict architecture and offer interesting contrasts between powerful masses and slender elements. The liners' saloon type decks are pure, clear, clean, and healthy. Indeed, underneath a photo of the Canadian Pacific *Empress of Asia*, Le Corbusier places his definition of architecture as the masterly, correct and magnificent play of masses brought together in light. The steamship, he concludes, is the first stage in the realisation of a world organised according to the new spirit. It has the same aesthetic as that of a briar pipe, an office desk, a limousine, a lorry. (The insistence in *Towards a New Architecture* on the significance of the briar pipe escapes me.) It is the triumph of the new, of a beauty that is calm, vital and strong; of freedom from enslavement to the past, from a lazy respect for 'tradition'.[21]

Our dwellings, too, must make use of modern materials. At present they lag sadly behind. The house, says Le Corbusier in another to-be-famous saying, is a machine for living in. By using reinforced concrete, the roof can be suppressed and replaced by terraces, with windows going right round the 'square-built' house. Inside, remove the present clutter with built in fittings. Get rid of the old tapestry covered seats and install rush-seated adjustable chairs with a movable reading-desk, a shelf for the coffee cup, and an extending foot-rest. Get rid of the enormous chandeliers and install electric lighting, concealed, diffused, or projecting. Use modern plate glass instead of the small panes of old. Instead of a riot of all manner of things, demand bare walls in your bedroom, living room and dining room. Eliminate heavy furniture and thick carpets, keeping the house full of light and air; make sure you acquire a vacuum cleaner. Insist on one really large living room instead of a number of small ones. Take advantage of a refrigerator. In general, houses will be far more quickly built ('months of work are saved') in the factory, with standardised materials, as with cars, cannons, airplanes, lorries, wagons.[22]

Towards a New Architecture reveals a remarkable historical optimism, even utopianism. A 'great epoch has begun', conceived in a 'new spirit', the spirit of 'industrial production', which will create new cities, towns, quarters, dwellings, design. The great city is now part of a rising tide; in particular, we can start envisaging a City of Towers. We can think, for example, of bringing together at certain points, relatively distant, the great density of our modern populations and to build at these points enormous constructions of 60 storeys, using reinforced concrete and steel. Cafés and places for recreation would be transferred to the flat roofs. ('Cafés . . . would no longer be that fungus which eats up the pavements of Paris'.) There can also be roof gardens. All the windows would have an uninterrupted view of vast airy and sunlit spaces. At the foot of these towers would stretch parks, covering the whole town: Le Corbusier is not opposed to nature as such, only that building and façades themselves be geometric, with rich contrasts to the surrounding vegetation. There will be green sward, sportsgrounds and abundant plantations of trees. Well away from the towers would flow the noisy arterial roads, full of a traffic which becomes increasingly rapid. By such means shall we round Cape Horn into new horizons of town planning; we shall enter upon a period 'that no epoch has known'.[23]

What the Old World has to do is catch up to the New, in particular North America. *Towards a New Architecture* abounds with admiring references to and photos of Canadian and US grain stores and elevators. Such indeed, along with American factories, are among the magnificent first fruits of the new age, for the 'American engineers overwhelm with their calculations our expiring architecture', revealing the beauty and grandeur of geometric forms. The American skyscraper has also proved to be a vital constructional event, and opposite the title page of *Towards a New Architecture* is a provocatively placed photo of the Telephone Building, New York. New York's Equitable Building also earns a photo, opposite one of an American steel bridge; the next page has a photo of 'America', a high-speed racing car.[24]

The architectural new world represents 'evolution' for humanity. Civilisations 'advance'. They pass through the age of the peasant, the soldier and the priest, and attain what is rightly called culture, the flowering of the effort to select. Selection means rejection, pruning, cleansing, the clear and naked emergence of the Essential. Evolution is a move towards the establishing of an architectural and urban standard that is clearly 'rational'. Evolution is a movement from elementary satisfactions ('mere decoration') to the 'higher satisfactions' (mathematics). Evolution is a movement from the female to the male, from styles of architecture like the Gothic, to an architecture of graver ends, capable of the 'sublime', impressing the most brutal instincts by its objectivity, calling into play the highest faculties by its abstraction. It is a movement from the 'frivolous' to an art which is 'austere', of 'severe and pure functioning elements', which has 'discipline' and 'economy'. In these terms we can admire the airplane for its imagination and 'cold reason' (the same spirit, after all, that built the Parthenon). To build the new house and town we need men who are 'intelligent, cold and calm', governed by standards which are a matter of 'logic, analysis and precise study'. For Ruskin in *The Stones of Venice*, the Gothic included the grotesque, the ludicrous, play, laughter. For Le Corbusier, to attain austerity is to reach for the highest levels of mind and sensibility.[25]

The ideal city

In 1924 Le Corbusier published *Urbanisme*, which quickly went through many editions; the eighth French edition was translated by Etchells in 1929 as *The City of Tomorrow*. The translation includes Le Corbusier's Voisin plan for Paris which had been shown at the Exhibition of Decorative Art, Paris, 1925, and was named after the Voisin motor car company that had agreed to sponsor it (Peugeot and Citroen had turned him down). Le Corbusier notes that he experienced enormous difficulties in being part of the Exhibition at all.[26] The plan caused outrage, and in much of *The City of Tomorrow* we see Le Corbusier answering his critics and opponents. He evidently felt that he was unfairly being accused of ignoring emotion, the poetic, and nature.

While nature seems to us chaotic, the spirit which animates it is order, in particular the equilibrium that comes with the balance of the horizon, the horizontal, the straight line, with the vertical, giving us the right angle, and so the universal foundation of the geometric. The right angle has superior rights over all other angles, because it enables order, coherence, and so keeps before us the idea and possibility of perfection. In founding building as geometric, as in houses, or towns planned according to rectilinear patterns, we are at one with Nature's deepest law. With horizontals, prisms, pyramids, spheres and cylinders we enjoy serenity and joy, the Hellenic spirit.[27]

As well, the human body demands sunshine. Skyscrapers, for example, create a 'vertical city', rising upwards, open to light and air, clear and radiant and sparkling. Their immense geometrical façade, all of glass, reflect the blue glory of the sky. They are 'bathed in light'. Furthermore, skyscrapers, these 'clear crystals of glass', are set far apart, so that their outlines are softened by distance, and at their feet are parks, making the city 'one vast garden'.[28]

Here is Utopia, city of skyscrapers in the midst of green spaces. It is only when we are on high, looking down at a city from a skyscraper, or from the platforms of the Eiffel Tower, that we can see how geometric a town or city should be; and looking down from such heights gives us a moving feeling of comprehensiveness, a feeling so far enjoyed by Alpine climbers alone.²⁹

Le Corbusier was, however, irritated by his critics claiming that he wanted everyone to live in skyscrapers, up to 700 feet high. Not so, he wished to clarify. The skyscrapers are business offices only, appropriate (unlike adapted dwelling houses used at the moment) for the life of commerce. They contain the brains of the whole nation; everything is concentrated in them, from telephones, cables, radio, to the banks and the control of industry. The skyscrapers enable the model city, the 'new business city'. But, says *The City of Tomorrow*, the skyscraper, the office, has nothing in common with dwellings, which were never to be taller than roughly 160 feet. They provide the horizontal lines to balance the verticals of the skyscrapers. Le Corbusier includes a drawing showing long lines of flats, the buildings six double storeys in height, with every window of every room, on both frontages, looking onto open spaces.³⁰

At present Parisians delude themselves in thinking they live in an admirable city or in tolerable home conditions. Paris is a 'dangerous magma' of human beings gathered from every quarter by conquest, growth and immigration. Parisians live in the 'corridor-street', which must be broken up in order to create a city of the broad vista. Parisians are everywhere sandwiched between three or four neighbours; staircases are badly lit; there is no lift; servants are housed uncomfortably somewhere under the roof. And servants show how unfree Parisians really are. If they want company for an evening, the servants grumble, and there is a domestic crisis. In any case, the drawing room is small and neighbours expect to be asleep about ten. If you come back with friends for supper round about midnight, the servant sulks. As for physical culture, it takes people an hour to get to the gymnasium, where they are heavily charged.³¹

In Le Corbusier's Voisin plan for Paris, whole such jumbled areas would be cleared, and blocks of dwellings on the cellular system (each flat a cube) would be constructed. Some 660 flats or maisonettes can be built and grouped together, making a 'sort of community'. A co-operative organisation or hotel syndicate could direct the catering and domestic services, so live-in servants were no longer necessary. The 'servant problem' would be solved. The concierge would vanish, replaced by reception rooms, pleasant and dignified. With the universal use of reinforced concrete, the attic can be done away with and replaced by a terrace. The roof becomes a sort of extra street, for strolling, sun parlours, gymnasiums, even a 1000-yard track for running.³²

The new blocks of apartments permit a flourishing of nature. Each apartment is divided by hanging flower gardens. The roof is available for gardens. At ground level there will be a massive planting of trees, far more than can survive at present in Paris' corridor-streets. Once the old corridor-street has given way to wide, noble and cheerful spaces, there will be a 'charming partnership between man and nature'. The presence of trees in the city is a kind of caress, a kindly thing in the midst of our 'severe creations'. The clear-cut shapes of the buildings will combine with the rounded forms of the foliage and the arabesques of the branches. The City of Tomorrow indeed could be set amid green open spaces. The outer suburbs can be replaced with Garden Cities. Men, women and children who wish to engage in sport should be able to do so: sportsgrounds will be just outside their front doors. Football, tennis, running tracks, basketball, are all now available. The green open spaces allow gardening as well. At present householders the world over tend to their little private gardens round their house, painfully caring for flowers, a few fruit trees, a tiny plot for vegetables: 'And the result of all this is a few pears and apples, a few carrots, a little parsley and so on. The whole thing is ridiculous.' Now, all such private gardens can be joined together, can be automatically watered, ploughed with tractors, and systematically manured, the whole supervised by a farmer who employs methods of intense cultivation, standardised and scientific, and does the heavy work while the inhabitants, for example, the shorthand typist, are at work. When the inhabitants come home from office or factory, they can enjoy themselves doing light work in the garden, and gathering the produce that can feed them for most of the year. Between the gardens and houses are orchards.[33]

Further, Le Corbusier maintained, his Voisin scheme for Paris would respect the city's historical past, indeed would rescue it. The ancient churches, certain historical monuments, arcades, doorways, carefully preserved because they are pages out of history or works of art, or a fine Renaissance house, would now be shown off at their best by being surrounded by verdure, by green grass, trees, woods.[34]

Le Corbusier was evidently stung by charges that he wished Old World cities like Paris to be torn down and reconstructed as American-type cities. In *The City of Tomorrow* he is appreciably more ambivalent about America. At the beginning, he rounds off the italicised foreword by exclaiming that Europe is not old at all, it is still full of power, it is alert and inventive. While America's strength is in its youthfulness, Europe's is in the head: 'If in America they feel and produce, here we think!' Europeans must, nonetheless, have the courage to admire the way America is confronting the problem of town planning, planning of a whole urban space, in its rectilinear cities like Minneapolis. We must also continue to admire the skyscrapers of New York, but only the skyscrapers, for New York has no beauty, which only comes with geometric order; New York is all confusion, chaos, and upheaval, a barbarian city. New York is both exciting and upsetting, as are the Alps, as is a tempest, as is a battle. The skyscrapers crowd each other, creating congestion, heavy masses that stifle and oppress, mutually robbing each other of air and light, rather than being set amidst parks, as in the City of Tomorrow. Manhattan doesn't show straight lines and right angles; the line of its horizon is broken, jolted, irregular, lacking rhythm. Manhattan, indeed, Le Corbusier declares near the end of *The City of Tomorrow*, is the exact opposite of what his Voisin plan envisages for Paris.[35]

Le Corbusier was also clearly stung by an accusation that he was too admiring of a supposed German spirit of order. On the contrary, he replied, it was Germany and the countries of northern Europe that practised an architecture and town planning stressing the curved line, which he dismisses as the Pack-Donkey's Way of constructing a city, all zigzags, crowdedness, and confusion. It is northern Europe which produces baroque, rococo, disjointed Gothic; and the farther north you go, the more you will be depressed by cathedrals reflecting the agony of the flesh, hell and purgatory, or forests of pines seen through pale light and cold mist. It is French cultural history which gives us the beauty of geometric order, as in Louis XIV and the Louvre, Le Nôtre and the Tuileries and the Invalides and Versailles and the Champs Elysées. The Hellenism, the serenity and joy produced by geometric forms, is unknown to the Gothic.[36]

Le Corbusier admired an architecture and town planning of geometric forms wherever it occurred in the world. Throughout *The City of Tomorrow* there are warm references to Stamboul, the domes and minarets of its mosques, a 'suave melody of very gentle forms'. Everywhere Stamboul's houses, noble examples of architecture, are surrounded by trees. But for Le Corbusier, in an image very much drawn from a century of Orientalist thought and assumption, Stamboul, with 'Allah watching over all', is also 'orientally immutable', historically static. The corollary is that European history is dynamic, is always open to change, and, in the twentieth century, can change, can produce the City of Tomorrow, possessing a beauty based on uniformity and unity, mass production, the machine age, and – speed. Staring at the speeding traffic on the Champs Elysées, Le Corbusier felt overwhelmed by an enthusiastic rapture, the rapture of power.[37] He knew he was in love with his epoch; but that epoch could only come into its own when decorative art, such as that shown in the 1925 Paris Exhibition by other architects and designers, was swept away. The new city has to be 'made for speed'. Between its spaced-apart skyscrapers run roads for fast traffic.[38]

Our outdated cities must adapt to the age of speed, in all things. Speed will have utopian effects. The skyscraper, for example, will speed up daily communication, expediting business so much that there will almost certainly be a shorter working day. By such means will our epoch be revolutionised, though Le Corbusier was irritated that he was being called a revolutionary by those who wished to maintain society as it was. He records with amusement, however, that various Communist Party organs were refusing him the title of revolutionary; they praised the technical side of his proposals, but severely criticised him for not labelling his buildings the People's Hall or Soviet or Syndicalist Hall, and did not crown his overall plan with the slogan 'Nationalization of all property'. *The City of Tomorrow* ends with Le Corbusier declaring that his architecture and town planning were not political, were neither dedicated to the existing capitalist society nor to the socialist project, but were properly only technical.[39]

If his proposals were accepted, Le Corbusier felt sure, the twentieth century in Europe may well see the magnificent ripening of civilisation. And not only Europe, for the mass production of houses and buildings, based on standardisation, could be internationalised; indeed local architecture will disappear. He suggested that it would be a good thing if the centre of Paris was internationalised, the gigantic towers of glass of the City of Tomorrow being financed by American, English, Japanese and German capital. Such countries would then take good care never to permit Paris' destruction.[40]

As so often in cultural history, what was shocking and enraging at its beginnings, became powerful and widely accepted. Along with the Bauhaus, Le Corbusier's kind of architecture did indeed become international, the International Style, refashioning and remodelling cities, architecture, design, throughout the world.

CHAPTER TWO

Literary Modernism

Unreal City,
Under the brown fog of a winter dawn,
A crowd flowed over London bridge, so many,
I had not thought death had undone so many.
Sighs, short and infrequent, were exhaled,
And each man fixed his eyes before his feet.

T.S. Eliot, The Waste Land, *1922*

In support of the belief that the modern phase of human
history is unprecedented it is enough to point to the
machine. The machine, in the first place, has brought about
change in habit and the circumstances of life at a rate for
which we have no parallel. The effects of such change may be
studied in *Middletown*, a remarkable work of anthropology,
dealing . . . with a typical community of the Middle West.
There we see in detail how the automobile (to take one
instance) has, in a few years, radically affected religion,
broken up the family, and revolutionised social custom.
Change has been so catastrophic that the generations find it
hard to adjust themselves to each other, and parents are
helpless to deal with their children.

F.R. Leavis, Mass Civilisation and Minority Culture, *1930*[1]

While Le Corbusier disavowed any necessary political affiliation for
modern architecture, he was not shy in putting forward proposals that
he thought were best for humanity, that fulfilled humanity's supposed
universal basic needs. The implication of both *Towards a New Architecture*
and *The City of Tomorrow* was that the architect could and should decide
on humanity's behalf the true course of history. Early in *The City of
Tomorrow* Le Corbusier rebukes an opponent for criticising him in a
daily paper: 'You have no right to use the newspapers in order to impose
your own stupidity and pretence on the more or less ignorant average

reader.' *The City of Tomorrow*'s final gesture is a reproduction of a painting, *Louis XIV Commanding the Building of the Invalides*. Beneath it Le Corbusier hails the king as a great town planner, a despot who conceived immense projects and realised them by an edict from on high. (*The City of Tomorrow* also admires the ancient Romans as 'great colonizers', everywhere establishing rectilinear towns.)[2]

In England, a year after Etchells' translation of *The City of Tomorrow* appeared, a Cambridge University literary critic, Frank Raymond Leavis (1895–1978), always known as F.R. Leavis, then in his mid-thirties, brought out a pamphlet, a manifesto, *Mass Civilisation and Minority Culture*, similarly confident about humanity's true needs, this time in relation to literature and mass culture. Leavis, the journal *Scrutiny* that he edited (from 1932 to 1953), and the critical school he inspired, which came to be quickly known as the Leavisites, were destined to be highly influential in the development of twentieth-century literary and cultural criticism, in Britain as in its ex-colonies. As I've recorded in an essay entitled 'How I became a teenage Leavisite and lived to tell the tale', I was for a time a devoted disciple, when a young undergraduate and postgraduate in the 1960s.[3]

Strangely, given my then keenness for reading and re-reading every word my master wrote, I can't recall ever looking at *Mass Civilisation and Minority Culture*, nor at *For Continuity*, the 1933 volume of essays in which he reprinted the pamphlet. I was of course in no danger of being seduced by anything mass. I instinctively knew that one only read the highest literature, that is, English, European and a few approved American novels; anything else was beneath notice, was gross and vulgar. I spent much of the inner life I possessed fantasying how different my sensibility was from anything constituted by and in mass culture and the masses and indeed wishing I could live elsewhere, in some finer civilisation like Italy in touch with a noble past, rather than on these vulgar antipodean shores.

As an apprentice Leavisite in faraway Sydney (and then later Melbourne, for my postgraduate work), I could read Leavis' books like *New Bearings in English Poetry* (1932), *Revaluation* (1936), *The Great Tradition* (1948), *The Common Pursuit* (1952), *D.H. Lawrence: Novelist* (1955), and learn not only a manner, a way of talking with enormous certainty, but the canon, the poets and novelists worthy of discrim-inating attention. Reading *Revaluation*, for example, I realised I should value what Leavis articulates as the line of wit, seventeenth- and eighteenth-century poets from Donne and Marvell to Dryden and Pope, whose verse combined intelligence with passion, the sardonic and poig-nant, the flippant and intense. At the same time I learnt that nine-teenth-century poets like Shelley were merely emotional and rhetorical, and that poetry only recovered suppleness and sinewiness with late nineteenth-century poets like Gerard Manley Hopkins (who also earns high canonical ranking in *New Bearings in English Poetry*), and then Ezra Pound and T.S. Eliot. (It was only much later, in studying popular radical verse like Shelley's witty and passionate *The Masque of Anarchy*, inspired by the Peterloo riots, that I came to appreciate that Leavis' judgment on Shelley was a travesty.)

To be a Leavisite was to feel oppositional, resistant, to know oneself as sternly apart from any conventional literary judgements, just as Leavis had been from the beginning of his career. *New Bearings in English Poetry* (1932) challenged the conventional criticism of the day by championing the claims of the new modernist poetry of Eliot and Pound. Here we can point to similarities with Le Corbusier's architectural project. Where Le Corbusier disliked the decorative arts movement and what he took to be the intrusive styles of the late nineteenth century, seeing them as sentimental, lightweight (like a feather on a woman's hat) – as it were feminine – Leavis similarly disliked the verse of the same period for lacking toughness, being too emotional, too much into special poetical styles. Like Le Corbusier, Leavis called for a modern poetry in touch with modern life, with contemporary speech idioms, as in Eliot's *The Waste Land* and Pound's *Hugh Selwyn Mauberley*.

Like Le Corbusier in relation to architecture, Leavis revealed a lifelong aggressive certainty about the high place and central importance of literary criticism in solving the crisis of the twentieth century. Leavis wished to establish a true way, a single comprehensive standard for all English literature, a canon of works which realised true values, values of life (responsiveness, vitality, fineness, intelligence, vigour, subtlety, wit) that are at the same time literary values.

The key difference is that Leavis believed the modern world should be invoked not to pay homage to it as with the French architect, but in order to criticise it, criticise it with unending and relentless sharpness. It is in these terms as well that Leavis would write approvingly about Pound and Eliot in *New Bearings in English Poetry*. *The Waste Land* is to be acclaimed a great poem because of its representative status, because it reveals the modern world as like Dante's Hell, marked by futility and failure, a drying up of the wellsprings of hope and renewal, even unto sex, which is sterile, breeding only disgust; dreams of romantic love can end only in desolation. Similarly, a key to *Hugh Selwyn Mauberley*'s greatness is that it has a 'representative' value, 'reflecting' the absence of direction in the modern world and its uncongeniality to the artist.[4]

In this sense, of modernism as the critique of modernity, Leavis' *Mass Civilisation and Minority Culture* is much much closer than Le Corbusier's 1920s manifestos to the way modernist media and cultural studies developed in succeeding decades. Indeed, reading Leavis' manifesto now, I'm astonished at how much it anticipates later attitudes and positions.

Culture, *Mass Civilisation and Minority Culture* argues, is always vital to the whole of society, indeed to life itself. Only a minority, a 'very small minority', possesses in any period a discerning appreciation of art and literature. The minority is the 'intelligent' few, those who are capable of 'adult' judgements and discriminations in terms of ranking what artistic and literary works are superior, which inferior.[5]

This 'very small minority' forms a 'centre', the centre of what should be the society's collective mind and temperament. Leavis approvingly quotes Matthew Arnold's *Culture and Anarchy* (1869) on the value of just such an ideal centre of correct information, taste and intelligence. The minority does not belong to an isolated aesthetic realm; on the contrary, as a centre, it keeps alive the values and standards that order the 'finer living of the age'. The minority keeps alive the very language, the 'living subtlety of the finest idiom' upon which in turn 'fine living' and the finest heritage of the past depends. And in being capable of appreciating not only Dante, Shakespeare, Donne, Baudelaire, and Hardy but also their contemporary successors, the minority constitutes the 'consciousness of the race'. (What quite Leavis means by 'the race' is unclear; he was always very concerned to establish the value of some kind of essential Englishness, but from the authors quoted here, he seems to mean a presumed European race.)[6]

The 'very small minority' are the few in society at any time who are capable of 'unprompted, first-hand judgment' on literary and artistic works. They represent proper 'authority' in maintaining standards. What should happen is that the cultural minority set standards for a somewhat wider 'cultivated public', and from there such standards radiate outwards and downwards to the public at large.[7]

That's how it was in Shakespeare's day. Shakespeare wrote plays that were at once popular drama, and could yet be appreciated by an educated minority as poetry: '*Hamlet* appealed at a number of levels of response, from the highest downwards.' True culture necessarily works at several levels, like a pyramid. Yet now the work that expresses the 'finest consciousness of the age', as in *The Waste Land, Hugh Selwyn Mauberley, Ulysses* or *To the Lighthouse*, is accessible only to a minority.[8]

In the early twentieth century, the 'very small minority' finds itself in a crisis. For its efforts on behalf of the society and race, it is conscious of facing not merely an uncongenial but a hostile environment: 'The minority is being cut off as never before from the powers that rule the world.' Not only that, but it is being displaced as a cultural élite by a false centre, by those claiming to be authorities on literature, arbiters of taste, yet who reveal only debased standards.[9]

Leavis' example is the novelist Arnold Bennett, who could be observed in the late 1920s writing literary articles in the mass circulation *Evening Standard*, articles which, unfortunately, made Bennett the most powerful maker of literary reputations in England. Bennett praises bestsellers, so that people mistake them for 'literature'. In terms of literature proper, Bennett can mention in the same breath D.H. Lawrence and a novelist called R.H. Mottram! That Bennett's association of Lawrence with R.H. Mottram is not greeted with a roar of laughter graphically shows that there is no longer an informed, cultivated and discriminating public.[10]

How can we explain why the 'very small minority' is no longer being listened to, is no longer the centre, authority, standards-bearer, keeper of the mind of the race? Leavis explains this 'catastrophe' by pointing to the phenomenon of Americanisation, the way American practices have been all too willingly accepted in England, almost as if by a fifth column. America leads the way in introducing into the world 'mass-production and standardisation', whose most obviously sinister effect lies in the 'levelling-down' that has occurred in the realm of the press, advertising, film, and broadcasting.[11]

Here is disaster. We can see the process of levelling-down in the all too successful career of press baron Lord Northcliffe. In the last half-century Northcliffe broke down the then prevailing idea that newspapers should appeal to the intelligent few; now the *Daily Mail* is read by everyone in British society, in the third-class railway compartment as in the first-class, in the big country house's kitchen and pantry as at the hall table. Throughout the society, then, the debased coin of the tabloid press has allowed the reign of established prejudices, the primitive feeling and impulse. In something called the national temperament, the bad has driven out the good.[12]

The success of Hollywood film has been even more disastrous, because films have so much 'potent influence' on their audiences. The film, it pains Leavis to observe, now provides the main form of recreation in the 'civilised world', for the film involves 'surrender, under conditions of hypnotic receptivity, to the cheapest emotional appeals, appeals the more insidious because they are associated with a compellingly vivid illusion of actual life'. A primary part of the potency of film lies in its stress on the visual sense, on the pictorial – something Leavis also detects in bestsellers, as in the Edgar Rice Burroughs Tarzan series of novels – leading to a diminished reliance on other senses and faculties, reading in particular, that are more fruitful for culture and thought.[13]

Leavis is unconvinced by the argument that attempts are being made to use film as a serious medium of art, just as he rejects the view that broadcasting should be supported because people claim to have heard good music and intelligent lectures. Both Hollywood film (engaged in purely commercial exploitation) and British state broadcasting involve the same processes of standardising and levelling-down. Because both involve mainly passive diversion, they make active recreation, especially active use of the mind, more difficult.[14]

Standardisation has also invaded the critical reception of books. The British public is not only going to false authorities like Arnold Bennett in newspapers and weeklies for guidance in their reading. They are also following an American practice in dealing with the problem of what to read among new books, using the Book of the Month Club, or Book Society, or Book Guild, which regularly put out for their members Recommended Lists. Such organisations now possess 'sovereign power' over their members. The very terms by which books of the month are recommended reveals an insidious Americanising, in the use made of the American adjective 'worthwhile' with its atmosphere of 'uplift and hearty mass sentiment'. And, from the same vocabulary, comes the term high-brow. High-brow, says Leavis, is an ominous addition to the English language, for the book clubs use it to disparage serious criticism as merely snobbish. Detective novels can, for example, be blithely recommended to book club or guild members by saying, don't listen to the objections of high-brow literary critics.[15] Detective novels! What next?

There's another insidious American influence: the creation of mass psychological control of audiences and readers in the 'unprecedented use of applied psychology'. Here is something new in history, the deliberate exploitation of the 'cheap response' which characterises twentieth-century society, in the praising of the bestseller, Hollywood film, the press, broadcasting, and, not least, advertising. Leavis quotes with alarm various proponents of advertising who argue that advertising, through market research, can now scientifically direct the public mind. This is a 'catastrophe' in debasing not only the realm of culture but the language, Shakespeare's English, as a whole. Arnold Bennett has obviously been infected by advertisers' language in the 'gross' critical vocabulary he uses in his newspaper columns, as in phrases like 'value for money' or such and such a book has 'chunks of horsesense'.[16]

The attempt, as in the behaviourism beloved of advertisers, to control the individual, is related to attempts by others in British society to replace the older 'unscientific traditional ways' with a reliance on science, a science preferred to literature and in particular poetry.[17]

For *Mass Civilisation and Minority Culture*, it is poetry above all that keeps alive in life and society active use of the mind and verbal expression at its finest. (Leavis' stress on Shakespeare's plays as poetry led to decades of neglect of the plays as performance, as meanings created in interaction with audiences.) Leavis quotes a pioneer of modernist criticism, I.A. Richards in his *Practical Criticism*, to the effect that a general insensitivity to poetry, the kind of insensitivity revealed in the turning away from fine literature to film and broadcasting, means a low level of general imaginative life.[18]

But poetry and imagination have little hope in the age of industrialism, the age that exalts 'the machine'. That which Le Corbusier delighted in is precisely what Leavis sees as at the root of the historical crisis. Because of the machine and its associated mass production and standardisation, we are in a period of decline, the kind evoked by Spengler in his *The Decline of the West*. Where Le Corbusier in *The City of Tomorrow* (at this point praising speed, commerce, and the skyscraper) argued that we should celebrate a utopia of the new and not regret any Golden Age,[19] Leavis feels that there is nothing in the new that can interest us, and that we are in danger of losing contact with tradition, the heritage of literature and culture of pre-industrial times. Where Le Corbusier anticipates a sharp, even revolutionary break with the past, Leavis cherishes 'continuity', the 'delicate traditional adjustments, the mature, inherited codes of habit and valuation'.[20]

For Leavis, another reason why we should prefer past to present lies in the sheer plethora of reading 'of all kinds' as well as other 'distractions' that beset the mind. In Wordsworth's day, there was but a 'limited set of signals', making 'severe thought' and acquaintance with the best models of literature more widely possible than now. But in this century the variety is so overwhelming that readers 'dissipate' themselves amid the 'smother of new books', losing a sense of the distinctions and boundaries that are necessary, and that only a 'serious critical organ' can provide. (*Scrutiny* would become this organ.) Here is the 'plight of culture', and we must act now.[21]

The belief in, the nostalgia for, a presumed simpler age when mental maps were clearer would become a major theme of modernist cultural criticism. Is there also a touch here, in the fear of that which distracts, makes one dissipate one's attention and concentration, and smothers one, of an image of mass culture as female, as indeed a kind of bewitching succubus, overwhelming the masculine concentration and nerve that is necessary for true discrimination if the historical crisis is to be faced and thought through?

A kind of puritanic rationalism does become important in modernist cultural criticism, the necessity of 'severe thought' about the plight of the epoch, last bulwark against the pleasures, the dissipating distractions, of the deluge of bestsellers, newspapers, film, broadcasting, advertising. Important also would become Leavis' kind of dislike and fear of what he takes to be the predominance of the visual sense in modern mass culture, with its dangerous capacity to be hypnotic, to mesmerise. So would Leavis' assertion (based on what evidence it's not clear) that Hollywood film aims for an illusion of realism (a 'compellingly vivid illusion of actual life').[22]

Important too would be the dislike of pluralism. So too would be the critical method whereby contemporary cultural figures or works are treated either with enormous respect as critical, as condemnatory, of the modern age, or, when not condemnatory, as themselves symptoms of the crisis. And so would cultural pessimism, as in Leavis' final pronouncement that the prospects for culture are 'very dark', mixed with a kind of desperate hope that the machine age can still somehow be defeated and a cultural élite, an élite which knows history's true cultural values, can regain attention, respect and authority.[23]

Doubts

Leavis' claims to magisterial knowledge, knowing that he was a member of the 'very small minority' in possession of the finest consciousness of the (English or European) 'race', who knew the finest culture of the past and could detect its modern successors, and who know precisely what humanity should read for their own good, might strike us as a little curious today. Leavis could not be more confident in *Mass Civilisation and Minority Culture* in telling us that a cultivated public should have roared with laughter when Arnold Bennett associated an R.H. Mottram with D.H. Lawrence. Yet we might now perhaps smile at Leavis himself, when in the final chapter of *New Bearings in English Poetry*, he praises as magnificent the verse of a young poet of his time, a Mr Ronald Bottrall, and says his work sanctions high hopes for the future[24] – Mr Ronald Bottrall, who sank without a trace.

Thinking of *New Bearings in English Poetry* as a whole, we might now also smile at how Leavis could possibly grant greatness to Pound's *Hugh Selwyn Mauberley*, everywhere so showy and tricksy. Certainly my fourth-year supervisor (in 1966), Tony French, smiled in puzzlement at Leavis' judgement here, arguing that the contrasts in Pound's poem between a tawdry present and an idealised past are naive, are too easily assumed, are too simple.[25]

In *Mass Civilisation and Minority Culture* Leavis associates Thomas Hardy with Dante, Shakespeare, Donne and Baudelaire, an association which might be worth a guffaw, particularly as Leavis himself, in later proclaiming the great tradition of the English novel, not only signally leaves Hardy out, but writes that attempts to take Hardy seriously in the 1920s were comical.[26] Was he thinking about his own ranking of Hardy in *Mass Civilisation and Minority Culture*?

Those novelists who provide the canon of true fiction in the 1948 *The Great Tradition* are but five, Jane Austen, George Eliot, Henry James, Joseph Conrad and D.H. Lawrence; yet Leavis early in his career had not thought highly of Lawrence, and admits in the preface to *For Continuity* that he cannot read his initial work on Lawrence 'without wincing'.[27] In *The Great Tradition*, Dickens, except for *Hard Times*, is slighted, especially for being melodramatic.[28] But later on again Leavis would drastically revise upwards his opinion of Dickens, so that by the 1967 *Anna Karenina and Other Essays* we find him acclaiming Dickens as one of the successors to Shakespeare, if, as we should, we conceive the novel as a dramatic poem. (The others now are Jane Austen, Hawthorne, Melville, George Eliot, Henry James, Conrad, and Lawrence).[29] And by 1970 he and Q.D. Leavis have published a full-length celebratory book, *Dickens the Novelist*. Perhaps it is the certainty of modernist élites, so confident at any one time of the true value and place of all culture, that deserves a refreshing roar of laughter.

CHAPTER THREE

Modernism versus Popular Literature

> . . . generations of country folk have lived to some purpose
> without the aid of books other than their Bible. But these had
> a real social life, they had a way of living that obeyed the
> natural rhythm and furnished them with genuine . . .
> interests – country arts, traditional crafts and games and
> singing, not substitute or kill-time interests like listening to
> radio and gramophone, looking through newspapers and
> magazines, watching films and commercial football, and the
> activities connected with motor cars and bicycles, the only
> way of using leisure known to the modern city-dweller. . .
>
> Q.D. Leavis, Fiction and the Reading Public, 1932 [1]

Strangely again, while in the throes of being an agog teenage Leavisite, I
never read the major work of Frank Raymond Leavis' wife, Queenie
Dorothy Leavis. I was far more interested in pursuing writers F.R. Leavis
had recommended as worthy of serious adult attention (though not the
unfortunate Mr Ronald Bottrall), such as Marvell, Pope, Henry James,
Joseph Conrad, T.S. Eliot, Lawrence, than in reading about bestsellers.
Looking at it now, I realise that *Fiction and the Reading Public*, like *Mass
Civilisation and Minority Culture*, anticipates later modernist critiques of
mass culture like an unfolding pattern.

In her introduction Q.D. Leavis tells us of the method she'll adopt in
her book. It won't, she says, be a work of literary criticism proper, for
literary criticism studies literature. The mass of fiction she will be dealing with is not worthy of being called literature, and certainly not worthy
of detailed analysis, the kind of analysis, the close study of literary texts,
for which Leavisites would become famous. Consequently she will adopt
a method she calls anthropological, sending questionnaires to various
popular writers like the creator of *Tarzan* and analysing their replies for
cultural attitudes.[2] She will also do what anthropologists do, go out in

the field and be a participant-observer; to this end she tells us that she has occasionally visited circulating libraries and newsagents to observe how the mass of English readers acquire their reading.

The late nineteenth and early twentieth century was witness to numerous brave social explorers who would penetrate the abyss of London's East End, edging along the streets, often in disguise, staying a night in a doss house, then reporting back to polite society how brutalised by poverty, overcrowding and drink were England's poor and outcast; we can think of American writer Jack London's *The People of the Abyss* (1903).[3] We don't know if Q.D. Leavis wore disguise when she descended from Cambridge to visit London's circulating libraries and newsagents; but she does espy enough to be able to report back on her field work with confidence. She also says in her introduction that she will for the most part observe, without passing any value judgements on what comes before her. This is comical.[4] It's soon more than obvious that she's like an old-style colonialist ethnographer, staring with distaste at the barbaric ways of strange and unknown people.

The key finding of *Fiction and the Reading Public* is that the mass of people in present-day England are not so much being brutalised by their social conditions as coarsened by their reading and viewing, often entwined as in the novels that accompany Hollywood 'super-films'. What is to be observed, Q.D. Leavis argues, is that most of the English public do not go to bookshops to buy books, but borrow or hire them from municipal or subscription libraries of various kinds; and what they mainly read is fiction, in particular detective, thriller, and romance, with women being the main borrowers of these 'worn and greasy novels'. Some of the romances she mentions, as in Joan Conquest's *Harem Love* and *Desert Love*, along with the more well-known *The Sheik*, by Edith Maude Hull, are set in the Orient, though this does not rouse her interest. The majority of the public also go to newsagents, where they can be seen purchasing story magazines, many of them American, including *Black Mask*, devoted to detective stories, as well as film magazines. Detective fiction, she notes, is enormously popular.[5]

At one point *Fiction and the Reading Public* quotes *Mass Civilisation and Minority Culture* to the effect that in any period it is upon a very small minority that the discerning appreciation of art and literature depends, and throughout she agrees with F.R. Leavis on the importance of judging 'sensibility', the kind and level of a writer's sensibility as revealed in a novel. As nineteenth-century European colonists were wont to think in terms of a scale of humanity, with, naturally, whites on top, so *Fiction and the Reading Public* implies a notion of a scale of sensibility. When we deal with the small group of modernist novels, that which constitutes the true life of contemporary literature, as in the work of

Lawrence, Joyce's *Ulysses*, Woolf's *To the Lighthouse*, Forster's *Passage to India*, we know we are seeing in action a first-class fully-aware mind.[6]

What sort of values, mind and sensibility does an assured member of the very small minority – referred to here as the 'sensitive minority' – find in popular writing and mass culture generally, from 'cheap fiction' to the cinema to jazz to advertising to tabloid journalism? Everywhere Q.D. Leavis observes on show a 'crudeness of sensibility', sometimes amounting to 'the fatally crude', as well as the 'second-rate mind', the 'gross', 'cheap thinking', the 'semi-educated', the 'uneducated ear', the 'emotionally uneducated', the 'almost always . . . vulgar'. In short, we see a sensibility that is dangerously 'crude, impoverished, and narrow' and hence 'typical of the level at which the emotional life of the generality is now conducted'.[7] An abyss, of taste.

How did this appalling situation come about? Here *Fiction and the Reading Public* fills out the narrative of historical decline sketched in by *Mass Civilisation and Minority Culture*, a narrative based on the assumption that culture ideally proceeds from the top down, in a unified society, within an homogeneous, pyramid-like, public. This apparently was the situation before the cultural destruction wrought by the modern world. Q.D. Leavis tells us that when, for example, in the sixteenth and seventeenth centuries the mass of people went to see *Hamlet*, it was almost certainly 'only a glorious melodrama' to them, but they were nonetheless living at that moment in terms of Shakespeare's blank verse, his plays as poetry. Consequently their ear and mind were being educated 'unconsciously', to such effect that their standard of mental alertness and concentration has never been reached by the London public since.[8]

The eighteenth century too was a period worthy of keen nostalgia, different from the previous centuries in being, while less innocent and lusty, more fine. Here was another peak of English cultural history. For one thing, there was a unified reading public, likely to read every novel published, all living in the same mental world and the 'same code', shared by reader and writer. It was an age of the common reader, where common was not, as it is now, a derogatory term. Indeed in the eighteenth century the reader was anything but common. The prose of Aphra Behn, for example, implied a shared background that was 'cultured', a code of manners, wit, polite intercourse, good breeding. Her stories reveal an exquisite poise, the poise of an aristocratic society, an 'aristocratic culture' that properly stressed the elegant, the polished, the refined. The educated class was scattered up and down Britain, from Edinburgh to Cornwall, forming little centres of culture, each pursuing its own sober round of duties and pleasures, meeting in the evenings to sing, read aloud the latest books, discuss politics, and keep in touch with each other's thought through the critical review and the 'dignified newspaper'. The governing class then was cultivated.[9]

The achievement of the eighteenth-century also lay in the creation of what we would now call the public sphere. In particular, the journalism early in the century of Steele and Addison's *Tatler* and *Spectator*, in a language that was lucid, urbane, and polite, established common standards of taste and conduct. These 'serious standards', 'adult and critical', were also shared by writers later in the century and into the first part of the nineteenth, from Richardson to Scott to Jane Austen. Eighteenth-century taste and 'sensibility' was happily controlled by decorum, a decorum at once emotional and rational. The eighteenth-century public was 'still homogeneous', and the century's 'literary map' still possessed a reassuring 'simplicity'. The public, the 'one public', through the reviews which were so intelligent, serious and critical, took its standards 'from above'.[10]

For those low in society, peasants and craftsmen, life from the sixteenth through to the early nineteenth century was also preferable to how the majority live in the present. Reassuringly, standards of behaviour and judgement were traditionally set for them by the 'select, cultured element'. Most could not read, but this was a fortunate state of affairs. *Fiction and the Reading Public* quotes one such oldtime craftsman who managed to survive into the twentieth century, George Sturt in *The Wheelwright's Shop* (1923), a favourite Leavisite witness. Before the age of the machine, skilled hand-work, even if the hours were very long, up to twelve, was in intimate touch with the materials of life, with iron, timber, clay, wind and wave, horse-strength. Here was that literary-modernist utopian ideal in practice, a 'genuine community'.[11]

In the sixteenth and seventeenth centuries, reading did not play much part in the lives of the majority, who, when they weren't unconsciously benefiting from Shakespeare' poetry, were involved in 'active participation' in music, in catches, ballads, whistling. Further, the community inherited a body of traditional lore, rich in 'proverbial wisdom', local and national proverbs, traditional similes and dicta, tested by generations of use and pooled to form a common stock of social wisdom, which prevailed almost up to the present day. It is a pagan folk idiom 'rooted in the soil', as were the religious works read by those who could read, the Authorised Version of the Bible and, for the Puritan 'respectable poor' of the seventeenth century, Bunyan's *Pilgrim's Progress*.[12]

Bunyan's great work reveals a subtle morality that was a triumph of Puritan culture, and showed that his sensibility was on the side of the high-brow (a term that Q.D. Leavis adopts, without worrying if it is an Americanism, as does F.R. Leavis). From low to high and back again there was unity and complementarity, not fatal disjunction. Further, even into the nineteenth century, journeymen and peasants and trades-men were guided by the surviving Puritan tradition, and read poetry, novels, history and criticism to serious purpose, as did mid-century working-class radicals like the Chartists.[13]

Clearly for *Fiction and the Reading Public* the rot set in in the latter half of the nineteenth century. Oh that that century had never happened! The destructive forces were so many. There was, for a start, a turning towards romance (or 'romantic idealism'), melodrama, and the sen-sational in many novels. We only have to compare Jane Austen as representing the best of the continuing eighteenth-century tradition, with Charlotte Brontë's *Jane Eyre* (1847). Austen, with her 'code of good taste and good sense', preserves a delicate distance from the emotional situations she handles. But Brontë is too close to such situations, and consequently exhibits a 'shameful self-abandonment to undisciplined emotion'. *Jane Eyre* is but a fable of wish-fulfilment, a form of self-indulgence appealing to the 'commoner daydreams'. Unfortunately, it was Charlotte Brontë's 'crudities of feeling' which helped shape popular fiction during the Victorian period, alongside writers like Dickens and Thackeray, with their 'vulgarity and puerility'.[14]

Dickens' sensibility is judged harshly in *Fiction and the Reading Public*. Dickens, again in contrast to the sophisticated, gentle code of the eighteenth century, stands for a set of 'crude' emotional exercises (crude is a favourite word). Dickens indeed discovered the laughter-and-tears formula that has been the foundation of practically every popular success since, in the bestseller as in the Hollywood film. The alert critical mind can, however, cut such tears off at the source 'in a revulsion to disgust'.[15]

Emotionally, Dickens is not only uneducated, he is also immature. He represents the uninformed and half-educated writing for the un-informed and half-educated. But more: Dickens, in helping to pioneer and establish cheap serial publication, had to abandon patient cumul-ative construction of a novel for immediate sensational effects. Hence melodrama was introduced into the world of letters, with its violent incidents, stagy dialogue and use of coincidence. In the lack of restraint of *Jane Eyre*, and the serial form and closeness to stage melodrama of Dickens, we can see the beginnings of the split between popular and cultivated taste, between the educated and the general public.[16]

Then there was the coming of the popular press late in the nine-teenth century, which hastened the erosion of the Puritan tradition, a process we can sum up as the replacing in popular taste of the Bible and *Pilgrim's Progress* with *News of the World* and the *Sunday Express*. As in F.R. Leavis' *Mass Civilisation and Minority Culture*, Northcliffe figures largely in this story of disastrous decline. Periodicals before Northcliffe were, it might be conceded, occasionally dull; after Northcliffe they have almost always been 'vulgar'. Before 1850 the standards of popular journalism were set from above; after Northcliffe came a new breed of journalists, more akin to businessmen, using applied psychology to secure readers, and introducing tabloid styles which influenced not only newspapers but popular fiction as well. Today, it is not easy to draw a line between the popular novelist, the journalist and the advertising copy writer.[17]

Another primary destructive force was industrialism itself, brutal in the early part of the nineteenth century, but releasing the majority into hours of leisure by its end and into the twentieth century, when the older polite society and the old craft ways had been all but destroyed. Here *Fiction and the Reading Public* offers a now familiar contrast between modern industrial society (*Gesellschaft*) as mechanical and alienating and standardised by mass-production, and premodern society as genuine or organic community (*Gemeinschaft*) – the distinction that has been so influential in the development of sociology.[18]

Fiction and the Reading Public was an important contribution to the sociological tradition, arguing that the older village and small town communities have now been replaced by cities, cities composed of units whose main contact with each other outside the home is in the dance-hall, the cinema, and the theatre (she presumably means the popular theatre). In cities people lead lives of desolating isolation, and such amusements, including reading the press and bestsellers, compensate for the 'poverty of their emotional lives'. How modernists like Q.D. Leavis know that people in modern cities are poverty-stricken in their emotional lives I don't know. She refers to letters readers have written to their favourite popular novelists saying they like the way the novels have created characters that live for them, that are real and like friends. Actually, she quotes only one such letter.[19] Becoming involved with characters in a story doesn't strike me as substantial evidence of emotional desolation. Quoting from a single letter from an unknown unidentified person is the only evidence Q.D. Leavis offers for an assertion that is supposed to cover millions and millions of people's lives. She certainly doesn't claim, despite her being an anthropologist for the purposes of the book (without revealing any professional training in anthropology or ethnography), to have visited multiple numbers of people in their homes, and to have observed and then run some sort of tests for emotional poverty.

Modernists like Q.D. Leavis don't have to do such research or run such remarkable tests. The argument of *Fiction and the Reading Public* is circular. There is no direct evidence. But since what the majority of people now read is crude and vulgar, we can therefore deduce that their emotional lives are desolate and empty – that's why they need to read such fiction in the first place, as compensation, as a substitute for the richer 'first-hand living' their ancestors led before 1850 or so, before the past of villages, small towns, Puritan religion and folk wisdom disappeared. Much of *Fiction and the Reading Public* dwells on this point, this linking of mass reading (and viewing and listening) to a kind of mass psychology. People don't really read for enjoyment; they read because they psychologically have to.[20]

Lacking the strong inner morality of old, the majority now accept passively what is given to them by way of popular fiction; and those who read the new journalism or attend the cinema or listen to the gramophone and wireless are also passive. Q.D. Leavis knows they're 'passive' because in libraries she sees that they don't ask questions about the books they borrow. (Perhaps the customers have noticed a strange, obviously cultured lady staring at them.) In any case, it's clear to the observer at these libraries, says Q.D.L., that the public is 'failing to exercise any critical intelligence' in their borrowing and reading. Indeed, the reading habit has now become so compulsory it's like a 'drug habit'.[21]

But these are not soporific drugs. Rather, they overheat. The bestseller now provides 'wish-fulfilment' and 'self-indulgence'. We can certainly see this in romance, from Charlotte Brontë's *Jane Eyre* to present examples like *The Sheik*, which, in the year of its publication, was to be seen in the hands of every typist. *The Sheik* embodies the typist's day-dream. The habit of fantasying, of castle-building, of 'vicarious living' engendered by romance is more dangerous a diet than reading detective stories because it can lead to maladjustment in actual life.[22]

Another reason why the bestseller is less a case for the literary critic than for the psychologist is an obsession with sexuality, often emerging as unconscious pornography, or emotional orgies, or the lasciviousness of the syncopated rhythms of song and dance records. Bestsellers and Hollywood films offer a kind of moral uplift (constituted by cheap responses) that is at the same time largely masturbatory. Into the bestseller the author (usually female, Q.D.L. notes) pours her own day-dreams – 'hot and hot' – and the reader is then invited to share the debauch.[23]

It's clear, *Fiction and the Reading Public* argues, that the mass literacy of the modern world, coming in with the education acts of the late nineteenth century and with compulsory schooling, is very much to be regretted. The world was better when the mass of people couldn't read, for now they read the popular novels which substitute an emotional code which is 'inferior to the traditional code of the illiterate'.[24]

Furthermore, mass literacy and state education have given the mass of people of the modern world a sense of alternatives they shouldn't have. The ideal historical situation is as it was in pre-industrial pre-mass culture times. In the Elizabethan era the majority of the audience 'had to take the same amusements as their betters'. In seeing *Hamlet* they were 'receiving their amusement from above' instead of being specially catered for as now by journalists, film-directors, and popular novelists. Again, in the eighteenth century critical standards were so firmly 'imposed from above' that the 'mere idea of any serious challenge to them was almost unthinkable'. And even up until about 1850 there was properly only one kind of journalism, the dignified kind, its standards also set from above, so that if other classes found them dull, they must go without: 'there was no choice'. For many centuries, Q.D. Leavis happily feels, there was on the part of the majority an 'unquestioning assent to authority'.[25]

When the majority have no choice, their sensibility develops along with the cultured minority that guides their lives by putting them in touch with the best that is written at any time: the novel, the true novel, can 'deepen, extend, and refine experience by allowing the reader to live at the expense of an unusually intelligent and sensitive mind, by giving him access to a finer code than his own'. In this ideal situation, the 'average man' attains 'normal development'.[26]

In the twentieth century, however, such 'normal development' is prevented by the leisure time spent in cinemas, looking through magazines and newspapers, and listening to jazz. In addition, the normal place of the 'sensitive minority' at the top of the cultural hierarchy is now being menaced. Because the cultural élite is no longer respected as the only authority on culture, the only source of standards for a single homogeneous public, it is threatened with 'extinction'.[27] It is no longer being permitted to raise society to its finer level.

No more than *Mass Civilisation and Minority Culture* is *Fiction and the Reading Public* an old quaint text, to be exhumed only for curiosity and diversion. Like F.R. Leavis' pamphlet, Q.D. Leavis' book prefigures guiding assumptions in modernist mass culture study and teaching. We can list them.

• Cultural history is a matter of clear oppositions.
• Popular fiction and mass culture in general provide 'cheap and easy pleasures'[28] for a mass public which, because of a sociological situation, of mass city living and the destruction of small-scale communities, has a need for vicarious or substitute life satisfactions.
• Mass culture is not worthy of being analysed as true or authentic literature or culture; rather, it is a reflection of the state of the mass

mind, and we must now look to a psychology or psychoanalysis of the mass reader or popular audience member to explain it.

- Mass culture offers fantasies for people whose 'normal impulses', once satisfied in pre-industrial times, are being starved.[29] Here is an idea to become prominent in media studies, that mass culture and advertising somehow cater to false needs, as against true or normal human needs which are presumed to exist or to have once existed. Modernists know what true, normal human needs are because of their knowledge of the finest values in human culture, past and present. Only the modernists themselves represent and embody the truly normal in the twentieth century. The mass, the herd, that modernists have so sharply to distinguish themselves from, is unfortunately a now corrupted form of humanity.

- The cheap and easy pleasures of mass culture are based on genres, in particular, romance, melodrama, and detective, that should have stayed low, very low, in any proper hierarchy of forms, for they have no aesthetic value in themselves. It's interesting to observe that Q.D. Leavis includes writing in the American *Black Mask* as examples of contemporary contemptible bestseller literature. Despite her claim that the critical minority always recognises the new, she signally failed to notice that *Black Mask* was permitting and encouraging talents and work in the hard-boiled detective and thriller genre, including that of Dashiell Hammett, Raymond Chandler and Cornell Woolrich (who wrote *Rear Window*, to be made into the famous Hitchcock film starring James Stewart and Grace Kelly), that would help make the modernist hierarchy of genres look more and more absurdly narrow, restrictive, and untenable.

- Romance and melodrama in particular offend against the primary aesthetic values of control, restraint, and 'rational' distance. Such values were prominent in the eighteenth century, in its literature, periodical journalism, and public sphere, the realm of dicussion and debate, conducted in an atmosphere of politeness and decorum, that could be seen in action in, for example, the London coffee shops. The eighteenth century would be idealised and projected forward as utopian examplar in just such terms in subsequent modernist thought; and the values of distance, rationality, control, restraint, would become approved modernist values, ways of count- ering what was seen as the emotionality and sensationalism of late nineteenth- and twentieth-century genres like romance and melodrama.

- The cheap and easy pleasures of mass culture prevent critical thought, thought that is critical of the modern industrial world and of mass culture. In being critical, the ideal modernist text will cause 'disturbing repercussions in the reader's emotional make-up'. By contrast, the bestseller, argues *Fiction and the Reading Public*, doesn't unsettle common preconceptions and beliefs, and so leaves the mass reader 'with a comfortable state of mind', washed in 'reassuring sentiment'. Consequently, the bestseller and the cinema, Q.D.L. tells us in a favourite phrase, appeal to the 'herd-instinct'. They are always on the side of 'social, national, and herd prejudices'. Her main evidence seems to be that popular fiction is 'completely stereotyped in its demands' and usually has a happy ending, which apparently encourages 'conformity'. Modernist writing, however, is properly pessimistic and tragic, hence necessarily disturbing.[30]

- The cheap and easy pleasures of the bestseller and song and dance records and so on have led to an eroticising of contemporary mass culture, an eroticising that is not innocent and lusty, as in the past, as in Elizabethan times, but is lascivious, unhealthy because over-stressed. Even when the bestseller deals with religion, it mixes religion with melodrama, and so emerges as a kind of 'religio-erotic stimulant', a fusion that is 'necessarily disgusting to the sensitive'.[31]

- The cheap and easy pleasures of the bestseller and so on are accepted passively; they don't encourage or demand 'active participation' (as music did in the past, as in Elizabethan times).[32]

- The cheap and easy pleasures of the bestseller, pictorial papers and the cinema lead to an over-emphasis on the eye, on the visual, which is necessarily inferior to reading.[33]

- The bestseller exists only for a single 'purpose'. In the case of *The Sheik*, for example, this is to provide a means for fantasy, that denies 'thinking'.[34]

- The bestseller, journalism, advertising, and cinema, organised by commercial methods in 'mass-production conditions', have assumed a 'monstrous impersonality' that has become 'terrifying'. The only hope is blanket opposition, 'resistance by an armed and conscious minority'.[35]

- The conscious minority has become a victim of the possibly uncontrollable directions that the modern world and mass culture are taking. This strain of victimology, this ever-present note of plaint against the world, of lament, shades into other directing modernist moods, an expectation that history will be tragedy, that modern life (and love and relationships) will be failure, defeat, bleakness, loss. Curiously, however, at one point, *Fiction and the Reading Public* contradicts such victimology when it notes, almost as an aside, that in the late nineteenth century some high-brow novelists, including Henry James and Conrad, were influenced by contemporary French novelists like Flaubert to cultivate the novel as an art meant only for an initiated audience. Here, Q.D. Leavis is suggesting, it was the modernists who took the initiative in separating themselves from the 'ordinary reader', in choosing their isolated state. Elsewhere in *Fiction and the Reading Public*, however, such isolation occurs because of the withdrawal of the herd from proper culture, led by popular novelists who 'exhibit a persistent hostility to the world of letters which is quite unprecedented'.[36]

- In terms of teaching, education must always be directed against mass culture. Such an education will train a 'picked few' who, in a 'missionary spirit', can go out into the world organising 'conscious resistance'.[37]

  Part of this resistance will be directed against American influences, which include not only mass culture but the American attitude to democracy that challenges the 'many centuries of unquestioning assent to authority' that once distinguished Europe.[38] In general, liberal democracy is of no interest to *Fiction and the Reading Public*, since the mass of people's lives in modern cities are emotionally poverty-stricken (as we know from their liking of mass culture and their general demeanour).

- We should oppose cultural plurality or relativism in aesthetic judgements, the existence of more than one reading or viewing public, since it is the modernist élite, the critical minority, who should take the acknowledged lead in setting new cultural standards.[39] What is good for the cultural minority, the avant garde, is good for the world.

- Cultural maps are needed, as in the 'simplicity of the eighteenth-century literary map', when novels were still being published in 'manageable numbers'. We must have an 'accepted scale of values', set for all by the magisterial modernist élite, more intelligent, sensitive, rational, far-seeing, perceptive and discriminating than anyone else in contemporary society. They know their sensibility is finer because they alone can respond to their own modernist culture.[40]

- Finally, *Fiction and the Reading Public* exhibits historicism, the perception of a period or age, whether it be the Elizabethan, the eighteenth century, or the modern (the later nineteenth and into the twentieth), as dominated by a single force or mode or mood: the ascription of singular characteristics, a single spirit, as in the 'temper of the age', the 'sensibility of an age', the 'tone of the age'.[41] Such visions and language of unity and totality are, we might think, disproved by the deep contradictions within twentieth-century modernism itself, as in the conflict between literary modernism and Le Corbusier's architectural modernism as well as avant-garde movements like the

Cubist or Constructivist or Futurist, which extolled the possibilities of the machine age, of new technology, engineering, and cities.[42] Each modernism was ever wont to identify its version and vision with modernism as such.

Yet it was literary modernism that was most preoccupied with mass culture, and, as we shall now see, almost all subsequent literary modernist analyses of mass culture are but footnotes to *Mass Civilisation and Minority Culture* and *Fiction and the Reading Public*.

CHAPTER FOUR

The Frankfurt School versus Walter Benjamin

> Pleasure always means not to think about anything, to forget suffering even where it is shown. Basically it is helplessness. It is flight; not, as it is asserted, flight from a wretched reality, but from the last remaining thought of resistance. The liberation which amusement promises is freedom from thought and from negation.
>
> *Adorno and Horkheimer,* The Culture Industry'[1]

In the inter-war period literary modernists like the Leavisites engaged in frequent debate with a new generation of Marxist critics and cultural theorists. In *For Continuity* (1933) F.R. Leavis says he supports the utopian vision Marxists have: 'I agree with the Marxist to the extent of believing some form of economic communism to be inevitable and desirable.' He also believes that a 'serious' educational movement would aim at fostering an anti-acquisitive and anti-competitive moral bent. He disagrees, however, with the way Marxists discount the possibility of a unified culture that might (as in the past) transcend social divisions, a culture to be fostered by a new critical centre and an associated (serious) educational movement. Criticism and education would, he thought, do more to oppose present society than the class warfare urged by Marxists.[2]

Curiously, the Frankfurt School, the most influential group of Marxists to emerge after World War I, would produce theories and positions that were not at all dissimilar from those of the Leavisites.[3] They too assumed that a 'very small minority' should be at the centre of the age, of mind and consciousness. In effect, the Frankfurt School married Marxism to modernism, and in the process Marxism emerged very different from what it had been, in particular in attitudes to class and class consciousness, to revolutionary optimism, and to the working class as the ideal bearer of the future, the basis of a new society.

Like the Leavisites, the Frankfurt School was profoundly affected by the inter-war context. For the Leavisites, this largely meant feeling displaced and menaced by what they saw as the explosion of mass culture in the early twentieth century, from newspapers to cinema to bestsellers to jazz, much of it American or American in style. The Frankfurt School, too, felt threatened by the perceived flood of new mass culture; but they also were responding to the growth of fascism and Nazism on continental Europe from the late 1920s, political developments that affected them personally as well as intellectually.

Largely composed of German Jewish intellectuals centred in a social research institute in Frankfurt, the school wrote in a European tradition of speculative philosophy. This usually means long passages of argument rarely interrupted by supporting examples. They included figures who would become prominent in twentieth-century social thought like Theodor Adorno, Max Horkheimer, Herbert Marcuse. With the rise of Nazism, Adorno, Horkheimer and Marcuse became exiles in the United States; the Institute of Social Research was re-established in New York.

The culture industries

The writings of Theodor Adorno and Max Horkheimer represented the mainstream of the Frankfurt School, and were to prove immensely influential in modernist mass culture theory.[4]

In *Dialectic of Enlightenment* (1944), Adorno and Horkheimer made a break with the traditional Marxist view that saw history as hope, as inevitable progress towards revolution, with the working class succeeding the capitalist class and then establishing a classless, free and abundant socialist future. They could see little in the twentieth century to support such historical optimism. The experience of fascism and Nazism seemed to show that the working class in Europe was all too ready to accept and be guided by totalitarian ideas. What Adorno and Horkheimer saw in America, land of democracy, was hardly more reassuring. For weren't the working class and the mass of people in America accepting, even willingly accepting, a mass culture whose underlying theme was social conformity, a social conformity so pervasive that it was dangerously authoritarian? In Q.D. Leavis' terms in *Fiction and the Reading Public*, America above all represents the threatening 'superiority of the herd'.[5]

I'm not arguing that Adorno and Horkheimer were specifically influenced by the Leavisites. But they were influenced by the general literary-modernist stress on the power of culture in the modern world, along with its pessimism about history. It was not so much social conditions that now oppressed people, as cultural. In their most influential essay, 'The Culture Industry: Enlightenment as mass deception', a chapter in *Dialectic of Enlightenment*, Adorno and Horkheimer delivered a scathing indictment of American mass culture of the 1920s and 1930s, the mass culture of the society that had given them haven. The unleashed entrepreneurial system of American capitalism, whose monuments are a mass of gloomy houses and business premises in grimy, spiritless cities, has in fact created effective monopoly conditions. Under such monopoly, all mass culture is 'identical', part of an 'iron system'. Movies and radio programs need no longer pretend to be 'art', for the obvious truth is that they are just businesses, industries, with their makers part of the market, as is clear from published information about their managers' incomes.[6]

The culture industry is no more than the achievement of standard-isation and mass production. We all know that the differences between various makes of cars, such as Chrysler and General Motors, are illusory: they are all alike in the end. The same applies to the apparent differences between Warner Brothers and Metro Goldwyn Mayer productions. For automobiles, there are such differences as the number of cylinders, cubic capacity, details of patented gadgets; for Hollywood films there are the number of stars, the extravagant use of technology, labour, equipment, and the introduction of the latest psychological formula. As with film, as in thriller or detective or adventure movies, so with songs, stars, (radio) soap operas, and the 'idiotic women's serial': the details are interchangeable, they recycle rigidly invariable types and formulas. For the purposes of mechanical reproduction, everything has to be stereotyped. Differences between, say, A or B movies, or magazines with different prices, are simply ways of 'classifying, organising, and labeling consumers'. The culture industry presents a 'ruthless unity'.[7]

With mass culture, the individual has become subservient to the 'absolute power' of capitalism. Unlike with the telephone, from radio onwards there has been no machinery of rejoinder. Particularly with the takeover by the sound film, movie-goers see the world outside as an extension of the film they have just left: 'Real life is becoming indistinguishable from the movies'; the film 'forces its victims to equate it directly with reality'. With the sound film, sustained thought is out of the question, for the spectator has to keep up with the relentless rush of facts. No scope is left for the mass media consumer's powers of imagination, which are becoming stunted.[8]

All the other films and products of the entertainment industry (such as jazz, which is no more than stylised barbarity) have taught spectators what to expect from any one product. Hence to any example of the culture industry spectators react 'automatically'. The culture industry as a whole, Adorno and Horkeimer feel, has 'moulded men as a type unfailingly reproduced in every product'. Consequently, the 'might of industrial society' is lodged in people's minds.[9]

With mass culture, there is too much smoothness of style, too much unity of form and content, indicating a unity of individual and society. Here indeed is the 'secret', the single purpose, of mass culture, 'obedience to the social hierarchy'. The superiority of modernist art, as in Schoenberg and Picasso or the Dadaists and Expressionists, lies, however, in a lack of harmony and unity, a 'discrepancy' between form and content that permits criticism, a negation, of modern society.[10] The Frankfurt School itself became known simply as Critical Theory, as a theory that negated present liberal capitalist society.

Like F.R. Leavis in *Mass Civilisation and Minority Culture* and Q.D. Leavis in *Fiction and the Reading Public*, Adorno and Horkheimer feel that we are in an age dominated by advertising and publicity. The culture industry needs advertising because it is always in danger of satiating the audience. Advertising strengthens the bond between consumers and the big combines, for it is only the big networks that can afford its costs. Economic power in the culture industry is more and more centred in the same hands, not unlike, they argue, a totalitarian state. The repetition of the same culture product is the same as that of the propaganda slogan, as with the German fascists. Furthermore, advertising has permeated the style, the very idiom, of the culture industry. Advertising and the culture industry are merging at such a rate that it is now difficult to distinguish them, as a 'quick glance' at, for example, advertisements, editorial and text will reveal of American magazines like *Life* and *Fortune*. The merging makes of advertising, publicity and product a procedure for manipulating people, a form of 'psycho-technology'.[11]

Modern America is to be compared unfavourably with traditional European society. It worked, for example, to pre-fascist Europe's advantage that democracy was slow in coming. From the time of princes and feudal lords to their successors in the nineteenth century, culture, as in Germany's universities, theatres with 'artistic standards', great orchestras, and museums, enjoyed protection. In particular, 'art' was free from the pressures of the market, of supply and demand.

Such demand in modern American society is, Adorno and Horkheimer are sure, illusory in any case, since consumers are moulded by the American social system to have the same 'manufactured needs' for the same culture industry products: 'Capitalist production so confines them, body and soul, that they fall helpless victims to what is offered to them.' Adorno and Horkheimer agree with the verdict of the French thinker Alexis de Tocqueville when he visited America in the mid-nineteenth century, that democracy means conformity, conformity to the majority, otherwise you will be treated as an outsider, and the 'most mortal of sins is to be an outsider'. Liberal democracy means mere mass conformity: the 'deceived masses' themselves insist on the very ideology which 'enslaves' them. Tocqueville's analysis has proven 'wholly accurate'.[12]

Some doubts

Adorno and Horkheimer's argument in 'The Culture Industry' relies on the kind of iron system of binary oppositions that structured the work of the Leavisites.

There is the sure opposition of true and false cultures. False art as in the culture industry emphasises sexuality and desire, in the naked torso of the athletic hero or breasts in a clinging sweater, but erotic situations are never allowed to go too far. True art, however, knows that in the realm of sexuality fulfilment is always a broken promise: 'Works of art are ascetic and unashamed; the culture industry is pornographic and prudish'. Indeed, love in the 'pleasure industry' is downgraded to romance, whereas true ecstasy always involves 'pain', the pain that is also found in ascetism. True delight is 'austere'.[13]

Adorno and Horkheimer know what true art is, that it always involves the tragic, assumed to be an aesthetic absolute, unarguable. The only time Adorno and Horkheimer come close to approving of anything in Hollywood is in a reference to the 'tragic Garbo', though her presence, as Hollywood has gone on, is being replaced by the non-tragic, by Mickey Rooney.[14] Always, in modernist cultural history, there is the same unfailingly reproduced narrative of decline.

Not only do Adorno and Horkheimer know what true art must always involve, but they also know that the culture industry denies 'truth', for example, the 'true kind of relationships' human beings should have, but can't, in democratic America. They know that the culture industry is colouring the very 'language and gestures of the audience and spectators' – even though, they admit, as if it's a minor and forgettable problem, that such can't be yet shown experimentally. They can't show it, but they know it. They know what 'girls in the audience' feel in the cinema.[15]

Here is a passage from the concluding paragraph of their essay, commenting on the 'most intimate reactions of human beings' in contemporary America:

> The way in which a girl accepts and keeps the obligatory date, the inflection on the telephone or in the most intimate situation, the choice of words in conversation, and the whole inner life as classified by the now somewhat devalued depth psychology, bear witness to man's attempt to make himself a proficient apparatus, similar (even in emotions) to the model served up by the culture industry.[16]

How can Adorno and Horkheimer conceivably know such things? How do they know how millions of young American women accept a date? Did they listen in on their conversations, or tap their phones? How could they know what the mass of Americans possess for an inner state when in the 'most intimate situation'? How did they become such privileged observers? Did they go around observing millions of people making love? Even so, would such observation (however attained) give them access to the masses' 'inner life'?[17]

The level of evidence for such propositions is, then, not only disturbingly casual and even laughable. It is also complacent, and therefore repellent. 'The Culture Industry' was written in the early 1940s, and presumably represents their reflections on 1930s Hollywood film. Yet while there is an occasional reference to Hollywood stars, no titles of any movies are mentioned: there was no invitation by Adorno and Horkheimer to readers to check the claims being made about Hollywood with any actual examples. In a monologic way, readers are positioned by the Culture Industry essay as passive, as having automatically to accept as received truths their totalising judgements.

Nevertheless, it is headscratchingly difficult to think of examples from the 1930s to support their key propositions, for example, that with the coming of the sound-film movie-goers see the world outside as an extension of the film they have just left, that 'Real life is becoming indistinguishable from the movies', that the film 'forces its victims to equate it directly with reality' because it is 'intent upon reproducing the world of everyday perceptions'.[18] What conceivable examples from the 1930s could be brought forward in support? The 1930s was the great age of genres, of the western, the gangster film, the hard-boiled detective, the screwball comedy, the musical, the family melodrama. Such genres inherited conventions from nineteenth-century popular American (and travelling English) theatre, from vaudeville, from dime novels, from romantic ballads.[19] They called attention to themselves not as reality but precisely as genres, created under the sign of a general melodramatic mode, enjoying to the full their genre characteristics and conventions, always reproducing and yet varying and playing with those conventions. Furthermore, the painterly effects, the dramaturgy, and the melodrama music of classic Hollywood were extravagant, lush, excessive, extreme, the very reverse of realism. Are we supposed to think that the astonishing choreography of Busby Berkeley's 1930s musicals was indistinguishable from real life outside the cinema? Adorno and Horkheimer's claims here are merely preposterous, ludicrous.

Where is the empirical support from 1930s Hollywood for another of their propositions, that film, insisting on conformity, can never positively entertain the outsider?[20] Let's think of an example ourselves, one of the first Hollywood technicolour films. The 1936 *The Garden of*

Allah, a romance-melodrama, stars Marlene Dietrich and Charles Boyer. Dietrich plays Domini, a wealthy young Catholic woman who is restless and dissatisfied with the great world of Europe; she travels by train to the edge of the Sahara in Algeria, where she meets and falls in love with Boyer's character, Boris Androvsky, another European traveller. They marry and journey into the desert for their honeymoon, where Domini learns that Boris is really a Trappist monk who has fled from a monastery elsewhere in Algeria, fled because he can no longer tolerate a life of silence and ascetic retreat from the pleasures of the world. At the end, there is no easy resolution; an agonised Boris returns to the monastery, and an equally agonised Domini is driven off in a carriage. Both Boris and Domini are clearly outsiders, and indeed the film is peopled with Europeans drawn to the desert, because closeness to it generates a life and challenge far from the stifling ways of Europe. Boris and Domini experience the desert as metaphysical, as testing their deepest desires and fears. *The Garden of Allah* revels in its non-realist dramaturgy, with Dietrich's face (for we never doubt Domini is both a character and always and already 'Dietrich') like a mask, the intense stylised mask of melodrama. Visually, the film is fascinated by whatever is not European, by its construction of Arab crowd scenes and of the Sahara, effects that recall nineteenth-century Orientalist paintings.

We might even hazard that a feature of Hollywood, in the 1930s as before and since, is a fascination with outsider figures, a fascination that is rarely if ever conformist dismissal. We only have to think of the most popular Hollywood film ever, the 1939 *Gone With the Wind*, with Clark Gable as Rhett Butler, clearly an outsider to the South and the North in the Civil War, critical of both. Rhett is a rogue figure (Scarlett O'Hara calls him a varmint), a gun-runner, a trickster at home everywhere, including in a house of ill-repute, a bandit recalling centuries of admired criminal figures, a descendant of Robin Hood and Dick Turpin. (We can think as well of the 1940 version of *The Mark of Zorro*, with Tyrone Power, Linda Darnell, and Basil Rathbone; Power plays Zorro, the masked bandit and Robin Hood figure.) The film's sympathies flow towards those low in society, the black slave Mammy, the prostitutes, the wage-slaves employed and harshly treated by Scarlett in the industrialising of the South after the war. Rhett himself embodies friendship and loyalty, not manipulating people, contrasting with the caste and class attitudes of Scarlett, as in her contempt for the prostitute or assorted white trash. At the end, as Rhett walks out into the night, dejected and rejected by her, the pathos is all with the outsider figure, not the respectability-seeking Scarlett.

No admiration in Hollywood for outsider figures! Only three years after *Gone With the Wind* audiences could study Humphrey Bogart as

Rick in *Casablanca*. You really have to wonder how much acquaintance with Hollywood, with the empirical material, Adorno and Horkheimer allowed themselves. Are their generalisations based on gross, massive and culpable ignorance? Did they not have to see, because they already knew? Was their argument the long unfolding of an a priori judgement?

There are other worrying features of the Culture Industry essay. It is reflectionist, assuming that mass culture like Hollywood film simply reflects American social and industrial life. It is thereby also functionalist, assuming a smooth fit between aesthetic forms, images, representations and non-aesthetic realms, between culture and society, as if the capitalist world was a smoothly functioning totality, without divergence, disjunction, conflict, contradiction, questioning, challenge, reversal, inversion, messiness, inexplicability, enigma. It offers a mechanical theory of what Adorno and Horkheimer refer to as 'social control', manipulation and domination from the top.[21] In assuming a single mass spectator, the subject of psychology and psychoanalysis, it undercuts any sociology of viewing groups, groups divided by tensions of race, class, gender, age, religion, region, nation. Its method is what we can call structuralist, in its vast reduction of the complexity and diversity of mass culture to a single ideological meaning. And its contemptuous theory of standardisation ignores how much Hollywood's creation of genres can be seen as a great aesthetic achievement of twentieth-century popular culture.

Also disturbing are some comments in 'The Culture Industry' that come very close to a desire for censorship. At one point Adorno and Horkheimer entertain the idea of closing down the movie theatre, 'this bloated pleasure apparatus'. Such closures, they say, would not be 'reactionary machine wrecking'. The only use of cinemas they can see is for the housewife to snatch a few hours while nobody is watching, and for the unemployed to find coolness in summer and warmth in winter.[22] This flirtation with the idea of massive censorship and cultural control is in curious tension with their proclaimed anti-authoritarianism. They dislike what they see as the conformity of mass culture. Do they thereby wish, however, for the masses to conform to another culture, that approved for them by Adorno and Horkheimer, by a modernist élite?

Adorno on TV

In the 1944 Culture Industry essay Adorno and Horkheimer can feel no confidence that the imminent coming of television would stave off the 'aesthetic barbarity' that mass culture was threatening. Rather, television, as a synthesis of radio and film, promised drastically to intensify mass culture's impoverishment of aesthetic matter. After television had been going for a few years in the US, Adorno, in his 1954 'Television and the Patterns of Mass Culture', offered a critique, with the help of psychoanalysis, of its 'nefarious' effects upon the spectator's personality.[23]

Much of the argument is familiar from the earlier essay. Adorno feels that the archetypes, the key continuing features, of present popular culture were set early in the development of 'middle-class society', a couple of centuries ago, at the turn of the seventeenth century and early part of the eighteenth, in England. At this time, in the works of novelists such as Defoe and Richardson, literary production became geared to the market. By this century the commercial production of cultural goods has become so streamlined that it has seized all media of artistic expression and become a system. Even when popular forms appear to have little in common on the surface, like jazz and the detective novel, they in fact reveal an amazing parallelism in their basic structure and meaning.

This system is now the 'prevailing ideology of our time', and is wreaking major changes in social and moral values. Even those formerly aloof from modern popular culture, the rural population on the one hand and the highly educated on the other, are 'somehow affected' – a levelling-down is occurring. Adorno argues (adopting the terms of David Riesman's 1950 book *The Lonely Crowd*) that earlier generations of Americans, especially in the eighteenth century, were inner-directed, internalising the values of their parents, in particular middle-class Protestant values of concentration, intellectual effort, and erudition. Modern popular culture appears to preserve and still promulgate such values. But what we can more and more notice is that these values of early middle-class society lie only on the surface. The 'hidden message' of modern popular art is other-directed, towards the 'norms of an increasingly hierarchical and authoritarian social structure'. This hidden message is one of adjustment and unreflecting obedience, and it seems to be dominant and all-pervasive today. For the modern mass media, society is always a winner, and the 'individual is only a puppet manipulated through social rules'. The message is 'invariably that of identification with the *status quo*'.

Adorno argues that the culture industry has taken over a feature of true, authentic art, what he calls polymorphic meaning; authentic works of art can never be boiled down to a single unmistakable meaning or message. The 'rationalised products' of television have been designed as multi-layered structures, attempting to enthral spectators on various psychological levels. The explicit surface of a TV show may even be anti-totalitarian. But there will always be a hidden message, escaping the controls of consciousness. We know, says Adorno, that political and social trends of a totalitarian nature feed on irrational and frequently unconscious motivations. What the majority of TV shows do is channel audience reaction at an unconscious level so that they produce in the spectator the smugness, the intellectual passivity, the gullibility that fit in with totalitarian creeds. Consequently television, along with the rest of modern mass culture, has become a medium of undreamed-of psychological control.

Spectators don't even know that such 'indoctrination' is present. This effect is strengthened in the way TV aims for a kind of 'pseudo-realism', which permits in the spectator a 'direct and extremely primitive' form of identification. Because of this kind of realism, crime shows, for example, create an atmosphere of the normality of crime, so that there is, Adorno thinks, a grain of truth in the old-fashioned view that the mass media incite criminality in the audience, even though the overt morality of such programs is one of crime and punishment. In television, the heroic role of the big-shots of crime is silently endorsed even if they are pictured as villains.

Adorno is quite concerned about changing historical perceptions of gender. He argues that the concept of the purity of women is one of the invariables of popular culture at any time. In the eighteenth century, in Richardson's *Pamela*, we can see a conflict being played out between the ideal of chastity and bodily desire. Yet in today's popular culture there is no such inner conflict, and the invariable idea is that the nice girl gets married and that she must get married at any price. Also changing are women's erotic attitudes. Formerly, in the eighteenth century, men were presented as erotically aggressive, with women on the defensive, but this pattern has been largely reversed in modern mass culture. The stereotype of the nice young girl with unimpeachable morality remains, even if, in a particular (unnamed) show she is a crook. Such stereotyping tends to confirm in young girls exploitive, demanding, and aggressive attitudes, a character structure we know from psychoanalysis as oral aggressiveness.

He notes that on American television the stereotype of the haughty, egoistic, yet irresistible girl, playing havoc with poor dad, has become an institution. On the surface she exploits her father and is aggressive to him. But we can see from psychoanalysis that she is indeed an example of oral aggressiveness, that underneath she is really dependent on the father. Far from being the pretty girl who can do no wrong, as the surface of American TV shows suggests, she is really an example of reversion to infantile development phases.

For Adorno, then, television aims at a kind of pseudo-realism. It is full of stereotypes and formulas. It has an unvarying deep structure of ideological meaning. It offers its spectators a primitive kind of identification with what is on the screen, and it binds them to an 'infantile need for protection', a child-like search and desire for security and conformity that can be explained psychoanalytically.

Adorno's TV essay mechanically reproduces the positions of 'The Culture Industry', within an overriding modernist assumption, that we saw before in Q.D. Leavis' *Fiction and the Reading Public*. We can read off knowledge of audience responses and reception – the human condition of the mass of the population – from our (presumed) knowledge of mass culture texts. Knowledge that rarely even encompasses the title of a TV program.

Who was Walter Benjamin?

We come to Walter Benjamin (1892–1940), another famous German-Jewish cultural theorist, who had settled in Paris in the 1930s; his writings, particularly on Baudelaire and the Paris arcades, reveal dread and fascination, lament and delight in the French metropolis. When the Nazis invaded France he tried to escape to Spain, cross to Portugal and then travel to the United States. Tragically, he took his life on the Spanish border when refused entry, the Spanish having just that day closed access. Benjamin swallowed fifteen tablets of a morphia compound and died in agony. It was the 26 September 1940.[24]

Benjamin could perhaps be seen as a kind of rogue or dissident member of the Frankfurt School, yet he was not really a firm member of any set school of thought, or certainly not for long or without introducing dissolving doubts. There is no single unified 'Walter Benjamin'. Throughout his writing life he could be seen trying to work through contrary and competing positions, from nihilism and anarchism to surrealism to Brecht's Marxist theatre to Jewish mysticism to mainstream Frankfurt School theses. From work to work, essay to essay, he often reveals quite opposed attitudes, to progress, cultural tradition, technology, mass society, the city. A deeply ambivalent and contradictory figure himself, Benjamin shows how ambivalent and contradictory a phenomenon modernism has been.[25]

In some writing, especially in the 1936 essay 'The Work of Art in the Age of Mechanical Reproduction' – to which Adorno and Horkheimer's Culture Industry essay is a reply[26] – Benjamin can be seen as outside the pessimistic modernist positions that have become classic with the Leavisites and the Frankfurt School. Benjamin argues that what the mass of people most enjoy in art, and always have enjoyed, is 'simultaneous collective experience'. Such collective enjoyment is possible with public architecture, with the epic poem in pre-capitalist times, and the movie today. The long bourgeois era, however, introduced individual ownership of art. Paintings, for example, were now known to have an individual author, with an 'aura' of uniqueness and private ownership about them, and mass audiences were restricted from viewing them by the excluding associations of ownership and class.

Modern technological developments changed this situation by introducing media like photographs and film. Because they were mechanically reproduced, because there was no single photo or movie print, they did not permit the aura of uniqueness and individual and class possession that accompanies high art, the art of the salon, the art museum, galleries. Benjamin argues that it is for this reason that mass audiences still won't respond to paintings or to avant-garde movements which are 'politically progressive', even those of Picasso or the Surrealists. But they will respond positively to a 'grotesque' movie or to a Charlie Chaplin film, because in a cinema they can organise and control their own conditions of reception; in a salon or gallery no such control was permitted. Photos and especially film could be enjoyed and participated in by mass audiences as they wished. Benjamin, then, was far from seeing mass audiences as passive.

Benjamin argues in this essay against the view that the pleasures and supposed distractions of popular culture mean that readers and audiences can't also think and reflect. For Benjamin, popular audiences are not unconscious and hence totally uncritical in their response to film: 'With regard to the screen, the critical and the receptive attitudes of the public coincide'. Popular audiences combine both enjoyment and conscious discrimination and choice. He returns, then, a positive verdict on the relationship between popular film, audience response, and psychoanalysis. Film does for optical and acoustical perception what Freud's *Psychopathology of Everyday Life* did for perception of hidden depths in ordinary conversation. The camera, Benjamin said, introduces us to 'unconscious optics as does psychoanalysis to unconscious impulses', bringing about a general 'deepening of apperception' for film audiences. Cinema explores the unconscious and deepens perception, rather than making it empty and shallow.[27]

How rare indeed in this century of modernist culture theory is Benjamin's eloquent defence of popular audiences. Indeed in the 'Work of Art' essay he is defending audiences that modernism, as recent critics like Andreas Huyssen and Patrice Petro have argued, so often perceived as female - the 'girls in the audience' in Adorno and Horkheimer's derisory commentary.[28] In the reference to popular audiences preferring 'grotesque' movies, Benjamin is also, at least by implication, defending popular interest in melodramatic and sensational genres.

For a long time after his writing became well known, from the middle 1950s, 'The Work of Art in the Age of Mechanical Reproduction' was dismissed by orthodox modernist mass culture theory as technological determinism (which it clearly wasn't). But it was always a threat to the developing modernist orthodoxy.[29]

Benjamin also wrote of the modern city with a complexity and ambivalence that modernists rarely permitted themselves. Unlike Adorno and Horkheimer in the Culture Industry essay, so remote from the phenomena they so harshly judge, Benjamin in the fragments of analysis that constitute his book on Baudelaire makes close textual acquaintance with nineteenth-century urban scenes, spaces and technologies, with the arcades, photography, the street, and diverse media from the diorama to panorama literature to 'physiologies', a genre that investigated the 'inexhaustible wealth' of human types to be encountered in the marketplace. Benjamin is interested in detective fiction and in the journalism that was like detective fiction, with both the journalist and the detective drawing on the skill of the *flâneur*, the purposeful Parisian gentleman stroller, in moving among the crowd.[30]

At one point Benjamin refers to a passage where Baudelaire says how he prefers the backdrop paintings of the stage where his, Baudelaire's, 'favourite dreams' are treated with 'tragic concision', and their falsity, their illusion (like the 'crude magic' of the dioramas of old) are displayed as false, as illusion. Baudelaire sees such theatricality as much closer to the 'truth' than 'our landscape painters' who are 'liars, precisely because they fail to lie'. Baudelaire, Benjamin adds, goes so far as to judge landscapes by the standard of paintings in the booths at fairs.[31] Now recall how Adorno and Horkheimer had posed against Hollywood and the culture industry a notion of a 'true kind of relationships' – a notion that Baudelaire was scorning as a form of lying, as perilously close to a truth somehow prior to representation (though representable in an approved representation), the myth of a truth that is not endlessly deferred by representation.

Benjamin of course doesn't say he agrees with Baudelaire. He cites the passage as 'curious' and wonders about it. And such teasing citing, such agnosticism about absolute positions, are characteristic of the way he explores Baudelaire's fascination, mixed liberally with repulsion, for the big city crowd, and of how he works through other nineteenth-century writing about city life, as in Poe viewing the big city crowd as barbaric, arousing fear, revulsion and horror. Engels is also quoted from *The Condition of the Working Class in England in 1844* on the 'brutal indifference' and 'unfeeling isolation' of Londoners.[32]

The city is feverish, yet where each in the crowd is locked in isolation. In the nineteenth century we can see the city becoming standardised,

more administratively controlled, the crowd more 'uniform'. If the
flâneur does surrender to an intoxication with the crowd, as he moves
through the arcade or bazaar, it is like the intoxication with the
commodity, with the 'soul of the commodity' as Marx would have it,
which partakes equally of the spirit of 'drugs' and of prostitution, the
'prostitution of the commodity-soul'. Benjamin argues that the *flâneur's*
empathy with the crowd, the crowd he abandons himself to, is
comparable to the way, in Baudelaire's phrasing, the poet is 'a roving
soul in search of a body', who 'enters another person whenever he
wishes'.[33]

Benjamin would appear to be aligning himself with a history of
discourse where the modern city is characterised as abyss, as social
death. But his text allows doubts and qualifications to appear and
surround and tug at this discourse. The spirit of the city may be like
prostitution, yet Benjamin can refer to a Baudelaire poem where a
courtesan refers to her heart as 'bruised like a peach, ripe like her body,
for the lore of love'. He admits that Marx's allusion to the soul of the
commodity was a 'jest'. He slyly notes that Engels' comments on
London are by someone who hails from a Germany that was still
'provincial'. He tells us that when Dickens went travelling he repeatedly
complained about a lack of the street noises that were indispensable for
his writing, and that Baudelaire hated Brussels because there were no
shop-windows that would allow for strolling: as Benjamin says,
Baudelaire loved solitude, but he wanted it in a crowd.[34]

We might say that in the Baudelaire book Benjamin ponders the
implications of modernist mass-culture theory with an ambivalence that
Baudelaire himself would surely have admired as properly vertiginous.
Benjamin's writings accept neither a linear narrative of pessimism nor
of optimism, of bleakness or of hope.

I was introduced to the work of the Frankfurt School in the same
popular culture discussion group that urged me to read Benjamin. But
whereas I found Benjamin's thoughts and speculations immediately
beguiling, mainstream Frankfurt School theory struck me, just as
immediately, as everywhere astonishingly crude and even fantastical in
its generalisations. I was soon to learn, however, that to write critically in
the early 1980s of the Frankfurt School was to earn immediate censure:
how could one dare to treat so disrespectfully such modern masters of
thought (from Europe), when what they were saying about mass culture
was so obviously true?[35] It was like being ill-mannered at the dinner
table.

Yet I still think that whereas Benjamin was admirably independent-
minded in his thinking about cultural history and contemporary

culture, Adorno and Horkheimer were coming out with positions that were emerging as modernist dogma. They dwelled in safety, in conformity.

As we shall see, Benjamin's playful textuality, his theatrical staging of arguments – questioning any magisterial presumption of knowledge of history and humanity's true needs; permitting competing contradictory voices, discourses, writings, moods, to speak to each other, to unsettle, jostle, joust, and duel – can be seen as anticipating poststructuralist theories as well as various motifs of postmodernism.

CHAPTER FIVE

Flowering of an Orthodoxy

Most mass-entertainments are in the end what D.H. Lawrence described as 'anti-life'. They are full of a corrupt brightness, of improper appeals and moral evasions. To recall instances: they tend towards a view of the world in which progress is conceived as a seeking of material possessions, equality as a moral levelling, and freedom as the ground for endless irresponsible pleasure.

Richard Hoggart, The Uses of Literacy, *1957* [1]

The girls we have spoken to at the Birmingham Youth Centre constantly make jokes among themselves for the sole purpose of confusing or misleading the researcher who may well be infringing on their territory by asking personal questions, or whose presence at the weekly disco they resent. For example, one group of three fourteen year olds explained to us that the fourth member of their 'gang' had male genitals. The 'joke' lasted for about ten minutes with such seriousness that we were quite convinced until one of the girls said 'Dickie' came from Middlesex. The girls shrieked with laughter and the interview came to a halt.

Angela McRobbie and Jenny Garber,
'Girls and Subcultures', *1977* [2]

Until the late 1970s, mainstream modernist mass-culture theory after the Leavisites and Adorno and Horkheimer displayed a kind of ruthless unity. We can drop in on classic moments in French and British writing, though we should recognise that the intellectual traditions and methods drawn on by various thinkers could be very different. The ruthless unity came from the shared literary-modernist positions and assumptions.

51

French structuralism

1957 was a good year for modernist mass-culture theory. Roland Barthes' *Mythologies* appeared, a collection of magazine articles he'd written between 1954 and 1956; the essays ranged widely over the various phenomena of everyday mass culture, from wrestling to toys to a plastic exhibition to advertising. As Barthes explains in his preface to the 1970 edition, he had just read Saussure, and was trying to apply semiology to the products of mass culture, seeing wrestling or an advertisement as a language, a sign-system that could be analysed in detail. Barthes was granting to mass culture the dignity of detailed textual analysis that cultural criticism, as in the literary studies of the Leavisites, had previously reserved for 'high' literature. Here *Mythologies* is path-breaking and admirable.

But granting the dignity of detailed analysis did not mean that Barthes in any way approved or supported mass culture; *Mythologies* was no 'The Work of Art in the Age of Mechanical Reproduction'. In his 1957 preface, Barthes told his readers that the starting-point of the various essays was an impatience with the way newspapers, art and common-sense itself pass off reality as natural, as if not formed and shaped by history and ideology. He would track down such 'ideological abuse', the attempt by mass culture in 'our bourgeois world' to represent History as Nature.

'The World of Wrestling', the first and, I think, by far the most interesting essay in *Mythologies*, concerns popular wrestling, often taking place, says Barthes, in squalid Parisian halls. Here is an activity and mode of performance that seem far removed from an image of an enveloping bourgeois world. Indeed, Barthes begins by launching himself with some irritation at those presumably bourgeois people who disdain popular wrestling for not being a sport, like boxing or judo. Wrestling, Barthes ripostes, is not a sport but a spectacle. It is a spectacle of excess, of emotion without reserve, and he calls on a long ancestry of similar spectacles, in Greek drama and the masks of antiquity, in bullfights, *commedia dell'arte*, pantomime, Molière. Wrestling is a genre, obeying conventions well known to the audience, and evidently also to Barthes, for he implies that he is not a rare visitor, that it is not uncommon for him to be there listening in to the comments going on around him.[3]

Each wrestler is a character in a drama, and each body represents a grandiloquent sign. Fauvin, for example, an obese fifty-year old, treacherous, cruel and cowardly, displays in his sagging flesh the sign of an amorphous baseness; he is the *salaud*, the bastard-octopus, provoking nausea and disgust; the public calls him *la barbaque*, stinking meat.

Other wrestlers represent passivity, or grotesque conceit, or the *salope*, an effeminate, a bitch. Some of the wrestlers, Barthes notes, are great comedians, delighting the audience by their theatricality and extremes.

By the end, Barthes has nonetheless arrived at a stern judgement. Wrestling, he decides, is a drama of Good and Evil, of suffering, defeat, and justice. It seeks 'above all' to unveil the idea of justice, the justice that finally meets treachery and unfairness. This story of suffering and justice is what the public wants and has always wanted, this is the 'age-old image of the perfect intelligibility of reality'. In the clarity of its signs, popular wrestling presents an understanding of the moral universe that is without ambiguity, without contradiction, each character rounded like a 'univocal' Nature, without any allusiveness, representing only a single sign. This, says Barthes, is the public's mythology, an eternal return of desire for moral certainty and simplicity.

Yet for all the certainty of Barthes' own conclusion, 'The World of Wrestling' remains a puzzling performance. For much of it Barthes, modernist critic, almost seems to be admiring popular wrestling as highly successful theatricality – though he never admits to actually enjoying it. Further, he occasionally appears to suggest that this example of popular theatre is not necessarily so simple, is not necessarily desiring to see reality as perfectly intelligible. At one point he writes of this 'spectacle of excess' that some fights end in a kind of baroque confusion, a sort of unrestrained fantasia where the rules, the conventions of the genre, the referee's attempts to censure and the limits of the ring are abolished. They are all swept away in a 'triumphant disorder' which overflows into the hall and carries off pell-mell wrestlers, seconds, referee, and – the spectators.[4]

What is clear, however, in this essay is that Barthes has no theory of such excess in popular theatre and comedy. He has no theory that could suggest that excess, grandiloquence, extremes, in their play of parody and self-parody, are attractive to audiences precisely because they are the reverse of a certain, unvarying and immediately intelligible view of the world.

For Barthes to entertain such a theory would represent a major break with literary modernism's image of the mass as conformist and idolatrous, in contrast to the modernists themselves, who can ever entertain ambiguity and contradiction and enjoy the uncertainty of allusiveness, of meanings and references that need time and concentration and contemplation to unravel. The disdainful conclusion of 'The World of Wrestling' is the sudden reassertion of the mainstream literary-modernist myth, an abiding certainty about what the mass public supposedly always expects and wants from mass culture.[5] No more than Adorno and Horkheimer in their writing does Barthes in *Mythologies* feel any need to

test his own certainties, to try to research (apart from a bit of eavesdropping) the mass audience's responses and values.

The literary modernists have always taken it upon themselves to
decide on the psychological state of mass audiences. Yet the
contradictions in 'The World of Wrestling' prompt questions about the
psychological state of modernist critics. Does the constant reassertion
about the mass audience's limited capacities reveal in the mainstream
modernist a kind of infantile need for protection, for certainty, for
reassurance, for the security of a distance, for superiority? Was Barthes
fascinated by, did he take pleasure in, popular wrestling, despite his
modernist self? Was this pleasure repressed and displaced as stern
judgement, wrestling as ideological abuse?

Barthes' observation in 'The World of Wrestling' of the mass
audience's enjoyment of 'a triumphant disorder', 'the most baroque
confusion', 'unrestrained fantasia', also contradicts his structuralist
method. Along with anthropologist Claude Lévi-Strauss, Barthes was
part of the structuralist movement in the 1950s that challenged the
influence in French intellectual life of existentialism and inter-war
Marxism, both of which in different ways tended to focus on
consciousness (grievously alienated in our bourgeois world) rather than
institutions or structures. Structuralism looked back to the early
twentieth-century linguistics of Ferdinand de Saussure, but made a
particular interpretation of it, stressing that the surface of language,
how people talked (*parole*), was directed by a deep inner structure or
code (*langue*). The characteristic structuralist method was to assume
and search for, in any phenomenon, from myths in traditional
communities to mass culture in American and European societies, the
langue, the single deep structure that would explain it. In focusing on
the operations, in society and culture, of definite identifiable structures,
rather than hazy notions of alienation, structuralism could hopefully
approach science, could yield scientific knowledge.

Mythologies is a manifestation of such structuralist method, seeking
out, as Barthes put it in his preface to the 1970 edition, the operation in
ads or wrestling matches or magazine photographs of a single force, the
'essential enemy', the 'bourgeois norm'. The danger of the structuralist
method would be to minimise or ignore in a phenomenon evidence of
contradiction or ambivalence, by trying always to arrive at a single
underlying essential meaning. This is precisely what does happen in
'The World of Wrestling', where Barthes' conclusion – that the mass
audience of wrestling wish only for certainty – has to repress what he's
already cocked an eye at, that the audience is delighted by 'triumphant
disorder'.

The structuralist method in general had always to repress contradiction and ambivalence in popular culture texts. But as we saw with
Adorno and Horkheimer, or Q.D. Leavis in *Fiction and the Reading Public*,
reduction of mass culture texts (remember Q.D. Leavis talking of the
'purpose' of popular fiction) to a single meaning or psychological
function, was an already well-established move in mainstream modernist
cultural studies, a move almost natural to make, like commonsense
itself. *Mythologies*, an immensely influential text, was part of, but also
gave new life and direction to, a developing modernist conformity.
Literary modernism was becoming a machine, a psycho-technology,
unfailingly reproducing modernists in its own image.

British cultural studies

In 1957 another landmark work appeared, Richard Hoggart's *The Uses
of Literacy*. Hoggart was trained as a literary critic, and was influenced by
the Leavisites, but not in a conservative direction. By the 1950s
F.R. Leavis had become notoriously querulous, suspicious of most of his
former followers, gloomy and deeply pessimistic about the modern
world and the state of criticism. Hoggart, however, like Raymond
Williams in *Culture and Society* (1958), wished to use the methods of
Leavisite literary criticism, particularly the close analysis of texts, but
now not necessarily in relation to literary works alone. The approach
became known as 'left-Leavisite'.

In *The Uses of Literacy* Hoggart deploys the kind of ethnographic
approach claimed by *Fiction and the Reading Public*, particularly where
Q.D. Leavis extolls the folk wisdom, the age-old sayings and dicta, of the
respectable lower classes, even unto the early twentieth century.
Brought up in a working-class community himself, in Leeds in the north
of England, if now educated and a university teacher, Hoggart will
return as an anthropologist, a participant observer, to report on the
cultural values, and judge the condition and level of sensibility of the
people to whom he once belonged. He will do a close analysis of their
lives, sayings and thoughts.

We can see *The Uses of Literacy* as a post-World War II sequel to Q.D.
Leavis' *Fiction and the Reading Public*, each turning on a contrast between
older and newer cultural ways. In the first part of his book, Hoggart
evokes the older order of working-class life, the order he will remember
and reconstruct from his childhood and family. As he recalls it, it is a
culture centred on family and neighbourhood, on oral tradition, on the
best elements of the English Puritan tradition, and on perceptions of
the world that emphasise the personal and the concrete. The older

working class would make a traditional distinction between us and them, between their own communities and those above them, employers, civil servants, local authorities, teachers, the school attendance man, the local magistrates.[6]

Hoggart insists, however, that he doesn't wish to idealise the past, here implicitly disagreeing with *Fiction and the Reading Public*. He notes that the enclosed group life favoured by working-class communities can sometimes impose a harsh pressure to conform, and can also be cruel to those perceived as outsiders, for example, a foreign wife. Working-class life could also be 'coarse and savage'. It possessed a strain of 'insensitivity'. He remembers his own grandmother was often 'harshly crude'. But he also remembers that, in common with many in her generation, she could reveal an admirable gentleness and fineness of discrimination. (Here we are very close to the language of the Leavisites.) Such gentleness and discrimination was the product of centuries, breeding a reasonableness, a quiet assumption that violence is the last ditch.[7]

Hoggart is also harsher than the older Leavisites in his judgement of oral tradition, arguing, for example, that working-class views on religion and politics are marked by prejudices and half-truths. But in the realm that working-class people make their own, the personal and local, the intimate, sensory and detailed, their conversations are like those of a novelist. They are fascinated with individual behaviour, and every anecdote is told dramatically, with a wealth of rhetorical questions, supplementary illustrations, significant pauses, alternations of pitch. Working-class people are themselves 'dramatists'. The guiding values in their conversation are qualities of friendliness and decent-heartedness, of directness, openness, frankness. For this very reason, working-class people can be innocents, are as babies when approached by appeals to their own values, as in advertisements aimed at them. Then they are easily duped.[8]

Hoggart is still very much the older superior kind of Leavisite as he makes his round of judgements on working-class sensibility. When, for example, he writes that most working-class people, preoccupied with the local and personal, are 'non-metaphysical' in their outlook, it's hard not to think he's being enormously patronising, especially when he notes himself that working-class women often discuss some of the 'great themes of existence' (marriage, children, relations with others, sex). He also observes that the working class reveal a positive belief in fate and destiny, a belief that emerges in a fondness for gambling, astrology, fortune-telling at fairs, prophecies in old almanacs. Here is a 'supernaturalism that has survived for centuries'.[9]

Hoggart stresses another long continuity in lower-class life, a hedonism, going back to the Wife of Bath, Shakespeare's clowns, Moll Flanders, the nineteenth-century music-halls. Part of this hedonism is what he calls a 'sprawling, highly-ornamental, rococo extravagance', a love in working-class people of splendour, abundance, lavishness of colour, the baroque, the grotesque, often expressed as an attraction to the Orient, conceived as exotic and elaborate. The interest in abundance can be seen too in working-class hobbies, for example, in the 'wild grotesqueries of fretwork'. Such observations cast an interesting light on Barthes' noting of the love of spectacle and excess, theatricality and the grotesque, in popular wrestling. And when Hoggart tells us that most working-class pleasures tend to be mass-pleasures, where everyone 'wants to have fun at the same time',[10] we are with observations in 'The Work of Art in the Age of Mechanical Reproduction', when Benjamin talks of popular preference for simultaneous collective enjoyment.

Benjamin's point in that essay was that older modes of collective enjoyment could be enabled and sustained by newer forms of mass media like movies. *The Uses of Literacy*, however, makes no such radical departure from mainstream literary-modernist suspicion, indeed fear and hatred, of the new mass media of the twentieth century, particularly when that media comes from or is modelled on the American. Part two of the book, 'Yielding Place to the New', offers little that we could not already predict from *Fiction and the Reading Public*. The new forms of mass publications, media and recreation are looming as a disaster for the older English working-class ways, so (overall) affectionately constructed in part one of *The Uses of Literacy*.

To move in *The Uses of Literacy* from the past to the present is to travel in an almost Manichean way from light to darkness, warmth of spirit to coldness, cultural richness to poverty. The new mass media manipulate the working class by appearing to appeal to their values. Yet what popular journalism, for example, is really about is trying to turn the strong sense of group identity in the working class into a callow democratic egalitarianism (de Tocqueville contra America is quoted in support here). Popular journalism is calling on a cant of the common man as against the high-brow, leading to a 'levelling-down', an injunction always to feel part of the 'main herd', which then becomes an excuse for 'gross insensitivity'.[11]

A particularly worrying trend is the creation by the new mass culture of differences between the generations. The latest cinematic spectacle has a dangerous appeal to young working-class people, inviting them to see the present and future as always preferable to the past. The new media are glorifying the young themselves, as in the advertising which appeals to the American mythology of the teenage gang fond of jive and boogie-woogie, leading to a kind of shiny barbarism, a new callowness. Furthermore, the popular press is now over-emphasising the visual, ousting what is to be read by what is seen, for example the comic strips aimed at the young.[12] (Recall the fear of the visual in *Mass Civilisation and Minority Culture* and *Fiction and the Reading Public.*)

At the lowest level this turning away from reading can be noticed in the sales in Britain of American or American-type comic books, where for page after page, Hoggart tells us, big-thighed and big-bosomed girls from Mars step out of their space-machines, and gangsters' molls scream away in high-powered sedans. For the young, such comics represent a 'passive visual taking-on of bad mass-art geared to a very low mental age'. In his endnotes Hoggart refers us to the American Fredric Wertham's *The Seduction of the Innocent* (1953) for the 'most thorough analysis of American comic books'.[13] Wertham's book was part of a worldwide movement in the early 1950s of protest against popular American comics, a movement that was frequently pro-censorship. Worryingly, Hoggart expresses no reservations in this regard.[14]

Then there are the milk-bars, which, in their glaring showiness, indicate a complete aesthetic breakdown. The records coming out of the juke-boxes are almost all American, and the young men present, Hoggart enigmatically notes, waggle a shoulder or stare 'as desperately as Humphrey Bogart, across the tubular chairs'. Exposed to the mass trends of the day, such young men, sub-Bogarts inhabiting the milk-bars night after night, have no aim, no ambition, 'no protection', no belief. How do we know? We can tell from their facial expression, how they 'stare'. (Perhaps they were staring at Hoggart staring at them, at his ethnographic gaze.) These 'juke-box boys' are, unfortunately, the typical readers of the new-style popular journals. They are also likely to read American crime stories where the interest and excitement remain all with the gangster, or the detectives who are temperamentally gangsters. As with Q.D. Leavis and Adorno and Horkheimer, Hoggart puts the detective genre very low in the mainstream modernist hierarchy of taste. Hoggart offers no actual instances of such writing; rather, he strangely tells us, 'my examples have had to be invented'.[15] We are back with the problem of what the literary modernists consider as evidence for their claims about mass culture.

In general, Hoggart concludes, the new mass publications, the cinema, sound broadcasting and television (particularly when commercial), and large-scale advertising, are encouraging in working-class people an unconscious uniformity and a high degree of passive acceptance. The only sources of 'resistance' lie in the persistence of the older decent local, personal, and communal way of life. Such can still be observed in working-class speech, in forms of culture like the working-men's clubs, styles of singing, the brass bands, the older types of magazine, and group-games like darts and dominoes. There still exists a mode of cheerful debunking. And marriage and the home are still important. So too are hobbies, in cage-bird breeding and fancying, as with pigeons.[16]

To Birmingham

Hoggart is a considerable figure in British cultural studies. In 1964 he became the founding director of the Centre for Contemporary Cultural Studies at the University of Birmingham, which gained worldwide attention as a centre of new theory under his successor, Stuart Hall, especially in the 1970s.[17] Hall and those he influenced like Paul Willis, Richard Johnson, Angela McRobbie, Dick Hebdige, inherited Hoggart's interest in ethnographic study of working-class cultures, and the dangers of conformity to what *The Uses of Literacy* referred to as 'all the canned entertainment' of postwar capitalist society.[18] They also inherited Hoggart's interest in sources of 'resistance' to the media and mass culture.

The 1970s Birmingham Centre was, however, responding to a very different postwar world to that experienced by Hoggart in the 1950s. It was a world that was witnessing an explosion of student protest and radical critique, as in women's liberation and gay liberation, as well as anti-racism, for 1970s Britain was multicultural and multi-ethnic in ways unknown to the world of *The Uses of Literacy*. Yet such protest and critique, its most spectacular expression the May 1968 student riots in Paris against bureaucracy, hierarchy and authoritarianism, had not dislodged the capitalist system and what appeared to be its ruling ideologies. How to explain such survival?

The Birmingham Centre could still perceive resistance in lower-class cultural life, though such resistance did not take the homely form of pigeon-breeding or dart clubs as in Hoggart's constructions. The Birmingham Centre would now see resistance in much more con-temporary activities and styles. The most well-known example here would be Dick Hebdige's 1979 *Subculture: The Meaning of Style*, with its gallery of rastas, mods, teddy boys, rockers, skinheads, punks. Such subcultures are evoked much as Hoggart evoked older working-class culture, as living texts, susceptible of detailed analysis. Hebdige and the Birmingham Centre, however, now looked for their methods of textual analysis to semiology, from Saussure, the 1920s Russian circle that included names like Volosinov, to Roland Barthes.

Subculture: The Meaning of Style and the Birmingham Centre in general saw such resistant subcultures as always being under threat from commercial entertainment produced by the market, which absorbed resistant modes and styles and so incorporated them into dominant ideologies. Commercialism diluted and destroyed the true oppositional resistance of the subcultures. Was mass culture, then, the key way the dominant values of capitalism held their sway?

Here the Birmingham Centre was on familiar modernist ground, making familiar moves. But it felt it required more sophisticated notions of power than previous theory had yet made available, an explanation of how cultural representations, as in the media, are related to dominant ideologies and the working of capitalist society. It turned to a vibrant European Marxism rather than the faded English left-Leavisite tradition. The Birmingham Centre would try to develop a Marxism that was not economic determinist or crudely reflectionist, that didn't simply see the ruling ideas of society as a reflection of the ruling productive forces.

We can take as our example an essay by Stuart Hall, the towering figure of 1970s Birmingham.[19] Hall is known not so much for any particular book of his own, but for essays and introductions to collections that were significant interventions in ongoing debates, guiding Birmingham work through various theoretical minefields; like so many others, I found such essays stimulating and challenging, the first I'd turn to in the various Birmingham volumes. For more sophisticated versions of Marxism, Hall looks to Italian theorist of the 1920s, Antonio Gramsci, imprisoned for most of his adult life by the fascist authorities, and 1960s French philosopher Louis Althusser, a kind of structuralist Marxist.

In 'Culture, Media and the "Ideological Effect" ', Hall spends most of the essay working out problems of Marxist theory; the media only gets attention at the very end. Gramsci's notion of hegemony is, Hall argues, pivotal and commanding. By it Gramsci means that in liberal-capitalist societies the dominant classes usually exert authority over other classes by consent rather than direct coercion. The dominant classes strive to frame all competing definitions of reality, all sense of available alternatives, within their own horizon of thought. Hegemony, ideological leadership, works through institutions like the family, the education system, the church, the media and other cultural forms. But hegemony is sustained not by a single unified ruling class, but by particular unstable alliances; further, hegemony is not a permanent state, but always has to be actively won and secured by these dominant class factions. Accordingly, it can also be lost.[20] Nevertheless, the overall tendency is that liberal-capitalist societies are structured in dominance; the whole of social, ethical, mental and moral life actively conforms to the requirements of the productive system.

Althusser is to be admired for his theory of 'domination', which, Hall argues, stresses the key notion of reproduction. Althusser criticised the early Marx for seeing society as a simple structure, its every level everywhere obeying determination (in the last instance) by the economic; society for the early Marx is an expressive totality, reducible to the unfolding of a single principle. For Althusser, the social formation is a set of complex practices, each with its own specificity, its own relative autonomy; neither the economic, the social, the political nor the ideological can be reduced or collapsed into each other. But, nevertheless again, we must not think that these various modes have total independence from each other, are autonomous and unrelated. It is true that each mode is not determined by any other single mode. But the ideological is indeed determined by the whole complex of effects (the notion of over-determination), so that the social formation as a whole is, in Althusser's terms, structured in dominance. There is no simple functionalist fit between the different spheres of capitalist society. They can be and are diverse and contradictory. But – but, says Althusser (and Hall) – they are nonetheless still unified, unified under a ruling ideology.

Althusser gives pride of place to the school and family as key apparatuses sustaining the ruling ideology. Hall, however, shifts attention to the importance of the mass media, which first appeared in their modern forms, he argues, in the eighteenth century, with the development of the literary market, the artistic product becoming a commodity. Hall here takes a swipe at the conservative Leavisite tradition for idealising the eighteenth century, rather than seeing it as inaugurating the reign of the market, that satanic force. By the twentieth century, the mass media have so colonised the cultural and ideological sphere that they have assumed leadership, hegemony, dominance. The media are now responsible for providing groups and classes with images, information, knowledge, concerning their own lives and the lives of other groups. They intervene in what appears to be the bewildering complexity of our modern lives, by classifying images, within certain preferred meanings and interpretations. This ceaseless ideological work of classifying permits consensus and consent to emerge out of apparent plurality: 'This forms the great unifying and consolidating level of the media's ideological work.'[21] The production of consensus, the construction of legitimacy, is not so much in any finished product, but in the process of argument, exchange, debate, consultation and speculation which it carries forward. Here is the 'generative structure' beneath the media's massive investment in surface immediacy, the phenomenal multiplicity of the social worlds in which the media traffics. Hall is coming very close to the structuralist model of language, the deep structure that controls and determines the surface of a phenomenon.

The Birmingham Centre is alive, as the Frankfurt School generally wasn't, to the possibility that audiences may in their own ways decode the 'dominant discourses'; their responses are not necessarily automatic, as Adorno and Horkheimer assumed. The dominant ideologies encode the media with preferred meanings, presenting explanations of the rush of events in the world as if they are natural and rational. The audience might decode in a counter-hegemonic way, Hall allows for a moment; but it doesn't, it usually accepts the preferred meanings, meanings supported by the repertoire of dominant discourses sustained by the media as a moving whole. The audience does feel it is decoding in its own way, but such decodings are usually only negotiations within the dominant codes. Because they feel they are decoding in their own way, the audience thereby gives consent to the media as a system. It receives popular legitimacy.

The media, then, is part of a structured ideological field, a complex unity, which comes from terms of reference the media shares with the society as a whole. There will, says Hall, referring to Gramsci, be counteracting tendencies, and the dominant ideologies also struggle and contend among themselves. But, overall, the media (quoting Althusser) is structured in dominance.

What interests Hall in this essay is trying to work out how dominant values dominate. There is never any doubt that there are dominant ideologies, nor that they do indeed dominate. The argument of the essay looks as if he's playing out the possibilities of contradiction and complexity, even of a hegemony that may be lost. Yet the essay keeps circling back to modernist certainty, to the insistence on underlying unity, dominant ideology, dominant discourses. When we come to it we're not at all surprised by Hall's conclusion, when he speaks of the systematic tendency of the media to 'reproduce the ideological field of a society in such a way as to reproduce, also, its structure of domination'.

Rereading Hall's essay now you get the feeling he was not really interested in the media. He refers only to television news, and he never gives specific examples. He appears to dislike, disdain, the media in traditional modernist style and assumption. This feeling is confirmed for me by the conclusion of another essay, 'Deconstructing the Popular', where Hall says he doesn't 'give a damn' about popular culture except in so far as it enables analysis of domination and provides a possible basis for political resistance.[22] Isn't this remark as élitist and contemptuous of mass culture as the stances of Adorno and Horkheimer and F.R. Leavis and Q.D. Leavis before him?[23]

From this distance Hall's 'Culture, Media and the "Ideological Effect" ' also appears written in a dry, excessively severe, ascetic, even monkish mode; it is also curiously androcentric, his gender frame of reference being 'men', 'he' and 'him'.[24] It's perhaps little wonder that feminist members of the Birmingham Centre through the 1970s began to object to the way male members were focusing on the cultural rituals and resistance of male subcultures, rastas, teds, mods, bikies, punks and so on; writers like Angela McRobbie pointed out that while teenage girls, for example, were not so publicly visible, their cultural expression and experience still needed ethnographic investigation.[25]

Yet feminist Birmingham Centre investigators also, like their male counterparts, firmly judged mass publications for young women to be written under the sign of dominant ideologies of femininity.[26] In 1970s Birmingham material can be seen actively at work the literary modernist distinction between cultural experience, practices, rituals, sympathetically explored as resistance, and mass culture as inevitable conformity to mainstream (and malestream) society.

In the 1970s, then, Hall and the Birmingham Centre, through all their negotiations with more supple versions of Marxism, never really strayed too far from decades-long orthodoxy; the leash was long, but they always allowed it to pull them back. They looked as if they were embarking on dangerous seas of uncertainty and indeterminacy; but, however shaken, however insecure, they always slipped back to home port.[27]

CHAPTER SIX

Myths of Origin: 1970s Screen Theory and Literary History

I want . . . to attempt to define the structure which typifies the nineteenth century realist novel and to show how that structure can also be used to describe a great number of films. The detour through literature is necessary because, in many ways, the structure is much more obvious there and also because of the historical dominance of the classic realist novel over much film production . . . The structure I will attempt to disengage I shall call the classic realist text and I shall apply it to novels and films.

Colin McCabe, 'Realism and the Cinema:
Notes on some Brechtian Theses', 1974 [1]

It is said that analysing pleasure, or beauty, destroys it. That is the intention of this article.

Laura Mulvey,
'Visual Pleasure and Narrative Cinema', 1975 [2]

A feature of belief systems in many traditional cultures is a fear of representation, an implicit notion that representation of people or things might involve a danger to those represented - by giving power over the subject to those representing. This fear is steeped in the customary framework of many societies. It seems to be shared by many of our society's 'revolutionary' artists and art theorists when they ascribe almost magical powers to the 'realist' art object, and describe the insidious ways in which the object can cast its spell for evil purposes.

Lorraine Mortimer,
'Godard and Reflexivity . . .ivity . . .ivity', 1982 [3]

1970s Screen Theory, a radical version of modernism based on the London journals *Screen* and *Screen Education,* rushed into a gap left by Birmingham Centre approaches, a lack of actual analysis of mass culture texts in favour of evoking subcultures. Unlike the Birmingham Centre, Screen Theory had no interest at all in ethnographic study of sub-cultures or working-class cultural experience. Its (formalist) focus was on a kind of generalisable visual text and the relation of this text to the film (or television) viewer.

In an early 1980s discussion group in Sydney, I was told I must read an essay exhibiting the virtues of 1970s Screen Theory, Colin McCabe's 'Realism and the Cinema'; whatever you think of it, the group assured me, it's important, crucial, seminal, influential, even, already, canonical. As a relative outsider, a nervous new chum to media studies, with my previous work in literary criticism, cultural history, intellectual history, what immediately struck me was that McCabe's construction of literary and cultural history, his 'detour through literature', a pillar of his argument, would surely sway and fall at the first touch. How, I thought, could such flimsy cultural history (however sophisticated and 'difficult' the manner of writing) be so influential in cultural theory, how could it have launched a thousand essays not only in *Screen* and *Screen Education* but in journals across the Anglo-Australo-American world? How could its key terms, especially the Classic Realist Text, be so confidently and blindly repeated for years after as articles of faith? I expressed some of this puzzlement in an early 1980s essay, 'In Defence of Popular Culture', as a statement of resistance to what I took to be, along with Adorno and the Frankfurt School, the reigning orthodoxy, the inherited 1970s media studies doxa. Law.[4]

In 'In Defence of Popular Culture' I compared McCabe's essay to Adorno's early 1950s 'Television and the Patterns of Mass Culture'. I felt both Adorno and McCabe shared an enthusiasm for seeing popular audiences as the mere subjects of psychoanalytic analysis (from the top), a working-class consciousness bound by infantile identification with dominant bourgeois values. And like Adorno, McCabe turns to the bourgeois novel as setting the main pattern for things to come, arguing that the bourgeois aesthetic domain is dominated by the 'classic realist text', based on the nineteenth-century realist novel, as in George Eliot's *Middlemarch*. Just as Adorno called attention to the 'fake' realism of mass culture, so McCabe is at pains to point out that the 'classic realist text' is also a pseudo or pretend realism. Such texts in fact are simply narratives that do not call attention to themselves as articulation, as a particular interpretation of reality, a discourse like any other: 'the whole text works on the concealing of the dominant discourse as articulation'. The narra-tive tries to be transparent, like a window onto the real, and readers or viewers feel that in reading or watching this or that narrative they are seeing things as they really are. What they don't know is that the narra-tive is a concealed ideological discourse, to which their unconscious has responded, in what Lacan calls the mirror phase of infantile recognition of itself in the world. What followed was the depiction of popular culture as an epiphenomenon of psychological study of presumed audience response. In McCabe as in Adorno before him, what was proposed was a smoothly functioning system of fake realist surface text, with an underlying psychological effect, the easy insertion of the viewer into capitalist ideological patterns ensuring cultural passivity, psychological subjection, social control. Mass obedience was secured by mass culture – what I would now evoke as the familiar literary modernist narrative.

In 'In Defence of Popular Culture' I felt that McCabe's argument (as Adorno's) could be convicted of various sins of social theory: functionalism, that is, a mechanical theory of ideological reproduction; a crude theory of social control as manipulation and domination from the top; and a denial of relative autonomy to an area of culture (film and TV reduced to presumed audience psychological effects).

But I also thought McCabe's assertion that film (his followers quickly extended this ambit claim to TV) tries to present itself as if it is reality itself, as natural and predestined, rather than calling attention to itself as art, as articulation, was quite fantastic. To say that twentieth-century popular visual forms are modelled on high bourgeois novels like George Eliot's *Middlemarch* struck me as astonishing. To the contrary, we can see that this century's media of film and TV inherited, developed and transformed nineteenth-century, and earlier, popular forms, chiefly of the theatre. Such theatre was not dominated by realism – indeed realism was the last form and effect it wished to achieve. Its staple fare, I rushed on, consisted of melodrama, romance, vaudeville, farce, adult pantomime, nautical comedy, fantasy, magic, Shakespearian adaptations, and the unrealist like. There were, I readily conceded, programs like the BBC period dramas which conform more to McCabe's model of the 'classic realist text', but that was because they consciously acknowledged a debt to nineteenth-century realist literature. What this meant was that TV and film enjoyed a wide variety of forms, in which realism and naturalism are minor and certainly don't predominate.

Further, twentieth-century film and TV inherited the star system from nineteenth-century theatre; a system of publicity about the personalities and actors which, if anything does, precisely and glaringly calls attention to the whole enterprise of film and TV as a construct, a creation, art and entertainment. How can one watch a movie with Jane Fonda in it without being aware that one is responding to the character she is playing (say, Bree in *Klute*, one of McCabe's examples), *and* that this is Jane Fonda playing a character? Audiences in watching film or TV are responding to that film or TV show's imaginative world: not everyday reality but a world they recognise from their knowledge of forms and genres (comedy, musicals, detective, western, crime, horror, mystery, spy, and so on). That is, popular audiences know they're watching art because such art is as convention-laden, as intertextual, as any so-called authentic or autonomous art. Indeed, some shows like the American spy comedy *Get Smart* are almost totally structured on allusions to previous spy movie conventions; and in *Raiders of the Lost Ark* much of the enjoyment comes from recognition of how much scenes and actions refer to previous western conventions, like those of the Lone Ranger, but in a new context involving twentieth-century technology, science fiction, and the supernatural (Indiana Jones also being a scientist-explorer like Dr Who).

But the nineteenth-century theatre of visual spectacle is not the only influence on twentieth-century film and TV. A major twentieth-century source is at the very opposite end of the conventional cultural scale from the high bourgeois novel – comics. Films and TV shows and cartoons featuring superheroes like Superman or Spiderman or the Incredible Hulk, or Princess Leia or Luke Skywalker and Han Solo in the Star Wars movies, derive from and interact with comics (for example, the Marvel Comics Group). Further, mentioning superheroes reminds us that a great deal of popular culture reveals elements which are recognisably mythological, cultural elements that are of pre-capitalist, indeed of ancient, lineage. McCabe was arguing that *Klute* was a 'classic realist text'. But how can it be when it so signals its conventions to the audience, in particular, the detective as moral centre, a type of superhero. In terms of the relation of detective film to detective novel, Sam Spade in Dashiell Hammett's *The Maltese Falcon* (1930), is clearly a species of mythological figure, as are the clown-like, demented searchers after the jewel-laden falcon. Brigit O'Shaughnessy, Wilmer, Joel Cairo, Gutman, are all mythological figures of permanent evil. Such figures have no immediate social context; they come out of nowhere, and move restlessly round the globe, in a search for the holy grail of Mammon. They are symbols of forces which can be defeated but will always reappear. In this sense the world of *The Maltese Falcon* is similar to that of the TV version of *Batman and Robin*, where their enemies like the Joker, the Penguin, the Riddler, or Catwoman, are caught but always escape from jail. They symbolise an anarchic humour at the service of evil, in conflict with permanent good, the slightly ridiculously solemn dynamic duo.

Characters like the detective are not social realist in conception but are *figures*, trailing a mythological ancestry but also important as social explorers, as in TV shows featuring doctors, forensic scientists, nannies, vets, police – heroes who have to receive or visit or contact anyone in society as part of their daily work, who can thus reveal and explore the multiple aspects of class and the ubiquity of subcultures in modern society, plumbing family and psychological depths.

Nineteenth-century narrative

For a first go at media studies, 'In Defence of Popular Culture' was certainly rough around the edges, its theoretical tools undeniably clumsy. It was rude and crude; and, tying popular culture to the working class, it talked more about class than I ever seem to these days. But, looking at it now, I don't think it was too wrong about McCabe's canonical essay. I probably should have outlined his argument more carefully, in the way he says the classic realist text proposes a hierarchy of discourses. Yet McCabe's own example here always struck me, as it has struck others, as curious, even bizarre.[5] He quotes as his prime example of the 'classic realist novel' a passage from *Middlemarch*, where, he says, no discourse is allowed to speak for itself except as framed by the narrative, a narrative that is concealing its status as narrative, and claiming to present us with the truths of human nature.[6]

Yet in the very passage he quotes from *Middlemarch* the narrator is to be observed explicitly drawing attention to the narrative as narrative. ('Some who follow the narrative of this experience may wonder at the midnight darkness of Mr Dagley. . .'). The narrator is also making it clear, in an amused and quizzical tone, that she or he is sharing this knowledge, of a story being told, with the reader – indeed, is including the reader in a common 'we' – contemplating not the present but a shared attempted understanding and speculation ('wonder') about the past. The narrator and the novel never hide that they're trying to construct a past state, of provincial England, and, as in this passage, the narrator is concerned that the reader may be disagreeing with her interpretations: the reader is being addressed and argued with.

The nineteenth century was a great age of narrators and narratives revealing themselves as narrators and narratives, in almost any novel you think of, social realist or romance or romance-melodrama or adventure-romance or Gothic or science fiction or whatever. We only have to call up Jane as narrator in Charlotte Brontë's *Jane Eyre* ('Reader, I married him').[7] Texts revelled in calling attention to themselves, and readers, we can suspect from the easy, confiding way they were addressed and appealed to by narrators, relished the revealing, the game, the mutual understanding. Such direct address of narrator to reader is not that surprising, given that the nineteenth century was also the great age of novels, often appearing in serial form, being read out aloud in group situations.

Further, social realism in the nineteenth century was but a minor phenomenon, compared to the other novel genres, especially those influenced by the century's thriving melodrama theatre and aesthetic.[8] The last thing melodrama wanted to do was conceal itself as discourse, as art; on the contrary, it was ever eager to call attention to itself as theatricality, as a poetics of excess, as performance, as genre.

Nineteenth-century popular literature enjoyed toying with narrative modes. Take the immensely popular detective and mystery novels of Wilkie Collins, like his friend Dickens a master of serial fiction, yet far more witty, he of *The Woman in White* (1860), *No Name* (1862), *The Moonstone* (1868). The brief preamble to *The Woman in White*, for example, tells the Reader that 'the story' which follows will be like a trial, with the reader in the position of judge, listening to and weighing up various accounts by various witnesses; for that reason, the preamble goes on, there will be no single narrator at all, but various narrators offering or revealing what they know, accounts that must be necessarily partial and fragmentary. The first narrator, the Reader is told, will be Walter Hartright, teacher of drawing, and when he is not telling us things 'he will retire from the position of narrator'.[9]

Much of the delight of *The Woman in White* comes from the variety of narrative contributions, in the form of statements, letters, dreams, reported conversations, diary extracts, letters quoted within diaries, eavesdropping, memories, reminiscences, interviews. We are given, for example, the diary entries of the wonderful Marian Halcombe, and then told in a note: 'At this place the entry in the Diary ceases to be legible. The two or three lines which follow contain fragments of words only, mingled with blots and scratches of the pen'. Then follows a postscript to her diary by the less than admirable Count Fosco, villain extraordinary, into whose hands Marian's diary has fallen after he has made her ill with his evil arts, the Count being nonetheless a great admirer of Marian, only regretting that their interests were so 'at variance'.[10]

When Marian's cantankerous, grotesquely misanthropic uncle, Frederick Fairlie, begins his story, there is a footnote telling us: 'The manner in which Mr Fairlie's Narrative, and other Narratives that are shortly to follow, were originally obtained, forms the subject of an explanation which will appear at a later period': *The Woman in White* is ever on the delicious edge of self-parody. There is even a tombstone inscription ('The Narrative of the Tombstone').[11] There are indeed narrative contributions from everyone more or less involved, from the heroes of the story (Hartright and Marian Halcombe) to a lawyer, a doctor, a housekeeper, to the Count, to Count Fosco's cook. This is narrative as collage.

The Nineties

Was the *fin de siècle*, seed time of twentieth-century cinema, characterised by the Classic Realist Text?

As I noted in my 'In Defence of Popular Culture', the 1890s was an extraordinarily diverse cultural period which saw a growth not only of symbolism and transitions to modernism, but a vivid interest in a speculative literature of horror, cataclysm and disaster, which offered an imaginative equivalent of formal psychoanalytic theories of unconscious depths, Freud's theories also thriving in and from the 1890s. The late nineteenth century was a period of utopianism and anti-utopianism, of H.G. Wells' science fiction, of a revived Gothic, and of a vivid interest in split selves, as in Robert Louis Stevenson's 1886 *Dr Jekyll and Mr Hyde*. Some of the first films made, with remarkable special effects, were horror and monster movies (the unconscious manifested as a monster arising from the deep), drawing on a long tradition of popular literature going from Mary Shelley's *Frankenstein* to *Dr Jekyll and Mr Hyde* to Bram Stoker's *Dracula*.[12]

If anything, there was an intensification of experiment with narrativity in 1890s literature. Think of Stoker's Gothic *Dracula* (1897), where, again, there is no single narrator, and where the story proceeds by a collage of letters, newspaper cuttings, diary notes, journal entries. The young lawyer Jonathan Harker's notes, we are told, were initially transcribed in shorthand – the text here calling attention, as does *The Woman in White*, to the materiality of discourse. In the latter part of the novel, in the pursuit of Count Dracula across Europe as he tries to reach the safety of his castle, our resourceful heroes intercept through hypnosis the long-distance telepathic communications between heroine Mina and the vampire-king (Mina had been attacked by him, thereby becoming, at least in one part of her consciousness, his follower and communicant). *Dracula* foregrounds its own fantastical modes of narrative.

Now think of *The Turn of the Screw*, published a year after *Dracula*, where Henry James turns his hand at popular mystery writing, at Gothic terror. *The Turn of the Screw* begins by evoking a storytelling situation, with a group of sceptical, amused listeners sitting 'round the fire', commenting on various stories being told; clearly it is an audience used to enjoying and judging stories and storytelling. One of their number, the author's friend, Douglas, prepares to tell his tale 'with quiet art', but first has to write to 'my man' in town to send up the manuscript, which, he explains, was written not by him but in 'old, faded ink, and in the most beautiful hand', by a woman who has been dead some twenty years. Douglas further explains that the woman, once his sister's governess, was herself talking about events that had happened many, indeed forty, years before, when she was a governess to two children, orphans, in a semi-deserted Gothic mansion.

The telling of the governess' story is like a 'serial', told over several nights. We're initially led by Douglas' admiration for her, when they were both young, to believe that she must have been reliable, sane, steady, eminently likeable. But Douglas is the only authority his listeners have that she is sane, and as her own account goes on in her own words, they as listeners and we as readers are ever teased with various suspenseful possibilities. The children might, as she claims, be in dire danger of being possessed by ghostly devil-like forces. Yet she might be imposing fearful ghost fantasies onto the children. She might not be their protector but their jailer. Exalted with power as governess and protector against evil, she is perhaps waging psychological terror on them, is trying to possess them totally, with tragic results. *The Turn of the Screw* is an interrogation, a questioning, of the claims to truth of the governess as she tells her version of events, asking us, as listeners and readers, to be sceptical of her as narrator, to work out from the internal evidence of the story different motives, different interpretations and explanations, yet never knowing for sure, never finally being able to reach any certain Truth.[13]

In popular theatre the 1890s was a great age of spectacle, not only in melodrama, burlesques, variety, extravaganzas, comic operas, musical comedy, and not only in decidedly non-realist stage pictures and scene paintings (think of the remarkable pantomime transformation scenes, visual explosions), but in the magic shows which were also nurturing some of the first attempts at film. Film historian Tom Gunning points to a primal myth in film criticism that when spectators first saw Lumière's 1895 film *Arrival of a Train at the Station* they were terrified, showing that film spectators were credulous before the power of the film image then, and have been ever since.[14] Gunning argues to the contrary that cinema's first audiences, in the 1890s and turn of the century period, were far from naive; they were sophisticated urban pleasure seekers knowledgeable in the ways of the stage illusionists of the magic theatre, the same showmen who were now producing the illusions of early film.

The productions of Méliès at the Théâtre Robert Houdin in Paris, or Maskelyne at London's Egyptian Hall, were at times accompanied by exhibitions of freaks and artifacts of natural history: Gunning's position is that the first cinema was part of an 'aesthetic of attractions' that had developed in conscious opposition to an orthodox identification of viewing pleasure with the contemplation of beauty. (We can think of

both Barthes and Hoggart writing of popular attraction to the grotesque.) Increasingly such magic theatre was part of a wider theatre of
spectacle, a revue which would include music and live performance,
continually reminding the spectator of the act of watching by a succession of sensual assaults.

Gunning argues, then, that the first film audiences screamed with
astonishment and terror at *Arrival of a Train at the Station* because they
were exhibiting an undisguised awareness of and delight in film's
illusionistic capabilities, growing out of the astonishment and terror
they had already enjoyed in stage magic shows, and were coming to
enjoy in the frightening attractions of the new amusement parks, such
as the roller coaster. Just as the roller coaster employed new technology
to create its thrills, its terror, so audiences enjoyed the new technology
being deployed by the new cinema. Such research is speedily undermining the (literary-modernist) assumption in McCabe's essay that
cinema audiences gaze at film in a passive, credulous way.[15]

Structuralism: the reign of binary opposites

McCabe's argument rested on a Manichaean combine of binary oppositions, with the classic realist text on the dark side shaped as a uniform
'structure' ('the historical dominance of the classic realist novel over
much film production'), and on the golden other, a 'revolutionary text'.
The ideal revolutionary film would build on the work of Brecht and
Godard, where the narrative doesn't dominate, but simply serves as the
method by which various situations can be articulated together; the
reader has to produce a meaning for the film by analysing the
contradictions offered amongst the various discourses.[16]

The trouble with structuralism is that it is always creating, through its
oppositions, ruthless unities in each contrasting term. Yet as we've seen,
the nineteenth-century novel is vastly more varied than McCabe's
unifying (totalising) notion of 'classic realist text' can possibly suggest,
enjoying highlighting its own status as writing, narrative, storytelling,
and frequently being multi-narrative. The reader has indeed to work to
produce meanings, and some of the fascination of texts like *Dracula*, we
can speculate, is that they have become 'mythic' – mythic not meaning
(as Barthes wrote in his structuralist *Mythologies*) the passing off, the
naturalising, of ideology as if reality, but as the ever elusive, ambivalent,
puzzling, intriguing, uncertain, startling, inexhaustible.

McCabe's ideal revolutionary text was astonishingly prescriptive:
'much film production' (everything that constituted the 'classic realist
text') would now be deleted from the screen in the service of a grey
alternative, the one true text we should have for ever after, the one

singular narrow way. And indeed the Screen Theory project did appear to stimulate into production some alternative left-modernist screen texts. I recall some years ago going along in Sydney to a British example, *Song of the Shirt*, fulfilling the requirements of self-reflexivity and differing discourses and perspectives – it was mind-bogglingly dismal, tedious, and boring.

In his opposition between 'classic realist text' and ideal 'revolutionary art' McCabe is trying to get at a distinction between open and closed texts. It's the kind of distinction that interested Mikhail Bakhtin in his contrast of monologic and dialogic novels, as between Tolstoy and Dostoevsky. Yet Bakhtin never drew an absolute opposition between the monologic and dialogic, writing that a novel, to be a novel, must allow a dramatic minimum of diverse discourses (in terms of various 'languages') to speak and differ and contend and comment on each other.[17] I've had occasion to apply Bakhtin's distinctions to a perhaps unfortunate classic of popular literature, Leon Uris' *Exodus* (1959), a blockbuster, an epic, mixing melodrama with tract-like history.[18] Yet even in *Exodus* its attempted unified monologic language is interrupted by other languages, other voices, of doubt, distance and rejoinder to Zionism's settler-colonial fantasy – just as McCabe's monologic voice in 'Realism and the Cinema. . .' can't entirely repress the answering voice, as in the passage he quotes from *Middlemarch*, of the nineteenth-century novel.

McCabe is not only drawing absolute distinctions between his notions of closed and open texts, but is further identifying the closed with one particular aesthetic form, one particular genre, realism, and the open with one particular form, a highly rationalist self-reflexive alternative film. Yet the self-reflexive text by itself doesn't guarantee a discursive openness.[19] No genre in itself, realism or other, can ever be confined to a single ideological meaning: the monologic and the dialogic appear and compete within texts and genres anywhere and everywhere.

Screen Theory and screen studies

McCabe's nineteenth-century 'classic realist text', his 'detour through literature', was a mirage, a phantom, a fantasy. Its acceptance in screen and media studies as the undeniable truth of nineteenth-century literary and cultural history by those whose knowledge of literary and cultural history was usually nil, must surely stand as a remarkable episode in recent intellectual history. Perhaps it needs to be explained in terms of 1970s radical modernists' infantile desire for certainty, certainty about the single essential truth of mass culture and the necessity to oppose it in absolute ways.

Perhaps also its easy acceptance can help serve as a parable of what happened to screen studies, which tried from the 1970s to constitute itself as an autonomous discipline, like a Department of English. The assumption was that to establish itself as autonomous, screen studies had to sever any lingering connection with literary study, and indeed screen studies did attract scholars from outside traditional English departments, from philosophy, sociology and such like. Such scholars were, however, highly vulnerable to McCabe's theory of the classic realist novel – they were in no position to disbelieve it, to maintain a dialogic interest in scepticism and doubt. Wide-eyed, they swallowed it whole. I recall a conversation with a philosopher-turned-screen-studies person, who looked at me with pity when I said that from my knowledge of literary and cultural history McCabe was talking bunk. No, said this philosopher, the classic realist novel, that's what the nineteenth century was about.

In the 1970s and well into the 1980s screen studies pursued its ambition to be autonomous, with the inevitable result that it became so over-specialised and narrow that it bored even its own practitioners, who either went off to make their own screen texts, or dived into policy studies, this latter signalling a return of the repressed, of the economic, governmental and regulatory contexts of cultural activity suppressed by Screen Theory's formalist focus on film and a universal film spectator. When the structuralist project of Screen Theory collapsed, screen studies collapsed, so confined had its theoretical spaces become.

At this distance what also now seems clear about 1970s Screen Theory is how conventional a literary-modernist project it was. In particular, it followed F.R. Leavis and Q.D. Leavis of the 1930s and Adorno and Horkheimer of the 1940s in the importance it placed on the visual in mass culture, seeing mass culture as primarily concerned with creating an illusion of realism, and fearing the visual as overwhelmingly powerful for common viewers, apparently defeating their consciousness, reason, capacity to think, laying their unconsciousness and sensibility open to massive social and psychological conformity. The visual sense is powerful, evil, satanic. Thought, reflection, cannot coexist with visual pleasure, so it's obvious which has to go.

There is a trace here of the alarm of the Leavisites, that the new mass culture, in its visual aspect (for the Leavisites this also meant a popular literature that over-emphasised the pictorial), was displacing what the cultural minority knew best how to do, a culture of reading, calm and rational, the culture that had once assured them (so they felt) of cultural and intellectual authority and centrality. For Screen Theory, that ideal rational past would be re-created anew in the future, in the revolutionary, grey, rationalist film.

Laura Mulvey's structuralist gaze

If McCabe's argument rests on a massive assertion concerning the formative influence of the nineteenth-century novel over 'much film production', Laura Mulvey's feminist version of 1970s Screen Theory, 'Visual Pleasure and Narrative Cinema', similarly rests on a bald massive assertion: cinema, Hollywood cinema and all it has influenced, is a direct growth of the unconscious in childhood.

Have we here another myth of origin? The argument goes something like this, proceeding by a sequence of unitary terms. The unconscious, which is 'formed by the dominant order', structures 'ways of seeing and pleasure in looking' by male children and men, a structuring which in turn shapes classic Hollywood narrative realist film. What Mulvey explicitly offers here is reflection theory: Hollywood's 'formal pre-occupations reflect the psychical obsessions of the society which produced it'.

The 'magic', the 'formal beauty', of mainstream film, of Hollywood, is its manipulation of visual pleasure, which codes desire, the erotic, into the language of the 'dominant patriarchal order'. Such visual pleasure arises from two main aspects of 'scopophilia', the voyeuristic and the narcissistic. Scopophilia is taking other people as objects, subjecting them to a controlling curious gaze. Mulvey tells us that Freud says this is what children do in a voyeuristic way, but she will apply it to the way the spectator in the cinema, who is apparently always male, gazes at the female on screen as object of desire. There is also scopophilia as narcissistic, as 'identification with the image seen', when the (male) spectator identifies with the male hero of the film whose object is to control and dominate the female.

But it is to French psychoanalyst Jacques Lacan that Mulvey looks, not Freud, for her account of male psychic formation, that originary moment in childhood that then explains the whole unfolding development of cinema this century. Lacan argued (Mulvey says 'described' as if it's an observable process) that the moment when a child recognises its own image in the mirror is crucial for the constitution of the ego. This moment, the mirror phase, which predates language, occurs at a time when the child's physical ambitions outstrip 'his' motor capacity, with the result that his recognition of himself is joyous in that 'he' imagines 'his' mirror image to be more complete, more perfect than he experiences his own body. Recognition is thus overlaid with mis-recognition, of an ideal ego, which then somehow 'gives rise to the future generation of identification with others', that is, enables the entry of the subject into language, into what Lacan calls the social symbolic order – or what we can recognise as that literary-modernist orthodoxy, mass conformity. The pleasure of the film image is to satisfy this primal moment of recognition and mis-recognition, recognition by scopophilia, and mis-recognition in terms of the star system, which produces ego ideals for the members of the dominant patriarchal order, cinema's spectators.

In Hollywood film, then, woman is the image, man is bearer of the look, the gaze. Woman is always 'passive', man always 'active', always furthering the narrative, making things happen. The 'determining male gaze' projects its desires onto the female figure, who is created only in order to be looked at, for her 'to-be-looked-at-ness'. She is the erotic object for the male characters within the film, and for the (always and only male) spectator within the auditorium. Since the spectator identifies with the male protagonist, the male in the film is 'the bearer of the look of the spectator': the spectator recognises his ideal self, his ideal ego, in the male hero just as in the 'original moment of recognition in front of the mirror'. The presence of woman is an indispensable element of spectacle in 'normal narrative film', though her visual presence tends to work against the development of a story line, to freeze the flow of action in moments of erotic contemplation.

What is the alternative to Hollywood? Well, technological advances, with for example 16mm film, permit the possibility of artisanal rather than capitalist production. The 'alternative cinema' now possible is presumably to be created only by women, since all men are subject to the mirror stage and therefore presumably must all their lives be in thrall to the uncontrollable desires of scopophilia.

What, Mulvey argues, radical film-makers are now doing against Hollywood and mainstream film is to establish reflexivity (the film referring to its own materiality as a recording process) and to permit the 'critical reading of the spectator' – that is, 'passionate detachment', as in the Frankfurt School, the absolute negation of the 'magic' of Hollywood. Alternative cinema calls for the 'destruction of pleasure as a radical weapon'. The pleasures of traditional Hollywood film will thankfully be destroyed, and our only pleasures henceforth will come from attending alternative cinema with its 'passionate detachment'. Hurry upon us, grey world.

Like McCabe's 'Realism and the Cinema', Mulvey's 'Visual Pleasure and Narrative Cinema' was enormously influential in feminist psychoanalytic theories of film. Yet many might be our doubts and mis-givings. We might ask with philosopher-critic Martin Barker, discussing feminist-psychoanalytic theories of comics, if the account of the uncon-scious adapted from Lacan isn't wildly improbable. As Barker notes, in such psychoanalysis, present-day desires are stored up versions of childhood desires. But, he then asks, even if we accept the account of childhood, why should it follow that adult life in an *identical* way is an unfolding development of an initial experience? He points to an analogy in the growth of plants, in the way the first leaves, those that break the soil, are crude and bear little relation to the complex forms that subsequent leaves take. Why, Barker asks, shouldn't we see a similar relationship between childhood and subsequent desires?[20]

The relationship Mulvey proposes between child and adult experience is one of supremely linear development, identical at every stage. Everything develops from a childhood moment of formation for the male (so early it predates language) into a rounded system, of dominant patriarchical order and Hollywood cinema, a series of perfectly reflecting mirrors. But, we might ask, is there a single dominant ideology? Is there a single 'dominant ideological concept of the cinema'? Is there a single seamless patriarchal order? It would seem doubtful that any system could be so flawless, could function so well and so completely. Mulvey extolls the virtues of 16mm film as permitting radical feminist cinema. But if the patriarchical order was working so perfectly, it seems strange that it would permit the invention and availability of a technology that could lead to the questioning of one its support systems, Hollywood cinema. Unless 16mm was invented only by women. . . And how could all spectators of Hollywood film be male? Were they? Are they?[21]

Mulvey's own examples from Hollywood, a brief discussion of Sternberg and Hitchcock, add to the doubts one might have about the ruthless unity of her concepts.[22] Sternberg, says Mulvey, provides many pure examples of fetishistic scopophilia, for example the cycle of films featuring Marlene Dietrich. Mulvey has to point out, however, that in such films the men are so weak that they're effectively absent from the movies' key moments involving Dietrich (the 'male hero misunderstands and, above all, does not see'). But this absence doesn't matter, Mulvey tells us, even though it means the Sternberg Dietrich movies are therefore *not* 'characteristic of traditional narrative film', which she says she's talking about. The male protagonist being so weak or absent means that the male spectator can then enjoy unmediated erotic contemplation, possession, and control of Dietrich.

In this account we have improbably to believe that Marlene Dietrich is merely 'passive', mere 'sexual object', and is not active in narratives. In the 1936 *The Garden of Allah*, however, which we glanced at in relation to Adorno and Horkheimer's image of Hollywood, Dietrich as face and eyes (almost like a masked figure of carnival) is featured as part of the intensity of high melodrama moments of agony and decision, and her character is certainly not passive in the narrative. It is she who takes almost every initiative in the development of her relationship with the male protagonist, the escaped Trappist monk Androvsky, who, slowed by guilt, tries to resist her interest. And it is she who finally deposits him back at his monastery.

Mulvey's Hitchcock example, *Vertigo*, is even more odd. In *Vertigo* the 'blatant' voyeurism of chief male figure Scottie is, Mulvey herself argues, precisely the focus of the film, as the spectator watches Scottie attempt to create for himself a perfect image of female beauty and mystery. But Scottie's voyeurism is exposed as precisely that, voyeurism, so that what the spectator is presented with in *Vertigo* is, Mulvey admits, an 'uneasy gaze'. The spectator's erotic involvement with the look of the male protagonist becomes, Mulvey tells us, 'disorientating', the spectator's fascination being 'turned against him', until the spectator sees through Scottie's look and 'finds himself exposed as complicit, caught in the moral ambiguity of looking'. *Vertigo* therefore, Mulvey says, exposes as 'perverted' the power of 'established morality', of the 'symbolic order', of the 'patriarchical super-ego', that is embodied in Scottie – the policeman, the representative of law, that at the beginning of the narrative the spectator was supposed confidently to identify with.

Mulvey ends 'Visual Pleasure and Narrative Cinema' with a ringing declaration that Hollywood film prevents the spectator 'from achieving any distance from the image in front of him'.[23] Yet by her own argument Hitchcock's *Vertigo* is exposing, studying, examining, laying bare, analysing, tracing, pursuing the male protagonist's deadly fantasies of constructing the female in his desired image: in so doing *Vertigo* is 'disorientating' the spectator: the 'disorientating' that is the ideal of Screen Theory, what Screen Theory says Hollywood and mainstream film cannot do. More, by her own account, *Vertigo* is doing what the whole literary-modernist tradition from the Leavises through to the Frankfurt School says mass culture cannot do, offer detachment, negation, critique. And remember who *Vertigo* is 'by' – Hitchcock, for decades Hollywood's most famous director of immensely popular films. (Is, then, such 'disorientating' characteristic of what Mulvey calls 'normal narrative film'?)

Even more curiously, in her discussion of *Vertigo* Mulvey is unwittingly agreeing with Walter Benjamin in 'The Work of Art in the Age of Mechanical Reproduction' where Benjamin argues that popular film brings about a general 'deepening of apperception' for film audiences, that there is a positive relationship between film, audience response, and psychoanalysis, that film allows for deeper perception of the workings, fears and desires of the unconscious. Mulvey's unitary notions of Hollywood begin to unravel by her own hand, as does her absolute opposition between mainstream film and alternative radical cinema. Perhaps the most interesting question for those interested in psychoanalysis is: why did Mulvey's unconscious choose the very example that would make vulnerable her argument?

Indeed, we might say, what Mulvey's argument does is not strengthen but help undo structuralism itself. At its moment of triumph in the middle 1970s, modernist film theory was scattering the seeds of its own deconstruction.

PART TWO

Modernism and Postmodernism

CHAPTER SEVEN

Architectural Postmodernism:
Learning from Las Vegas

Learning from the existing landscape is a way of being revolutionary for an architect. Not the obvious way, which is to tear down Paris and start again, as Le Corbusier suggested in the 1920s, but another, more tolerant way . . .
  The architect becomes a jester.
  You can like billboards without approving of strip mining in Appalachia.
  . . . the Bauhaus vanquished Art Deco and the decorative arts.[1]

From the latter 1970s on, the power of modernism – appearing to be overwhelmingly persuasive, like commonsense itself, setting the agenda for how mass culture was to be approached as theory as well as in terms of teaching and research in the burgeoning fields of media and cultural studies – waned. This doesn't mean modernist approaches simply booked out, to be noticed now only in byways as fallen idols, replaced by a new, single, approved, pure 'postmodernism'. Cultural history is, thankfully, never so linear, never so unidirectional. When 'postmodernism' emerged, it came not as a sleek new god, perfect in form and shape, but as many-headed, multi-armed, waving in different incompatible directions, at once old and new.

The most visible change came with 'postmodern' architecture, especially in the United States, in structures and design that built on decades of modernist uses of technology, yet were suddenly playful, whimsical, eclectic, jumbling together different architectural modes and languages and past and present styles. Postmodern architecture recalled Art Deco, Art Nouveau, Victorian clutter, reintroducing elements of the ornamental, decorative and pictorial that modernism had for decades tried to purge and eliminate. Architectural modernism in the 1920s threw up a polemical figure in Le Corbusier. In Robert Venturi,

Denise Scott Brown and Steven Izenour's *Learning from Las Vegas* (first published in 1972, revised in 1977), architectural postmodernism furnished its manifesto (written and visual, with collages of photographs) that anticipated and provided much of the theory of the new movement. In their preface to the first edition the authors told their readers that the book was the result of a studio conducted in 1968 at the Yale School of Art and Architecture and had involved work in the field, a ten-day visit to Las Vegas with their students.

When they wrote, 'postmodern' was obviously not a term that had entered vocabularies in the known critical world. Venturi, Scott Brown (a town planner) and Izenour contented themselves with offering a critique of 'Modern architecture', and they stressed in the preface how intense was their admiration for its early heroic period when its founders, sensitive to their times, proclaimed the right revolution. *Learning from Las Vegas* was to be directed against the irrelevant and distorted prolongation of that old 1920s revolution into the 1970s. Yet there is ambivalence here, as we can notice from the epigraphs, where *Learning from Las Vegas* is as critical of founding father Le Corbusier as it is of the spawning of post-World War II International Style architectural modernism.

In what would become a well-known quote from this rumbustious performance, *Learning from Las Vegas* suggests in its opening paragraph that Modern architects are 'out of the habit of looking nonjudgmentally at the environment'. Modern architecture has been 'anything but permissive', preferring to 'change the existing environment rather than enhance what is there'. In short, 'orthodox Modern architecture is progressive, if not revolutionary, utopian, and puristic'. Modernist architecture is universalist, ignoring and overriding local, vernacular environments.[2]

Learning from Las Vegas is indeed a full-frontal assault on the cardinal principles of architectural modernism, as they flow from its foundational figures, from Le Corbusier to Bauhaus names like Mies van der Rohe and Walter Gropius. It sees modernist architecture as everywhere trying to create and impose a singular language, particularly in defining architecture as enclosed space. Space becomes hallowed as Modern architecture's unique medium, the 'essential ingredient that separates architecture from painting, sculpture, and literature'. Because space is 'sacred', a sculptural or pictorial architecture became unacceptable, forbidden, the other, that which would remind architecture of the dread cultural history it freed itself from, nineteenth-century eclecticism, or the picturesqueness, the mixing of styles and media, in Gothic churches, Renaissance banks, Jacobean manors. Modern architects, says *Learning from Las Vegas*, in constituting architecture as the expression of structure and function, 'abandoned a tradition of iconology in which painting, sculpture, and graphics were combined with architecture'. In a modernist building, if there were painted panels, they floated independently of the structure ('one did not paint *on* Mies'). If there were sculptured objects, they were in or near but seldom on the building. Modernist architecture gloried in uniqueness and purity, a single true 'universal' way anywhere and everywhere all over the world, a preoccupation with 'total design' that results in universal 'deadness', at once 'strident' yet 'empty and boring'.[3]

The modernist building, however, *Learning from Las Vegas* argues, while it wished to expunge decoration and ornament from its surfaces, became itself an ornament, became symbolic, as in Le Corbusier, Mies, Gropius, the Bauhaus, of the Industrial Revolution and its 'brave new world of science and technology'. Early modernist architecture, as in the 'abstract geometrical formalism' of Le Corbusier, was not only 'nautical-industrial', in its interest in steamships and cylindrical grain elevators (*Learning from Las Vegas* reproduces a photo from Le Corbusier's *Towards a New Architecture* of a North American grain elevator). It was also attempting to adapt the language of early twentieth-century modernist painting, in particular Cubism, to architecture. Early modernist architecture symbolised a 'Cubist-industrial-process'. It is a matter for lament, not satisfaction, that the association with modernist art continues in post-World War II architecture, influenced by and trying to adapt 'abstract expressionism'.[4]

Learning from Las Vegas proposes that architecture should learn from the everyday vernacular, including suburbia. From suburbia?! For Venturi, Scott Brown and Izenour, what modernist architects cannot accept, because of their assumption of the universal and unchallengeable rightness of 'uncluttered architectural form', is precisely the clutter, the variety, of suburban houses, in their mixed and ornamented Regency, Williamsburg, New Orleans, French Provincial, or Prairie-Organic modes. Modernist architects find 'distasteful' the symbolic decoration of suburban houses, seeing in them the debased, materialistic values of a consumer economy where people are brainwashed by mass marketing and have no choice but to move into such visually polluting ticky-tacky dwellings that bruise modernist architectural sensibilities.[5] *Learning from Las Vegas* here ties in architectural modernism with the long heritage of high literary modernism, in its totalising concept of consumerism or the consumer society, its dislike of market-driven mass culture.

Modernist architects also wish the Modern building to stand out from, to soar above, the everyday vernacular of the commercial strip, with its architectural language of billboards, advertising, signs. Yet it is popular commercial art, in its heraldry that extends from the advertising pages

of *The New Yorker* to the super-billboards of Houston, that has pr⟨
kept alive a 'continuing iconology' descending from nineteenth-cenι⟨_,
architectural eclecticism. It is the American commercial strip, in its
aesthetically unselfconscious way, driven by the pressures of competition
in the market, that has allowed modernist architecture's repressed other
to remain abroad. Further, the commercial strip has introduced and
helped the technology of the late twentieth century, 'current electronic
technology', not least in the fantastical spread of neon lights, to
flourish.[6]

Venturi, Scott Brown and Izenour explain that their attempt to
develop a postmodern architecture not of space, form and function but
of 'iconography', the 'ironic richness of banality', was helped by the
'sensibilities of the Pop artists' of the early 1960s, who had revolted
against abstract expressionism by turning to commercial art and
advertising. Admiring references to Pop Art recur throughout *Learning
from Las Vegas*. Pop artists, the manifesto argues, questioned the
authoritarian demand of modernism that art be always new, original,
scorning the everyday. Pop Art revived pre-modern traditions where
'creating the new may mean choosing the old or the existing'. Pop
artists show the value of 'unusual juxtapositions of everyday objects' and
of the cliché changed in scale or distorted in shape or used in a new
context (as in the soup can in the art gallery) to achieve a new meaning,
to make the common uncommon: the 'familiar that is a little off has a
strange and revealing power'. It shows the complexity of the relations of
'modernism' and 'postmodernism' that Venturi, Scott Brown and
Izenour can feel that such a Pop Art procedure, of mimicry with
difference, looks directly back to the practice of early twentieth-century
literary modernism, to T.S. Eliot and in particular to Joyce in *Ulysses*,
a sensitivity to the idioms, rhythms and artifacts associated with
contemporary urban environments.[7]

Because Pop artists mimic the everyday commercial, this does not
mean their techniques 'reproduce the content or the superficiality' of
such. Lichtenstein borrowed the techniques and images of the comics
to convey 'satire, sorrow and irony' rather than 'violent high adventure'.
In a similar way, postmodern architecture can suggest qualities like
'sorrow, irony, love, the human condition, happiness, or merely the
purpose within'. Following Pop Art, we can see the postmodern architect as designing buildings that are 'multivalued', with a sense of
paradox and irony and wit, using a 'joke to get to seriousness' – in a
quote I rather like, the 'architect becomes a jester'. *Learning from Las
Vegas* sees Pop artists as, compared to modernist architects, 'non-
authoritarian' in temperament, showing the way in how to create art
and architecture for a 'pluralist society'.[8]

Route 66

Why Las Vegas? What do Venturi, Scott Brown and Izenour learn in their unlikely journey to and exploration of the famous gambling city and desert oasis that might provide a new postmodern architectural language and aesthetic?

Pop Art's enjoyment of the modern city as exciting, with Manhattan as exemplar, and in particular its ironic enjoyment of the advertising signs and billboards which help create Manhattan's visual excitement, leads *Learning from Las Vegas* to reflect that the contemporary commercial strip is not as contemptible as modernism has always suggested. 'Often the brightest, cleanest, and best-maintained elements in industrial sprawl, the billboards both cover and beautify that landscape'. Nor is the billboard unique to this century. Ancient Roman architectural history is not as unheterogeneous as early modernists like Le Corbusier claimed, a story of pure geometrical forms as in the Colosseum. The series of triumphal arches in ancient Rome, like those advertising the victories of Constantine via inscriptions and bas-reliefs, can be seen as the prototype of the twentieth-century billboard. *Learning from Las Vegas* also points out that the Roman Forum was, like the Las Vegas Strip, formally a 'mess' – yet it too was, symbolically, a 'rich mix'.[9]

Driving to and through Las Vegas nonetheless does involve a late twentieth-century element, perception at speed, a notion of carscape or autoscape: 'Time travels fast today'. In Venturi, Scott Brown and Izenour's view, modernism has an 'antiautomobile bias'. Roadside and highway signs, perceived at speed, provide an eclecticism that interrupts modernist purity. Such signs make verbal and symbolic connections through space, communicating a complexity of meanings, hundreds of associations in a few seconds. In this carscape, symbol becomes more important than form, so that roadside signs come to herald an architecture of 'communication' over space, over that element projected as the defining essence of modernist architecture.[10]

The casinos of Las Vegas also represent a triumph of the pictorial, frequently reaching back for inspiration, allusion and playful recreation to past modes. On the Las Vegas Strip, the front of the casino predominates, a dazzling array of signs, a 'vulgar extravaganza' as against the usually long low buildings extending behind (hotels, gambling rooms, shopping malls). Isn't, they ask, the medieval Gothic cathedral very similar to a Las Vegas casino? Isn't Amiens Cathedral, with its heavily decorated and inscribed front and relatively unadorned low building behind, a 'billboard with a building behind it'? And just as through continuous work over decades and centuries the facades of Gothic cathedrals evolved and became ever more extravagantly symbolic, so too do Strip casinos like the Flamingo, the Desert Inn, the Tropicano or Caesar's Palace accumulate more and more signs, until they become in their façades almost all sign. The Stardust Hotel has become 600 feet of 'computer-programmed animated neon'. The Las Vegas sign uses mixed media, words, pictures, sculpture, the same sign working differently at night or during the day. In these terms, Strip architecture has restored the 'decoration of construction' that Ruskin called for in his admiration of Gothic.[11]

Here, then, in so 'American' a spot in the world, is an exuberant rediscovery of the European and Middle Eastern architectural past, and not only in the façade. In the Middle Eastern bazaar, reflect Venturi, Scott Brown and Izenour, communication works through proximity, as along its narrow aisles buyers feel and smell the merchandise on offer; in the medieval town, persuasion is also mainly through sight and smell. The Las Vegas casino shopping mall now calls on memories of the oriental bazaar, except that graphic packaging has replaced the oral persuasion of the merchant. In a similar way, the pedestrian malls of the off-highway shopping centre return their customers to the mode of the medieval street, in what *Learning from Las Vegas* now provocatively refers to as 'medieval or Strip architecture'.[12]

The Gothic cathedral, in terms of a blatant disjunction between façade and building behind, lacked the organic unity prized by modernism. For this, say Venturi, Scott Brown and Izenour, we should be ever thankful. Strip architecture also is to be valued precisely because it is so ununified, contradictory, paradoxical, because it is so eclectic and allusive, because it is so fantastically inclusive of diverse competing conflicting styles. The Aladdin Hotel and Casino is, for a startling example, Moorish in front yet Tudor behind. Caesar's Palace, like the Roman Forum, is replete, in its various signs, statues, wings, landscaping, fountains, with an asymmetrical accumulation of styles, from Early Christian to Neo-classical Motel Moderne; statues of Roman centurions stand next to Etruscan plastic columns. Yet Caesar's Palace styles also encompass the modernist, in massive 'Miesian light boxes': postmodernism here freely includes the modernist as one of its possible elements and perspectives, that comment on, talk to, quiz, interrogate and parody each other.[13]

Here is a point that *Learning from Las Vegas* very much wishes to stress, that the 'order of the Strip *includes*'. The spectator, the participant, is not dominated by the expert, as with modernism, is not rendered passive, but is more like a late twentieth-century embodiment of Walter Benjamin's notion of the *flâneur* as attentive, watchful stroller playing with multiple heterogeneous urban meanings. Las Vegas as architecture is certainly close to chaos, but as near-chaos it gains in vitality, and the spectator and participant, the 'moving eye in the moving body', is allowed a space and freedom to interpret a variety of changing incongruous contradictory juxtaposed orders.[14]

Las Vegas shows that 'even architects' can have 'fun', can be 'jester', trickster, wise fool, turning every conventional notion of building and design upside-down: a comment perhaps that could be made of *Learning from Las Vegas* itself. Architecture can take on a dimension of the European carnival of old, as in the 'statuesque' figures outside Caesar's Palace, carrying trays of fruit, suggesting the 'festivities' that beckon within. In Las Vegas, in its inclusiveness and allusiveness, its intertextuality, visitors can be *flâneurs*, explorers, rediscoverers of the architecture of the past. Architecture becomes a reaching out to, a play with, the other, continually suggested by the idea of the town as desert oasis, with the desert oasis' classic fundamental elements: courts, water, greenery (frequently palms), intimate scale, enclosed space. Las Vegas becomes a liminal space, of between and betwixt, where anything can happen, the oriental oasis in the desert where usual identities from the rest of the United States can be sloughed off: 'for three days one may imagine oneself a centurion at Caesar's Palace, a ranger at the Frontier, or a jetsetter at the Riviera rather than a salesperson from Des Moines, Iowa, or an architect from Haddonfield, New Jersey'.[15]

Learning from Las Vegas is one of my favourite books. I like the way it opposes the modernist claim to authority, to a single truth universally applied. I like its suggestion, taking off from Las Vegas – and Rome – of a postmodern aesthetic as inclusive, contradictory, extravagant, excessive, 'flamboyant'. Venturi, Scott Brown and Izenour argue that postmodern architecture is not afraid, like the modernist is afraid, to have fun, to attempt wit. But they are clearly irritated by the suggestion that such an architecture is thereby socially conservative or complacent, that it lacks social concern or responsibility (Denise Scott Brown refers to this charge in her preface to the revised edition; the authors have also been accused of being Nixonites). They certainly accept the presence of the market, the commercial strip, advertising, in a way that would be anathema to high modernism's blanket, foundational, anti-market credo. But they see no necessary reason why the methods of commercial persuasion and the skyline of signs 'should not serve the purpose of civic and cultural enhancement'. To accept the presence and activity of the market is not to be complacent or merely accepting, as they point out in relation to Pop Art, to Lichtenstein's play with images from comics, suggesting wit shaded by satire, irony, sorrow.[16]

What modernist architects wish above all to reject is the 'very heterogeneity of our society', that heterogeniety that is always the enemy of modernism's magisterial ambitions, that which they desire most to control, to purify, to rein in as the reserve of the 'expert', the modernist architect as 'authoritarian' judge of what cityscapes and the mass of people everywhere truly need.[17]

CHAPTER EIGHT

From Las Vegas to Sydney

I could not sleep for excitement over a fresh adventure in life. The lovely spectacle of the harbour jewelled with its fore-shore lights, the bulk of an unknown city beyond them, the ferries trailing brilliant reflections back and forth across the harbour, and most of all, a full-rigged ship discharging cargo by the light of kerosene flares immediately below me, kept me up half the night . . . I am not yielding to a nostalgic illusion of charm over that Sydney of the eighties and nineties, which lasted into the nineteen hundreds. When I arrived there (in 1901) it was at its best, a city that will never again be seen on earth – a sailor-town city, a free-trade city, a pre-mechanised city, in which one jostled in lower George Street and the Quay sailors from all the earth, and glimpsed over wharves and the roofs of harbour-side houses the tall spars of sailing ships. Its population was of sharply differentiated types and classes, so that one knew at a glance which social stratum each one belonged to . . . At least it is pleasing to recall that the two best prose writers of my generation have left vivid sidelights on the Sydney of my youth, Conrad in his *Mirror of the Seas,* and Stevenson in *The Wrecker.*

Norman Lindsay, My Mask [1]

In the middle and later 1980s controversy came to my home town, Sydney, capital and port city of its state, New South Wales. The business and retail heart of Sydney has always had the potential to be an exciting cityscape, to match its harbour, its coat-hanger bridge, its famous Opera House shaped like sails. At least in my view, such potential was denied by the triumph of modernist high-rise international style in the 1960s and 1970s, planting brutally assertive buildings that devastated a previous complex architectural heritage, ranging from nineteenth-century eclectic to early twentieth-century stylish and witty Art Deco. By the early

1980s, resistance to modernism, with its support from government and municipal town planning and its apparent open invitation to 'developers' to run rampant and destroy what was, had manifested itself in a vigorous green movement for conservation and restoration; it combined commentators from the 'public sphere' with trade union greenies, a rare and unusual breed that flourished briefly amongst Sydney's builder's labourers. Because of the public strength of the movement, in terms of protest and publicity, many older neighbourhoods and buildings were saved, in particular the historic Rocks area next to the Harbour Bridge, near where the British colony began in the late eighteenth century.

In 1983–4, the by then eight-years-old social-democrat Labor government of New South Wales, led by Neville Wran, embarked on a strategy for a fifth term of office. The strategy would centre on capital works like a tunnel under Sydney harbour (with an increased toll on the Harbour Bridge to help pay for it), and the construction of an 'urban park' at Darling Harbour, with an associated monorail that people could use to move between Darling Harbour and the central business district. Darling Harbour was an ex-railway goods line area, on the western side of the central business district, near Sydney's thriving Chinese quarter. Wran, an ex-lawyer, smooth-talking and flamboyant in terms of traditional images of Labor Party politicians, promised that Darling Harbour would be his government's present to the people of Sydney and New South Wales for the 1988 Bicentennial, the commemoration of the beginning (in Sydney) of the white colony.

Darling Harbour had been important in Sydney's maritime history as a port area for the new colony, where sailing ships continuously called with provisions and for trade. To be built over a four year period, the urban park at Darling Harbour would recall this history by mixing its open space and cool quiet areas of native trees (including palms) with artificial canals, waterfalls, shallow water for little children, a Maritime Museum, and moored old ships. There would also be an aquarium below water level, Chinese gardens, exhibition buildings, and a festival marketplace building replete with restaurants, eateries of every ethnic sort (Sydney is strikingly multi-ethnic in its food tastes), and many retail shops. There would be wandering clowns, acrobats, jugglers, to entertain those invited to stroll.[2]

The politician chosen by Wran to push these projects and visions through was Laurie Brereton. Brereton had been appointed to Cabinet in 1981 and given the health portfolio. He immediately proved himself an energetic and tough minister, best remembered for his transfer of nursing education from hospitals to colleges, and for his 'beds to the west' program, moving hospital services from the inner city to the massively populated but severely under-serviced western areas of Sydney. He oversaw and opened a major artificial recreation lake at Chipping Norton in Sydney's west, fashioned from disused pits that had been dug for sand-mining; the scheme also involved restoration for public use of an 1880s homestead. In 1984 he was promoted to the portfolios of public works and roads and ports, and entrusted to guide to completion Darling Harbour with all due haste, given how large a building project it was, with the 1988 Bicentennial as the looming deadline.

Brereton, however, quickly proved a controversial minister in his new high-profile role. Many and passionate were the things said against him: he was of the NSW right wing of the Labor Party, with a questionable past in local branch politics; his approach was relentless, bullying, impervious to criticism; he wore expensive suits and sounded like a simulacrum of his mentor Mr Wran; he was pro-development and developers, and therefore was betraying traditional Labor values. So controversial did Brereton and Darling Harbour and its monorail become, among conservationists, environmentalists, town planners, certain (but certainly not all) architects, and media commentators and journalists, especially in 'quality' 'public sphere' newspapers like the *Sydney Morning Herald,* that his career, along with the chance of re-election of the Labor government, was threatened as the years went on. As it turned out, Brereton was sacrificed, losing in late 1987 his ministerial position (from rooster to feather duster, as the journalists the next day said), though the Labor government, even *sans* Brereton, would easily lose the following election.[3]

Through 1987 there had been a chorus of scorn, alarm, agitation, formation of protest groups, and a number of street demonstrations, opposed most immediately to the construction of the monorail, but also to Darling Harbour and everything associated with it. In the street marches, demonstrators, some wearing Mickey Mouse ears, shouted slogans against Darling Harbour and the monorail as bringing the degradingly frivolous spirit of Disneyland to central Sydney. Protest spilled into the media. In mid-October the ABC, child of the BBC and rationalist 'public sphere' state-funded broadcasting, showed a *Four Corners* documentary program, 'My City of Sydney'. In time-honoured *Four Corners* monologic style, the journalist Tony Jones had already decided the single truth of Darling Harbour and the monorail. He showed graphic footage of machinery portrayed as speeded-up dinosaurs tearing down the insides of old buildings in the centre of Sydney's retail area – not in Darling Harbour – and then brought forward commentators like Neville Gruzman, then visiting professor of architecture at the University of New South Wales, as a talking head to reinforce what was apparently a pellucid case of wanton destruction. Gruzman told us that the uncontrolled development happening in Sydney, including at Darling Harbour, was the 'biggest disaster that has ever happened to any city anywhere in the world'. Another talking head, James McClelland, ex-minister from the early 1970s years of the federal Labor government, trowelled scorn on Brereton as in any sense representing the traditions of the labour movement.

The *Four Corners* program was written up favourably in the *Sydney Morning Herald*, Richard Coleman in his weekend review column saying that simply showing visual evidence of the monorail was enough to convict it. (Coleman did, however, point out how single-minded and already decided the ABC program was.) In his regular column in the *Herald*, James McClelland kept up a running mordant commentary, with supreme assurance, unshaded by doubt, on new architectural developments in Sydney. The developers were creating havoc, he said, and he singled out for derision the Coopers and Lybrand tower in George Street, across from Sydney's main cinema area. The Coopers and Lybrand edifice just happens to be one of my favourite postmodernist buildings in Sydney, tall and of glass as in modernism, but in playful blues and pink, with Art Deco touches at the top, perhaps referring us to New York's Art Deco masterpiece the Chrysler Building. In McClelland's eyes, my favourite postmodernist building outside Darling Harbour was the ultimate bad joke, a 'vulgarity', a 'Disneyland castle'.[4]

The next month McClelland focused on what he referred to as his own special *bête noir*, telling us that the 'main argument against it has always been the aesthetic one', that it is an 'eyesore' destroying what remains of Sydney's beauty. He brushed aside a *Herald* telephone survey that suggested a majority of Sydneysiders accepted the monorail. December of 1987 found McClelland bewailing Darling Harbour. He agreed, he said, with Neville Gruzman, that Darling Harbour should have been a park, surrounded by low-income houses with supporting amenities, people living in or near the central city area bringing new life and animation to it. He could only see 'ugliness' in one of Darling Harbour's main structures, the Exhibition Building. Also in the *Herald*, in his then regular Saturday column, Sydney University literary critic Don Anderson wrote that the monorail was 'indefensible', turning (here he called for help on French philosopher Jean Baudrillard) the central business district into 'Disneyland'.[5]

Throughout 1987 I found myself puzzled by the furore. When I saw Brereton on TV, he struck me as rather stiff, slightly reminiscent of a programmed android, and indeed a little comical, talking like his mentor, Premier Wran.[6] Yet it could be argued, I thought, that Brereton possessed a broad vision for Sydney, and was prepared to see the project through despite what turned out to be enormous personal cost.

A number of my friends were involved in the various protests. Some, associated with off-Broadway-style theatre and describing themselves as inner-city and left-labour, read out at a birthday party poems, songs, lampoons, limericks, haikus, frequently with apologies to authors perhaps remembered from undergraduate days (Chaucer, Spenser, Blake, Shelley). The contributions were printed for the occasion – its twenty or so pages, loosely bound, with accompanying cartoons and visual gags, were almost exclusively directed at Brereton and his various perceived faults. There was the rare glance at the monorail itself:

> How much is that monorail station
> The one o'er a spindly pylon
> With glitz and graffiti and mirrors
> And v. nasty decoration.

> How much are those blue painted girders
> That snake round each mis'rable street
> That snarl and block and snag all the traffic
> That crawls at their miserable feet . . .

The burden of the songs, however, was set by the cover, with a cartoon showing Brereton as Napoleon, overreaching himself and attempting a dictatorial grandeur he was ludicrously incapable of. Here a poem drew on Shelley's 'Ozymandias':

> My name is Laurie Brereton, Minister for Public Works,
> Look on my works, you lot and despair.
> Nothing beside remains. Round
> The decay of that monumental folly, boundless and bare,
> The rubble stretches far away.

Another looked to Blake's 'Tyger':

> Laurie! Laurie! Burning bright
> In the factions of the right,
> What infernal hand or eye
> Decreed this monorail on high?

All the contributions were read out to much laughter, and a cake was cut with a drawing in icing of Brereton wreathed by his monorail, the evil angel of urban death.

In general there were many points of critique. The monorail and Darling Harbour were perceived as being pushed brutally through, despite considered opposition, ignoring due process, an example of state coerciveness. Brereton was like a dictator of old, a Caesar: he came, he saw, he insisted on building. Local Sydney people were being ignored in favour of overseas tourists, who would be the main, perhaps the only, users of the monorail and Darling Harbour. As the monorail journeyed past offices, especially in narrow Pitt Street, office workers in the buildings would feel under surveillance from strangers looking uninvited at them. Safety issues in relation to people walking underneath the monorail had not been properly addressed, nor had there been serious consideration given to alternatives, like a moving walkway. The urban park at Darling Harbour, with its exhibition halls and food and retail shops, would erase the working-class history of the site, as a goods line, a rail junction important to trade: yet more of Sydney's history and heritage would be lost.

I didn't and don't wish to minimise or dismiss such arguments. Yet some of them struck me as entirely misplaced. I couldn't understand why concerned citizens like James McClelland, claiming to represent the public interest and the true spirit of Sydney, did not *welcome* the Coopers and Lybrand building because it was so different from the 1960s/70s common fare of modernist monoliths. Whenever I see it, its flamboyance and wit make me laugh, particularly when compared to the spectacularly boring grey functional modernist office buildings that surround it and that it is obviously contesting and parodying: in terms of *Learning from Las Vegas*, the architect as jester, as wise fool.

I watched the *Four Corners* program, 'My City of Sydney', and found bizarre its linking of alleged new high-rise development in Sydney's retail heart with Darling Harbour – which did not have any high-rise modernist buildings. Furthermore, nothing of Sydney's architectural heritage had been torn down at Darling Harbour, which for years had been an area of desolation, large, disused, derelict, an emptiness. Since it was the very reverse of a return to modernist high-rise or international style, I again thought, why isn't it being welcomed as such?

I defend the monorail

I also decided, looking at photos of the monorail cars and then going to see the rail itself, the ribbon of sky-blue steel winding through some of Sydney's streets, that I liked it. I could concede that there might be transport problems and lost transport opportunities associated with it, since it didn't link up with existing railway stations. There might, too, be cause for worry in that the monorail was being privately financed, built, and managed: by TNT, a large Australian company run by prominent businessman Sir Peter Abeles. (Recent information suggests that the establishment cost for TNT was $65 million.)[7] I also thought there might be cause for concern in the monorail coursing along Pitt Street, because of its narrowness, though I wasn't convinced this was a problem. And I was worried the monorail might prove noisy (a needless fear, I now think).

Some of the objections to the monorail I found predictable-modernist, particularly the fear of Americanisation – that fear that courses back to F.R. Leavis and Q.D. Leavis and Adorno and Horkheimer in the 1930s and 1940s – raised in the oft-repeated cry, we don't want Disneyland in our city. The strangely puritanic and rationalist assumption here seemed to be that the non-utilitarian spirit of fun that the monorail could provide was inappropriate in the Central Business District, as if that were all sober commerce and government administration, rather than the crazy mix of business and government offices with department stores, shops, arcades, cinemas, coffee shops, cafés and restaurants it already was. Why should an additional pleasure be seen as Americanisation? Americanisation was, I thought in any case (and still think), a prime modernist myth.

I really liked the idea of the monorail (the service was not to open until 1988), and strongly felt that what was announced by James McClelland as the main objection to it, the aesthetic, was wrong, that the monorail was indeed aesthetically defensible, in terms of postmodernist values. I began to chance my arm to people I talked to at various gatherings, outlining my defence, to universal intense opposition. This spurred me on, and I decided to write an article for the *Sydney Morning Herald* 'op ed' page (its page of commentary, opinion and features facing the editorial and letters page). On Monday, 26 October, I awoke to find my article printed, the *Herald* giving it the title 'And now for the I-love-the-exciting-monorail party trick' as well as an inflaming sub-heading, 'Sydney's monorail is an aesthetic triumph, writes John Docker'. Here's how it went:

> Over the past few weeks at parties I've been perfecting an obscene performance for astonishing the other guests. I defend the monorail on aesthetic grounds. I usually say I need at least 10 minutes before objections crowd in. I've learnt to do this after finding that if I don't, no-one will let me say more than a sentence.
>
> My defence goes like this. The monorail is, after all, only a single blue rail, it's not actually very long, it doesn't take up much visual space. I like it, I say, because it is a horizontal ribbon winding its way through and across vertical structures.
>
> In this way, it reminds me, I say, of the beginning of Fritz Lang's *Metropolis*, showing a futuristic city with a monorail curving its way among tall modern buildings. The Sydney monorail is, I go on, similarly futuristic. It is exciting, creating interesting patterns of space and time.
>
> Since it moves just above the awning line, passengers will have access to Sydney's architectural past and present, able at the same time to see older architectural styles above the awning, and contemporary Sydney at street level below it. It will restore a sense of the layers of the city's architectural

history. It will return to Sydneysiders views usually closed to them as pedestrians, so that they can enjoy historically significant buildings and façades long denied them by the Awning Revolution.

It's also likely that with the coming of the monorail the façades will be cleaned and restored. To show just how much I disagree with the views common to the people I know, I then say that the way the futuristic monorail winds near and past the already restored Queen Victoria Building will be particularly exciting.

I then tell the by now open-mouthed and irritated guests that they should welcome the monorail because it is an example of Post-Modernism. In helping to create and highlight a mixture of styles in Sydney, it represents an example of what some say Post-Modernism is about, restoring pastiche and collage and whimsy and pleasure and fun to architecture and aesthetics.

I say that I think the monorail cars are beautiful, sensuous, erotic, and, I ask rhetorically, what's wrong with people coming to Darling Harbour and catching the monorail up to the QVB and enjoying themselves? Also, I go on, for decades Darling Harbour has been a dead part of Sydney. Now it will become interesting and accessible and be joined in an exciting way to the rest of the city.

I then suggest that I've gots lots more arguments, but I'll finish with the ringing declaration that it's the sign of a dynamic city that it is not frozen in time, but develops the new at the same time as it restores and makes accessible the old.

The objections then certainly do burst forth, but so far none, I think, has answered me satisfactorily. They usually switch the point of attack, and give their rather low opinion of Mr Brereton. They don't answer the aesthetic argument, even though that is, or is supposed to be, their main objection.

To show just how crazy I am, they begin to suggest I'll be defending the tunnel next. Mmm, the tunnel . . .

Feelings for and against will be running as high as the monorail as it goes into its trial runs around the city in the next few months. I wonder, actually, if one has to be entirely for or entirely against.

We pro-monorailers could agree that there may be certain problems, such as noise, though I'd like to take a wait-and-see attitude on that, as they say. Anti-monorailers might agree that the monorail has a certain aesthetic and entertainment and practical appeal.

I predict most people in Sydney will love the train and the views and the ease of getting around and will use it to the full. In five years time I'll be able to say, I told you so.

Looking back now, some years later, I don't in the least regret my defence of the Sydney monorail. The monorail has, I think, proven popular, though it has suffered from the business crashes that closed the decade of the Booming Eighties. Two stations were planned for large commercial developments (World Square and Park Plaza) that have never been built.[8] I still think it's highly defensible as embodying a postmodernist aesthetic, particularly in terms suggested by Venturi, Scott Brown and Izenour's *Learning from Las Vegas*. Going round the monorail permits perception at speed, allowing the passenger to be a *flâneur* above ground level, interpreting a 'variety of changing, juxtaposed orders',[9] reflecting on times past, present and future (the futuristic monorail itself) in terms of architectural styles and modes. For a few minutes, passengers can inhabit a liminal space and time, lifting them out of the city as business- or purpose-oriented, allowing them to feel as if in a magical movie world. And I still think the monorail cars are sensuous, erotic.

If the monorail allows contemplation, a recovery, of Sydney's architectural past above the awning line, so too does Darling Harbour as urban park, where crowds can course as strollers, traditional *flâneurs* on foot, active participants in a varied scene. As in Venturi, Scott Brown and Izenour's evocation of Las Vegas buildings behind the façades of signs, the buildings of Darling Harbour are mostly long and/or low. They are not of a tall inhospitable phallic hardness, as in the modernist mono-lith, but rather welcoming, receptive, warm, including, approachable. The Crystal Palace-like Festival Marketplace (by architects Clarke Parry Blackmore), with its outrageous waterfall and dolphins, enjoys a visual extravagance that parodies modernist austerity, but which is also, like Pop Art, so flamboyant that it also self-parodies.

The story of the Festival Marketplace is interesting. It is a great popular success, drawing large and constant crowds to its restaurants, cafés, foodbars and specialty shops, and doing a roaring trade in postcards of the marketplace building itself. Yet its path to existence was rocky indeed. In 1983 Premier Wran asked Tom Hayson if he would contribute to the Darling Harbour project, Hayson being the only property developer in Sydney to express an interest in assisting the government with its idea of an urban park. Hayson travelled in late 1983 and early 1984 to the United States and came across Baltimore's harbourside marketplace, which he thought could be a prototype for a similar building at Darling Harbour. Hayson contacted James Rouse, the inventor of the festival marketplace format in America, who had built Harborplace Baltimore, which, after intense opposition from those in the community who believed public space should not be alienated by commercial interests, had proven immensely popular and helped reinvigorate the city's harbourfront. It was estimated that on its opening day 400,000 people jammed Harborplace and the Inner Harbor and that there were 18 million visitors in its first year of operation. The ethnic food sold at Harborplace related to Baltimore as a port city with a rich mosaic of cultures, Jewish, Greek, Italian.[10]

Hayson invited James Rouse to Australia to try to involve him in the Darling Harbour project. Rouse gave a lecture in Sydney in May 1984 to some five hundred people, property developers, financiers, local government planners, architects, in the Regent Hotel Ballroom, Rouse being introduced by Laurie Brereton. A week before Rouse arrived in

Sydney, however, Tom Hayson had had a heart attack, and responsibility for the visit largely devolved to Bob Perry, of Clark Perry Blackmore/Architecture Oceania, the architects commissioned by the Hayson Group to design the festival marketplace building. Rouse decided to join the Hayson group in constructing the building, the first time Rouse had entered into a joint venture outside the US.

But things then seemed to stall. Later in 1984 Rouse's principal designer Mort Hoppenfeld came to Australia to help present the proposed building to the government so that it could be included in the masterplan for Darling Harbour. The masterplan, however, was published the day before Hoppenfeld arrived – without the festival marketplace in it. When Laurie Brereton visited Baltimore as part of a world tour looking at harbourside projects, Hoppenfeld told him Darling Harbour would fail unless it included a festival marketplace building. As it happened, Brereton was very taken with Rouse's Harborplace Baltimore, and took an executive decision to freeze the government's masterplan; he then appointed Hoppenfeld as the master planner for Darling Harbour. But in late 1985 Mort Hoppenfeld died.

Architecture Oceania (principally Robert Creed as well as Bob Perry) worked with Rouse's Enterprise Development Company in Baltimore to design the building, two pavilions linked in the middle (with what came to be known as the Crystal Galleria), with restaurants and cafés along the front, on both of its levels. Architecture Oceania were also engaged to do all the interior design. Baltimore's Inner Harbor, with its mix of National Aquarium, Science and Technology Museum, and festival marketplace, drew 80 per cent of its visitors from Baltimore itself. It was hoped that Darling Harbour, with its mix of exhibition halls, convention centre, aquarium, maritime museum as well as festival marketplace building, would also appeal principally to Sydneysiders.

The Harbourside Festival Marketplace was designed to catch the eye of the stroller promenading in Darling Harbour by its impressive Crystal Palace-like galleria; as you get closer to it, the building has the effect of diminishing in size, becoming more intimate, an effect of its soft edges, its restaurants and cafés at the front, its balconies, and its various openings, so that the public feel it owns its spaces, can effortlessly move in and out. On the first floor are observatories with views out over Darling Habour. The marketplace was to be a kind of a giant theatre in a festive setting, but a theatre without a separate stage area. All could be players, so that when you are sitting in a restaurant or café at the front, you can not only look at the waterfront and the city but also the passing crowd as they are looking at the building and at you.

Inside, as in the markets and bazaars of old, the various foodbars and specialty shops are not visually closed off from each other. The interior is highly communicative, with extravagant shop signs and a profusion of artwork, for graphic artists were engaged to create decorative arts for the building. As with the terrazzo floors, such arts are for daily use – shades of William Morris' late nineteenth-century art-and-craft ideals, art as useful, the useful as art. An essay in *craft arts international* tells the story of the terrazzo floors, their ancestry in ancient Roman techniques of cement paving. Sydney is home to the modern terrazzo style – skill in terrazzo was carried to Australia in the early years of this century by Italian immigrants. The families of Melocco, Venier, Togno and Guigni, from northern Italy, have been operating in Sydney for some sixty years, and their company, Terazzo and Co. Pty Ltd, combined with Suzanne Holman, of the Public Art Squad, to execute the designs. Holman's experience and background were in theatre and circus, costume, mask and puppet-making, and murals and community projects, such as the designing and building of children's playgrounds. Along with the Terazzo and Co. artisans, she translated original linocut images from graphic artists, for example, Bruce Goold's *Waratah* and *Currawong*, Zig Moskwa's *Gecko* and *The Carp Pool*, and the four designs by Aboriginal women artists Banduk Marika and Thancoupie, including Marika's *Snake Floor*.[11]

The construction of the terrazzo floors was under the overall direction of Bob Perry, as were the other decorative arts in the building, over fifty artists creating, in a spirit of festival and theatre, ceramic and painted murals, sculptures, silk banners and flags, large earthenware pots, mobiles, and laminex table tops. Some of the pots designed by Thancoupie, a potter and ceramic artist from Cairns, were snapped up by the National Gallery in Canberra. Bob Perry saw himself as trying to stimulate into being a kind of 'choreographed anarchy', a collective adventure: the architect as *bricoleur*. Here there is a contrast to the slight touch of modernist monumentalism in the grandeur of some of the other Darling Harbour buildings, a monumentalism calling attention to the buildings as authored, the architect as *auteur*.

The festival marketplace building was intended to be highly allusive, not only most obviously to London's famous Crystal Palace and to the nineteenth-century arcades that so intrigued Walter Benjamin, but to specific features of Sydney's architectural heritage. A brochure put out by the architects tells the story of the Oceania Fountain, a large waterfall in the central galleria, where people often congregate and take photos. A sign OCEANIA is drawn on the wall behind the waterfall, which at night is illuminated and can be noted from across the bay. The overall form of the fountain is that of the outline of a stained-glass window of old.

The brochure explains that the inspiration for the Oceania Fountain came from *Australia*, a highly coloured stained-glass window that was created on the south side of the Sydney Town Hall to celebrate the 1888 Centennial of New South Wales. The window was designed by a French-born artist, Lucien Henry, who at the age of twenty-one had found himself transported to New Caledonia for his involvement in the Paris Commune of 1871, a convict history that recalls the beginnings of New South Wales. Following a political amnesty in 1879, Henry journeyed to Sydney, where he became a key figure in art education in Australia, teaching sculpture, modelling, painting, terracotta, architecture, and design. He advocated the use of Australian fauna and flora, in particular the waratah flower, which fascinated him. The brochure reproduces Henry's spectacular *Australia* window, which features in its central panel the powerful figure of a young woman, boldly looking at us and the future, behind her head glowing rays of the sun; she holds a trident and a miner's lamp, with fleece and ram horns on and around her hair, an iconography suggesting the colony's wealth in wool and minerals and connection to the treasures of the sea. In the panels beside her are pots with potent red waratahs (as in Bruce Goold's terrazzo design). She stands on top of the upper part of the earthenware-coloured globe, with OCEANIA inscribed on it.

In the Oceania Fountain the globe that peeps from below 'Australia's' robust sandalled feet is released into wholeness, now of swirling whites and blues as if a map of the Pacific Ocean writ large. Around and away and upwards from the globe move dolphins and amongst them a slim androgynous human figure swims as if part of the dolphin family and the life of the sea: a human figure no longer dominating the planet and this part of the world as in the late nineteenth-century stained-glass window. In the Oceania Fountain, Australia is not tied to its past relationship with its interior, has ceased to be inturned and insular, as it looks outwards in a lyrical utopian way to seas, oceans, futures beyond.

Darling Harbour in general breaks with modernism's international style and welcomes the local and vernacular, which includes a multi-ethnic and multicultural history and presence, as with the Oceania Fountain's intertextual referencing of French-Australian Lucien Henry,[12] or the marketplace building's mix of cafés and foodbars, reputedly far more ethnically diverse than Rouse's building in Baltimore. (James Rouse came to the opening of Darling Harbour, and thinks its harbourside project the world's most exciting.) The Chinese Gardens recall the long presence in this part of Sydney of Chinese immigrants, in restaurants, shops, and businesses. The Exhibition Centre and the Maritime

Museum were designed by prominent local architect Philip Cox. When a Philip Cox Exhibition was held at the Art Gallery of New South Wales in the middle of 1992, captions to various drawings and plans explained that in his Maritime Museum the 'constant visual relationship between interior spaces, the external ship display and the working port on the opposite shoreline' were a 'deliberate endeavour to relate history with contemporary maritime activity'; the roof, suggesting 'billowing sails or rolling waves', was designed to create a strong identity for the building in 'Sydney's urban fabric'. The inspiration for the Exhibition Centre came partly from Paxton's 1851 Crystal Palace, and also from the European tradition of great lightweight exhibition centres set in public gardens; its skeletal mast-and-cable structure was designed to complement the background of massive woolstores and warehouses; the structure was also intended 'as a nautical metaphor giving the feeling of a great docked ship'.

Such buildings, with their ship-like spars and sails, help create Darling Harbour itself as a liminal space, between land and sea. They refer outwards to Sydney Harbour in general as a port saturated with a nineteenth- and twentieth-century history of ships that crossed the world's seas, the port that once enchanted, as artist, novelist and cartoonist Norman Lindsay, then fresh from Melbourne, notes in our epigraph, writers like Robert Louis Stevenson and Joseph Conrad.

> . . . in Sydney, where, from the heart of the fair city, down the vista of important streets, could be seen the wool-clippers lying at the Circular Quay – no walled prison-house of a dock that, but the integral part of one of the finest, most beautiful, vast, and safe bays the sun ever shone upon . . . the general cargo, emigrant, and passenger ships of my time, rigged with heavy spars, and built on fine lines, used to remain for months together waiting for their load of wool. Their names attained the dignity of household words. On Sundays and holidays the citizens trooped down, on visiting bent. . .[13]

CHAPTER NINE

Are We Living in a Postmodern Age?

So far we have been considering what we might call 'aesthetic post-modernism', a phenomenon manifested particularly in architecture and associated theory, as in Venturi, Scott Brown and Izenour's *Learning from Las Vegas*. 'Postmodernism' as a term also usually covers what I would prefer to call visions of postmodernity, visions that are relevant not so much to the aesthetic realm as to social and political theory. Indeed, such visions have been spread before us by theorists like Baudrillard and Lyotard who in terms of aesthetic theory are themselves determined modernists, and are continuing long modernist traditions.

We can see 'postmodernism' in this sense as a *fin de siècle* genre, as social and political theory informed and shaped by literary tropes, suggestive modes of narrative. In his *Century's End* (1990), American author Hillel Schwartz argues that in European cultural history *fin de siècle* periods have only gradually become more important. There was no mass panic during the 990s, anticipating the first millenium. What Schwartz calls centurial excitement gathered pace after 1300. *Fin de siècle* versions of utopias were written. Various popes began to celebrate a century's end, with papal jubilees promising the inauguration of universal peace. Sinners were offered an amnesty. Sometimes heretics, like Giordano Bruno in 1600, were burned at the stake as an example of the kind of person authorities didn't wish to encourage in the new century. In the nineteenth century the Romantics complained of *mal du siècle*, century sickness, nauseated by the century they lived in. The expression *fin de siècle* apparently made its debut in 1886.[1]

Fin de siècle periods are unusually intellectually turbulent and self-questioning, a curious effect, as if in a self-fulfilling prophecy, of the very self-consciousness of being at the end of a century. *Fin de siècle* periods are liminal, jumping out from between centuries, looking back on the old and forward to the new, placing past, present and future in unexpected, unforeseen, suddenly different relationships. Such periods are usually awash with futuristic glimmerings, prophecies, the new and unpredicted. Yet also and equally are they times of Gothic, forebodings, sinister omens, *unheimlich*, forecasts of disaster, history as relentless drift into living death.

As such an apocalyptic genre 'postmodernism' creates a new historical period, 'postmodernity', a period of the post-industrial, a new age of information, computers, mass media, mass communication.

Baudrillard

> Certain central themes spring up repeatedly in cyberpunk. The theme of body invasion: prosphetic limbs, implanted circuitry, cosmetic surgery, genetic alteration. The even more powerful theme of mind invasion: brain-computer interfaces, artificial intelligence, neuro-chemistry techniques radically redefining the nature of humanity, the nature of the self.[2]

In his well-known essay 'The Ecstasy of Communication', Jean Baudrillard draws explicitly on a language of 'science fiction'.[3] Our world, it appears, has been invaded by the awful omnipresence of communication, especially as embodied in television and advertising. Television has invaded the once-private home, changing our habitat into a kind of archaic envelope, a vestige of human relations whose very survival remains perplexing. Our bodies waste away as our minds in our living-rooms lock into the televised screen. We become part of mass communication's circuits, part of a realm and era of connections, contact, contiguity, feedback, generalised interface, an era that is 'obscene' yet 'lunar' cold. The new era of communication invades our minds in a pornographic way, ejecting all interiority, injecting the exterior world of television and information. We succumb to a state of terror proper to the schizophrenic, of too great a proximity of everything, the 'unclean promiscuity of everything which touches, invests and penetrates without resistance'.

The curiously erotic language of Baudrillard's essay here, of contact that is obscene yet lunar cold, penetrating without resistance, reminds me of a remarkable moment in another *fin de siècle* Gothic text of a century before, Bram Stoker's *Dracula*, when young lawyer Jonathan Harker, trapped within the Count's castle in Transylvania, is close to seduction by a vampiress. The light is lunar, and Harker feels a deadly fear mixed with a wicked, burning desire that she should kiss him:

> 'I was afraid to raise my eyelids, but looked out and saw perfectly under the lashes. The fair girl went on her knees and bent over me, fairly gloating.

There was a deliberate voluptuousness which was both thrilling and repulsive, and as she arched her neck she actually licked her lips like an animal, till I could see in the moonlight the moisture shining on the scarlet lips and on the red tongue as it lapped the white sharp teeth. . . . I closed my eyes in a languorous ecstasy and waited – waited with beating heart.'[4]

In the late twentieth-century imagery of 'The Ecstasy of Communication', we might say that Postmodern Man has to suffer the embrace of communication also conceived as a succubus, a witch, a vampiress on top, fatally attractive, all conquering, smothering – death so near by undesired ecstasy.

Outside the home, now not a home but a 'lunar module', advertising also 'invades everything', so that public space (the street, monument, market, scene) disappears. As in post-nuclear, but here post-communication, science fiction films, we are left in a devastated, empty, eerie, primitive-again world. Every prior distinction and value – of public and private, subject and object, the social and the political (as in the lost public sphere of argument and debate), and even any vestige of the pre-industrial past (based not on commodity production but on free symbolic exchange of the gift, as in potlatch communities) – have gone, even 'the real' itself. Instead of 'the real' we have everywhere only the simulacrum, a world so pervaded by media images that we see only images of images, copies of copies.[5]

Baudrillard offers a classic modernist narrative, history as a linear, unidirectional story of decline. But whereas the early twentieth-century high literary modernists could dream of an avant-garde or cultural élite that might preserve the values of the past in the hope of a future seeding and regrowth, no such hope surfaces in Baudrillard's vision of a dying, entropic world. It's not even possible to write in a rational argumentative form, for that assumes a remaining community of reason.

In his mid-1980s book *America*, evocation of his journey into the New World, Baudrillard finds *fin de siècle* humanity's ultimate lunar-cold future, its desolate dystopia. The strategy of the narrative we can call structuralist, the search beneath supposed surfaces for an ultimate structure, for essences that, once discovered by the observer, the narrator, explain a phenomenon conceived as a whole, a unity. In *America* Baudrillard as narrator tells us that he went in search not of social and cultural America, not the America of mores and mentalities, but what he calls 'astral' America, the America of the 'empty, absolute freedom' of the freeways. Such he can perceive in the screenplay, in television, in the succession of signs on the road. But its 'finished form' – the 'future catastrophe of the social' – he will find as he drives through the desert. The 'inhumanity of our ulterior, asocial, superficial world' finds its form in the geology of the desert, cold and dead, yet filled with heat (Baudrillard is here calling on traditional images of the inferno). The desert has an essence, it is 'simply' a form of disappearance. Its geology suggests the 'desertification' of what used to be a meaningful society.[6]

We have, then, says Baudrillard, to search beneath the 'superficial diversity' of America, its apparent complexity, hybridity, and inter-mingling, to detect that 'deep down' America is 'fundamentally primitive', for its essence is 'emptiness', a void whose visible sign is the surreal, empty 'lunar' desert. In the desert, as in 'doubtless all of American culture', is to be seen, as we travel at speed across it, the 'extermination of meaning', revealed in sexual terms. Baudrillard's *America* is insistently gendered. The female is associated with the primitive, the geological, and the barren. In the desert, 'man' is in danger of losing his 'resistance' to its emptiness, its 'total availability', its 'transparency'. In a moment of 'vertigo', man is sucked into the 'vacuum'.[7]

The vacuum of the desert is the essential void of the rest of the United States, again imaged in female terms, from Las Vegas as 'that great whore' (O what modernist cliché), to its metropolises like New York, where the aggressive advertisements are like 'wall-to-wall prosti-tution'. In New York the plumes of smoke are reminiscent of 'girls wringing out their hair after bathing', the city for a moment alluring, an association quickly followed by those other dangerous lures, Africa and the Orient. The narrator notices everywhere 'Afro or pre-Raphaelite hairstyles', and Manhattan strikes him as like a city of Pharaohs, all obelisks and needles.

America here performs a return to the primitivism of early twentieth-century modernism, as in 1920s Paris, with its negrophilia, its fascin-ation with Josephine Baker as traditional African *sauvage*. *America*'s narrator refers to the 'beauty of the Black and Puerto Rican women of New York'. The 'pigmentation of the dark races' produces a beauty that is 'sublime and animal', 'esoteric', with a 'ritual potency'. To read of such modernist fantasy, such racial essentialising, in the 1920s is of historical and anthropological interest. To witness it espoused with such unabashed innocence in a late twentieth-century text is merely embarrassing. (It also doesn't surprise when Baudrillard as all-knowing modernist mandarin tells us that the Navajos possessed a 'terribly cruel religion' that was apparently needed to exorcise the desert's awful power.)[8]

The assemblage of modernist cliché brought to bear on New York is in general embarrassing. The narrator is struck by the 'terrifying divers-ity' of New York faces. Yet the metropolis is 'desert-like' in its banality.

People in the big city suffer such solitude that they have 'cirrus clouds in their heads or coming out of their eyes, like the spongy vapours that rise from earth cracked by hot rains'. We are obviously not far from the images of desert and of urban ghosts who walk in *The Waste Land*. Indeed, we might say that Baudrillard's text here is a simulacrum of a century of modernist writing about the modern metropolis.

The narrator writes, as if attracted to them, that New York's streets are intense and vital. He then claims, apparently from a glance, that only tribes, gangs, mafia families, secret societies, and 'perverse communities' can survive in New York, 'not couples'. (That 'perverse communities' is strangely moralistic terminology, suggesting norms that all humanity should abide by.) In a futuristic science-fiction image of social death, the narrator tells us that New York is an anti-Ark, where 'each one comes in alone – it's up to him or her each evening to find the last survivors for the last party'. New York's violence, he is soon telling us, is a violence of 'all relations', including the sexual, which no longer has time to realise itself in human love-relationships.[9] We can remind ourselves here of Adorno and Horkheimer in *Dialectic of Enlightenment* also claiming to know the most intimate situations of human beings in America. How does Baudrillard acquire the knowledge that no couples, no relationships, survive in New York?

Also embarrassing are the European/New World tropes of comparison, the accumulated clichés of a long European sociological tradition, constructing a binary opposition of modern impersonal alienated societies of contract, of *Gesellschaft*, to traditional communities, with their supposed binding relations of collectivity, neighbourhood, kin, friendship, love, *Gemeinschaft*. In this tradition, 'America' becomes the extreme form, the dread future, of such *Gesellschaft*, of the lonely crowd. 'Why do people live in New York', asks *America*'s narrator. 'There is no relationship between them'. Further, in their New World society Americans are 'lacking a past through which to reflect on this', on their own emptiness, which is why they are so 'fundamentally primitive'. They lack any Old World knowledge of previous *Gemeinschaft* traditions by which to understand themselves.[10]

It's of little surprise, then, that Baudrillard sees the New World very much as de Tocqueville saw it last century, as high on democracy, low in 'civilization', its freedom really only conformity and emptiness. The narrator of *America* comes to his object of enquiry as a superior European. 'We in Europe possess the art of thinking, of analysing things and reflecting on them', he tells us without any self-irony towards such pomposity I can detect. 'No one disputes our historical subtlety and conceptual imagination.' We certainly cannot look to American intellectuals to analyse their society's 'naive extravagance', for they are 'shut away on their campuses'.[11] The all-seeing Old World modernist can tell at a glance that all American intellectuals all over the US are shut away in their campuses; perhaps Venturi, Scott Brown and Izenour's field trip to Las Vegas, empirical correlative of their *Learning*, didn't occur.

There is ambivalence in *America*, a perception of the New World as the 'dawning of the universe'. But such is the ambivalence of the *fin de siècle* futuristic genre itself, a science-fiction-film sense of the new, shadowed by Gothic foreboding. The freeways possess a 'magic', but the fascination is one of 'senseless repetition'. American cities have sparkle as well as violence. But there is 'no human reason' to live in New York, except the 'sheer ecstasy of being crowded together'. Nothing could be 'more intense, electrifying, turbulent, and vital than the streets of New York'. But in them the 'mad have been set free', as the city 'acts out its own catastrophe as a stage play'.[12]

Baudrillard in America, in search of catastrophe: where, as so often in modernist writing, 'America' functions, predictably and repetitively, as the sign and endpoint of all those cultural processes that are destroying the world.

Lyotards

Jean-François Lyotard, best known in relation to this debate for his *The Postmodern Condition: A Report on Knowledge* (1979), in general agrees with his fellow French theorist that the postmodern age is post-industrial, is the age of knowledge production, of media, computers, information, data. But Lyotard is critical of Baudrillard's nostalgic social theory, his innocent glance back at an ideal pre-commodity society of the gift. For Lyotard, such nostalgia is the product of Western anthropological desire, desire for the 'good savage': Baudrillard, in postulating a traditional community somehow free of power and political economy, is still in search of an unproblematic realm of truth.[13]

In *The Postmodern Condition* Lyotard criticises Baudrillard for such a 'paradisiac representation of a lost "organic" society', with its linked view that the present is a relentless uniform total system. 'No one,' says Lyotard, 'not even the least privileged among us, is ever entirely powerless over the messages that traverse and position him at the post of sender, addressee, or referent'. Lyotard argues that the limits imposed by institutions on people's potential language moves are also never established once and for all. People in postmodernity are never completely powerless in relation to communication or to bureaucracy and social structures.[14]

Lyotard is perhaps best-known for his critique of what he calls Grand Narratives. In the postmodern age we no longer have a positivistic science that claims to know the truth; rather, science, as in the new quantum mechanics associated with Chaos Theory, now tells stories, competing stories, as in any other area of knowledge.[15] We can no longer call on a tradition of speculative philosophy, as in Hegel, that claims to see society and history in their totality. We can no longer see society as a uniform whole, as in Parsonian systems theory. Nor can we relate to Marxism, theory of an outdated industrial society, for Marxism postulated society as working only on a duality, a single difference, as between labour and capital.[16]

In postmodernity we are also now re-examining the Enlightenment idea of history as capable of being guided towards a single ideal goal, the establishing throughout human societies of a universal model of reason, embodied in a hopefully triumphant agent or subject, whether this be the working class or the state or European Reason itself. Lyotard is particularly harsh on what he takes to be German philosopher (and heir of the Frankfurt School) Habermas' search for universal consensus, a search Lyotard identifies with a terroristic conformity. Lyotard prefers a vision of postmodernity as a search for dissent and the recognition of heterogeneity, of a multiplicity of arguments never arriving at agreement, of 'language games' and moves as agon, as contestation, jousting, scoring points as in taking tricks, language as duelling, as performance.[17]

In general, Lyotard opposes any notion of teleology in history, rather seeing postmodernity as dispersed narratives foregoing universalising, globalising ambitions.

Lyotard's theorising, as Julian Pefanis argues, is closely related to his political involvements, his engagements and disengagements, over the last few decades. Lyotard has had a long history in French Marxism and syndicalist and libertarian socialism, in the *Socialisme ou barbarie* group. In 1964 Lyotard broke with *Socialisme ou barbarie*, suffering a loss of political faith in socialism and in Marxism. His disillusion was confirmed only a few years later, in May 1968, when the organised militant left failed to respond to the student-led revolt.[18]

We can, perhaps, relate the social and political theory of *The Postmodern Condition* to the late 1960s, early 1970s New Left, which spurned any older left idea that class was the central category of contemporary societies, and that the left could integrate the various struggles around class in terms of a coherent political vision and a cohesive organisation, a single party. The New Left by contrast, influenced by sources of anarchism and libertarianism that reached back into the nineteenth century, erupted all over the world in various unforeseen movements, in student protest against bureaucracy and hierarchy (including within older left parties) and in the liberation movements, black, women's, gay. There were student demonstrations and riots, intense activity and momentum, the counter-culture, theories of a new consciousness that could transgress and possibly replace the conformism induced by capitalism and its dominant ideologies, a conformism shared alike by the capitalist class and the traditional working class. The correlative of the New Left in social theory was a dispersal of the categories of analysis; class took its place alongside race, ethnicity, gender, sexuality, power, age, as only one of the forces that at any one time and in any particular situation could be influential and shaping. Such forces were not fixed, were unstable, were unpredictable in their combinations. There was a pluralising and equalising of categories and concepts.[19]

Lyotard in *The Postmodern Condition* appears similarly inspired by a vision of people engaged in heterogeneous contradictory actions and issues, without, however, the insurgent optimism that characterised the New Left in the late 1960s, early 1970s, a sense that an aging system could be confronted and conquered by a new radical consciousness: an optimism that now almost seems like the past as a foreign country.

In aesthetic terms, however, Lyotard is certainly not a postmodernist. As Pefanis observes, Lyotard still believes in the long modernist project of the intellectual and artistic avant garde that is the bearer of the radical and transgressive, the key source of innovation in a society facing intellectual death by majority culture.[20]

In the essay, 'Answering the Question: What is Postmodernism?', appended to *The Postmodern Condition*, Lyotard tells us that mainstream culture is concerned with realism, a desire for a shared communication code that will guarantee the 'addressee' a 'recognisable meaning' and an identity, a consciousness, that is approved by others.[21] Mass communication as in cinema and photography is an enclosing circle connecting mass culture and its audiences, it is but 'mass conformism', it is art debased to 'therapeutic uses'. When Lyotard in the main part of *The Postmodern Condition* was disagreeing with Baudrillard's relentless pessimism, he wrote of people never being completely powerless. Now, however, deep in the discourse of aesthetic modernism, of mass-culture theory, obeying its every move, Lyotard happily ventures that all the mass want is psychological reassurance, 'therapeutic uses', from mass culture.

In this analysis Lyotard acknowledges that he is simply updating Adorno (and Benjamin, he adds without qualification), reproducing the familiar tropes and contours of an 'interpretation' which is, he informs us, 'correct in its outline'. Adorno's correct interpretation of mass culture, however, has to be supplemented by Lyotard's conception of the avant-garde. Where mass culture wishes to present reality as unified, simple, communicable for the approval of all others and so offering 'comfort', the avant-garde will negate such mass culture by experimenting with emotions which are 'equivocal', which carry a pleasure derived from pain. The true aesthetic will not present reality: on the contrary, it will withhold any such presentation.

Lyotard tells us that Kant says that the commandment from *Exodus*, 'Thou shalt not make graven images', is sublime in that it forbids all presentation of the Absolute. Here, says Lyotard, is the basis of the avant-garde aesthetic, the aesthetic as a negative. The avant-garde will disavow photography and film, the highly visual aesthetic media favoured by mass culture, instead favouring painting and the novel. Avant-garde painting will 'therefore' (the language of commandment?) avoid figuration or representation, it will be abstract (an example would be a square of white). In the novel, as in Joyce and Proust, allusion will prove 'indispensable' to the true aesthetic. The early twentieth-century avant-gardes were caught, Lyotard believes, in a tension between nostalgia for lost presence, as against the 'jubilation', as in Dadaists like Duchamp, of inventing new rules of the game, which prevent the 'formation and the stabilisation of taste'. On such a difference, Lyotard feels, depends the 'fate of thought'.

I find Lyotard's argument for an avant-garde staggeringly authoritarian, ascetic, puritanic, and prescriptive. All mass culture is consigned to the rubbish bin of aesthetic history in one easy totalising and psychologising gesture: it and its recipients only want solace, comfort, reassurance. As usual, how modernists like Lyotard know such mass inner states is never revealed. Rather the assessment is asserted as a kind of positivistic truth, unassailable fact – the very kind of positivism that Lyotard says in *The Postmodern Condition* we should disregard as an oppressive Grand Narrative.

Another Grand Narrative Lyotard says in *The Postmodern Condition* we should disregard is that of teleology, a story of progress for the whole of humanity. In 'Answering the Question: What is Postmodernism?', Lyotard similarly tells us that in the era of postmodernity we must severely re-examine the Enlightenment idea of a 'unitary end of history and of a subject'. Yet in this essay Lyotard now relates a narrative of progress for art and thought (from Kant's sublime to early twentieth-century modernism). Here is surely a Grand Narrative which posits a unitary end of history for the aesthetic and all culture (modernist experimental art as the only true art). And this end, this telos, certainly has a privileged subject (the avant-garde). Lyotard is offering us a Grand Narrative of aesthetic, philosophical and theoretical progress, with approved thinkers, writers and artists whose thought and methods are deemed essential to no less than the 'fate of thought'.[22]

In Lyotard's narrative of progress, it is apparently mandatory that there be a steep almost skyscraper-like hierarchy of media in the world, with painting and the novel on top, photography and film low as low. Painting should be non-representational, and so stress the pain of that which is conceivable but not presentable, not to be visualised. The visual, as in photography and film, can yield only comforting pleasure. Lyotard's commandment here not only works by a single standard, it is also curiously Eurocentric. The only true art is that European tradition, theologically derived via Kant's Protestant dislike of the visual in religion, manifested in early twentieth-century modernist avant-garde works. Little wonder that African-American critic Cornell West has argued that European postmodernists like Lyotard, while seeking to highlight notions of difference, marginality, and otherness, conduct the debate about postmodernity and the aesthetic in such a way as to further marginalise actual people of difference and otherness, for example, African-Americans, Latinos, women. The debate is confined in a narrow way to European modernism, and so ignores any transgressive potential in the distinctive cultural and political practices of oppressed peoples, not least African-Americans, whose cultural production focuses on linguistic innovativeness as well as performance and pageantry, style and spectacle in music, sermons, and certain sports. West observes of Lyotard's 'postmodernism' that its aesthetic project, of non-representational experimental techniques, is a kind of European navel-gazing, insulated, parochial, provincial.[23]

Cornell West feels that contemporary African-American culture is closely related historically to black religious practices.[24] But given Lyotard's acceptance of the Biblical injunction against graven images (why isn't he, a modernist, embarrassed to associate himself with such received Law?), the highly visual character of African-American religious and cultural performances would have to be outlawed as not true culture.

Lyotard tells us that the 'axioms' of the modernist avant-gardes prevent the formation and stabilisation of taste. The true artist or writer or philosopher is 'he' who disestablishes 'familiar categories'. Yet surely the history of modernism this century has been precisely that, the stabilisation of taste in painting and literature around modernist criteria, 'familiar categories' supported by critical authority and prestige, institutionalised in art galleries, museums, publishing, university departments of English, underwritten by wealth and power. Lyotard himself in this essay is doing little more than rehearsing orthodox modernist 'axioms' (which he also disarmingly refers to as 'instructions'). He can refer admiringly to early Dadaist major figure Duchamp, without any sense that Duchamp was also an inspiring figure for the late 1950s, 1960s, neo-dada Pop Artists, who rebelled precisely against the standardisation and institutionalisation of modernist art, not least in the stale abstraction that Lyotard still lauds and prescribes.

Curious gender aspects also suggest themselves in Lyotard's aesthetic theory here, drawing him closer to Baudrillard by a thread of erotic imagery. The 'addressee' of mass culture is invariably a 'he' - as is the avant-garde writer, artist, philosopher. As in Baudrillard, it would seem mass culture is for anxious Postmodern Man a dangerous enveloping female presence. Lyotard knows everything there is to know about the 'consciousness' of the mass of postmodern men, who have succumbed to a culture which sets out to 'seduce' them. He writes in another essay:

> The enemy and accomplice of writing, its Big Brother . . . is language [*langue*], by which I mean not only the mother tongue, but the entire heritage of words, of the feats and works of what is called the literary culture. One writes against language, but necessarily with it. To say what it already knows to say is not writing. One wants to say what it does not know how to say, and what it should be able to say. One violates it, one seduces it, one introduces into it an idiom which it had not known. But when that same desire to be able to say something other than what has been already said – has disappeared, and when language is experienced as impenetrable and inert rendering vain all writing, then it is called Newspeak.[25]

This is very interesting. Mass culture language, the language of Newspeak – 'America' again the exemplar – is associated with authoritarianism (Big Brother) and the mother. This authoritarian mother is always becoming a dead, inert, 'impenetrable' weight. The male writer then, in a kind of incestuous Oedipal act, has to summon up a 'desire' that 'violates' and 'seduces', and so 'introduces' into the mother an alien substance (a new idiom). Only by such violence, even rape, can writing, true writing, the only writing Lyotard will countenance, be delivered into the world.

We can observe that the tyranny of the new that Lyotard the orthodox magisterial modernist wishes to impose on the world, not only ignores the standardisation of modernism, it also practises massive exclusions. By such a criterion, all popular genre writing would be refused the name of 'writing'. Yet surely the history of genre writing, in everything from romance to adventure to detective to science fiction, is witness to a remarkable inventiveness and resourcefulness; genres both continuously reproduce conventions while they transform them, play with them, turn them inside out, reverse them, parody them, self-parody. Such genres are always introducing new idioms by playing off, interacting with, contesting, each other.

Lyotard's absolute oppositions possess the simplicity, unity, agreed communicability and lack of contradictoriness of all binary pairings, of all structuralist binary thought. It cannot allow for an unpredictable criss-cross between terms, between cultures.

Lyotard: have absolute aesthetic categories, will issue decrees, commandments, instructions, prohibitions, axioms, truths, injunctions, ordinances.

CHAPTER TEN

Mapping Frederic Jameson's
Grand Narrative

Jameson, author of the influential, oft-debated, and strikingly panoramic essay, 'Postmodernism, or The Cultural Logic of Late Capitalism' (1984), is that very unusual phenomenon, an American Marxist.[1] The American context is important, because the rise of postmodernism in North America in the 1970s was associated with postmodern architecture and its direct challenge to the project of the modern movement or International Style, stemming from Le Corbusier and the Bauhaus of the 1920s. We can see postmodern architectural theory, especially as told so engagingly by Venturi, Scott Brown and Izenour in *Learning from Las Vegas*, advocating values that appear very close to Lyotard's vision of postmodernity in *The Postmodern Condition*. The postmodern poetic would be design that is heterogeneous, contradictory, ambivalent, inclusive – including of modernist modes. It might quote from diverse historical forms, allowing different periods to speak to each other, to contest and parody and argue. It is interested in relating to vernacular cityscapes, to local narratives. The architect is a jester, and, as in Lyotard's notion of language games, the postmodern building jousts and duels with the buildings around it, in a wit, a 'deep play', that can call on pathos, sadness, seriousness.

Learning from Las Vegas' language of heterogeneity is also close to European poststructuralism, with its stress on multiple meanings, discontinuity, fragmentation, contradiction.

By contrast, Jameson pulls sharply back from welcoming either postmodern architecture or poststructuralism, seeing them as representative of a postmodern age he for the most part (except ambivalently for postmodern literature) intensely distrusts and dislikes. In 'Postmodernism, or The Cultural Logic of Late Capitalism', Jameson is very like Baudrillard in 'The Ecstasy of Communication', presenting a vision of postmodernity from deep within modernist tradition.

Jameson, however, remains a Marxist. He does not see the post-modern era as Baudrillard and other recent social theorists like Lyotard have done, as post-industrial. Rather, he follows the Marxist economist Ernest Mandel in seeing postmodernity as but the latest phase of the capitalist world system. The virtue of Mandel's *Late Capitalism*, this 'great book', is that it allows us to discern definite historical periods, in a tripartite movement from the nineteenth to the twentieth century. First came market capitalism, then the age of monopoly and imperialism, and now we're in the era of multinational or consumer capitalism, perhaps the purest form of capitalism yet to have emerged. Mandel's contours of capitalism are, says Jameson, not at all inconsistent with 'Marx's great 19th-century analysis'.[2]

Jameson also tells us that Mandel inspired him to put forward his own 'tripartite scheme', his own 'cultural periodization'. There are aes-thetic forms that clearly correspond to Mandel's economic periods: realism, modernism, postmodernism. We might wonder why there is only one cultural form permitted for each stage of capitalism, but Jameson assures us that the one-to-one correspondance follows on from his 'method', which is to isolate in each historical period a 'cultural logic', or 'systemic cultural norm', or 'hegemonic norm'. This logic and norm is a 'cultural dominant', a conception which, Jameson says, allows for the presence in each historical period of a range of 'very different, yet subordinate features'. So, after realism, which for Jameson is the realism defined for us by Hungarian Marxist Lukács, to be witnessed in the bourgeois historical novel, we move into modernism, and here Jameson's text fairly glows with affinity, support, admiration, nostalgia, even anger that modernism's canonical tenets, aesthetic, political and pedagogical, no longer prevail.[3]

Modernism critiques the modern world. Edvard Munch's painting *The Scream*, for example, is a 'canonical expression' of the 'great modernist thematics of alienation, anomie, solitude and social fragmentation and isolation', a cry that is yet cathartic in its desperate communication. Modernism usually combines critique with suggestions of a utopian alternative. In Van Gogh's *Peasant Shoes*, for example, also a 'canonical' work of modernist art, we can see that the painting reworks, transforms and appropriates a whole 'object world' of rural poverty and misery. At the same time the painting's glorious materialisation of pure colour is a 'desperate' utopian gesture and compensation. Modernist buildings, as in Le Corbusier's 'great *pilotis*', are 'vast Utopian structures' that explicitly, violently, repudiate the degraded city fabric around them. Modelled on the steamship, the motor car and the machine gun, they create a 'new Utopian space', beacons for a desired 'protopolitical Utopian transformation'. And, in political modernism proper, as in Brecht, we can see, presumably as an extension of such utopianism, the necessary 'cognitive and pedagogical dimensions' of culture, the 'teaching function of art'.[4]

Then came the fall, the dread dead hand of postmodernism. Here Jameson's essay moves towards the kind of *fin de siècle* Gothic that Baudrillard has made us familiar with. Postmodernist culture lets itself loose in a range of phenomena. There is the unprecedented level of commodification and commodity fetishism. There are the media and advertising; Andy Warhol and Pop Art; Hollywood and its commodified stars like Marilyn Monroe; the breakdown of the older modernist distinction between high culture and mass or commercial art and taste; the alienation of daily city life felt as hallucinatory exhilaration; the loss of reality in images, pseudo-events and spectacles; and fundamental alterations in our experience of time and space, history and the present.[5]

We cannot look for assistance to 'contemporary theory', for we soon come across the poststructuralist abandonment of the very concept of truth, and a perception of the present as sheer heterogeneity, random difference, a coexistence of a host of distinct forces whose effectivity is undecidable. Such theory is but a 'symptom' of postmodern culture, is part of the problem.[6]

The problem overridingly is that while modernism protests against the contemporary world, postmodernism is complicit with it. We can see this in Pop Art. Andy Warhol's 'great billboard images' of the Coca-Cola bottle or the Campbell's soup can foreground commodification and commodity fetishism, but without any detectable political or critical edge: whereas they '*ought* to be powerful and critical political statements'.[7] That interesting 'ought' word.

That visit

Let's follow Jameson as he journeys, in time-honoured modernist ethnographic style, to John Portman's Bonaventure Hotel in Los Angeles. Getting into the building, Jameson's key example of postmodern architecture and space, is, however, far from easy. Its entrances are almost lateral and backdoor, as if the postmodern building is striving for a new form of 'closure'. Once 'you' – Jameson, Modernist Man, universal rational subject – have managed to get inside, you realise the purpose of such difficulty of entry. The Bonaventure aspires, Jameson feels, to be a total space, a complete world unto itself. The 'great reflective glass skin' of its four towers, with their 'absolute symmetry', acts to repell the city outside, dissociating it from its neighbourhood. There are 'real pleasures' to be registered in Portman's hotel, particularly the escalators and elevators which like gondolas ceaselessly rise and fall. But such leisure-time space is nevertheless merely 'complacent', and the movement of the escalators and elevators, he quickly realises, acts to replace older forms of movement, especially walking, the promenade. We are no longer allowed to promenade on our own.[8]

Even more alarming is the experience of space you undergo, especially in the lobby or atrium, with its unnerving busyness and hanging streamers. Here you experience a feeling of packed 'emptiness', a 'bewildering immersion' in a kind of 'postmodern hyperspace', immersed up to 'your eyes and your body'. In such a state of bewilderment and immersion – presumed by Jameson to be experienced by everyone there – you lose a sense of distance that enables perception and perspective. The result is that the 'individual human body' can no longer map its position in a 'mappable external world', and such forced incapacity is symbolic of the wider 'incapacity of our minds' to map the 'great' global multinational communicational networks of the postmodern world.[9]

In the new space of postmodernism, then, bodily and critical distance have been abolished. We can see this disaster in other postmodern cultural phenomena. People now are immersed in 'image addiction', especially in the way television images transform 'older realities' into the logic of the simulacrum (the identical copy for which no original exists). Jameson, indeed, is very concerned about our loss of the real. If we compare, for example, Van Gogh's *Peasant Shoes* with Warhol's *Diamond Dust Shoes*, we see that whereas we can reconstruct for *Peasant Shoes* a past 'object world' (rural misery), we cannot construct from Warhol's work any such depth of reference to reality. Consequently, we see in Warhol a new kind of 'superficiality', a 'depthlessness' that is the supreme formal feature of postmodernism. Instead of political passion, as in Van Gogh or in modernist architecture, or emphasis on the pain of anomie and alienation that has to be heroically overcome in utopian gestures, we are left with mere 'decorative exhilaration', with 'gratuitous frivolity'.[10]

When postmodern culture does attempt to turn to history, as in the 'complacent eclecticism of postmodern architecture' – Jameson cannot here be thinking of the invariant glass towers of the Bonaventure Hotel – it merely cannibalises all the architectural styles of the past, combining them, he notes, into 'overstimulating ensembles'.

We arrive here at perhaps the most well-known of Jameson's formulations, a distinction between parody and pastiche. The modernists like

Wallace Stevens or D.H. Lawrence all apparently had a 'personal *style*', in a modern age which still believed in a subject, an ego, even if cruelly alienated. This style could then be parodied. But in the postmodern world, the subject has disappeared, and in the explosion of private styles in literature there has occurred a 'linguistic fragmentation' to the point where 'the norm' itself is eclipsed, reduced to a 'neutral and reified media speech'. You can only have parody and satire where such a 'healthy linguistic normality' still exists, as with the modernists or as in the eighteenth century, when there is a known distinction between a normal and an 'abnormal tongue'. But where no such normality exists, you only have pastiche, mere neutral mimicry, mere imitation of dead styles.[11]

The 'random stylistic allusion' of postmodern pastiche is at one with what the postmodern mass wants, an historically original consumers' 'appetite for a world transformed into sheer images of itself'. The result is again discouraging, for in the postmodern attempt to refer to the past through 'glossy' images and fashion, we find the end of 'genuine historicity'.[12]

The strange case of the Bonaventure Hotel

Evoking and evaluating postmodern architecture is crucial to 'Post-modernism, or The Cultural Logic of Late Capitalism'. Jameson argues that we find the decisive instance of postmodern culture in architecture, because it's so close as a practice to the economic, to multinational consumer capitalism. Indeed, Jameson tells us, it was debates around architecture that principally inspired his own conception of postmodernism. Further, the modernist era was concerned with the temporal, the elegaic mysteries of memory. Now, in the postmodern era, we find that 'our' daily life, 'our psychic experience', our cultural languages, are dominated by categories of space rather than of time. Here again, architecture remains the privileged aesthetic language, making manifest the new postmodern space emerging around us.[13]

If Jameson's key instance fails, his whole argument is in jeopardy. What is the representative status of John Portman's Bonaventure Hotel, Los Angeles, USA?

There are some strange uncertainties (linguistic abnormalities?) in Jameson's text. Jameson introduces the Bonaventure as a 'fullblown postmodern building' (for reasons that are unclear, he chooses to call it the Bonaventura). Curiously, however, Jameson admits that the hotel is 'in many ways uncharacteristic' of the postmodern architecture we associate with names like Venturi – though Venturi and references to *Learning from Las Vegas* and its 'populist rhetoric' figure in the essay as major examples of postmodern architectural complicity with consumer capitalism, mass culture, and the 'tawdry and commercial sign-system' of the contemporary city. Nevertheless, a page later, Jameson is confidently talking of Portman's Bonaventure Hotel as a 'characteristic' postmodern building.[14]

How confidently can we take the Bonaventure as an example of postmodernist architecture? The sociologist Margaret Rose notes that architectural historians like Charles Jencks refer to the Bonaventure as a Late-Modern building, pointing to the defining presence of the cylinder-like shapes of its glass towers.[15] In these terms, we can indeed see the Bonaventure as an extreme development of Le Corbusier's advocacy, in his 1920s manifestos, of primary geometric forms; we can remember his loving reproduction of photographs of North American wheat silos. Further, the way the glass towers reflect, but don't interact with, the surrounding urban landscape, is the kind of standard modernist mode scorned by Venturi, Scott Brown and Izenour in *Learning from Las Vegas* for its lack of involvement with the local and the vernacular. Jameson refers to the 'absolute symmetry' of the Bonaventure's towers. But a key point of *Learning from Las Vegas* is a postmodern delight in asymmetry, in heterogeneity and contradiction and inconsistency of architectural styles.

Jameson writes that the Bonaventure is characteristic of post-modernism in that it almost conceals its points of entry. Yet *Learning from Las Vegas* regards Las Vegas as suggesting a new postmodern architectural language that is open, welcoming, festive, a feast of signs for all to read and interpret. Jameson tells us of the Bonaventure as postmodern architecture ('fullblown') that the complacent entertainment provided by its escalators and elevators abolishes older forms of movement, as in walking, the 'narrative stroll'. Yet *Learning from Las Vegas* suggests that the long low buildings of Las Vegas, especially in the shopping arcades, recall older forms of strolling as in the Eastern bazaar or the narrow medieval street: an observation we could extend more generally to the contemporary shopping mall, heir of the nineteenth-century arcades that so fascinated Walter Benjamin. (When Roselands Shopping Centre, reputed in its day to be the largest in the southern hemisphere, was opened in Sydney in 1965, the then NSW Premier, the usually dour Mr Askin, was moved to call it a 'rival to even the fabled Persian bazaars'.[16])

Certainly we can say that the enclosed cylindrical towers of the Bonaventure are not characteristic in the least of Darling Harbour, Sydney's postmodern urban space, where its Chinese Gardens, low long exhibition buildings, maritime museum, aquarium, and food hall extravagantly invite entry and participation. Darling Harbour doesn't repell its surrounds. Its monorail runs every few minutes to the business and retail heart of Sydney, while its canals and harbourside exhibits and moored boats participate in Sydney as a port city. Darling Harbour as a whole, with its park and walkways, also precisely permits the narrative stroll of the *flâneur*, the reflective contemplative promenading of a crowd appreciating postmodern humanity's fertility of difference.

Jameson's announced affection for walking is in any case curious. He tells us that when he was in the Bonaventure he didn't actually see the hotel's residential rooms, but 'one understands' that they 'are in the worst of taste'.[17] The modern ethnographer doesn't need the assistance of walking, he can understand without seeing. And there also apparently exist absolute standards of aesthetic 'taste' which the magisterial modernist ever understands. I love that phrase: 'one understands that the rooms are in the worst of taste'. Is this Modernist Prim?

Doubts and queries

Jameson admires norms, bearings, maps, the canonical, a 'healthy linguistic normality', and the 'ought' word. Experience has to be 'coherent'. We must not break the 'signifying chain'. We must 'unify' the past, present and future of the sentence. We must 'unify' our psychic life. We ought remember the modernist avant-garde, which could formulate for humanity a 'collective' future. We need a political art and culture that will be 'cognitive', and not succumb to mere decorative 'glossy' 'over-stimulating' pleasures in which we can only fear 'bewildering immersion' up to our eyes.[18] Postmodernity is contaminated by a mass culture that is yet again demonised as dangerously female, as seductive succubus, as an abyss of gloss.

The new culture we need, recalling a past paradisiac world of normative reason, will be 'pedagogical', will teach humanity about the new global system. This astonishingly rationalist 'aesthetic of cognitive mapping' can be guided by the 'great Althusserian' definition of ideology as the representation of the subject's imaginary relationship to his or her real conditions of existence. Marxism is the 'science' which can distinguish between the imaginary and the real.[19] In particular, Jameson, magisterial modernist, knows what is real history, genuine historicity. He'll teach us, and we'll happily become part of the collective project he'll map for us, so we can recover reality, true historical consciousness, and the normal way.

Is our author, nonetheless, a necessarily reliable guide to what he so confidently refers to as 'genuine historicity'? He claims that postmodernism in architecture is a spurious return to history. At the same time he looks back with nostalgia to 1920s architectural modernism – whose explicit project was to deny history, to be purely new. Yet postmodern architecture, which seeks to recover historicity, to make past and present converse, is decreed by fiat, on the basis of Portman's Los Angeles glass cylinders – a building of more than dubious postmodernist provenance – to empty history of meaning.

Jameson's binary distinction, that the modern era was concerned with time, the postmodern with space, looks decidedly infirm. I'm not denying that the spatial is a prominent interest in postmodernity, perhaps in part because there has been such widespread questioning of grand narratives of linear progress. But the spatial can also inscribe history in narratives that are not necessarily linear, that question the linear, as in postmodern architecture, collage, and modes of contradictory juxtaposition more generally.

If Jameson's postulated binary opposition, of modernist time as against postmodernist space, wobbles and falls, then maybe all the other binary distinctions that structure the argument are beginning to lean dangerously. Jameson tells us that in the modern era the subject was centred or unified, even if alienated. In the postmodern era, however, the self has been decentred and fragmented. In aesthetic terms, this binary opposition means that in the modern era, in the 'high-modernist conception', there were 'unique' and 'personal' styles. In the post-modern era, with the primacy of mechanical reproduction, there are now only 'free-floating and impersonal' feelings, an 'increasing unavailability of personal *style*'.[20] That modernism stressed the centred subject and the personal is a peculiar proposition indeed.

I'm thinking of D.H. Lawrence's feeling, in his well-known letter to Edward Garnett of June 1914, that the contemporary novel should get away from past notions of unity and consistency in the conception of character. Lawrence was in Italy at the time, wondering what ideas he could draw out of Marinetti's futurist manifesto. He tells Garnett that he can see something worthwhile in Marinetti's argument for an intuitive physiology of matter. He too is fascinated by the 'non-human in humanity'. Such, he feels, is more interesting than the old-fashioned mode of novel writing, which causes one to conceive a character in a certain moral scheme and 'make him consistent'. It is the 'certain moral scheme' he objects to, as now 'dull, old, dead': 'You mustn't look in my novel for the old stable ego of the character. There is another ego, according to whose action the individual is unrecognisable, and passes through, as it were, allotropic states'. He pulls back from Marinetti's pronouncement that matter, as in metals, is more interesting than a woman's smile or tears. But he does toy with the idea that such allotropic states are variations of an unchanged element, as in carbon in relation to diamond, coal and soot. Then Lawrence reaches for another image. The characters of the new kind of novel will fall into the form of a new rhythm, as when one 'draws a fiddle-bow across a fine tray delicately sanded', and the sand takes lines 'unknown'. Lawrence hopes he's not being boring, pleads with Garnett not to get 'chilly and disagreeable', and in a postscript asks him to keep the letter because he might want to write something on futurism.[21]

I'm also thinking of what is surely a formative essay in modernist aesthetics, T.S. Eliot's 1917 'Tradition and the Individual Talent', questioning Victorian notions of poetry as personal expression, as an outflowing of the feelings of the author. Eliot argues that the poet has 'not a "personality" to express, but a particular medium, which is only a medium and not a personality', in which impressions and experiences combine in unexpected ways: 'Impressions and experiences which are important for the man may take no place in the poetry, and those which become important in the poetry may play quite a negligible part in the man, the personality.' What counts is the combining of such impressions and experiences, whereby a 'new art emotion' is produced. Like Lawrence, Eliot reaches for images drawn from chemistry. During the combinatory process, the poet's mind and personality should stay inert, neutral and unchanged, rather like platinum in a chamber containing oxygen and sulphur dioxide: a famous trope for an impersonal theory of poetic creation.

In 'Tradition and the Individual Talent' Eliot also comments that poets should continuously surrender themselves, their personality, to a 'historical sense', which involves writing with a feeling that the 'whole of the literature of Europe' from Homer to the present 'has a simultaneous existence and composes a simultaneous order', an order which is altered by the new ('the really new') work of art among them.[22] This famous formulation, issuing from high *literary* modernism, is a long long way from the urging and practice of modernist architecture. But it is, interestingly, not all that distant from the plea in *Learning from Las Vegas* that postmodern architecture should reject the rejection of historical reference in modernist architecture. Rather, postmodern architects should acquire the historical sense, that compels architects to create with a feeling that the whole of European architecture has a simultaneous existence and composes a simultaneous order.

Jameson may object that postmodern design is not 'really new'. (Given Jameson's belief that a Late-Modern building like the Bonaventure is postmodern, we can't be entirely confident that Jameson can recognise the new.) Yet it would certainly appear to be answering to Eliot's view that the 'important thing is the combination' of 'numberless feelings, phrases, and images' in 'artistic production':

these would appear to be comparable terms for postmodern architecture as a combining, a quoting, of diverse architectural feelings, phrases, and images.

It's certainly true, in a more mundane sense, that the modernists had particular and distinctive styles. We don't mistake Eliot for Pound, Lawrence for Joyce. But then we don't mistake Warhol – even while playing with mechanical reproduction – for other Pop Artists, for Lichtenstein, Rauschenberg, Oldenburg. As for mechanical reproduction in general, as in Hollywood film, we also don't mistake the work of one Hollywood filmmaker for that of another, even when they're working in (have surrendered their personality to) the same genre.

Jameson makes no distinction between modernisms. Nor does he consider that postmodernism, as in the new history-mindedness of postmodern architecture, may be continuing aspects of particular modernisms. He can't so consider, since his 'method' assumes that each leading aesthetic form is unified.

More niggling doubts

Jameson's periodising, then, is dubious indeed. It's a return to the long history of historicism in cultural studies, seeing a cultural period as an expressive totality, where texts are symptoms of an unfolding unified state. Given that each period is unified around a 'cultural logic', a 'systemic cultural norm', a 'hegemonic norm', a single text can then be taken as representative of that unity. In architecture, Jameson's unfortunate example is the Bonaventure building. In art, we can apparently compare a single Van Gogh painting as representing all that's admirable in the modernist age, with a single work by Warhol, *Diamond Dust Shoes*, as representing all that's alarming about postmodernity, especially frivolous decoration. Yet Jameson also reminds us, almost laterally, as in an afterthought, of Warhol's series on traffic accidents and the electric chair. Wouldn't these Warhol works suggest that it is dangerous to take but one text as representative of an age?

Jameson tells us that such Warhol works, seemingly referring to pain, death, and terror, are 'debased and contaminated in advance by their assimilation to glossy advertising images'. In general, Jameson adopts a reflectionist view of culture for postmodernity. Modernist culture protests against modernity. Postmodernist culture, however, reflects postmodernity. If Jameson doesn't like something or other in the contemporary world, he dismisses it as a reflection: it's 'symptomatic' of despised times.

In these terms he dismisses poststructuralism, and any other perception of history that might stress elements of 'sheer heterogeneity, random difference, a coexistence of a host of distinct forces whose effectivity is undecidable'.[23] But a theory has to be engaged within its own domain, as theory; it can't be refuted by finding its meaning in another domain. Would Jameson say of Chaos Theory, with its interest in a perceived play of disorder and order, randomness and pattern, instability and unpredictability, that it is a mere reflection of the age, and therefore should be discounted? Warhol's works, including the electric chair series, might reveal a complex, perhaps contradictory, range of meanings and attitudes. Such range and complexity can't be explained away by claiming they are part of a context which Jameson doesn't like. I always thought that reflectionism, the reduction of a cultural phenomenon to a predetermined and prejudged context, was a Vulgar Error, something to which Marxist cultural theory was particularly prone, and indeed a major reason for the fall of the house of Marxism in the last couple of decades.

Jameson's 'method', his 'cultural periodisation', assumes that each historical period has representative features that clearly mark off one from the other. Is cultural history so clear, so lacking in fragmentation, contradictoriness, messiness?

Jameson argues that for the first time in history we have parody and satire without a sense of the normal. Jameson has to claim such newness because he's claiming that the features of postmodernity are unprecedented in history, a new stage of capital and of culture.

It's always a risky procedure to advance the historically unprecedented. Philosophies featuring fragmentation, heterogeneity, randomness, have been quite common in intellectual and cultural history. We might also recall the menippean satire of antiquity, conventionally dated to Menippus of Gadara in the third century BC. Unlike other satire which criticises people and activities from a fixed standpoint of morality, menippean satire was always undermining any certainties of position and outlook. Bakhtin relates that menippea were usually fantastical and experimental, testing high philosophical ideas against the everyday low world, freely mixing disparate genres, exploring unusual moral and psychic states, as in insanity, unrestrained daydreaming, passions bordering on madness; there was an interest in the split personality and the double, with characters losing their finalised quality, their unity.

Bakhtin argues that menippean satire was created in an epoch when national legend was in decay, amid the destruction of the ancient ethical norms. But he doesn't then argue that such satire was expressible only in such periods. Bakhtin sees menippean satire as, along with carnivalesque, a key part of the continuous generic history that contributes to the dialogic and polyphonic aspects of the novel, in particular leading to Dostoevsky, where we as readers participate in an unresolved clash of aesthetic modes and ideological values.[24]

Cultural history, that is, may reveal long and surprising continuities as well as discontinuities. We've already seen that there may be continuities between postmodern architecture and literary modernism in terms of historical allusiveness, a foregrounding and relishing of intertextuality.

Sharp questions have to be asked of Jameson's historicist method. Why should we, for example, take a *literary* form like realism (the realist historical novel) as the 'cultural logic' of the main part of the nineteenth century? In earlier discussion of the British Screen Theory thesis that something called the classic realist text dominated in the nineteenth century, I pointed to the importance in nineteenth-century cultural history of melodrama, its influence ranging from the stage to the novel. I don't wish to substitute melodrama for realism in Jameson's scheme, since I think we must unpick the very notion of a single logic or norm for a period. I would rather talk of fields of force, of always-already competing, antagonistic, interacting cultural forms.

What does a 'cultural logic', a 'cultural dominant', a 'systemic cultural norm', mean historically? In the 1920s modernism was certainly insurgent, exciting, quickly influential. But Hollywood was also becoming predominant, and was also exciting, insurgent, quickly influential as it established new genres, styles, modes, technologies, part of a mass-culture wave from radio to new newspaper styles, entertainment parks, popular literature, advertising. Why for the 1920s should we take modernism as the 'cultural dominant', and not Hollywood and the new electronic mass culture? Why does Jameson take 'high culture' forms only as his cultural logics? We might rather say that modernism, in the 1920s and later, was indeed highly important in twentieth-century 'high culture', at the same time as it – or at least high literary modernism – positioned itself in an antagonistic relationship to mass culture. Another bubbling volcanic field of force.

So dedicated is Jameson to the singular that he also defines the concerns of cultural forms in highly limiting terms. Modernism, he tells us, is concerned with the 'great' thematics of alienation, anomie, solitude, social fragmentation, isolation. Such appears a peculiarly Eurocentric view.[25] We might think also of the 'great' modernist thematics of the construction of the non-European other in primitivism, exoticism, Orientalism. We might also think that such thematics are entwined, given that since Byron at least, in the history of romanticism that leads to modernism, the non-European other has been looked to as alternative to a European self felt to be dead, anomic, alienated. Modernism, that is, might be far more varied than Jameson's method permits him to consider.

Orientalism and, for that matter, melodrama, are continuing presences in cultural history, from the late eighteenth century on, into the modern and then postmodern periods. Such continuities mock Jameson's assumption of self-enclosed periods, his essentialising mode of periodisation.

Conclusion

In comparing similarities between Jameson and Baudrillard in their characterisations of postmodernity, Margaret Rose comments that the time has come to ask how arguments such as Baudrillard's in his 1977 'Beaubourg-Effect', that the crowds visiting the Pompidou Centre were actually showing their hatred of it by unintentionally wearing it out, could ever have been taken seriously.[26]

I can't quite see why Jameson's essay has been so influential. I was bewildered for a while by the strange and insistent, not to say faintly irritating, use of 'great'. Almost anything or anyone that moves in the essay is 'great', whether Jameson admires them or not. Then I thought: its deployment helps create a clash of titanic forces, an apocalyptic struggle upon which the very fate of thought depends. In particular, modernist thought. Perhaps we can see 'Postmodernism, or The Cultural Logic of Late Capitalism' as therapy, as reassurance for afraid, angry, nostalgic modernists, who can now take comfort that one of their own has masterfully shown that postmodernism lacks what they still possess, a sense of genuine historicity. Their cultural authority, as arbiters of the true course of society, history and culture, has been reaffirmed.[27]

Jameson accuses postmodern architecture and leisure-time entertainment of being 'complacent'.[28] But we might wonder if his own essay is entirely free of such, of complacence in the exercise of modernism's conventional tropes and moves: its discourse of certainty, of singular truths, of the already known and decided upon. In particular there is throughout 'Postmodernism, or The Cultural Logic of Late Capitalism' a near automatised distaste for mass culture. When Jameson tells us that we really don't have to think about Warhol's series on the electric chair and car accidents because they are 'debased and contaminated in advance by their assimilation to glossy advertising images', he is enjoying all the comfort of the easy a priori judgement.

Terms like 'commodification' and 'commodity fetishism' and 'consumer capitalism' are eased into the argument as if they couldn't possibly be open to questioning, as if they're fixed coordinates of Jameson's cognitive mapping. Yet when Jameson relates Warhol's billboard images of Coca-Cola and Campbell's soup to 'commodity fetishism', we might wonder if the term, so central to the Marxist tradition, especially where it joins modernism in a critique of mass culture, could be at least provisionally unpicked. What does the 'fetishism' in 'commodity fetishism' mean? It appears to be a psychological term, perhaps drawing on nineteenth-century anthropological images of the primitive. It seems to assume that if people, consumers, feel they need or enjoy certain consumer items, then they are only doing so because, in a primitive ritualistic way, they are fetishising them, have surrendered to them as false gods. This might strike us as a crude psychological reductionism, a massive totalising judgement, imperious and patronising, on choices made out of reason and desire. The notion, or trope, of 'commodity fetishism' assumes that the theorist knows what are humanity's authentic needs, even if fallen consumer humanity doesn't and, given their immersion, their addiction, couldn't.

Finally, following on from the assumption of knowing humanity's true needs, there is that dangerously authoritarian distinction between the culturally 'abnormal' and 'healthy linguistic normality'. Is Frederic Jameson the F.R. Leavis of the postmodern world? Is 'Postmodernism, or The Cultural Logic of Late Capitalism' yet another rewriting, in the modernist palimpsest, of *Mass Civilisation and Minority Culture*?

CHAPTER ELEVEN

From Structuralism to Poststructuralism

> . . . the structurality of structure . . . has always been
> neutralised or reduced, and this by a process of giving it a
> centre or of referring it to a point of presence, a fixed origin.
> The function of this centre was . . . to make sure that the
> organising principle of the structure would limit what we
> might call the *play* of the structure . . . And even today the
> notion of a structure lacking any centre represents the
> unthinkable itself.
>
> *Jacques Derrida*, 'Structure, Sign and Play' [1]

> . . . in reading Derrida's work we marvel at what keeps the
> ideas of Western metaphysics there in all the texts at night
> and during the day, for so long a period of time. What makes
> this system Western?
>
> *Edward Said*, 'Criticism Between Culture and System' [2]

> It is less common today than it once was to speak of 'the East',
> but we still make casual reference to 'the West', 'Western
> culture', and so on. Even theorists of discontinuity and
> deconstruction such as Foucault and Derrida continue to set
> their analyses within and against a Western totality.
>
> *James Clifford*, 'On Orientalism' [3]

At some time in the 1980s, the middle years I think, I changed my mind
about poststructuralism. I'd been pretty tough on the phenomenon in
my *In a Critical Condition* (1984), about struggles for control of literary
criticism in Australia from the 1950s to the early 1980s. My argument
was that an older radical nationalist approach in the 1950s – that
'Australian literature' expressed a certain essential character (optimism,
egalitarianism, laconic humour, anti-pomposity, anti-pretension, self-
irony, self-deflation, iconoclasm) – was combated and defeated by a
combined New Critical/Leavisite assault. I drew on Foucault to evoke

129

the Australian New Critics and Leavisites as a discursive formation. 'Australian literature' was now to be recognised as exhibiting a new essential character, turning on a modernist-tragic spirit of alienation, desolation, solitude, loneliness, defeat, madness, terror. The New Critics and Leavisites won the high critical ground, instituting, in Foucault's terms, a regime of truth, a regime that was certainly productive of kinds of knowledge about Australian literature largely ignored or minimised by the radical nationalists, yet at the same time limiting of plurality, of diversity of approaches. In particular, its procedures, rules and edicts assumed that criticism should concern itself with metaphysical values, should indeed see other kinds of concern, social, political, ideological, historical, as extra-literary, and so not the business of the true critic. A dubious distinction between the literary and non-literary became inevitable truth, given institutional force in university teaching and supervision of research: Foucault's drama of knowledge and power was being enacted on the antipodean critical stage.

In a Critical Condition constructed a narrative whereby the new regime of truth was from the late 1970s showing definite signs of the sclerotic, was being perceived as narrow, exclusive, and debilitating. But help, I speculated, was arriving, theoretical assistance in the form of poststructuralism, performed in the name of Derrida and the later Roland Barthes (especially the Barthes of *S/Z*). In this guise, however, I felt, poststructuralism was but continuing the New Critical project, giving new and sophisticated authority, drawing on semiology, to its formalism, its assertion of the true character of literature as beyond ideology and history. Poststructuralism, with its stress on indeterminacy of meaning, was being used to refer the essential enterprise of literature and criticism to language, where language becomes a new metaphysical ground of being. Literature was to be released from any binding ties to history and society into language as the infinite play of difference, of ambiguity and ambivalence: the lined face of New Criticism was re-emerging, smiling, grotesquely youthful.

During the writing of *In a Critical Condition*, I came across Frank Lentricchia's *After the New Criticism* (1980), and was delighted to find there a similar narrative for North American criticism. I was fortified to see that Lentricchia was also suggesting what I gingerly proposed in my conclusion, that criticism be freed to consider literature in all its aspects, context as well as text, the historical, political, social, and ideological as well as the metaphysical. There could be a return of the repressed, to historical approaches which yet respected the literary, to a precarious balancing act over what had become a deep gulf between text and context.

In a recent interview Lentricchia wryly notes that despite the 'whipping' his *After the New Criticism* took (I know the feeling from reviews of *In a Critical Condition*), from 1980 on a move towards historical approaches became increasingly evident.[4] But poststructuralism and especially various uses of Derrida continue to figure largely in such moves. Derrida himself, who spends half a year in Paris teaching philosophy, half at Yale teaching comparative literature, has said that he feels his work is better received in America than in France.[5] It would appear that if in the 1970s he was vastly influential in literary studies, in particular amongst those critics known as the Yale Derrideans, or Yale deconstructionists, or Yale Mafia (Paul de Man, Geoffrey Hartman, J. Hillis Miller), in the 1980s and into the 1990s Derrida's influence has broadened considerably.[6]

The influence of Derrida is showing itself in interactions between literary study and cultural history and theory. The New Historicists, critics largely of Elizabethan culture, challenged the way the Yale deconstructionists appropriated Derrida to privilege high literary texts, seen as maximising indeterminacy of meaning. The New Historicism situated literary texts within broad textual fields, at the same time rejecting an older Marxist model where texts reflected or expressed a set, known historical context: context as a stable, unified background. Contexts became another series of texts, texts that are ever ambivalent and finally undecidable – a conception of text and context which I now find interesting and helpful.[7]

Under Derrida's influence, poststructuralism has put into general intellectual play concepts like heterogeneity, fragmentation, discontinuity, multiple and conflicting and contesting meanings and values in a text or society or period or epoch. In these terms Derrida has influenced anthropologists to critique an older structural-functionalism where traditional societies are constructed as stable, unified wholes; in the postmodern world, cultural identities are perceived as multiple, fragmented, contradictory.[8] Marxism itself has not survived unaffected. Writers influenced by poststructuralism have critiqued the Marxist tradition for its claims to total understanding of historical epochs, for its discourse of certainty (as in notions of objectivity or Marxism as science), for determinism. Marrying Derrida as marginal, liminal figure, a kind of intellectual trickster, to Bakhtin as evoker of carnival, new interpretations of Marx's writings are offered in the light of 'carnivalised' texts like *The Eighteenth Brumaire of Louis Bonaparte*. Here Marx is seen as creating history as heterogeneous, ambivalent, absurdly repetitious, as farce. The American historiographer Dominick LaCapra argues that Marx's own writing in *The Eighteenth Brumaire* exhibits a kind of polemical invective, where the aggressive, negative, critical abuse directed at its sorry object is almost Rabelaisian in its exuberant parody, perhaps prefiguring in its language a different future than that usually stressing Marx's insistence on modes of production. Further, Marx in this remarkable text is suspicious of the power of the state as it tries comprehensively to enmesh, control, superintend and tutor every relationship and detail of civil society. Marx is being broken up into multiple Marxes.[9]

It may seem like joining the rush, but in recent years I've felt increasingly attracted to poststructuralism precisely as a critique of structuralism, for I now see structuralist assumptions everywhere in the various influential approaches in cultural studies, received and continuing, with which I've been arguing from the early 1980s.

Derrida demolishes

When Derrida was invited in 1966 to give a paper to a conference intended to introduce structuralism to the American university intelligentsia, he delivered 'Structure, Sign and Play in the Discourse of the Human Sciences', which demolished structuralist theory.[10] Usually known as 'Structure, Sign and Play', it is perhaps the key formative essay of poststructuralism and deconstruction. Derrida set about opposing the prevailing French structuralist tradition (he targets Lévi-Strauss), which he sees as an extension of Western philosophy, for being essentialist. In structuralism a structure is conceived as possessing a centre, a fundamental ground, which supposedly explains everything about that structure, that totality, that phenomenon; the centre might be an arche, a claimed origin that everywhere unfolds, or a telos, a presumed destination that the structure, the phenomenon, is heading towards. Derrida also suggests that this centre is usually itself left unexplained as if it is beyond the structure it's in, so that the centre is both in the structure yet not in it. The centre, as Derrida characteristically writes, is not a centre. The centre governs the structure, but is itself beyond the play of meanings, of 'repetitions, substitutions, transformations, and permutations' involved in a fuller history of meaning. The centre maintains the structure as enclosed totality, as if it contains or exhausts all the meanings we can attribute to that structure.

The persistent search for a centre, a 'fundamental ground', maintains a given structure in a false state of immobility, of finality, of fixed truth. The search for a centre also betrays an 'anxiety', a 'desire' for a 'reassuring certitude'. The insistence on certainty, on a supposed fullness or 'presence' of meaning, Derrida usually refers to as logocentrism. If, however, we conceive of structures as without a centre, then we can see that they are always open to interpretation without end, unconfined, unreduced, unfinalised, untotalised, not continuous, not linear, where truth is never arrived at, is always involved in a play of differences that keep deferring its arrival, its full presence.

In 'Structure, Sign and Play' Derrida has heroes, thinkers like Nietzsche, Freud, Heidegger, who have shown the way beyond structuralism in Western philosophy, in terms of 'decentring', freeing structure into 'structurality', a play of structures. In particular, there is the Nietzschean 'joyous affirmation of the play of the world', joyous yet also always insecure, always an adventure. Derrida stresses that the inherited concepts of Western philosophy have to be used by such philosophers even in their critiques: 'we can pronounce not a single destructive proposition which has not already had to slip into the form, the logic, and the implicit postulations of precisely what it seeks to contest'.[11] We're always at once inside and outside the logocentric. We have to be self-watchful. We have to self-deconstruct.

Fateful alliance: Modernism and structuralism

We can, I now think, see a great many of the analyses we've been surveying in previous chapters in terms of 'Structure, Sign and Play'. A century of modernism has constantly searched in mass culture for a centre, a fundamental ground, that will explain the whole ghastly phenomenon. For F.R. Leavis and Q.D. Leavis, the mass of people saturate themselves in popular fiction, unvaryingly crude and vulgar, because their lives in the contemporary world are emotionally desolate and empty, deprived of the finer values of the non-industrial past. For Adorno, the centre of mass culture is mass conformity, and this centre enjoys a psychological origin, an infantile need for protection. For Barthes in *Mythologies*, the centre of mass culture is the bourgeois norm, again to be referred to an origin, a permanent psychological state, the mass populace's age-old desire for moral certainty and simplicity. For 1970s Screen Theory, as in Colin McCabe, Hollywood is an enclosed totalised structure, with the Classic Realist Text as all-governing centre; the curious origin of this centre to modern popular culture apparently lies in the nineteenth-century high bourgeois realist novel. Then recall that classic of 1970s feminist Screen Theory, Laura Mulvey's 'Visual Pleasure and Narrative Cinema'. We're to see Hollywood as a reflection of the dominant patriarchal order, and the fundamental ground of Hollywood and this wider order is to be traced to the male unconscious in childhood. In Derrida's terms, what Mulvey constitutes as a structure, Hollywood narrative film, has a centre, but that centre is not in the structure, it's in the supposed origin of the structure, in unconsciousness, a notion beyond any play of interpretation itself. In terms of modernist visions of postmodernity, we can see Baudrillard creating the postmodern world of the media and communication as a single structure uniformly informed and ruled by its centre, the all-suffusing simulacrum (images of images, copies of copies). Frederic Jameson treasures terms like cultural logic or systemic cultural norm or hegemonic norm that also clearly create postmodernity as a single structure, its all-explaining centre parody as mere pastiche, its origin in that strange concept, commodity fetishism, that apparently never requires problematising.

Derrida's position in 'Structure, Sign and Play' that we can never be free of the conventions, concepts and categories we wish to criticise, can also stand, I think, as a ringing of poststructuralist alarm bells for modernist notions of the avant-garde. The avant-garde, a sensitive cultural minority, is to be posed (even if in nostalgia) as the lonely, ever daring alternative to the contemporary world, ever at the cutting edge of time and experimentation, ever somehow purely oppositional, embodying in advanced form the ideal future. But, as we've been tracing, modernist oppositional thought has not been at all free of signal aspects of the modern world, of authoritarianism, institutionalisation, orthodoxy, routinisation, and the 'desire' in Derrida's terms for 'reassuring certitude' in its cultural judgements, its simple absolute opposition of Good (themselves) and Evil (mass culture). In terms of modernist art and architecture, there are the all too evident imbrications with wealth and power.

I hope I've explained my post-*In a Critical Condition* turn to poststructuralism: where modernist theory reduces mass culture to a simple single message, Derrida's stress on undecidability of meaning might restore to mass culture texts complexity, contradiction, difficulty, density, mystery.

Derrida's theory of history

While I find Derrida's critique of structuralism illuminating and extremely useful, I would not like to leave the impression – I trust it's not too late – that I've become that painful creature, a recent convert, now endlessly reproducing the same Derridean terms.

I'd like to suggest, in the spirit of Derrida's own warning that we're always inside the concepts we at the same time wish to critique, that some poststructuralism, not least Derrida's own, is unfortunately very much in danger of reintroducing into cultural theory notions of totality, singularity, linearity, unity, and binary opposites.

We can see such a return in the way Derrida himself constructs cultural and intellectual history, especially in his identifying what he dislikes most, logocentrism, with the history of Western philosophy and thought. Derrida does this in the name of anti-ethnocentrism, arguing that Western philosophy is a metaphysics, a

> white mythology which reassembles and reflects the culture of the West: the white man takes his own mythology, Indo-European mythology, his own *logos*, that is, the *mythos* of his idiom, for the universal form of that he must still wish to call Reason.[12]

But does Derrida's construction of the Western mythos of reason escape the inhibiting imprint of precisely those Western features he is ever ironic towards? Does Derrida's construction of Western thought perform as a fundamental ground, a 'transcendental signified', a centred structure, in his own writing?

We can explore Derrida's most sustained work, *Of Grammatology*, published in the late 1960s, much of it a long commentary on Rousseau's *Essay on the Origin of Languages* in terms of anthropology and what is usually called (in the Western mythos) prehistory. In the wide spaces of *Of Grammatology* Derrida can go more thoroughly into what he objects to in logocentrism. Logocentrism is the notion that study of language, as in the phonetic alphabet, should be based on a model of speech, on the spoken word, the logos. Logocentrism, says Derrida, is phonocentrism. Logocentrism is an ethnocentric Western concept, for phonetic writing is the 'medium of the great metaphysical, scientific, technical, and economic adventure of the West'. In philosophy and metaphysics from ancient Greece to modern times, from the pre-Socratic to the post-Hegelian, from Plato to Rousseau to Saussure to Lévi-Strauss, language is conceived of as based on speaking, on the presence of speaking subjects, whose immediate presence ensures a full presence of meaning and access to a true state of mind and being. Language based on speech is the Western logocentric dream, its illusion of 'pure intelligibility', of fullness and transparency of meaning – of certainty, truth, authenticity, all guaranteed by the presence of the speaking subjects.[13]

In Derrida's view, privileging speech situations as model of language and meaning is often, too often, accompanied by a desire to idealise such face-to-face speech situations. He is especially passionate against anthropological notions, as in the Romantic Rousseau and the structuralist Lévi-Strauss, of traditional societies alleged to be without writing and therefore without history, communities living idyllically in the immediacy of speech, with always clear agreed-on 'unanimous' meanings and values, communities that lead an authentic existence we in the West can only yearn for. In *Tristes Tropiques* Lévi-Strauss suggests, says Derrida, that traditional communities like the Nambikwara did not know violence or hierarchy, despite abundant 'evidence' to the contrary in *Tristes Tropiques* itself. And the Nambikwara knew and experienced hierarchy and violence precisely because they possessed what Lévi-Strauss said they didn't possess, writing. The error, the vulgar error, Lévi-Strauss commits is to identify writing with Western writing, the phonetic alphabet. But, says Derrida in one of his most controversial claims, writing in human history is much much broader than the Western notion of writing, especially as symbolised in the book, and this broader kind of writing came before speech.[14]

What is writing? How could it predate speech? Why, in Derrida's view, has it been repressed and excluded in the Western philosophical tradition as dangerous? Writing is not at all to be identified with the phonetic alphabet. On the contrary, writing designates the broadest of phenomena, writing is everything that gives rise to inscription, in any kind of markings as in the pictographic and the ideographic, the hieroglyphic, the cuneiform, from the past to the present, in choreography as in cinematography. Writing can be articulated in graphic substances, in materials (wood, wax, skin, stone, ink, metal, vegetable) or instruments (points, brush). Writing is aural as well as visual, the musical as well as the pictorial and sculptural.[15]

Writing, then, is to be found in anything which enables signifying references which 'supplement' the spoken word, which exceed immediate speech and whose meanings cannot be guaranteed or held down to or finalised in face-to-face speech situation. Writing is a 'play' of meanings that exceeds the immediacy of speech and language based on a model of speech. Whenever face-to-face speech itself has recourse to, or is prohibited from using, as in many traditional societies, certain proper names, there is a movement away from immediacy and transparency of meaning, since proper names always belong to systems of differentiation, of classification, which are open to dispute, a history of interpretation and reinterpretation, and hence to the possibility of violence, inscription within a system of linguistico-social differences.[16]

Indeed, for Derrida, writing and violence are born together in history. In every society, traditional to the present, naming and the prohibition of names is tied to inscribing within differences, the violence of difference. Writing, all that exceeds speech and refers to differences in and beyond speech, represents a violence to the human dream of full presence of meaning to the self. To compensate for this loss of full and controllable meaning, there arise attempts to conceal differences, deny them – another kind of violence, the suppression of difference, those differences, expressed in hierarchy, evil, war, indiscretion, rape, which yet ever recur. Drawing a long historical bow, Derrida argues that such relationships of knowledge and power have been with us since the neolithic age, in the creation of social, economic, technical, political and other structures upon which we still subsist.[17]

(Derrida's association here of knowledge with power is an interestingly Foucauldian touch, given Foucault's charge that Derrida ignores such relationships).[18]

Of Grammatology is, then, indeed a rewriting of Rousseau's *Essay on the Origin of Languages*. It is an essay on the universal origins of language and society. Derrida, however, is quick to argue in *Of Grammatology* that the origins he proposes are not origins, in the sense of a fundamental ground that can be identified and from which history can be seen as unfolding. Here we approach Derrida's notions of arche-writing, the trace, and 'differance'.

At the beginnings of human society is what Derrida refers to as 'arche-writing', the 'movement of differance', a swirling play of differences which surge into 'writing', whether graphic or non-graphic, material or spoken, as 'traces'. But there is no original trace that we can discover, there is only – in a famous phrase – 'always already' the play of difference, of meanings and values, of signifiers, ever disputed and involved with power. Traces born of 'differance' form together to constitute chains of signification, systems, texts, which never yield finalised truths, for 'differance defers-differs (*differe*)'. Differance or arche-writing also 'opens speech itself', the play of differences, of naming and classification, knowledge and power, within speech.[19]

The play of difference in human beginnings is also related to a psychoanalysis, an originary psychology of being, an ontology. Derrida is very wary of psychoanalysis in relation to textual analysis, if it means we refer the play of a text's meanings to a fixed reality outside the text, as in an author's presumed psychobiography, or some general designated psychological structure. We shouldn't in general, says Derrida, refer the text to any fixed referents outside the text, psychological or historical or metaphysical. Here Derrida produces his famous pronouncement: 'There is nothing outside of the text [there is no outside-text; *il n'y a pas de hors-texte*]'.[20] This is a move we can recognise as familiar in twentieth-century criticism, from the Russian Formalists to the New Critics' Intentional Fallacy to Barthes' declaration of the Death of the Author.

Yet in *Of Grammatology* Derrida is certainly interested in psychoanalysis, as supplement perhaps to his anthropological interest in the origins of language. Derrida ventures that the human subject, in sensing that the restless play of interpretation that is writing can't be controlled, faces a permanent threat to its power, indeed faces its 'death', end of its assured or 'absolute' self-presence and identity. In speech there is an attempt, out of the needs of 'auto-affection', to suppress differance. Here the desire for full presence of meaning appears born out of a primordial and constitutive human anxiety. When Derrida discusses Rousseau's *Confessions*, he talks, in another famous phrase, of the 'dangerous supplement', and the supplement, says Derrida, is 'another name for differance', of the restless play of unconfinable substitutions of meaning. Differance creates out of such restlessness, such 'non-satisfaction', the 'desire' in human beings for presence, for a reassuring certitude, stability of meaning.[21]

Perhaps, Derrida suggests, history and society can be defined as a play of supplements, of substitutions, that are attempts to resist the abyss (*l'abîme*) of unconfinable meanings by recovering the mother. We can speculate, in relation to Rousseau's onanistic fantasies about his lover when she is not there, whom he calls Mamma, that these fantasies, these substitutions for Mamma, are an attempt by the subject to regain that which it is impossible to regain, the 'self's very origin' with the mother, with Nature. The substitutions, the supplements, the fantasies, are an attempt to bathe again in 'originary perception', in the 'immediate presence' of the lost mother, even while the supplements continue in a chain, an 'infinite chain', that can never recover such unity, but only keep deferring it in more and more images. The 'desire for presence' is 'born from the abyss', that is, from the 'splitting of the self' from Nature into indefinitely multiplied supplements, or representations.[22]

In *Of Grammatology* there are strange uncertainties in relation to the notion of intention. Derrida warns that commentary should not try to reproduce a writer's 'conscious, voluntary, intentional' relationship to history. Rather the focus should be on how writing is worked by the system, laws and life of language (here is the structuralist inheritance in poststructuralism). A little later, however, we find him referring to the 'deep intention' of Rousseau's *Essay*, which must also apparently be distinguished from the work's 'declared intention'. In discussing Lévi-Strauss, Derrida also doesn't hesitate to refer to the older thinker's 'intentions', even a 'final intention' which 'the factual evidence' is oriented towards.[23] (What a positivistic, logocentric, touch that is, 'factual evidence'.)

An author's intentions, one might have thought, following Derrida himself, are not only outside the text but suspiciously look like an origin, a centre that is not in a structure yet directs it. Further, the notion of intention is surely uncomfortably close to desire, a notion crucial to Derrida's argument concerning Western thought. In 'Structure, Sign and Play' Derrida, we recall, tells us, again in a curiously positivist language of factuality, that the 'concept of a centred structure' in the 'history of the West' is 'in fact based on a fundamental ground', the 'desire' for a 'reassuring certitude' that tries to overcome 'anxiety', the threat of the unthinkable, of no centre to a structure.²⁴ In 'Structure, Sign and Play', I think, the concept of such a desire acts in the text as an origin for the structure Derrida is evoking (of structuralism), an origin that is itself not being opened by Derrida to any play of questioning.

In *Of Grammatology* Derrida is also keen to insist that the desire for presence, the desire to 'wrest' play and uncertainty away from language, is a peculiarly Western phenomenon, involved in the 'Western concept of language'. Yet, as we've been tracing, there are so many places in *Of Grammatology* where the text contradictorily constructs the desire for presence as either near-perennial or universal. In his anthropological discussions of the origins of language, Derrida argues that the desire for presence is apparent everywhere in the world for thousands of years at least since neolithic times. It works as an attempt to conceal differences as a way of controlling knowledge in relation to power, for example, in enforcing hierarchy, or claims to genealogy. Again in oddly positivist language, Derrida tells us (in disputing *Tristes Tropiques*) that it is 'now known, thanks to unquestionable and abundant information, that the birth of writing (in the colloquial sense) was nearly everywhere and most often linked to genealogical anxiety'.²⁵ And Derrida takes recourse to psychoanalysis, the origins of being, of split from the mother, to explain the logocentric. The desire for the logocentric here seems to be at one with the human condition. As Edward Said asks in our epigraph, why is logocentrism then specifically Western?

Derrida's text is so repetitive in its insistence that there is a permanent search for 'logocentric security' in Western philosophy and thought that we might wonder, in Derrida's own terms, if his own text is betraying an anxiety – his own desire that Western thought *should* be conceived as such, yet where so much of his argument points otherwise.²⁶

Of Grammatology indeed presents Western thought as a relentless uniform totality, a monolithic structure.²⁷ How it totalises! From the beginning we're told that from Plato to Hegel, from the pre-Socratics to Heidegger, the history of the notion of truth has 'always' involved the debasement of 'writing', a debasement that is the West's 'constituted normality'. For 'nearly three millennia' the West has been informed by such 'logocentric metaphysics'. Occasionally *Of Grammatology* does qualify its totalising vision by warning that we shouldn't neglect a 'very heterogeneous historical duration', that the 'linear norm' was never able to impose itself 'absolutely', only with an 'irregular and essentially precarious success'. But the burden of *Of Grammatology*'s language, its notions of structure and its metaphors, are overwhelmingly centred and indeed structuralist, Derrida's very object of critique. We're to agree that an 'entire epoch', that is, Western history, is a 'totality', 'the totality of the age of logocentrism'. Western logocentrism is a 'machine', it has an 'historical solidity', it's 'solidary' in its 'entire history', it has a 'structural solidarity'. Part of Western logocentrism is a concept of time as linear, and this 'linearism' is 'intrinsic to the totality of the history of the Occident', is the 'norm'. What we are dealing with here in the West is 'all metaphysics'.[28]

While Derrida says that he opposes the linear notion of time that is part of Western metaphysics, that he dislikes its 'continuist prejudice', his own history of the West quickly emerges in *Of Grammatology* as relentlessly linear and continuous. The text conceives of Western thought for 'three millennia' as a single thing, a single structure, enfolded in a desire for certitude, from the pre-Socratics through 'medieval theology' almost to the present. It is Derrida indeed who is everywhere constructing in *Of Grammatology* a 'linear norm', which has been 'dominating all philosophy'. It is Derrida's history of Western thought that is operating throughout on that which he derides, a 'linear model'.[29]

Of Grammatology presents the history of Western thought as a journey towards a desired destination, deconstruction itself, writing that permits the play of difference. We're to hail the appearance of a near-apocalyptic event, discernible in traditional (theological?) images of darkness, birth, light. For three millennia we can see that Western thought lives in its 'constituted normality', but a new 'future' is beckoning, even if we can only now present it as a sort of 'montrosity', what Derrida in 'Structure, Sign and Play' referred to as the unthinkable. Western logocentric thought is, apparently, approaching its own exhaustion, for we can see the coming of deconstruction as a 'glimmer' in a 'crevice'. We might be entering a new historical epoch, the coming of 'the first writing', that which makes visible the workings of Western metaphysics. The long 'night' of the Western norm is beginning to 'lighten a little', as we now recognise 'pluri-dimensionality'. Entry into the 'future epoch' (of differance) is heralded by philosophers like Nietzsche and modernist writers like Mallarmé and Ezra Pound. What *Of Grammatology* strangely parades, then, is a historical narrative of progress, theoretical progress, intellectual history as teleological.[30]

(As Said notes, in the hands of Derrida's disciples in literary studies, 'Derrida' quickly became a new orthodoxy: from the unthinkable, the monstrous, in the 1960s to doxa in the 1970s. In one oddly easy movement.[31])

To history as linear we can add historicism, in terms of Derrida's notions of representation, the way *Of Grammatology* constructs certain authors as exemplifying Western thought conceived as an unfolding totality. Plato, Hegel, Rousseau are to be read as 'landmarks' of the Western 'history of metaphysics'. Especially Rousseau. What *Of Grammatology* refers to as the 'exemplariness' of the '"Rousseauist" moment' is pivotal to its argument about Western thought as a whole, especially as we are to see that 'Rousseau repeats the Platonic gesture', the 'Platonic diagram', is the 'inheritor of Platonism'. We can identify Rousseau as a 'decisive articulation of the logocentric epoch'. Rousseau can also be taken more particularly as representing what is 'profoundly implied by the entire age' of Western thought from Descartes to Hegel, despite, Derrida says, all the different places and moments in the 'structure of that epoch'.[32] Here Derrida appears to be reintroducing the classic move of structuralist linguistics, to discern beneath an apparent heterogeneity of differences (*parole*) a deep invariant structure (*langue*), or, in his terms, a centre (Rousseau).

Clearly *Of Grammatology* is worried by such a move, Derrida noting that his regarding texts as 'symptoms' is regrettable and provisional, showing how much we are still caught within metaphysical concepts. But the caravan of worry passes by for the moment, *Of Grammatology* being left with treating Rousseau, and Lévi-Strauss as a kind of extension of Rousseau, as indeed symptoms of the 'dominant discourse'.[33] Ah, that prime structuralist notion, that trope of totality, the dominant. Yet it's not long before Derrida is again worried that he's playing down the density of texts in a rush to see them as functions of Western metaphysics. Indeed, it's this recurring anxiety in *Of Grammatology* that produces, I think, the famous proclamation that we must respect the textuality of texts, that there is nothing outside. But the proclamation is too late, far too late, given the general method of *Of Grammatology*, the way the texts of Rousseau and other figures are taken as illustrations of a prior set structure, Western Thought, outside their texts.

Of Grammatology is right to be so worried. Such reflectionist notions of representation are, as Said has protested, uncomfortably crude. Why should we, Said asks, talk of the age of Rousseau, why not the age of Condillac? Why should Rousseau's theory of language receive precedence over those of Vico, Sir William Jones, Coleridge? Said also points out that the writing Derrida takes as so representative is highly selective and rather conventional. In particular, Derrida tends to minimise narrative writing, a delimiting that is rather strange, since a key move in Derrida's writings is to draw attention to performative, theatrical elements in writing that exceed and therefore undo the attempt in Western thought to be transparently logocentric, complete in meaning. Said quotes a passage from *Great Expectations*, where Pip goes to see a farcical presentation of *Hamlet*, the irony going every which way, parodying *Hamlet* yet not denying its greatness. Said's point is that Dickens' comedy is doing very much what Derrida says cannot be done in Western thought, an open staging of deconstruction, a theatrical questioning of the idea of an origin to interpretation, a releasing and enjoying of a play of undecidable meanings, a destabilising of certainty around even an unquestionably great play such as *Hamlet*. In Said's view, an impressive range of novelists, before and after Dickens, from Cervantes and Sterne to Flaubert, Proust, Conrad, Hardy, Joyce, explicitly stage and explore as a constitutive aspect of their narratives the philosophic problems Derrida is concerned with. In these terms, Said probes on, how can Derrida construct allegedly universal characteristics of Western thought when so much Western narrative is already so deconstructive, so anti-logocentric?[34]

In *Of Grammatology* Derrida accuses Lévi-Strauss, in constructing traditional communities like the Nambikwara as models of original and natural goodness, of a 'suppression of contradiction and difference'. *Of Grammatology* can equally be accused of suppressing 'contradiction and difference' in Western culture and thought. Yet while the narrative of *Of Grammatology* is constructing the long night of logocentric darkness, there are traces in the text that suggest a more differentiated history, not only for Western cultural history but more generally in human cultures. There are, for example, references to tricksters in the discussion of Lévi-Strauss's exploration of Nambikwara society, and the quoting of a passage where Lévi-Strauss refers to 'play-acting'. In analysing Rousseau, Derrida notes at one point that Rousseau's text 'tricks with a gesture'; it calls to mind 'spectacles' and 'masques'. He also quotes a passage where Rousseau refers to originary 'festivals' in history.[35]

Such references, minor, scattered, marginal as they, are yet dangerous supplements to Derrida's text, exceeding and undoing its perception of a linear history of logocentric darkness; only in the latter nineteenth century did deconstructive thinkers come along, presented by *Of Grammatology* as history's first tricksters. Surely such references whisper of another cultural history, the history of carnival and carnivalesque, of tricksters, festivals and play-acting, as told to us by Mikhail Bakhtin: a history almost, but not quite, effaced in *Of Grammatology*. In his essay 'Forms of Time and of the Chronotope in the Novel' in *The Dialogic Imagination* Bakhtin argues that cultural figures like the rogue, clown, fool, and crank are enormously significant in the later development of the European novel. The masks of the clown and fool, says Bakhtin, came to the aid of the novelist, enabling characters who are life's perpetual spies, who can make private life public, who can be in life but not of it. These masks, rooted deep in the folk, are linked as well to the space and times of gatherings of the public square and with the trappings of the theatre.[36]

In contrast to *Of Grammatology*, we can say that Bakhtin, here and elsewhere, constructs a European cultural history where always already claims to truth and certainty are contested by such carnivalesque figures and masking, figures who parody conventionality at the same time as they parody themselves and their own claims to truth. Carnivalesque as a cultural mode, a cosmology, a philosophy, is continuously important from the mists of folkloric time onwards. Carnivalesque, ever reworking and transforming itself, is active in classical antiquity, in festivals and the festive in medieval times and early modern Europe, in later theatre and the novel, including Sterne and Dickens. (Here Bakhtin's history of the novel connects to Said's, though Said is curiously uninterested in Bakhtin – the Russian theorist's name doesn't register in *The World, The Text and the Critic*.) Further, Bakhtin notes that rogue, clown and fool figures were familiar not only in classical antiquity but in the ancient Orient. Bakhtin doesn't present a cultural history where the West is somehow magically sealed off from other cultural histories.

In Bakhtin's writings, European cultural and intellectual history emerges as the reverse of uniform, monolithic, and enclosed.

Poststructuralism – Modernist or postmodernist?

We can't simply say, as in structuralism to poststructuralism, so modernism to postmodernism. Poststructuralism is primarily a European phenomenon, an argument with an earlier history of structuralism, seen as orthodoxy. Postmodernism we can see as emerging from arguments in North America against a modernist heritage of art and architecture, seen as orthodoxy. I think poststructuralism and postmodernism clearly feed into each other, in stressing heterogeneity, difference, contradiction, indeterminacy, however much poststructuralism, as we've seen in *Of Grammatology*, repeatedly reproduces the structuralist procedures it is criticising.

Poststructuralism has also introduced into cultural play what is usually perceived as a postmodern writing consciousness (*écriture*), that there can be no objective text writing about other texts. All texts, including the philosopher's or critic's or historian's own, are suffused with tropes, metaphors, figural language that will always exceed claims to transparent truth.[37] The philosopher or historian or critic is acknowledged as a narrator in her or his own texts, texts shaped by particular genres and generic expectations. These texts, as much as the avowedly fictional, are susceptible to detailed 'literary' analysis, the revealing of narrative and metaphoric elements that undo any text's attempt to present itself as without inconsistency and contradiction.

In general we might say that poststructuralism suggests that the difference between fiction and non-fiction lies not so much in possession of truth (which for poststructuralism is ever deferred) but, in the case of scholarly writing, in the declared presence of certain agreed conventions and protocols, the referencing of previous work in a field, acknowledgement of sources, and so on. Poststructuralism has raised for us the difference of non-fiction and fiction as permanent question, enigma, the insoluble, aporia.

Yet poststructuralism, as Andreas Huyssen notes, has clearly associated its historical project with high modernism, particularly in terms of a continued contempt for mass culture. The African-American critic Cornell West has accused Derrida of situating his project within Eurocentric frameworks and modernist loyalties, highlighting the disruptive and transgressive as European-only, in Nietzsche, Heidegger, Mallarmé, Artaud.[38]

We have already noticed *Of Grammatology*'s admiration for high literary modernism, as in Mallarmé and Pound. *Of Grammatology*'s loyalty to Pound is perhaps rather odd, given the certainty and assertiveness, the brutal logocentric tone, of much of Pound's poetry. Pound also, along with the other high literary modernists, from fellow poets like T.S. Eliot to critics like F.R. Leavis, was nostalgic for the European past as an origin, of agreed meanings, reassuring certitude, *communitas*. Yet the myth of unanimous collective meanings in past communities is Derrida's derisive target when analysing Lévi-Strauss's *Tristes Tropiques*. And let's not forget the anti-semitic Pound doing broadcasts for Mussolini, providing texts that surely are just as worthy of consideration as his poetry. But Derrida is interested in Pound for a very particular reason, praising him in *Of Grammatology* for his fascination (under the influence of Fenellosa) with the Chinese ideogram, thus introducing a 'graphic poetics' that is the 'first break in the most entrenched Western tradition'.[39] The effacement of the range and complexity of Pound in order to enlist a selected aspect is, I think, characteristic of *Of Grammatology*'s approach to textuality.[40]

In *Of Grammatology* Derrida scorns *Tristes Tropiques* for, in relation to the Nambikwara, 'constituting the other as a model of original and natural goodness'. Yet it appears very much that *Of Grammatology* is close to constituting the Oriental other as a model of original and natural goodness, in Pound's admiration for the Chinese ideogram, and more generally, in the way the Chinese and Japanese have developed writing that is 'testimony of a powerful movement of civilization developing outside of all logocentrism'.[41] *Of Grammatology* is here swimming in the wake of early twentieth-century high modernism, conceiving the Orient (amongst various exotic others) as desired alternative to an alienated anomic dying-inside Europe. The West, conceived in essentialised terms (the 'entrenched Western tradition', apparent exclusive abode of 'all logocentrism') looks to an equally essentialised Orient: the kind of binary distinction, unifying the terms of an absolute opposition, Said has made us so familiar with in that Western game, Orientalism.

CHAPTER TWELVE

Cultural Studies: Transitional Moments from Modernism to Postmodernism

To ignore the wonderful tales that are told or declaimed by professional storytellers in the principal cafes of Istanbul would lead to an incomplete picture of the city's attractions and nocturnal enchantments during the month of Ramadan . . . You sit down, ask for a narghile or a chibouk, then listen to the tales which are drawn out for as long as possible, like today's serials, to the profit of the storyteller and the proprietor . . . I should mention that the cafe where we were gathered is in the working-class district of Constantinople, near to the bazaars . . . though a few elegant costumes were conspicuous here and there upon the benches and platforms. The storyteller whom we were about to hear appeared to be quite famous. Beside the customers inside the cafe there was a crowd outside jostling for a good position. The proprietor requested silence. A pale young man approached and sat down on a stool in a space about five feet square which was lined on all sides by the central benches. His features were extremely delicate, his eyes sparkled, and his long hair flowed down like a Santon's from under his cap, which was different from a tarboosh or a fez. A young boy, his personal assistant, served him coffee. Everybody prepared to listen attentively, for, according to custom, each part of the story would last for half an hour.[1]

It seems that the myth of the passive viewer is about to be shattered.[2]

By the 1990s the modernist mass culture orthodoxy, the 'left pessimism' that had held fast for decades, had crumbled, had lost its authority as automatic truth, though many of its positions and attitudes have run on into postmodern times, most noticeably in the writings of Baudrillard and Jameson. In America, as we've seen, postmodern architecture and

146

its associated theories, as in Venturi, Scott Brown and Izenour's *Learning from Las Vegas*, following on from Pop Art, mixing 'high' and 'low' genres, were placing a question over the primary modernist opposition of true culture and an ever-to-be suspected and despised mass culture.

Williams' challenge

In Britain a couple of years after *Learning from Las Vegas* there appeared Raymond Williams' valiant *Television: Technology and Cultural Form* (1974). There is a pathos in its publication at that time in that country. In the early middle 1970s what was becoming known as Screen Theory was pursuing a structuralist view that mass culture texts reveal a single underlying structure of meaning that secures the mass spectator's ideological subservience to, passivity before, dominant capitalist values. This view, reprising decades of modernist mass culture theory, in particular that of the Frankfurt School, if restated and reworked in then new or different semiotic and psychoanalytic languages, was sweeping all before it in cultural studies, was becoming truly octopoid. Looking back now, we can appreciate the independence and originality of Williams' contribution.[3]

Williams explains in his foreword that while he had written regularly about English TV for *The Listener*, he was writing the present book in California, in a very different television situation. The book is an exploration of contrasts. But while Williams disarmingly admits that he often felt bewildered by American TV, particularly the quick transitions from program to ad, he doesn't take the usual English and European 'high culture' (including radical high culture) road of derision and contempt: he is no Adorno and Horkheimer coming to the US and pronouncing its jazz to be 'stylised barbarity', its culture industry products, such as those of Hollywood, to be 'rubbish'.[4]

Williams distinguishes between two broad types of programming: a commercial kind that focuses on drama series and serials, movies, and general entertainment, and a 'public service' kind that provides news and public affairs, features and documentaries, education, arts and music, children's programs, plays.[5] What is radical about this book is that Williams doesn't then go on to say the British version of the second type of programming is obviously superior. Rather, he suggests that British-style television (in Australia, the ABC, child of the BBC) is based on assumptions that can be held up for questioning and scrutiny; in particular, that broadcasting should be pedagogical, should educate and instruct its audience. Williams observes that the 'characteristic definitions of public and general interest' which are advanced by British TV 'often, on analysis, show themselves as essentially abstract and at times merely passive'. He then relates the cultural project of 'public service' TV to 'quite evident class characteristics'. Williams was here wickedly turning a modernist assumption about mass culture audiences on its head: it was the professional middle-class audiences for educative programs on the BBC or the ABC in Australia who, on this argument, could be seen as too compliant, too accepting of what was offered to them. By contrast, American commercial TV, Williams argues, personalises its presentations more and permits participation by its audiences. His examples are serials and game shows.

Williams' highly heterodox contrast of the two broadcasting modes recalls the distinction in Walter Benjamin's 'The Work of Art in the Age of Mechanical Reproduction' between the forbidding aura of salon or gallery art and the collective enjoyment of popular cinema.[6]

Williams' distinction between public service and commercial TV questioned a key discourse of modernism as well as 'bourgeois public sphere' rationalism: the BBC represents true television; commercial TV and its popular forms and genres represent mere entertainment, the frivolous, the sensational, the mindless, mere pleasure; not knowledge, not information, not art. On the contrary, *Television* suggests, commercial TV has its own distinctive forms of knowledge. It doesn't simply lack what the BBC ideally possesses. It clearly favours fantasy forms, but why should fantasy be alien to knowledge?

Television also hung a question over the claim of 1970s Screen Theory that the popular visual text was the 'classic realist text', deriving from the nineteenth-century high bourgeois realist novel, such as *Middlemarch*. As one might expect from the author of *The Long Revolution*, Williams was familiar – as the *Screen* theorists appeared to be unfamiliar – with the history of English popular culture. In chapter three of *Television* he relates television to nineteenth-century serialised fiction, melodrama, music-hall, variety theatre: far more probable, we might feel, as ancestors of modern popular culture.

There are other suggestions and observations in *Television* that question modernist and rationalist public sphere assumptions, of the 1970s and since. Williams suggests that television, while building on previous popular traditions, is a new and distinctive cultural form. There is a distinctive televisual aesthetic in news, documentary, drama and variety as well as in various painterly effects: 'an experience of visual mobility, of contrast of angle, of variation of focus, which is often very beautiful'. He points out that television permits a scale and intensity of dramatic performance that is without precedent in the history of human culture. He notes the importance of TV, in its showing of old movies, as an archive for film history. He opens the question of the relationship of public-service-type TV to the state, when he argues that, in the case of the BBC, an equation of state and public interest shouldn't be accepted uncritically, since it relies on a consensus that has never been openly arrived at nor made subject to regular open review.[7] Here *Television* is asking questions relevant to arguments in Britain and Australia concerning state regulation of commercial television, since prevailing regulations enshrine the assumption that the kind of hierarchy of forms and genres on BBC/ABC-type television should be enforced on commercial television.[8]

Then there is the notion for which Williams' book is perhaps best known, that of 'flow', of television programming through the day and night. *Television* was here challenging how tightly conventional literary as well as screen studies were tied to analysis of the single, discrete text. 'Flow' recalls Mikhail Bakhtin's notion of culture as forms and genres continuously in interaction, tension, conflict, competition, where for genre we can in part read cosmologies, philosophies, discursive and ideological meanings.

We can, however, quibble with Williams in *Television* when he argues, in chapter four, that in all previous communication systems the essential item – a book, a pamphlet, a play – was discrete, whereas flow is perhaps broadcasting's defining feature. Theatre historians have made us aware that in nineteenth-century popular theatre there was also a flow of theatrical events, melodrama usually being followed by farce. In these terms we can see television flow as continuing and developing much older popular cultural forms.[9]

Williams goes on to say that 'we' find it very difficult to comprehend the implications of the flow of television because most of 'our habitual vocabulary of response and description has been shaped by the experience of discrete events', our modes of understanding and judgement being so closely linked to specific and isolated forms of attention. Television, on the other hand, emphasises what Williams describes as an 'increasing variability and miscelleneity of public communications'. He refers to the way the flow of items establishes the sense of a world of hurried surprising events coming in, tumbling over each other, from all sides. At another point he talks of the elements of speed and variety. These are part of a new general trend, a 'whole social experience': what we would probably now call postmodernity.

This is a fascinating suggestion. It might explain at least part of the reason why not a generalised 'we' but modernists and those who belong to the rationalist public sphere find postmodern popular visual culture to be so confusing, so bewildering. We only have to think of Baudrillard's 'The Ecstasy of Communication', or Jameson's 'Post-modernism, or The Cultural Logic of Late Capitalism', let alone John Berger's BBC series *Ways of Seeing* (1972), or Neil Postman's *Amusing*

Ourselves to Death (1987). They report feelings almost of nausea in relation to what Williams evokes as the tumbling speed and variety of contemporary communication. They argue that the ceaseless flood of media images overwhelms and destroys the real, the rational, older firmer bearings, older maps and charts of the mind, a mythical past where all apparently was comprehensible. What they cannot believe or grant is that the flow of mass culture may possess its own forms of reason, not reason in a rationalist sense, of attention to discrete ordered sequences of information and interpretation, but of sudden juxta-positions, swift contrasts, heterogeneity. Those who enjoy the post-modern world don't have any trouble with such a carnivalesque mode of understanding. It's been part of popular culture for centuries, it's part of their cultural capital. But those of the professional middle class, nurtured on the ideals and training of the bourgeois public sphere and of conventional literary and cultural studies, find it so baffling they have to evoke it as an absence, an epoch-threatening lack of the kind of reason they know and comprehend and which they believe is the only reason possible. They translate their own lack of cultural capital as universal nausea.[10]

Television: Technology and Cultural Form wonderfully resisted determ-inism and functionalism. It didn't choose structure over agency, and remained sceptical of the structuralist metaphysic that subjectivity is completely determined by discourses.

Its major limitation, perhaps, was a lack of attention to the textuality of television.

Revisiting the soaps

Another breach in the wall of modernist mass culture theory was the 1979 essay, 'The Search for Tomorrow in Today's Soap Operas', by the American critic Tania Modleski.[11] Modleski questions the view that soaps – melodrama made into a continuous narrative form – are trivial, noting that soap operas contain more references to social problems than do most other forms of entertainment. She points out that rape was recently an issue, and was 'for the most part, handled in a sensitive manner'. She argues that the pleasure of such popular narratives, daytime soaps like *Days of Our Lives*, should not be rejected, as it had been by feminist critics. Modleski rebuts the charge, for example, that soap opera merely reconciles women to the nuclear family as site of fulfilment. What the spectator sees in a soap, Modleski contends, is the direct opposite of her own isolated nuclear family; it is a kind of extended family, revealing a fantasy desire for community. Accordingly, Modleski argues, soaps should not necessarily be opposed by feminist aesthetics in favour of an alternative art.[12]

For Modleski, soaps are to be understood in terms of the lives of the women who are their audience. Soaps provide a specifically feminine narrative pleasure which is 'thoroughly adapted to the rhythms of women's lives in the home'. For one thing, soap operas never end, because each episode brings further complications that will defer resolutions and introduce new questions. Conclusions only lead to further tensions and suffering. Soap opera narratives place ever more complex obstacles between desire and fulfilment, making anticipation an end in itself. Hence soaps invest 'exquisite pleasure' in the 'central condition' of women's lives, which is 'waiting', for the phone to ring, or the baby to sleep.[13]

Modleski's essay also argues with 1970s Screen Theory's harsh judgement on popular screen texts that they insist on narrative and ideological closure. Modleski suggests to the contrary that soaps may be in the vanguard not just of television but of all popular narrative art, precisely because they provide multiple, decentred narratives, everywhere breaking the illusion of unity and totality offered the spectator by realism. By constantly presenting her with the many-sidedness of any question, by breaking identification with a single controlling character and providing multiple points of contradictory, ever shifting identifications, the soap opera undermines the spectator's capacity to form unambiguous judgements.[14]

Modleski herself is ambivalent about soap opera. At one point she feels that the multiple identifications that occur in soaps might well result in the spectator being divested of power, and so will reinforce 'feminine powerlessness'. At another, she judges that the extreme delight female viewers take in despising villain figures 'testifies to the enormous amount of energy involved in the spectator's repression', for the villainess is the negative image of the spectator's ideal feminine self. In despising the villainess, the spectator is despising her own hidden wishes to master her life, to deny feminine passivity. Also, the spectator, in repeatedly watching for how the villainess tries to gain such control, is participating in what Freud saw as the repetition compulsion, resulting from an individual's attempt to become an active manipulator of her own powerlessness. The spectator, Modleski speculates, comes to enjoy such repetition for its own sake, so reconciling her to the 'meaningless, repetitive nature of much of her life and work within the home'.[15]

Modleski believes, then, that the soap opera 'reflects and cultivates' the psychological disposition of the woman in the home. Here Modleski argues against Raymond Williams' notion in his *Television: Technology and Cultural Form* of program flow, for soaps, to the contrary, reinforce the very principle of 'interruptability' crucial to the proper functioning of women in the domestic sphere. The formal properties of daytime television thus 'accord closely with the rhythms of women's work in the home', as against watching film or nighttime TV shows which, Modleski appears to assume, is a male-only activity (engaging 'his' attention).[16]

Modleski's essay was a striking contribution to cultural studies debates, a break indeed. But, in terms of Derrida's dictum that we are always inside the concepts we attempt to critique, we might wonder if Modleski nevertheless reproduces certain routine features of modernist mass-culture theory. 'The Search for Tomorrow in Today's Soap Operas' is, for a start, unfortunately reflectionist in the way it positions the soap opera as mirroring American women's presumed lives in the home. The essay reads certain narrative features of soaps, like withholding of knowledge and deferring of resolutions, as reflections of the female condition, the experience of 'waiting' in the home. But such deferral of resolution, of interruptability, have been features of serialised melodrama since Dickens discovered the public's affection for it in the 1830s, with the serial publication of *The Pickwick Papers*. Dickens' friend, Wilkie Collins, author of *The Woman in White, No Name, The Moonstone*, once remarked of his readership in relation to the suspense and mystery generated by each new instalment of his narratives: 'Make 'em cry, make 'em laugh, make 'em wait'.[17]

Modleski's essay also appears rather patronising of the American housewife, who is created as a unitary figure, unvarying across the continent, untouched by difference, to be evoked in that prime universalist discourse, psychoanalysis. How wonderful psychoanalysis is. With its assistance you can know that there is a universal feminine condition, and you can see into the consciousness and unconscious of millions and millions of American women.[18]

In a formalist way, we can apparently read off knowledge of audiences from the text itself, though that text is continuously referred and reduced to a psychological structure (women's 'central condition') outside the text. In true modernist style, in choosing psychoanalysis as privileged carrier of knowledge of a universal (female) spectator, Modleski's essay reveals no interest in any kind of ethnographic research on actual audiences – even the brief Modernist Ethnographic Glance.

Further, Modleski at times is rather condescending towards the soap opera as art, as if looking down at it from a great aesthetic height. There is her magisterial language in judging that rape was for the most part 'handled in a sensitive manner', or her confident knowledge of the inevitable limitations of soaps, as in her a priori decision that an 'issue like homosexuality, which could explode the family structure rather than temporarily disrupt it, is simply ignored'.[19] If we extend our sense of soaps to include nighttime serial melodrama, which also enjoys large female audiences, then we can think of how homosexuality was sympathetically featured in the Australian soap *Number 96* and in the American *Dynasty, thirty something, L.A. Law.*

At the same time, Modleski's espousal of soap narratives as possibly being in the 'vanguard' of all popular narrative art might remind us of the modernist ambition of finding and enforcing the one true aesthetic way. Modleski makes it clear that while the soaps address real needs, feminists have a 'responsibility to devise ways of meeting these needs that are more creative, honest, and interesting than the ones mass culture has supplied'.[20] Soaps will be in the vanguard, but only once properly ideologically purified to make them more creative, honest and interesting – qualities and capacities, along with sure knowledge of people's true needs, the avant-garde always already possesses.

Modleski's essay was strongly supported by fellow American critic Robert C. Allen, who contends that the textuality and intertextuality of soaps demand enormous knowledge and competence of their readers/spectators, a cultural capital that high culture critics of soap operas usually abysmally lack. For Allen the soaps are open not closed texts, for not only do they usually defeat narrative closure since their stories are never completed, but in their multiple viewpoints they also resist ideological closure. Allen, perhaps a little breathlessly, believes that the soap opera represents an alternative basis for narrative aesthetic pleasure in general, valuing 'complexity, repetition, and speech over simplicity, telos, and action'. We might feel that there is a danger here as with Modleski, of reintroducing modernist notions of cultural hierarchy and of the single way.

Allen is, however, critical of Modleski's reflection theory, as if there is a direct metaphorical correspondence of soap opera and the presumed life of a housewife and mother. Allen points to research showing how much daytime serials are watched by college students, male and female, and he argues in general that the soaps offer complex fields of semiotic possibilities that their increasingly diverse audiences can use in a variety of ways.[21]

Ethnography

Sustained ethnographic research finally came to cultural studies: in the 1980s the modernist assumption of the mass viewer's passivity and subjection was confronted by some fascinating audience and readership studies. Here I will focus on the work of a member of the Birmingham Centre for Contemporary Cultural Studies, Dorothy Hobson's early 1980s exploration of the drama that erupted around the long-running

English soap *Crossroads*, produced by the Midland commercial television company ATV in their studios in Birmingham, not far from Hobson's home.[22]

Crossroads, which came to an end in 1988, was watched by an audience of some 15 million regular viewers. The soap revolved around a motel, run by Meg Mortimer, its chief character. On 22 June 1981 ATV announced that Noele Gordon, who had played Meg Mortimer for seventeen years, since the beginning of the program, was to have her contract terminated. The decision to end the character of Meg Mortimer was, it appears, taken by Charles Denton, ATV's director of programs, on the grounds that her centrality was impeding the development of new storylines and characters. There was suspicion amongst viewers, however, that Denton was responding to pressure by the IBA, the draconian Independent Broadcasting Authority which supervised independent television in Britain and was in its lordly way consistently critical of what it saw as the low production and acting standards of *Crossroads*. The IBA had already angered *Crossroads* viewers by deciding in 1980 that the program should be cut back from four to three nights a week.[23]

The unexpected announcement about Meg Mortimer/Noele Gordon was followed in the week of 22–27 June by public outcry in support of the actress, with wide media coverage. Hobson, as she explains in her introduction, was at the time studying *Crossroads*' programming policies, production processes, and audience attitudes for a thesis; she decided to respond to the crisis at the motel by writing an account of the events related to her research. She was also given access to the thousands of letters sent to a Birmingham paper by viewers. Hobson quotes from these letters, in chapter seven, 'Whose Programme is it Anyway?', and they are very moving indeed, in particular as revealing the writers' sense of powerlessness as old people in relation to decisions they feel are so important to their lives.

The overwhelming majority of the letters protested the decision by ATV. Many were written by middle-aged or elderly women signing their letters OAP and giving their age. Most also complained that neither ATV nor the IBA should have such power over what audiences like to see and feel is their own program. As one letter writer said: 'I would like to ask IBA who exactly the programs are made for . . . Crossroads is one of the few decent programmes that viewers obviously want to watch and it is constantly being attacked by IBA . . . Judging from their decisions, the wrong people must be in control at IBA.' The letter writers could not understand why the show's popularity did not count with either Charles Denton or the IBA. Why weren't they as the audience being listened to?[24]

Roy Rene, courtesy of the Sydney Opera House Trust

Graham Kennedy, courtesy of TCN Channel 9

Some of the cast of *Prisoner*, courtesy of Grundy Television

Coopers & Lybrand Building, with the Queen Victoria Building in the
foreground, courtesy of Coopers & Lybrand

Monorail, courtesy of TNT Harbourlink

Harbourside, Darling Harbour, courtesy Darling Harbour Authority

Children playing in front of the Darling Harbour Exhibition Centre,
courtesy Darling Harbour Authority

View of the Pyrmont Bridge walkway to the Maritime Museum, Darling
Harbour, photography by David Moore, courtesy of Philip Cox, Richardson
Taylor and Partners

The IBA maintains, as Hobson puts it, an icy blast of control in relation to commercial television, and a particular aura of disdain towards *Crossroads*. She soon realised that the IBA was working on the Reithian legacy of the need for broadcasters to educate, inform and entertain, and that what counted was its, the IBA's, assessment of the continuing value of *Crossroads*, with audience popularity irrelevant. Hobson's record of interview with a bureaucrat from the IBA makes chilling reading.[25]

Hobson has, however, more sympathy for ATV's Charles Denton, respecting the professional basis of his decision to cut the Meg Mortimer character. Nevertheless, the hurt, distress, and anger of the *Crossroads* public was largely directed against him.

Hobson's book explores the production processes associated with making a long-running soap. But it is also a warm study of audience interaction with a program they like and have continuously liked. In chapter six, 'Everything Stops for Crossroads – Watching with the Audience', Hobson reports on her participant-observation in people's homes in the evenings when the show comes on, at dinner time. The program is largely watched by women, who are at their frantically busiest time of the day, preparing the meal, often interrupted by small children. Sometimes they can only listen to the dialogue in the kitchen, or watch it on the black and white on top of the fridge, occasionally diving in to look at the colour set in the living-room when particular fashions are on show, or if there is a wedding or other sort of unusual occasion. Hobson feels that some of the repetition in *Crossroads* is mindful of the viewing conditions of its female audience, of half watching, half listening. It is not much watched by men, and sometimes the women have to watch it over the hostility of their husbands; some of the women viewers feel the men don't like the way the characters reveal their emotions so explicitly.[26]

Hobson explains that her method was to watch with a family, and to conduct 'unstructured' interviews after the night's viewing. (Even when men watched, it was usually only the women who would go to the kitchen with Hobson to talk about the episode.) She wished particularly to know why the program was so popular, and also about areas where viewers might have been critical. She was aware that her being present changed the viewing situation; but she felt it changed the situation for the better, sharpening their awareness of why they watched the program. She was also very aware that with a viewing population of 15 million there is no single representative spectator, but a vast range of different readings.[27]

Discussion of any particular episode quickly moved on to discussion of the history of the program and its characters and stories. The women approached each episode not so much as a discrete item but as part of a long composite flow of narrative and drama. The interviews were accompanied by much laughter, just as when watching *Crossroads* there were many asides and jokes. Hobson feels that much of the popularity of *Crossroads* came from the women's appreciation of that ancient art, continuous storytelling, as in the oral tradition. The stop shot, the last shot after the credits, would hold the suspense over until the next episode. There was also the enjoyment of being familiar with the characters, characters often known over a very long period, yet often involved in unexpected turns of the narrative. Familiarity with characters became part of shared knowledge amongst family and friends, a kind of cultural capital, with viewers sometimes playing in conversation a kind of game with the serial, talking about the characters and their possible fates and adventures as if they were live people – while knowing that they were fictional, that they were enjoying a fantasy interest in the characters. As Hobson reminded any of her readers who assume a 'critical elitism', it is 'actually fun to talk about the characters in a soap opera', not a sign of psychological disorder.[28] We are a long way here from Q.D. Leavis' *Fiction and the Reading Public.*

Viewers knew theirs was a threatened pleasure, and were very well aware that the critics – often in the popular press they also read – despised *Crossroads.* But they remained unimpressed by the opinion of those they saw as so-called experts. ('I've read things up about various things the critics have said have been marvellous, and I've thought it's been tripe.') They felt such critics should be less moralistic, more open and pluralistic. Yet some of the women did feel guilty and apologetic that they were watching a program that critics and sometimes their own husbands treated in a derogatory way.[29]

Viewers' interest in the stories was also continuously critical. Here Hobson struck a blow against the routine modernist view that popular culture was escapist, as if the audience were seeking to escape from their problems by inhabiting a fantasy world. Rather, the viewers would relate the stories to their own lives. This didn't mean they didn't enjoy shows like *Dallas* that they thought were glamourised and over-the-top: they enjoyed them for being over-the-top. But they enjoyed *Crossroads* in a different way as down-to-earth and set in their own society. The viewers frequently questioned, though benevolently rather than derisively, the way stories, particularly about social or moral problems, would develop. They liked the way the soap presented social problems in a personalised way, through characters they knew, rather than abstractly (a point that supports Raymond Williams' worry about abstraction in the manner public television often presents social problems). When they did make critical comments, they were usually constructive, offering suggestions how a story could be improved if this or that character would do something else. For example, some viewers felt that now Kath had returned to work (part-time in the motel's kitchen), she should be given stronger storylines, to show she is now more independent of her chauvinistic husband. One particular story involved Alison, a young woman, an orphan, who lived with her uncle, an extremely religious and bigoted man. Alison's life was completely isolated and protected, until she began to meet the other characters in the serial. As it turns out, Alison permits herself to spend the night with the unscrupulous Chris, becoming pregnant. *Crossroads* followed this revelation by presenting many arguments going back and forth for and against an abortion. As frequently occurs in soaps, there is a magical solution to the dilemma, Alison experiencing a miscarriage, but Hobson argues that for the viewers it was the *exploration* of Alison's story and the issues of unwanted pregnancy and of abortion that were interesting, not the magical resolution. Indeed, some of the women felt the story went on far too long. Hobson concludes that *Crossroads'* viewers are also its most knowledgeable critics, and that their opinion of *Crossroads* should be accorded immensely greater weight in the broadcasting process.[30]

Crossroads: The Drama of a Soap Opera was, I think, a pathbreaking book. It provided much, much more than the Great Modernist Glance, that rapid action, yielding generalisations of remarkable breadth about modern mass consciousness, performed by Q.D. Leavis in a circulating library, Richard Hoggart in a milk-bar, Jameson in a hotel, Baudrillard in New York. Hobson's book sharply questioned modernist dicta that popular narratives were escapist; she feels that they are fantasy forms that explore social and moral problems as difficult dilemmas, inviting audience discussion and dissension. Hobson is pluralist, arguing not for a new cultural hierarchy where serial narratives are suddenly the new approved aesthetic answer, but for enjoying cultural difference between serial melodrama, a single television play, or documentary.

Pluralism – how rare a creature that has been in modernist-influenced cultural studies!

If there is a criticism to be made of Hobson's book, it is that she, like Williams, tends to minimise discussion of textuality. Since, in her view, there are as many interpretations of *Crossroads* as there are viewers, she presumably sees no point in offering an analysis of the text where her analysis would be just another interpretation. This is an exceedingly difficult area of dispute; my own feeling is that that which is the occasion of audience readings has to be explored in its specificity, its playing with genre and convention and narrative modes and other texts, in order to understand more fully the interactions of that text with its audience – while agreeing that the critic's interpretation will always be haunted.

Also, much anthropology in the 1980s and since (as in the work of Clifford and Markus) has been anxious, self-conscious, self-reflexive, about the status of its narratives, concerned to undermine previous claims to objective transparent accounts of interviewees' attitudes. Hobson could perhaps have been more cautious about the difficulties of ethnography and its methods.[31]

But then again, any analytic approach to anything has methodological difficulties. We don't have to pronounce ethnographic evocations as thereby of no value. Those, for example, who place mystical faith in psychoanalysis seem to have no trouble in accepting its speculations about that great unseen, the unconscious.[32]

Champion of pleasure

I hope it's clear that I'm not proposing the various theories so far outlined in this chapter as the new true way for cultural studies, as if all theoretical problems have been neatly solved. We might be worried by such a danger, however, in the writings of the next theorist to be discussed, that peripatetic student of popular culture, John Fiske. Fiske's academic journey has taken him from Britain to Australia to the United States. Fiske is also peripatetic, with the occasional sharp u-turn, in a theoretical sense, travelling from conventional Marxist modernism in the 1970s and early 1980s to a kind of rebirthing into postmodern theory in the later 1980s.

Certainly in 1983, in an essay on TV quiz shows, Fiske, passing through the antipodes, was still your regulation modernist mass-culture theorist, reflectionist, functionalist, structuralist. There is a 'mutually validating fit' between texts and social experience, a neat functional interface that accounts for these shows' popularity, because they offer various kinds of psychological compensation for the people who watch them. The genre is structured on 'central discourses'. There is, for example, the 'economic capitalist discourse'. Another is an educational discourse, for the shows are easily perceivable as 'symbolic reenactments of the examination system', whose dominant ideology of striving for success 'validates the accumulation of economic capital'. The shows of course also turn on luck, but luck, or lack of it, says Fiske, is crucial because it provides the subordinate with an acceptable reason for their subordination in a class-structured, free-enterprise, supposedly equal-opportunity society. Audience attitudes can be deduced from the structure of the texts. (Quiz show viewers for Fiske appear to be male; at any rate, they are almost invariably referred to in this essay with a 'he' or 'his'.) The audience, the subordinate in society, the underachievers, participate by proxy in the achievement of the contestant, and in identifying with the contestant's success they accept the hegemonic discourse of a social system they should be rising up in a revolutionary way to change. Quiz shows perform a compensatory function, the viewer being led to accept and approve of the very social order that destroys his self-image and self-esteem in the first place. The usual relations of the 'dominant' and 'subordinate' are thus continuously reproduced by such manipulation of self-image and self-esteem. In short, TV quizzes 'reproduce social power', the 'dominant ideology'. So for quizzes, so for popular culture in general.[33]

So Fiske in 1983. But new currents were moving, in textual readings and ethnography, challenging cultural studies to see audiences as active not passive. I might interpose an autobiographical note here. My personal memory of John Fiske was at the Australian Communication Conference, held in Sydney in July 1983. There I'd given with Ann Curthoys a paper, '"Nothing but nasty people behaving nastily in a nasty situation": A Discussion of *Prisoner*' (known in the United States as *Cell Block H*).[34] *Prisoner* concerned a group of women prisoners, of various ages, divided amongst themselves, and ever trying to negotiate relations with the screws, the largely female warders. The show was conspicuously sympathetic to the prisoners rather than authority. Very much liking *Prisoner*, and following its two episodes a week, we'd long pondered over the implications of the prisoners being the sympathetic centre of its drama. We gingerly suggested in our paper that one reason for the popularity of crime drama and indeed much else in popular culture, both ancient and modern, might lie in a principle of inversion, inversion as the reversal of the usual and accepted in any society, here relations of authority and power between warders and prison system as against the prisoners, many of whom, including lesbian characters, were constructed as indeed strong figures. We noted that the literary historian Ian Donaldson in his *The World Upside-Down* (1970) pointed to how much seventeenth-century English comic drama shows magistrates as fools, judges as incompetent, the rich as idiots; and that he traces this kind of inversion back to drawings prevalent in the Middle Ages of the normal world as upside-down, and to the custom of 'carnival' in traditional societies, the one day of the year when all values of authority and respect are flouted. As soon as question time began, we stared as none other than John Fiske half rose from his seat, red in face, and shouted in true orthodox modernist style how wrong we were to talk about World Upside Down like that, since it was obviously but a mere safety valve. The poor man was quite agitated, though we did read with some amusement in the local paper the next day that he'd grabbed a headline by telling a journalist that parents and teachers shouldn't necessarily see *Prisoner* as bad for children, that soaps might do good in the world. Shouted at one moment, apparently agreed with the next.

Yet perhaps it was at that very moment that a metamorphosis in Fiske's attitude to popular culture began unconsciously to stir, grow, and struggle to be born. In any case, a few years later it was clear a New Fiske had emerged, in books like *Television Culture* (1987), and the 1989 twins *Understanding Popular Culture* and *Reading the Popular*. Fiske tells us that *Understanding Popular Culture* is theoretical, with *Reading the Popular* more a series of applications.[35]

Understanding Popular Culture sets out to oppose previous approaches to popular culture, which were either celebratory, thus ignoring relations of power, or so emphasised the forces of domination that it seemed impossible that a 'genuine popular culture' could exist at all. *Understanding Popular Culture* will suggest a third way, which sees popular culture as vital and creative, yet always embedded in a site of struggle. This approach recognises popular culture as 'progressive', though not radical in the macro sense of fundamental challenge to capitalist society. This approach is 'essentially optimistic' about 'the people': 'Popular culture is made by the people, not produced by the culture industry.'[36]

Understanding Popular Culture's third way also challenges the view – we saw it in Frederic Jameson – that late capitalism, characterised by the omnipresence of commodities, leads to domination by consumerism. Fiske agrees that the relationship between popular culture and commerce and profit is highly problematic, but argues that users don't simply passively consume a commodity, they actively rework it to construct their own meanings of self, social identity and social relations (his chief example is people tearing their jeans). For we can say that while there is a continuing 'economic base' there is also a rival 'cultural economy', the circulation around commodities of 'meanings and pleasures'.[37]

Understanding Popular Culture certainly does not wish to omit the dimension of power. In Britain, Australia and the United States we live in an 'industrial society', with an 'industrial proletariat'. These societies are fundamentally identical, for they all have a 'common ideology', which is white, patriarchal, capitalist. There is, then, a mode of 'domination', variously evoked as 'the dominant system', the 'dominant ideology', 'the dominant classes', 'the system', 'the power-bloc', 'the powerful', the 'hegemonic', and power that is 'top-down'. Opposed to the 'power-bloc' are 'the people', but *Understanding Popular Culture* follows what we might call post-New Left social theory in de-emphasising the unifying power of class. People are to be characterised as much by gender, race, age, region, as by class. The 'people, the popular, the popular forces', we learn, do not compose a stable sociological category. Rather various individuals belong to different popular formations at different times, and as 'active agents' therefore enjoy fluid 'nomadic subjectivities', capable of adopting, alternately or simultaneously, contradictory positions. Because of such social differences, popular texts also have a 'polysemic openness', hospitable to different readings.[38]

Nevertheless, the people are the people, and what unites them is opposition and resistance to the overarching 'power-bloc'. 'Women's tastes' and 'proletarian tastes' are, for example, similar because the people in both are 'disempowered classes'. The people resist by making popular culture, the culture of the 'subordinated and disempowered'. The power-bloc might try to incorporate this popular culture (for example, by marketing torn jeans), but such victories are never more than partial. Popular culture is always in struggle with domination, in a kind of semiotic guerilla warfare (Fiske calls on Eco here), as the people wrest their own meanings and pleasures from commodities and the shows and stars they like. So the 'everyday life' of the people is the art of 'making do' with what the system provides (Fiske here calling on de Certeau), a series of raids, of poachings, of trickery, pluralising the meanings of cultural commodities and their advertising. We can now talk of the 'vulnerability' of the system. And we can summarise what happens in everyday life in terms of a series of antagonistic relationships, where the bourgeoisie is opposed by the proletariat, hegemony by resistance, social discipline by disorder, and 'top-down power' by something rather odd called 'bottom-up power'.[39]

In short, in one corner we have 'the people', in the other 'the power-bloc'.

Understanding Popular Culture is, nevertheless, careful to argue that the culture of the people is contradictory, in that what is resisted is necessarily present in the resistance to it. In popular culture there will always be traces of the forces of domination. We will always see the ongoing struggle between domination and the resistance of the subordinate, the struggle that is 'central' to our social system. Take *Dallas*. What *some* readers may decode in *Dallas* are the elements of the power-bloc imprinted in the show, values that are racist, capitalist, consumerist, sexist. But such readers are not popular readers, are 'not part of popular culture'. A popular reading of *Dallas* will read the show as a criticism of capitalism and patriarchy. Hence in any mass-culture text we can separate the elements of the dominant system from the popular oppositional elements. This paring away leads Fiske to declare that 'popular culture is always on the side of the subordinate', for popular culture is 'formed always in reaction to, and never as part of, the forces of domination'.[40]

In the 1983 essay on quiz shows Fiske saw pleasure as a lure for the subordinate, ensnaring them into sealing their subordination in sub-mission to the dominant ideology. By *Understanding Popular Culture* the judgement of pleasure seems to be simply reversed, emerging now as wholly and unproblematically Good. Culture is defined as being concerned, along with meanings and identities, with 'pleasures'. The 'cultural economy' is the circulation of 'meanings and pleasures'. Popular pleasures 'oppose the forces of domination', and popular pleasures can be categorised into two types, those that centre on the mind, producing contrary oppositional meanings, and those that centre around the body, tending to cause offence and scandal. (A mind/body distinction that we might think is startlingly simple, if not impossible.) In chapter four, 'Offensive Bodies and Carnival Pleasures', Fiske argues (with the help of British historians Malcolmson and Stedman Jones) that in the nineteenth century, with industrialisation and urbanisation, there were attempts by the dominant to suppress or make respectable the pleasures of the body seen as threats to the social order. Such 'carnivalesque' pleasures continued to resist, however, and here Fiske calls on Mikhail Bakhtin's *Rabelais and His World* (or at least its introduction), to give a brief summary of carnival, forms of inversion and parody characterised by laughter, excessiveness (particularly of the grotesque body and its functions), bad taste and offensiveness, and degradation. Carnival creates a festive world without rank or social hierarchy. Carnivalesque as a mode can, Fiske argues, be then applied not only to the anti-moralistic popular culture of the nineteenth century but to this century as well, as in amusement parks, video games, and, especially, TV's rock'n'wrestling.[41]

Fiske then agrees with Stallybrass and White, in their *The Politics and Poetics of Transgression* (1986), that carnival cannot be essentialised as mere safety-valve; rather, the picture is more complicated, carnival sometimes working to strengthen the social order, at other times disrupting it. Fiske feels that the traces of carnivalesque in today's popular culture act as a 'pleasurable ideal' for 'the people', that is both utopian and counter-hegemonic. In this sense, we can see the grotesque body of the TV wrestler as a metaphor for the body of the people, the subordinated body that exposes the 'fragility' of the social order.[42]

I don't think I'm alone in feeling that the danger of positions more sympathetic to popular culture becoming codified, formulaic, moving to the rhythms of orthodoxy, is unfortunately present in Fiske's writings of the latter 1980s. In particular in *Understanding Popular Culture* phrases from de Certeau's *The Practice of Everyday Life* (about people making do against the system) are invoked in a strangely repetitive, talismanic, almost incantatory way, as if Fiske's text is speaking in the accents of theology, or the pedagogical lesson.

While *Understanding Popular Culture* appears boldly to reach beyond the older modernist mass-culture approaches its author once so enthusiastically followed, there are nevertheless strong traces of prior categories. The book is curiously old-fashioned in the way it characterises the 'late capitalist' world. 'We live', says Fiske, in an 'industrial society'.[43] Do we? We might be cautious about theories that say we've surely arrived in a post-industrial age of computers, data, information, media, yet such theories are pointing to phenomena that surely question and modify an older sense of an 'industrial society' – Fiske sounds here like Nineteenth-Century Man.

A kind of rampant structuralism also pervades in the way oppositions are created. Throughout *Understanding Popular Culture* we learn that there is in the world a simple binary opposition between two central forces, the dominant ideology and popular culture, the power-bloc and the people, the system and the subordinate, top-down power and 'bottom-up power'.[44] Are things so limpidly clear? Don't binary distinctions always strain to homogenise opposing terms, effacing difference and complexity? Terms like dominant and resistant are altogether too polarising, too bloc-like, too unitary and unifying, too unsupple as categories. Dominant discourses, if they exist in a contestatory world, are themselves not monolithic and single in character, but multifarious and contradictory. What happens in culture, 'high', radical or popular, is too ideologically 'mixed', too discursively messy, to be easily cast into the binary either/or boxes of domination and resistance.[45]

In the postmodern world, we might say, it is never easy to distinguish between the mainstream and the oppositional, the conforming and the unconventional, the majority and minority view – between centres and margins that are ever shifting and uncertain.

At one point we find *Understanding Popular Culture* arguing that 'racial dominance' is opposed by 'black separatism', and by the manner black high-school students opt out of the 'whitist' educational system, so that 'success in that system can be seen as a betrayal of blackness'.[46] Fiske is assuming that there is a single unified African-American position on the desirability of separatism or of opting out of an educational system that he refers to in a totalising, unitary way as 'whitist'. We might very well wonder if there is not, on the contrary, division, difference, debate, dispute, uncertainty, controversy, on such issues.

Understanding Popular Culture argues at another point that advertising usually fails in 'its tasks' (tasks presumably somehow set for it by some sort of central command-station of the unified power-bloc), which is to contain social diversity within the needs of capitalism. He gives as an example of scepticism towards advertising some Sydney school children turning a beer ad into a scatalogical playground rhyme. Then he offers another instance of successful resistance to advertising:

> Similarly, the kids who sang jeeringly at a female student of mine as she walked past them in a short skirt and high heels, 'Razzmatazz, Razzmatazz, enjoy that jazz' (Razzmatazz is a brand of panty hose, and its jingle accompanied shots of long-legged models wearing the brightly coloured products) were using the ad for their own cheeky resistive subcultural purposes: they were far from the helpless victims of any subliminal consumerism, but were able to turn even an advertising text into their popular culture.[47]

It's difficult not to feel uneasy reading this passage. A group of 'kids' (how old? of what gender? all male?) jeer at one of the author's female students because she is wearing a short skirt and high heels, and hence apparently reminds them of an advertising image of femininity which they wish to resist. Our author doesn't seem to feel the slightest sympathy for his female student as she's being publicly jeered at. But perhaps he shouldn't feel sympathy. The female student, in dressing as in an ad, had, according to the binary logic of *Understanding Popular Culture*, situated herself within the dominant ideology, and therefore gone over to the enemy: she now deserves to be excoriated, publicly humiliated. She's become a non-person, to be equated with the advertising image she's apparently accepted. She doesn't exist, she's just a walking ad. She's a mere signifier to be openly despised. Meanwhile, we're immediately to applaud the 'kids' because they have revealed that they belong to an opposing 'popular culture', and we admire that popular culture because it jeers at a female student, and, by implication, is telling her she shouldn't wear a short skirt and high heels.

(It's perhaps not that surprising that *Understanding Popular Culture*, while avowedly in opposition to patriarchy, can refer to a young woman in a jeans ad as 'a girl'.[48])

We're to applaud what the 'kids' are enjoying doing to Fiske's female student as a *pleasure* of popular culture, and such pleasures are always to be admired because they are so 'resistive'. It's hard to resist, as you read *Understanding Popular Culture*, a gathering feeling of unease about its insistence on the centrality of pleasure to culture.

Is pleasure an adequate term to evoke the textuality of popular culture? In 'The Search for Tomorrow in Today's Soap Operas', Tania Modleski notes that at the time of writing (1979) rape had recently been an issue in a daytime soap. Is drama about rape the occasion of 'pleasure', or do we perhaps need more nuanced, differentiated, heterogeneous terms? Amongst other traumas and suffering, *Days of Our Lives* has explored the long decline associated with alcoholism, with the young Hispanic character April Ramirez (Lisa Howard) declaring to an AA meeting, at the end of one episode, just before the credits, 'I'm an alcoholic'. Do we feel 'pleasure' as our response to this moment? Of course soaps involve pleasures, of mystery, suspense, cliffhangers, extravagance, excess, extremes, comedy, parody, self-parody. But equally they involve, in the continuous exploration of social, moral and psychological issues, pathos and sadness, the wrought intensity of melodrama. The ideals of community, friendship, love, fulfilment, which are counterposed to the harshness of fate, are continually deferred, or if achieved, almost immediately interrupted and threatened and destroyed again.

In general *Understanding Popular Culture* projects a happy world. People move between various subjectivities and identities in an easy nomadic way, enjoying the various pleasures of resisting and opposing. As Meaghan Morris has wondered of the New Fiske's writings, where in this happy world is deprivation, loss, pain, torment, anger, fear, defeat, death?[49]

For those of us interested in moving beyond the tired certainties of modernist mass-culture theory, the New Fiske's writings can perhaps serve as a spectacular negative exemplar, of admiring popular culture too easily and giving it a single ideological meaning, populism (the triumph of the people's culture). When I began in the early 1980s to offer positive analyses of quiz and game shows and then to apply Bakhtinian theories of carnival to popular literature, melodrama, television, I was so conscious of how powerful, how set, how imprinted, modernist judgements on mass-culture texts were as reproducing social conformity, that, looking back, I almost certainly on this and that occasion slid too far the other way, into the jaws of populism.[50] With the useful example of Fiske before me, the New Fiske as disturbing *doppelgänger*, I'll try, in the chapters that follow, not to be your Happy Postmodern Theorist, seeing only pleasure upon pleasure unto the bright horizon.

PART THREE

Carnival

CHAPTER THIRTEEN

Bakhtin's Carnival

True understanding in literature and literary scholarship is always historical and personified.

Mikhail Bakhtin,
'Toward a Methodology for the Human Sciences' [1]

The number of people in fancy dress begins to increase. Young men disguised as women of the lower classes in low-necked dresses are usually the first to appear. They embrace the men, they take intimate liberties with the women, as being of their own sex, and indulge in any behaviour which their mood, wit or impertinence suggests.

One young man stands out in my memory. He played the part of a passionate, quarrelsome woman perfectly. 'She' went along the whole length of the Corso, picking quarrels with everyone and insulting them, while her companions pretended to be doing their best to calm her down.

Here a Pulcinella comes running along with a large horn dangling from coloured strings around his thighs. As he talks to women, he manages to imitate with a slight, impudent movement the figure of the ancient God of Gardens – and this in holy Rome! – but this frivolity excites more amusement than indignation . . .

Since the women take as much pleasure in dressing up as men as men do in dressing up as women, many of them appear wearing the popular costume of Pulcinella, and I must confess that they often manage to look very charming in this ambiguous disguise.

Goethe at the Carnival in Rome, 1788 [2]

Women who masturbate . . . can only be finally cured through an operation on the nose if they truly give up this bad practice.

Wilhelm Fliess, On the Causal Connection between the Nose and the Sexual Organ, *1902* [3]

For much of this century, modernism has denied that mass culture, as the product of the industrial and now post-industrial eras, could have any significant positive continuities between its mass-produced images and the popular culture of pre-industrial times. Further, modernism maintains that history shows the necessity of aesthetic hierarchy, a hierarchy of forms and genres, with the tragic as supreme effect, the summit of art, answering to the fallen nature of the contemporary world, where time delivers defeat, fate destroys, and every relationship is destined to disappointment, menace, failure, loss. Until it knew better, modern mass culture would have to languish at the bottom of the pyramid of genres that constitutes true culture. When such cultural history and hierarchical notions of the aesthetic began to be questioned in the 1970s and increasingly in the 1980s, there was renewed interest in various thinkers of the past offering alternative visions, not least the Russian cultural theorist we've been alighting on in various chapters already.

Bakhtin

His biographers Katerina Clark and Michael Holquist tell us that Bakhtin (1895–1975) participated as a young scholar in the intellectual ferment of the Soviet Union in the 1920s, debating prominent theories of the time, Russian Formalism, Freudianism, and Marxism and the philosophy of language. Much of this early work appeared under other names. His study of Dostoevsky, this time in his own name, came out in 1929, but only after Bakhtin's arrest during a purge of Leningrad intellectuals. He was saved from certain death in a labour camp by a favourable review of the Dostoevsky book by Lunacharsky – just in time since Lunacharsky himself was about to be replaced as Commissar of Enlightenment. (In 1929 there was established a Committee for the Purging of the Institutions of the Commissariat of Enlightenment.) Bakhtin's sentence was reduced to relatively mild exile first in Kazakhstan, and then various provincial towns for the rest of his working life, until his retirement in 1961. Through the Stalin era, Bakhtin published only one article, about bookkeeping on collective farms, which appeared in a trade journal. At the end of the 1930s, when the worst of the great purges was over, he tried to re-enter the mainstream of intellectual life by writing a dissertation on Rabelais. But when the war came, defence of the thesis was put off. As well, publication of a book on the novel of education was terminally delayed, when the building which housed the publisher was bombed, with Bakhtin's manuscript destroyed. During the war years, when paper was scarce, Bakhtin used most of his own copy of the manuscript as tobacco paper. It was not until the early 1950s that the thesis on Rabelais was accepted. As Clark and Holquist say, in the eyes of the world, Bakhtin had effectively died in 1929.[4]

At the end of his teaching career, young Soviet scholars from the Gorky Institute of World Literature began to take renewed interest in Bakhtin, which led to the publication in 1963 of the second edition of the Dostoevsky book, under the title *Problems of Dostoevsky's Poetics*. Its reappearance, followed in 1965 by publication of the work on Rabelais, brought him to prominence. Bakhtin was able in the last years of his life to move to Moscow. In 1975, the year he died, appeared some of his essays on the novel that he'd first written in the 1930s (translated into English as *The Dialogic Imagination*). Translations of Bakhtin's works appeared in France in the late 1960s, followed by translations into English. By the 1980s Bakhtin's writings were being welcomed worldwide as fascinating theories of language, genre, carnival, making us wrestle with notions like the monologic, the dialogic, polyphony, heteroglossia, carnivalesque.[5]

As Clark and Holquist also make clear, it is important to recall the specific textual history in Russia of Bakhtin's arguments, why he wrote when he did, even if the work wasn't published until decades later. Bakhtin turned to the novel, for example, in the 1930s when it became the focus of government efforts to homogenise Soviet literary institutions. In 1932 all authors were required to join the new Union of Writers, and in the years following there was a concerted effort to install a stylistic as well as institutional unity, with socialist realism being declared the single necessary aesthetic for the Soviet state. Statements about socialist realism, including by Lukács, were published in 1934/5, and Bakhtin responded with his own theories. In his 1929 Dostoevsky book, Bakhtin had argued for the quality of 'polyphony' in Dostoevsky's novels, that they were multi-voiced, swarming with discourses that continuously collide without resolution, and where characters are, in Bakhtin's words, 'not voiceless slaves' but '*free* people, capable of standing *alongside* their creator, capable of not agreeing with him and even of rebelling against him'. Dostoevsky's novels are dialogic, keeping alive the interaction, interplay, interpenetration, the surprising recombining, of discourses, languages, genres, never resolving such play into a single finalised ('monologic') meaning.[6]

In 1929 Bakhtin hails Dostoevsky as the unique creator of the polyphonic novel. In his essays on the novel in the 1930s, however, Bakhtin came to see such polyphony as a culmination of what has always been present in the novel as a special kind of aesthetic energy or force. Bakhtin opposed conventional literary history, which suggests the novel is a recent form, arising perhaps with Cervantes, or with Defoe and

Richardson, until we recognise the novel proper in the psychological novels of the nineteenth century. For Bakhtin, the novel can be seen as possessing a long ancestry in European literature and thought, descending from antiquity, visible in the way Socrates emphasises the dialogic in discussion, and present in early genres like the menippean satire, the utopia, and the confession. The novel for Bakhtin is not defined so much in terms of any specific manifestation, as in the novelistic impulse in general, in 'novelness'. The novel is that heteroglot force in literary history that reveals the limits of any set system or hierarchy of genres, that witnesses the attack on higher forms by lower, that denies the purity of genres, dissolves their predefined borders, mixes them, 'novelises' them.[7]

Further, polyphony and the novelising energy are now extended by Bakhtin into general philosophical propositions about the nature of language, society, the world, particularly in the notion of 'heteroglossia', the operation of multi-voiced discursive forces at work in whole culture systems. For Bakhtin heteroglossia is clearly evident in the workings of language, where the fiction of a unitary national language is always trying to contain the stratification, diversity and randomness produced in the daily clash of professional, class, generational, and period utterances. Existence itself is heteroglossia, is a force field created in the general ceaseless Manichaean struggle between centripetal forces, which strive to keep things together, unified, the same; and centrifugal forces, which strive to keep things various, separate, apart, different. Bakhtin clearly relishes difference, variety, alterity, plurality, otherness, randomness, but he is very aware of the enormous power of forces which insist on system, structure, centralisation, hierarchy, unity. In the Soviet Union of the 1930s, in exile, often ill and short of food, unable to publish, for periods barred from teaching, anticlerical yet deeply interested in the philosophy of religion, prevented from entering within a 100 kilometres of Moscow, in the Stalinist night, it would be difficult not to be so impressed.[8]

Clark and Holquist argue that the thesis on Rabelais also had a specific textual history. Bakhtin's interest in the folk and in laughter was his response to the political importance being placed on such topics by the two leading Soviet intellectuals, Lunacharsky and Gorky. Lunacharsky, not long before his death in 1933, had set up a government Commission for the Study of Satiric Genres, and was himself at work on a book called *The Social Role of Laughter*; in 1935 his 1931 speech to the Academy of Sciences on the historical importance of satire and carnival was published. Lunacharsky argued that carnival is a safety valve for passions that might otherwise erupt in revolution; the lower orders would let off steam in a harmless, temporary event.

Meanwhile Gorky told the first All Union Congress of Writers in 1934 that culture workers should model their positive heroes on the heroes of folklore. Folk artists were urged to include Lenin and Stalin in their pictures in traditional style. Folk poets were to create epics singing the achievements of the new Soviet man, of Stakhanovite workers, of pilots. It was this official appropriation of folklore, folk culture being made to celebrate power and the state and the state's desires and designs and discourses and view of history, that sets the context for Bakhtin's thesis, begun in 1937, on Rabelais' great sixteenth-century novel *Gargantua and Pantagruel.* There was an appreciable degree of political allegory in the thesis and then book, *Rabelais and His World,* a silent comparison of the Holy Roman Empire and Catholic church/state nexus in France in the 1530s and the Soviet state of the 1930s. Bakhtin wished to restore a sense of folk satirical laughter as involving vigorous bodily imagery and as historically corrosive, not supportive, of state power, official discourse, puritanism.[9]

Carnival and folk culture

Rabelais and His World combines evocation of carnival and its market-place and public square games, feasts, processions, masks, dramas, its philosophies and cosmologies, and at the same time, discussion of the historical significance of these events and notions.

In the Middle Ages, *Rabelais and His World* argues, there were 'walls' between cultures, official and unofficial, including between languages – for example, Latin and the vernacular. The culture of folk humour had been shaped over many centuries, defending the 'people's creativity' in non-official forms, in verbal expression and spectacle. Throughout medieval times official Christianity had always to struggle with, and frequently recognise and permit, the continuing force of folk culture. The Church adapted the timing of Christian feasts to local pagan celebrations, celebrations linked to older cults and traditions of laughter, including the traditions of the Roman Saturnalia and other forms of Roman legalised folk humour.[10]

Certain religious cults, inherited from the East or from local pagan rites, were continued and allowed, often alongside official church rituals. There was, for example, the 'feast of the ass', which might take place near the precincts of the church. The 'feast of the ass' supposedly commemorated Mary's flight to Egypt with the infant Jesus, but the central protagonist of the story would be an ass, with each part of the mock mass being accompanied by braying, including replacing Amen with a good bray. The ass is one of the most ancient and lasting symbols of what *Rabelais and His World,* in a favourite phrase, refers to as the 'material bodily lower stratum', evident in the widespread ass-mimes of antiquity, prominent in Apuleius' *The Golden Ass*, and reverberating in medieval carnival and charivari. There was also the 'feast of fools' (stubbornly persisting particularly in France), celebrated by schoolmen and lower clergy, a parody and travesty of the rituals and symbols of the official commemorations they coincided with. Featured were boisterous masquerades, improper dances, gluttony, indecent gestures, disrobing, drunken orgies on the altar table. A clownish abbot, bishop, or archbishop was chosen for the day, and in churches directly under the pope's jurisdiction a mock pontiff was proclaimed. During the Easter season, following the period of lenten sadness, laughter, jokes, stories and anecdotes of a bodily kind were permitted even in church. Besides 'Easter laughter' there was also a tradition of 'Christmas laughter', involving extremely worldly songs, often sung to street tunes; sometimes religious hymns were combined with worldly tunes (which is why, Bakhtin says, the French Noël could later develop into one of the most popular genres of the revolutionary street song). Both Easter and Christmas laughter can be linked with the Roman tradition of popular Saturnalia.[11]

Parodic literature also flourished in the Middle Ages, produced by lower-class and middle-class clerics, schoolmen, students, and members of corporations. Parodies of the sacred were composed to be read out at times of school and university recreation, which usually coincided with feast days, in an atmosphere of freedom and licence. The oldest grotesque parody, 'Cyprian's supper' (fifth or sixth century) transformed all sacred history from Adam to Christ into a fantastic clownish banquet. In centuries following there were parodies of prayers, hymns, litanies, liturgy, gospels, monastic rules, ecclesiastical decrees, papal bulls and encyclicals, sermons, wills, epitaphs, of legal texts and laws, of proverbs and sayings of common wisdom. Not a single saying of the Old and New Testaments was left unchallenged so long as it could provide some hint of equivocal bodily suggestion. We find, says Bakhtin, this centuries-old culture of parody in abundant presence in Rabelais' novel, as in the figure of Friar John, the incarnation of the low clergy in travestied form. Friar John is a connoisseur of reinterpreting any sacred text in terms of eating, drinking and the erotic, including making jokes about noses, in an era where the size of the phallus was commonly (even by physicians) surmised from the size of the nose.[12]

Rabelais and His World suggests, however, that as the Middle Ages proceeded, activities like the feast of fools became only semi-legal, and by the end of the medieval period were banned completely from the churches, although continuing to exist in the streets and taverns, where they were absorbed into the merriment and amusements of carnival.

Laughter was eliminated from religion, from state ceremonials, etiquette, and from the genres of high speculation. Medieval ideology was constituted in asceticism, sin, atonement, suffering, as well as in the sombre character of the feudal regime itself, with its oppression and intimidation. The true, the good and the meaningful could only be sought by way of religious awe, humility, remorse, sorrow, in an overall tone of icy petrified seriousness.[13]

Medieval people had to become Janus-faced, leading two lives that coexisted in their consciousness: respect for the intolerant, the one-sided tone of seriousness characteristic of official culture, and a 'second festive life'. There were in effect two worlds, where, in parodic form, festive life built its own mock church and mock state. In medieval art, as in thirteenth- and fourteenth-century illuminated manuscripts, would be found pious illustrations of legends of the saints, alongside free designs representing chimeras, comic devils, jugglers, masquerade figures, and parodic scenes. The pious and the carnivalesque grotesque existed side by side, but never merged.[14]

In the Middle Ages, Bakhtin says, seriousness inspired distrust, but it also impressed people with its prohibitions and violence: 'As a spokesman of power, seriousness terrorised, demanded, and forbade.' It inspired fear, weakness, humility, and submission. The consciousness of medieval people could not free itself from such weakness and awe, except in the isolated occasions of festivity, which were often enough but 'mere festive luxury'. Bakhtin argues that for folk laughter to break out of its isolation, it had to enter the world of 'great literature'.[15]

For Bakhtin it was during the Renaissance, as the medieval feudal and theocratic order disintegrated, and the vernacular in literature was adopted, that the thousand-year-old tradition of folk humour broke into culture generally, in a remarkable flowering throughout the society, evident not only in the festivals of carnival, that might take up to some three months of every year in European cities and towns, but also in the 'sphere of great literature and high ideology', in Boccaccio, Rabelais, Cervantes, Shakespeare. Folk humour could now 'rise to the high level of literature and ideology and fertilise it', while being itself fertilised by humanist knowledge, science, worldly political experience, and advanced literary techniques, as in Rabelais (c.1494–c.1553). As 'lower genres' penetrated the 'higher levels of literature', official seriousness and fear could be challenged, could be abandoned in everyday life.[16]

In Bakhtin's view, from the interaction and mutual fertilising of medieval laughter and Renaissance high literature and learning, there developed a 'new free and critical historical consciousness'.[17] Rabelais' novel *Gargantua and Pantagruel* (c.1532–4) is the supreme meeting place for this encounter, and we know that for Bakhtin the novel, or novelising force, is the literary form most hospitable to such heterogeneity. We might also note that for someone living in a society of official socialism which was determined to eliminate the market from history, Bakhtin interestingly defends the market in early modern Europe, or at least defends the carnivalesque activities that are enjoyed in the marketplace. Indeed, he sees what we might think of as the cultural schizophrenia of the Middle Ages as inhering in the strict separation of official serious culture from the marketplace. The cultural heterogeneity of the Renaissance, the free mixing of genres and modes, bursts forth when this division breaks down.[18]

Carnival in the Renaissance

In *Rabelais and His World* Bakhtin recalls and analyses Goethe's description in his *Italian Journey* of the carnival in Rome of January 1788, a carnival that while late in European cultural history still revealed, Bakhtin feels, its 'central philosophy'.[19]

Goethe records his first-hand impressions made during the furious activity of the carnival. The Roman Carnival, Goethe points out, is not a festival given for the people, but one the people give themselves. The state makes very few preparations for it and contributes next to nothing. For the time of the carnival, the difference between the social orders seems to be abolished, everyone accosts everyone else, and the insolence and licence of the feast is balanced only by a universal good humour. Romans celebrate a victory over history, that Christianity did not succeed in abolishing the festival of the ancient Saturnalia.

Carnival assembles in the Corso, named from the horse races which conclude each day's entertainments. (The horses, *barberi*, foreign bred, are specially trained, and the prize is a *palio*, a pole with a piece of gold or silver cloth.) In the Corso of Carnival, long and narrow, packed with people, a person is both actor and spectator, unlike in the religious festivals in Rome. At a given signal, shortly after noon, festivities begin, people now having leave to be as mad and foolish as they like. Chairs are placed all along the pavements, and the street now looks more like a decorated gallery, a room full of acquaintances. People in masks and fancy dress appear, in enormous variety and exaggeration. They dress in the workaday clothes of other classes, or put on more elaborate fancy dress as peasant girls, women from Frascati, fishermen, Neapolitan boatmen, Greeks. Some put on masks of beggars or ghosts. Some dress in the *tabarro*, modelled on the black cassocks of monks. Young girls in masks mischievously flourish little brooms made from the blossoms of reeds in the faces of strangers and acquaintances who are not wearing masks. There are hundreds of Pulcinelle, and also people dressed as a *quacchero*, an imitation of the Quaker costume; the *quacchero*, looking very like the *buffo caricato* of Italian comic opera, usually plays the part of a vulgar fop, or a silly, infatuated, and betrayed old fool. One Pulcinella walks around as a cuckold, with moveable horns, stopping under the window of a newly married couple to shoot out both horns to their full length. Another Pulcinella has a birdcage instead of a cap on his head, in which a pair of birds, dressed as a monk and a lady, hop about. A group of Pulcinelle elect one of their own as a mock king, with a sceptre. Someone wearing a two-faced mask gets stuck in the crowd, and no one knows whether he is coming or going. As we saw in our epigraph from *Italian Journey*, women like dressing as men, and men as women. Goethe observes in a side street a group of young fellows, some dressed as women, who stage a grotesque drama, with one of them as if in an advanced stage of pregnancy; a mock fight breaks out, they attack each other with huge knives of silver cardboard, until the pregnant woman takes to moaning as if in labour, and brings forth a misshapen creature into the world, to the great amusement of onlookers. The carnival finishes with the *Moccoli*, the fire festival, where everyone carries a lighted candle, competes to blow each other's out, crying, 'death to you'; all ages and classes contend furiously with each other in the battle. The end of carnival comes with people leaving in a hurry to feast on the meat that will be forbidden them after midnight.

After the carnival is over, on Ash Wednesday, Goethe reflects on the experience. Carnival, he feels, is like life itself, unpredictable, unsatisfactory, problematic: the participant struggles in the thick crowd to retain a sense of free will; and carnival liberty and equality are only to be enjoyed in the intoxication of madness, desire only in the presence of danger. He is left feeling very uneasy.[20]

In *Rabelais and His World* Bakhtin writes with delight of Goethe's evocation, but he also criticises Goethe for trying, in his final Ash Wednesday reflections, to limit the philosophy of carnival to its meaning for how the individual as individual feels during the celebrations, rather than acknowledging collective, universal and 'cosmic' meanings: the broader meanings Bakhtin himself will draw out, as he tracks back and forth between the carnival of early modern Europe and Rabelais' novel.[21] The bulk of *Rabelais and His World* is devoted to exploring the philosophical meanings of various aspects of carnival's complex activities and images. What are these philosophical meanings, these cosmologies? What is the 'new free and critical historical consciousness' revealed in the nexus of folk laughter and high thought?

We can begin with the way Bakhtin analyses marketplace banquet imagery, of ancient and medieval provenance, but coming to historical fruition, to complexity, sophistication and rich nuancing, in Renaissance carnival and in Rabelais. Marketplace feasting has nothing in common, Bakhtin insists, with static private life and mere individual well-being. Carnival feasting is social, public and collective, a 'banquet for all the world'. Banquet images, of food, drink, swallowing, have a 'gay and triumphant tone'. Such feasting and associated legends with their hyperbole and fantastical exaggeration prefigure utopia, a utopia of 'abundance and rebirth'. There were many popular legends of giants (including the Gargantua story, the direct source of Rabelais' novel) involving utopian images of food, in lands of gluttony and idleness. Such lands, that might feature mountains of butter, rivers or seas of milk with pâtés and dumplings floating in them, and hot pies springing from the ground like mushrooms, belong to everyone. The Saturnian age had returned to earth.[22]

The official feast was a 'consecration of inequality', with a visual emphasis on rank. The abundance of the marketplace banquet was an inclusive utopia, a 'harvest' of equality and hence of 'social justice', as against class, privilege, and hierarchy. The spirit of feasting reveals a 'democratic spirit'.[23]

Images of food are connected to images of procreation, of fertility, growth, birth, and to the 'grotesque body', one of Bakhtin's key concepts in *Rabelais and His World*: the body in and of carnival, the collective body of the people as a whole, is always interacting with the wider natural world. In eating the body swallows, devours, rends the world apart, is enriched and grows at the world's expense. In eating, collective humanity's encounter with the world is not ascetic and suffering, it is triumphant, a victory over the world, devouring it without being devoured. Humanity in carnival is not afraid of the world, but defeats it in eating of it. The carnival feast celebrates this victory.[24]

Festive eating is always ambivalent, involving death, the devouring of the world through the mouth, and new life, regeneration. That ambivalence, of carnival as both destructive and creative, death and new life, Bakhtin will continually insist on. It is like 'time' itself, which kills and gives birth in a single act.[25]

The banquet can also be the occasion of a special carnival form of conversation, table talk, related to the antique symposium, as in Plato. Festive speech is free and jocular, including the right to be frank, a frankness that dooms and destroys the authority of all exalted and official genres, with their sanctimonious seriousness, their mysticism and 'abstract-idealistic sublimation', their fear and piousness. Speech, the word, is liberated into free play, especially free play with the sacred, nearly always including elements of parody and travesty of the Last Supper. Here was not the language of the church, palace, courts, of the

aristocracy, nobles, high-ranking clergy and the top burghers, dominated by hierarchy and etiquette. Marketplace language established a
realm of familiar speech, combinations of praise and affectionate
abuse.[26]

The 'grotesque symposium' of carnival freely blends the profane and
sacred, the lower and higher, the spiritual and the material.[27]

Bakhtin stresses the importance of the language of carnival generally.
Again, remarkably for someone living under socialism, Bakhtin
enthuses over early forms of advertising, especially the famous *cris* of
Paris, loud advertisments for merchandise called out by the Paris street
vendors, composed to a certain versified form, and popular for
centuries. At fairs in early modern Europe such cries had to compete
with the announcements of the barker, apothecary, actor, quack, and
astrologer. We must remember, Bakhtin says, that sound then played a
prominent role in everyday life and culture ('even greater than in our
days, in the time of radio'). Not only was advertising oral and loud, but
all announcements, orders, and laws were made in such form. The *cris
de Paris* would praise food and wines offered for sale, with every food
and dish having its own rhyme and melody. The cries represented in
themselves a noisy kitchen and a loud, abundantly served banquet, a
symphony of feasting.[28]

The marketplace of carnival had its own unofficial speech, of oaths,
curses, profanities and improprieties. Oaths were the more attractive to
use since they were often directly forbidden by the church and
government. Much of this language was scatological, seeing the human
in terms of the 'material bodily lower stratum'. Images of drenching in
urine and tossing of excrement were common in ancient times, as in
Heracles pictured on antique vases, lying drunk outside the door of a
paramour, with an old procuress emptying a chamber pot on his head.
Such images continued through medieval times and into the
Renaissance, as in an episode in Rabelais where Gargantua immerses
the pilgrims in his watery excess.[29]

Oaths and suchlike debased the person addressed by referring their
character to the lower bodily stratum, but the genital area was also the
realm of that which fertilises and regenerates, and so is always linked to
a positive element, to images of birth, fertility, renewal, welfare. In the
laughter of scatological language the terror of death is defeated.[30]

Images of inversion, world upside-down, topsy-turvy, vice versa, were
features of banquet festivity as well as of carnival activity in general,
symbolised in the king's attributes being travestied in mock royalty; at
nearly every popular banquet, especially in France, ephemeral kings
and queens were elected. Here again the Renaissance was continuing
medieval tradition, with stories where the king bears children while the

queen fights a war, a carnivalesque war, with cheeses, baked apples, and mushrooms. Revellers wearing clothes turned inside out, trousers slipped over the head, symbolised the overturning of hierarchy, not only in terms of class and caste, but also of men and women, fathers and sons.[31]

Indeed, in carnival man as husband and father is object of comic derision. Bakhtin refers in particular to French traditions which opposed the medieval ascetic view of woman as the incarnation of sin, the temptation of the flesh. In the popular conception woman possesses the carnivalesque ambivalence of the lower bodily stratum; she brings those who exalt themselves down to earth, lends a bodily substance to things, and destroys. But she is also the principle that gives birth. Woman is shown in contrast to the limitations of her partner, her husband, lover, or suitor; she is a foil to his avarice, jealousy, stupidity, hypocrisy, bigotry, sterile senility, false heroism, and abstract idealism. Woman represents the undoing of pretentiousness, of all that is finished and completed. Woman is the inexhaustible vessel of conception that dooms all that is old and terminated. In the imagery of cuckoldry, the old husband is uncrowned, the new welcomed in a new act of procreation: the old husband, symbolic figure of the old year, the receding winter, is stripped of his robes, mocked, beaten, and chased away. The laughter involving the young woman who cuckolds the old husband is at once mocking, destructive, and joyfully reasserting.[32]

In classical mythology and drama there is a fear of the son, he who will seize the throne from the king his father, in the Oedipus myth, or in the myth of Rhea, Chronos' wife, who not only gives birth to Zeus but hides the child from Chronos' persecutions, thus ensuring the new life of the world. The fear of the son is also embodied in carnival, as in the passage in *Italian Journey* where Goethe, observing the closing fire festival, sees a boy blow out his father's candle, shouting, '*Sia ammazzato il Signore Padre!*': Death to you, sir father! In vain the old man scolds him for this outrageous behaviour. The boy claims the freedom of the evening and curses his father all the more vehemently. Bakhtin notes that this admirable carnivalesque interjection of the boy merrily threatening his father with death and blowing out his candle needs no further comment.[33]

Masking was extremely important in carnival, in part to partake of world upside-down, in part to loosen any fixed daily identity, to enjoy identity as fluid and open, changing and changeable, as becoming not static being. The mask, descending from ancient cult and ritual, is, Bakhtin argues, of the essence of carnival's grotesque humour, intimately related to comic gestures, grimaces, caricatures, eccentric postures, parodies. In its intricate multiform symbolism it is the negation of

uniformity and similarity. It rejects 'conformity to oneself'. It is connected to 'gay relativity', to the joy of change and reincarnation, to
transition and metamorphosis. In this conception, masking permits
diversity and differentiation, a play with identities.[34]

Yet, Bakhtin argues, masking also enables collective and historic
meanings that Goethe in *Italian Journey* could not see. The carnival
crowd in the marketplace or streets, Bakhtin feels, is not merely a
crowd. It is the people as a whole, organised in their own way, outside of
and contrary to the usual forms of 'coercive socioeconomic and
political organisation', suspended for the time of the festivity. Through
costume and mask people can cease to be themselves, they can
'exchange bodies', and so become an indissoluble part of the collectivity and community. Further, in the pressing throng, the sensual
physical contact of bodies, individuals feel they are of the people's mass
body. The body of the people in the carnival square is aware of its
uninterrupted continuity and unity in time, is conscious of its 'relative
historic immortality'. In Bakhtin's view, Goethe could not see that such
awareness of time is related to the people's awareness of being part,
through the language of the lower bodily stratum, of the eternal
processes of the natural world, a cosmic relationship to the earth, sun
and star-filled sky.[35]

Another key philosophical element of carnival is self-parody. Carnival
imagery, talk, feasting, dramas, not only parodied official conceptions of
the world, they also laughed at themselves. Carnival laughter, Bakhtin
argues, differs here from the 'pure satire' of modern times, where the
satire places itself above the object being mocked. In contrast festive
laughter is also 'directed at those who laugh'. Even carnival marketplace
advertising was self-ironic. Festive laughter is always philosophically
ambivalent. It is aware of the relativity of all truths and conceptions,
including its own.[36]

What happened to carnival?

Clearly, for Bakhtin in *Rabelais and His World*, the sixteenth century
represents, as he puts it, the summit in the history of laughter and the
high point of this summit is Rabelais. Yet even in the Renaissance, if
still in confused and tentative ways, a 'hierarchy of genres' was
developing, by which carnivalesque authors like Cervantes and Rabelais
were increasingly regarded as merely amusing, merely comic, their
works but light irrelevant literature. By the end of the sixteenth century
Rabelais, descending lower and lower in the hierarchy of genres, was
finally driven out of the circle of what was considered great literature. By
the seventeenth century, the hierarchy of genres had become a fully

regulating force. Laughter, the laughter that interacts with seriousness in Cervantes, Rabelais, Shakespeare, was no longer seen as
philosophical.[37]

The seventeenth century was marked by the stabilisation of the new
order of the absolute monarchy, a stabilisation also effected in aesthetics
and philosophy, in classicism and rationalism. Like the ecclesiastic
feudal culture before the Renaissance, the intellectual culture was
authoritarian, insisting on stability and completion of being, and on a
single 'classical canon', with a single serious tone. The new exalted
genres of classicism were freed from the influence of the grotesque
tradition of laughter, with all its ambivalence. In the seventeenth and
eighteenth centuries there also developed a tradition of court festivals,
masquerades, and ballets. But in the removal of Rabelaisian imagery
from the marketplace to the court, popular festive forms acquired alien
elements of ornate and abstract allegory, with a consequent fading of
the popular spirit.[38]

As for the eighteenth century, in no other time was Rabelais so little
understood and appreciated as during that era, dominated by a
rationalist utopianism, a notion of the universal desirability of cognitive
reason; a mechanistic conception of matter; and a tendency to abstract
generalisation, typification, documentation. As Bakhtin says, the
Enlightenment tended to impoverish the world, to insist on the 'real
world' at the expense of archaisms, day-dreams, and fantasy. Enlightenment writers kept themselves busy expurgating and abridging past
masterpieces, especially of unruly authors like Shakespeare, Cervantes
and Rabelais. Voltaire scornfully wrote that Rabelais was unintelligible.
The sixteenth-century writer was now to be regarded as a mere drunken
buffoon: Voltaire could not understand, Bakhtin says, the traditional
link of 'wise and free speech' with food and wine, the carnival banquet
as symposium. Bakhtin notes that Voltaire does, nevertheless, use
carnival forms for his satirical writing, but laughter is reduced to bare
mockery, it has lost contact with the regenerating and renewing
elements of grotesque bodily humour.[39]

Carnivalesque goes through a series of destructive transformations in
Romanticism, which opposed the Enlightenment for the self-import-
ance of its classicism, cold narrow rationalism, didactic and utilitarian
spirit, and optimism. In response Romantic grotesque, as in German
Romanticism, turned for alternative conceptions to Renaissance
authors like Cervantes and Shakespeare, or to Sterne's *Tristram Shandy*.
But while it drew on some elements of carnival, Romantic grotesque
became the expression of an individualistic world outlook. (Bakhtin
feels that Goethe in his Ash Wednesday reflections in *Italian Journey*
prepared the way for such individualising.) The carnivalesque was

transposed into a purely literary and private realm. Laughter was cut down to cold humour, sarcasm and, especially, irony.

In Renaissance grotesque, festive madness makes people look at the world with different eyes, not dimmed by the supposedly normal, by commonplace ideas and judgements. In Romantic grotesque, madness acquires a sombre, tragic aspect of individual isolation. In Renaissance grotesque, terror appears as comic monsters, defeated by laughter. In Romantic grotesque, terror becomes central to an ordinary world seen as dubious, hostile, and meaningless: the world is alien to humanity, and if reconciliation does occur, it takes place in a lyric, mystic sphere. Romantic grotesque was interested in the mask of carnival, but now it becomes that which hides, conceals, deceives; behind the mask is nothingness. Where Renaissance grotesque occurs in ambivalent images of winter-spring, night-morning, light-darkness, Romantic grotesque is nocturnal, sinister, ghostly, ghastly.[40]

The cultural tradition of the grotesque, Bakhtin rather gloomily feels, is not entirely extinct. While it increasingly lost its living ties with folk culture, there persisted a line of carnival-grotesque in European literature and theatre. During the seventeenth and eighteenth centuries, it was preserved in *commedia dell'arte*, which retained a close link with its carnival origin; in Molière's comedies, which were related to *commedia dell'arte*; in the comic novel and travesty of the seventeenth century; in the tales of Voltaire and Diderot, and in Swift. It continued to live and struggle for its existence in the lower canonical genres, of comedy, satire, fable, and especially in genres like the novel and in burlesque and the popular stage, genres which were non-canonical and more or less oppositional. But this tradition still remained, and remains, within the limits of the official culture that has reigned since the seventeenth century, and so has been transformed and degraded.[41]

As for popular carnival itself in these centuries, we can observe, Bakhtin feels, from the seventeenth century to the present, a narrowing of the ritual, spectacle, and carnival forms of folk culture, which became 'small and trivial'. Increasingly the state encroached upon festive life and turned it into official parades, with the privileges formerly allowed the marketplace more and more restricted; at the same time, festivities were brought into the home and became but part of a family's private life. Carnival and its public character and feasting ceased almost entirely to be the 'people's second life', their 'temporary renascence and renewal'.[42]

Nevertheless, Bakhtin believes, the popular-festive carnival principle is 'indestructible'. Even if narrowed and weakened, it 'still continues to fertilise various areas of life and culture'.[43]

Conclusion: Bakhtin's conception of history

Since his reception in international cultural theory from the late 1960s, many have been the attempts to appropriate 'Bakhtin' for various critical movements, from Marxism to poststructuralism. In the introduction to their biography Clark and Holquist argue strongly, however, that there is no essential Bakhtin to be so appropriated, that Bakhtin himself disliked any attention that tried to seek a true or single identity for his writings, that he was embarrassed by agreement, and welcomed disagreement. Inevitably I have used 'Bakhtin', my own interpretations of his writing, for my own arguments about cultural history.

Bakhtin's view of cultural and intellectual history is, I think, admirably open, contradictory and undecided. There is no single narrative either of progress or decline. While, for example, Bakhtin is critical of the way Romanticism transformed the carnival-grotesque into its own individual-centred imagery, he also writes that Romanticism made its own important discovery, of the 'interior subjective man with his depth, complexity, and inexhaustible resources', an exploration of interior life unknown to the medieval and Renaissance grotesque tradition.[44] And while in *Rabelais and His World* Bakhtin is gloomy about the reduced survival into the present of carnivalesque, in *Problems of Dostoevsky's Poetics* Doestoevsky's novels are seen as a high historical point, a summit, for the presence and realisation of the dialogic, with its close relationship to carnivalesque.

Bakhtin does not see the Renaissance as a rounded totality. He argues for a conflict between carnival notions of the body as grotesque, and canonical Renaissance aesthetics which regarded the grotesque body as formless and hideous. Renaissance classical aesthetics, the aesthetics of the beautiful, drew on the literary and artistic canon of antiquity, conceiving the body as completed, finished, perfect, and also isolated, fenced off from all other bodies. All signs of the body as unfinished, its protuberances and offshoots, were smoothed out, its apertures closed: conception, pregnancy, childbirth, death throes, were almost never shown. The age represented was as far removed from the mother's womb as from the grave. Bakhtin emphasises, however, that he has no wish to assert the superiority of either the grotesque or classical conception of the body in the Renaissance, only their differences; further, the two canons were always experiencing various forms of interaction, of struggle, mutual influence, crossing, and fusion.[45]

Bakhtin is not like a modernist who sees history as linear, that before the rationalism of the Enlightenment and the utilitarianism of the industrial era there was a higher age of some kind for the human spirit, and since such time there has been but decline and devolution. We can think of Bakhtin's own contemporaries, Pound, Eliot, F.R. Leavis, Q.D. Leavis; in recent social theory we might think of Foucault (as in *Madness and Civilization* and *Discipline and Punish*). Certainly in *Rabelais and His World* Bakhtin dislikes the way the Enlightenment identified its own notion of reason as reason itself, failing to recognise that the fearlessness, frankness, freedom and laughter of carnival table talk was itself a mode of critical reason. Yet Bakhtin doesn't, as has happened in a great deal of contemporary social thought, modernist and postmodernist, from Foucault to Lyotard, return only a negative verdict on the Enlightenment. He still says in *Rabelais and His World* that the Enlightenment has its 'strong points'.[46]

Michael Holquist has protested at the way certain appropriations of Bakhtin see him only as the champion of carnival and carnivalesque, pointing to Bakhtin's lifelong admiration of Goethe. In a fragment from Bakhtin's unpublished manuscript on the novel of education, Bakhtin, says Holquist, honours in Goethe eighteenth-century virtues like measure, balance, and civic rectitude. In the fragment Bakhtin argues that the Enlightenment was always struggling against 'authoritarian' conceptions. Bakhtin also repeats what he argues in *Rabelais and His World*, that in rejecting previous literature with its fascination with other worlds beyond the known world, a literature of fantastical visions of ideal and utopian realms, the Enlightenment impoverished the mental world of the eighteenth century, compressed and reduced it, made it drier. But this diminution of fantasy had its own 'positive productivity', as we can particularly see in Goethe, in a new realism, the world graphically clarified, made 'real' and whole. By the second half of the eighteenth century there is a new sense of 'real time' and of space, as geographically and historically concrete.[47]

We have, says Bakhtin, been unfair to the Enlightenment in this respect. The Enlightenment did not lack a sense of historicity. On the contrary, it was an epoch of a great awakening of a sense of historical time. The theme of the ages of man, evolving into the theme of generations, loses a previous cyclical notion and begins to prepare for an awareness of historical perspectives, of the multitemporal, conceiving of the present as contradictory, with remnants of the past and rudiments and tendencies of the future. We can see, Bakhtin argues, such new conceptions developing more rapidly and profoundly in literary explorations, as in Goethe, rather than in the abstract philosophical developments of the Enlightenment. Everywhere Goethe's eye would seek out the movements of time, time as development, emergence, and history. The interest in time was also revealed in the interest in autobiography and biography that Goethe shared with his epoch, much of Goethe's own work being of these kinds, as in *Italian Journey*.[48]

Bakhtin, then, is not theoretically or historically absolutist. He is not like Derrida in *Of Grammatology*, totalising (and psychologising) Western thought as a uniform desire for certitude. He doesn't place a wall around Western culture. He differs from the modernist mass-culture theory of writers like Barthes, Esslin, Eco, when they argue that popular or folk thought has always insisted on a lack of ambivalence, on an age-old desire for certainty.[49]

Bakhtin to the contrary argues that from early in the history of folk culture the world has been seen in a sceptical 'double aspect'. Serious cults were coupled with comic cults which scoffed at the deity; serious myths were coupled with those that were festive-abusive; joined to stories of heroes were their parodies and doublets. In the comic dialogues of Solomon and Morolf which were popular in the Middle Ages, Solomon's sententious pronouncements are contrasted to the flippant and debasing dictums of the clown Morolf, who brings the conversation down to a strongly emphasised bodily level of food, drink, digestion, and sexual life. (Bakhtin compares the exchanges between Solomon and Morolf to the dialogues of Don Quixote and Sancho.) Bakhtin points out how ambivalent such doubling is, for carnivalesque humour, in degrading an object, does not therefore merely dismiss it, merely hurl it into a 'void of nonexistence'. Rather the parodied object enters into a comedy where there is transformation, new birth, new conceptions. And such comedy is also self-parodying, not a quality one often encounters in modernist culture theory.[50]

I will, in what follows, be disagreeing with Bakhtin's gloomy assessment in *Rabelais and His World* (entirely understandable in its appalling context) of the diminished force of carnival and carnivalesque. Certainly in European cultural history we can clearly see a diminution of carnival as a public festive event – though carnival continues strongly in South America and more recently has surfaced in Australia, in Sydney's annual Gay and Lesbian Mardi Gras. But I would argue that carnivalesque as a cultural mode still strongly influences twentieth-century mass culture, in Hollywood film, popular literary genres, television, music: a culture that in its exuberance, range, excess, internationalism, and irrepressible vigour and inventiveness perhaps represents another summit in the history of popular culture, comparable to that of early modern Europe.

CHAPTER FOURTEEN

Dilemmas of World Upside Down

His chiefest spite to the clergy was,
　that liv'd in monstrous pride . . .

No monks or friars he would let go,
　without paying their fees;
If they thought much to be used so,
　their gear he made them leave.
For such as they the country fill'd
　with bastards in those days;
Which to prevent those sparks did geld
　all that came in their ways.
                    'Robin Hood'[1]

The theory of carnival has been haunted by the fear that carnival is populist, idealising the people, constructing them as unified and wholly and invariably admirable in their inversionary values. Carnival might also merely be a safety-valve, a temporary release of contrary or dissident feelings and passions that, once humorously spent, actually strengthen the usual social order.

Populism?

In their biography Clark and Holquist suggest that in his desire to restore an oppositional quality to folk culture, in the political context he was in, Bakhtin was always going to be in danger of idealising carnival in general and the folk in particular, as inherently and instinctively anti-absolutist, pro-universal, anti-war, rebellious, and regenerative.[2]

Rather more sternly, Stallybrass and White in *The Politics and Poetics of Transgression* chide Bakhtin for what they see as his troublesome folkloric approach. Bakhtin's carnival is, apparently, always a populist vision of the world seen from below, always a critique, in the festive

186

inversion of hierarchy, of high culture. In particular, Bakhtin simplified the paradoxical, contradictory meanings of the marketplace and fairs in early modern Europe. Bakhtin succumbed to the separation of the festive and the commercial which is distinctive of capitalist rationality as it emerged in the Renaissance. Blinded by populism, Bakhtin could only see the fair as the potential space of popular and local subversion; the marketplace and the fair at carnival times were purely sites of pleasure, unconnected to any wider worlds. Bakhtin could not see what was obvious, that such fairs also involved economic forces, that they were at the intersection of the cultural and the commercial. He couldn't see that fairs were part of international commerce, which also involved a mixing of populations, as in Lyons, with its settlement of foreigners. Bakhtin was not only 'surely mistaken' in seeing the fair simply as the popular festival of rural life, he also ignored the way fairs could disrupt local and provincial habits and traditions by introducing a certain cosmopolitanism into Renaissance life, arousing desires in ordinary people of the time for exciting, exotic and strange commodities.[3]

Stallybrass and White are always in danger of essentialising 'Bakhtin', producing a portrait of a simple, lyrical, optimistic utopian, who naively conceives carnival as folk, rural, and local, to be admired solely as a culture emerging from below and as a critique of high culture. Where is the textual evidence for these claims? In *Rabelais and His World* Bakhtin certainly argues that carnival parodied official state and ecclesiastical claims to truth. But he doesn't say folk culture denied all 'high' knowledge and art. Bakhtin suggests that carnivalesque folk humour remained in the Middle Ages in an 'almost elemental condition' because of the separation of festive laughter in the marketplace from all official and serious thought. In the heterogeneity of the Renaissance, however, as this separation broke down, various kinds of interactions and mutual influencings took place. Folk humour could now rise to the 'high level' of literature and ideology and fertilise it, while being itself fertilised by humanist knowledge, science, worldly political experience, and advanced literary techniques, as in Boccaccio, Rabelais, Cervantes, Shakespeare.

In these new combinations, of 'lower genres' with the 'higher levels of literature', medieval laughter, Bakhtin argues, was transferred from its 'almost elemental condition' to a state of artistic awareness.

Rabelais and His World, that is, does not celebrate the folk as folk, but the interplay during the Renaissance of folk culture with more formal modes of literature and thought. Festive laughter can 'now rise to the level of literature and ideology', and only now could there develop, from this mutual interaction, a 'new free and critical historical consciousness'. Bakhtin himself, we might observe, retains in his historical argument in *Rabelais and His World* a sense of hierarchy, as if an intensely admirable, but 'elemental', popular folk culture can only come to consciousness in more developed, educated forms.[4]

Who in any case were the folk? Certainly *Rabelais and His World* does not identify the folk with the peasantry. When discussing the history of carnival in the Middle Ages, Bakhtin argues that the medieval culture of folk humour 'belonged to all the people', nobody 'could resist it'. In Bakhtin's narrative, however, carnival emerges both in the Middle Ages and the Renaissance as a largely urban activity, its home in the marketplace of town and city, with lower-class and middle-class clerics, schoolmen, students, and members of various corporations prominent in producing parodic literature and as participants in various activities like the feast of fools. Bakhtin also notes that particular towns and cities became famous for their festivals and fairs – including the French southern city of Lyon, with its large Italian colony. *Rabelais and His World* tells us that the Lyon fairs were held four times a year and each lasted fifteen days, that they represented one of the most important markets for publishing and bookselling in Europe, second only to Frankfurt, and that there were feasts of printers and the election of a prince of tradesmen. Bakhtin points out that Rabelais himself was closely acquainted with the fairs of Lyon, and also other famous fairs, like those at Fontenay-le-Comte, to which would come a great number of salesmen and customers, not only from France but also from other countries, including Germany. Attending as well were itinerant hawkers, gypsies, and the 'obscure *déclassés*, so numerous in those days'.[5]

For *Rabelais and His World* carnival was, then, not necessarily confined to a local community. It could be of national and international interest. The people who attended and participated could be highly heterogeneous, of every class and including those who always blur the boundaries of class, the numerous *déclassés*.

Indeed, Bakhtin insists on the prominence of a general historically self-conscious heterogeneity in the Renaissance, particularly in terms of languages. In the Renaissance the vernacular invaded all the spheres of ideology and worked to expel medieval Latin. The vernacular brought with it the 'free speech of the marketplace', although, Bakhtin adds, popular language was not homogeneous and contained some elements of official speech. The Renaissance also saw an attempt to re-establish Latin in its classical antique purity, and while this new-old Latin did not become a living idiom it revealed medieval Latin for what it was, ugly and limited.

Medieval Latin, *Rabelais and His World* argues, levelled all things. The marks of time in the Middle Ages were almost entirely effaced.

Consciousness seemed to exist in an eternal, unchanging world, and it was difficult to look around in time and space, to become aware of the peculiar traits of one's own nationality and homeland. But in the clash of languages in the Renaissance, of medieval Latin, classical Latin, and the vernacular, there developed an 'exceptional self-awareness' of historical difference, of the boundaries between periods in time. Such awareness could realise the present, contrast today with yesterday, become conscious of itself as contemporary time. The process of transferring philosophy into the vernacular and of creating a new system of literary media also led, Bakhtin argues, to an intense 'interorientation' of dialects within a particular vernacular language, though without 'concentration at a centre'.

Bakhtin observes a tension between such an intensified interest in dialects, with their local, provincial peculiarities, and the development of national languages, which inevitably entered into contact with other national languages. Some national languages, like Italian, had developed more quickly than others, like French, and indeed Italian and Italianisms so influenced French speech that a struggle soon developed between purists and Italianisers. The interaction and mutual clarification of national idioms led to a greater consciousness of concrete historic space. The language of the sixteenth century, and especially of Rabelais, has sometimes, Bakhtin notes, been accused of naivety. But it was the reverse. The complex intersection of languages, dialects, idioms and jargons involved struggle between languages, with languages being perceived as embodying concrete social philosophies and inflections of 'class struggle'. Bakhtin writes more generally at this point that if the 'creative spirit' lives in one language only, or if several languages coexist but remain strictly divided 'without struggling for supremacy', then linguistic dogmatism results. Bakhtin appears here to be extolling the virtue of competition in life – in the midst of a socialist society whose aim was to abolish it.

In the Renaissance, in this competition, language, even grammar, became plastic and there flourished a 'freedom from all speech norms'. Bakhtin compares such interweaving and struggle of languages and cultures to the hybridising Mediterranean culture of Sicily and southern Italy in antiquity. In the Renaissance the acute historical awareness of the heterogeneity of local and national languages enabled a 'new, self-criticising, absolutely sober, fearless, and gay life of the image'. By 'self-criticising' Bakhtin appears to mean that Renaissance people, aware of the 'active plurality' around them, could see their own media 'not only from the inside but also from the outside, in the light of other languages'.[6]

The problem of disunity

In *Rabelais and His World* Bakhtin certainly argues that the culture of carnival in the Renaissance belonged to all the people. But *Rabelais and His World* reveals here a degree of uncertainty and dilemma.

In *Italian Journey* Goethe observed class differentiations working through the Roman carnival. Some upper-class participants prefer the pleasure of losing themselves in the crowd. Others, however, while participating in carnival's world upside-down comedy, nevertheless retain a distinguishing distance from the mass festivities. Goethe says the carnival really starts with the opening of the theatres at the New Year, where one can see one of the 'Fair Sex, sitting in a box, dressed up as an officer and displaying her epaulettes to the public with the utmost satisfaction'. The wealthy also begin to drive their carriages up and down the Corso, although the footmen, dressed as women, haul up their friends, male and female, onto the back of the carriage, the master not minding. Fashionable society enjoys gathering in the neigh-bourhood of the Palazzo Ruspoli, again with lots of male-female inversions, and it is clear that Goethe himself prefers this area of carnival, 'where the company is so pleasant'. Mock battles between the carriages occur, with ladies and their escorts bombarding each other with confetti. Interestingly, he also notices that these merry mock battles sometimes, 'to one's amazement', turn serious, and 'personal jealousy and hatred' (here *within* the wealthy group) is vented in public.[7]

In his commentary in *Rabelais and His World* on *Italian Journey*, Bakhtin doesn't address Goethe's observations on the place and spaces of class differences in the Roman carnival. Yet Bakhtin doesn't invariably insist on carnival's unity of the body of the people. When discussing the importance of banquet images in marketplace festivity in *Rabelais and His World*, Bakhtin says that the traditional folk conception of the grotesque body, with its fat belly, gaping mouth, and giant phallus, represents the collective body of the people as a whole. But in the Renaissance such popular-festive imagery was ambiguously inter-woven with individual and class gluttony and cupidity. The fat belly of the demons of fertility and of the heroic popular gluttons, like Gargantua in folklore, could be transferred to private bodily life, particularly in the figure of the parasitical monk or abbot. The image of the grotesque body is split between these two extreme images.

Bakhtin points to the presence of such ambiguity in Rabelais' novel, where the figure of Gaster embodies both the positive, triumphant, liberating element of abundance that has a 'tendency to embrace all the people', and a contradictory image of monks as sluggards and gluttons,

Gaster as covetous, greedy, and unjust. The image of Gaster is complex, revealing a deep inward antinomy, which, Bakhtin says, Rabelais was unable to solve: 'Neither did he try to find a solution. He left antinomy and the complexity of life as they were . . .'[8]

Stallybrass and White, in their patronising view of Bakhtin as populist naif, have refused to *Rabelais and His World* elements that might be uncertain, complex, unresolved. They have smoothed the grain of his text.

Where is Caliban?

While *Rabelais and His World* insists on heterogeneity, awareness of the other, and self-criticality, it nevertheless plays down any opposing presence of ethnocentrism and hostility to foreigners or those conceived as outsiders. In *Italian Journey* Goethe tells us that strangers at the carnival in Rome had to resign themselves to being made fun of. German baker-apprentices had a reputation in Rome for often getting drunk, and Goethe could see carnival participants dressed up as German baker-apprentices staggering about with flasks of wine. Foreign painters, especially those who sit and draw in public and so are a familiar sight to Romans, would often encounter caricatures of themselves running about in the carnival crowd in long frock-coats, carrying huge portfolios and gigantic pencils.[9] Such parody appears benign, and, if we read it back as a feature of carnival in the Renaissance, may indeed answer to Bakhtin's observation that in the polyglot mixing of the time people were aware of the other, could be challenged by the other to be self-critical.

We can, nevertheless, readily agree with Stallybrass and White here that Bakhtin's approach does not recognise that carnival and its associated activities might on occasion have been disturbingly less than admirable in attitudes to ethnic and religious minorities.[10]

Enid Welsford in her classic 1930s study *The Fool* talks of the carnival plays in Germany in the fifteenth and sixteenth centuries, plays often featuring the appearance of a fool and his wife, who mock the other characters and engage in a dispute with each other which ends in the fool's wife departing in a rage, defying her husband and renouncing her wifely allegiance, apparently a stock episode of carnival comedy. In one play, the fool and his wife chiefly engage themselves in 'mockery of the Jews, whose iniquity is the main theme of the drama'. Peter Burke writes that the injustices and privations of life in early modern Europe often engendered frustrations on a massive scale, frustrations often displaced onto those perceived as outsiders to a community, such as witches,

Turks, Jews, or onto objects that could not easily defend themselves, like cocks, dogs, cats. The Roman Carnival included a race for Jews, offering a sadistic opportunity for throwing mud and stones at them as they passed. The May Day festival of 1517 was long remembered for turning into a riot against foreigners. Michael D. Bristol has drawn attention to the possible sinister side of plebeian culture in general, where feelings of resentment and grievance against the ruling élite could be, in a process of displaced abjection, deflected into hostility towards Jews, foreigners, prostitutes, actors. Stallybrass and White also argue that carnival could involve displaced abjection, where low social groups might demonise not those in authority, but those even lower, women, Jews, and animals like cats and pigs, such rituals of violence reaffirming rather than challenging traditional Christian perceptions.[11]

In his commentary in *Rabelais and His World* on *Italian Journey*, Bakhtin does not discuss Goethe's observations about parody of strangers. Nor does he, in the discussion of the heterogeneity of languages and awareness of the other, suggest that part of this awareness might involve knowledge of other races that Europeans were encountering and brutally colonising across the seas beyond Europe. Elsewhere, in the fragment of the book on the novel of education, Bakhtin discusses Goethe and the gathering specificity and concretisation of knowledge of the world's geography in the eighteenth century; but he does not mention that continuous colonisation by Europe of the rest of the world was advantaged by such exactitude.[12] Colonial expansion by Europe during the Renaissance and later seems not to impinge on Bakhtin's theories – he appears, in this sense, a Eurocentric figure, land-locked in his critical imagination.

I agree with Stallybrass and White that Bakhtin did not see that the fair could be a crucial point of intersection between the European citizen and the 'imperialist' spoils of the nation-state, where shows would increasingly include exhibition of exotic colonised peoples, from the West Indies to the South Pacific to Africa, as freaks and monsters. Stallybrass and White admit, however, even here, that the subordinate could feel an alliance with the exotic peoples on display, as common objects of the contemptuous, censuring gaze of the respectable strolling the fairs and shows. Amidst the grotesquerie, carnivalesque continued to destabilise any settled divisions in the world.[13]

Safety-valve?

Human cultures, past and present, traditional and modern, European and non-European, commonly reveal the persisting presence of liminal times and spaces of between and betwixt, where ordinary social rules and conventions are flouted, inverted, turned inside-out and upside-down. How do we interpret such longstanding and widespread, possibly universal, cultural practices? Certainly the safety-valve view appears unendingly popular as a formula of explanation. But then, what is the ancestry of the notion of the safety-valve?

Bakhtin's belief in *Rabelais and His World* that the popular-festive carnival principle is 'indestructible' and 'still continues to fertilise various areas of life and culture' was perhaps his enigmatic answer to the instrumentalist approach of Lunacharsky, Soviet Commissar of Enlightenment, that carnival is merely a safety-valve to be used by the ruling order of the day. For Bakhtin, the spirit of carnival, however crushed or restricted in human history, is part of human being itself.[14]

The safety-valve view is perhaps most strongly represented in post-World War II social theory by Max Gluckman in his 1956 work *Custom and Conflict in Africa*. Gluckman observed certain times and spaces in traditional African societies where there would be licensed rituals of reversal, women abusing men, or abuse of the king by his subjects. Gluckman concedes that such rites permit protest, yet feels they are 'intended' to preserve and even strengthen the established social order.[15]

Gluckman's letting-off-steam safety-valve approach was influential, even axiomatic, in postwar social theory and cultural interpretation. Certainly it was axiomatic for Ian Donaldson in his 1970 book *The World Upside-Down*. Donaldson evokes the various overturnings of hierarchy evident in seventeenth- and eighteenth-century English comedy, from Ben Jonson to Henry Fielding, dramatised in the lunatic governor, the incompetent judge, the mock doctor, the equivocating priest, the hen-pecked husband. Such, Donaldson argues, are the familiar and recurrent figures in the comedy of a society which nonetheless gives general assent to the necessity of entrusting power to its governors, judges, doctors, priests, and husbands.[16]

Donaldson writes, as does Gluckman in his reference to social intentions, as if a society is a kind of unitary being, a single personality with a single consciousness and a (final) single voice, giving assent, having wishes, intending to do this and that, and so on. Gluckman and Donaldson assume, in terms of classic functionalist social theory descending from Durkheim, that everything in a society, including the apparently dysfunctional, works towards social cohesion.[17] It's a social theory that presumes its answers. Such a priori theory was challenged in the 1970s by anthropologists and cultural historians who argued for seeing in society anti-structure as much as structure; conflict, contradiction, change, as much as order and stability. In the spirit of poststructuralism which was becoming important at the same time, we might call such new social and cultural theory postfunctionalist.

We can, then, see the enthusiastic reception of Bakhtin's *Rabelais and His World* as part of a wider movement, in the last few decades, amongst writers like Peter Burke, Le Roy Ladurie, Natalie Davis, David Kunzle, challenging the safety-valve view of phenomena like inversion, carnival, world upside-down, topsy-turvy, liminality. Two essays, by Davis and Kunzle, first presented in the early 1970s at a conference on phenomena of inversion and reversibility in human societies, bringing together anthropologists with literary and cultural critics, are important in these moves and debates.[18] In her contribution and by now well-known essay, 'Women on Top', the American cultural historian Natalie Davis argues that the female sex was thought the disorderly one *par excellence* in early modern Europe. In pictorial representation or at festival time she appeared as full of life and energy, clever, powerful, resourceful, lusty, saucy, licentious, witty, Amazonian, fighting for equality if not dominance.

The most popular comic example of the female's temporary rule was, Davis says, Phyllis riding Aristotle. The old philosopher Aristotle admonishes his pupil Alexander for his excessive attention to Phyllis, one of Alexander's new subjects in India. The beautiful Phyllis gets revenge before Alexander's eyes by coquettishly persuading Aristotle to get down on all fours and, saddled and bridled, carry her round the garden. Youth overthrows age, and sexual passion, dry sterile philosophy; nature surmounts reason, and the female, the male. (We might also add that the Orient here ridicules the ambitions of Western reason.)

Inversionary play with the notion of the antipodes, the reverse of the known world, figured as well, Davis notes, in seventeenth-century French literary utopias. Gabriel de Foigny's fictitious land of *Australie* (1673), for example, is inhabited by hermaphrodites. The Australian, in whom the sexes were one, compares notes with a French traveller about the condition of the family in Europe as against the antipodes. When s/he realises that in the European family the mother and child are subject to the authority of the father, s/he is appalled and dismisses the European family model as bestial.

In 'Women on Top' Natalie Davis directly challenges Ian Donaldson's view that cultural inversions have a single unidirectional meaning, to strengthen and support the given social order. She also disagrees with Donaldson's related assumption that the hierarchical societies of pre-industrial Europe were stable, rather than 'conflictual'. Davis argues that the cultural play with the topos of the woman on top was 'multivalent'. Images of the unruly or disorderly woman could indeed function to keep women in their place (she might do what the men *should* do). But such images could also prompt new ways of thinking and acting. They could widen behavioural options for women within and even outside marriage beyond the privileged time of stage-play and festive occasion. They kept alive alternative conceptions of family life and women's lives.

Davis points to the frequent ambivalence of festive performances for participants and audiences. The unruly woman on a float in carnival Misrule processions could be seen as shameful and outrageous, or vigorous and in command, with mockery turned against her martyred husband. The comedy of carnival was mixed, both exhorting the hen-pecked husband to take command and inviting the unruly woman to keep up the fight.

Davis argues more generally that the relation of woman to man, wife to husband, was a symbolic means of expressing the relation of all sub-ordinates to their superiors, of master–servant, sovereign–subject and the like. In societies that allowed the lower orders few formal means of protest, such cultural play could sanction political disobedience and riot for both men and women. At festive times men frequently disguised themselves as grotesque cavorting females (well-known English examples were the Bessy and Maid Marian). In the Saturnalian feast of fools, young clerics and laymen would mock official church life and the celibate priestly hierarchy by disguising themselves as women and making wanton and loose gestures. The image of the disorderly woman, in festive figures like Dame Folly, licensed widespread social criticism of unjust rule and rules. It also justified the attempted carrying out of popular justice. Women, and men dressed as unruly women, exercised the carnival right of criticism and mockery, which sometimes tipped over into real rebellion. At festival times women told off priests and pastors, were central actors in grain and bread riots in town and country, and participated in tax revolts and the other numerous rural and urban uprisings of early modern Europe.

The holiday rule of the woman-on-top, Davis tentatively concludes, confirmed subjection throughout society, but it also promoted resistance to it. The woman-on-top renewed old systems, but also helped change them into something new.[19]

Another contribution to postfunctionalism was given by David Kunzle, the major historian of narrative strips and picture stories in European broadsheets that were popular from the fifteenth to the early nineteenth centuries, in England, France, Italy, Germany, the Nether-lands, Spain, Russia. (The remarkable similarity of these broadsheet illustrations across so many different European countries helps us realise how international popular culture has always been.) Kunzle argues for a contrast in the popular culture of early modern Europe between proverbs, presenting a fatalistic resignation to the world as it is, and broadsheet images of World Upside Down, where every order of being, cosmic, human, animal, is fantastically inverted, reversed, toyed with.

In the comedy of World Upside Down prints, Kunzle says, we see the general cosmic reversal of earth and city above, sky and stars below. A church tower is inside a bell. There are ironic reversals of rich and poor, with prints showing a beggar giving money to a rich man, or a rich man giving a lift on his back to the poor man. The prints were bountiful in gender inversions. A husband sits, holding the baby, the wife stands, weapon in hand. Women are laying siege to a castle, firing rifles and clambering up walls. A hen is on top of a cock. There were frequent inversions of age. The child rocks the cradle wherein lies the father, or the child beats the father's bared bum, or the child feeds the mother. There are inversions in the usual relations of human to animal, and hunters to hunted. A carriage is drawn along by wealthy ladies, with a horse using the whip and horses inside as the passengers. A man is inside a cage, watched by a bird outside. A butcher is strung up and disembowelled by the animal he usually slaughters. A fox is chased by hens. A fish is on land, with a fishing rod, pulling a bird out of the water.

Like Davis, Kunzle argues for the 'essential ambivalence' of World Upside Down. The WUD prints, he says, don't in themselves ensure a set ideological meaning. Groups in society who are satisfied with the existing social order might take pleasure in the motif as mocking the efforts of those who wish to overturn that order. Discontented groups, however, might see WUD as a promise of revenge and a vindication of just desires. The World Upside Down broadsheet could be made to appeal to the political conservative, the dissident, and the lover of fantasy and nonsense. The same or similar aesthetic conventions could be used, deployed, developed, played with, in diverse, surprising and unpredictable ideological ways.[20]

Le Roy Ladurie has discussed just such differential uses of inversion in *Carnival in Romans*. In the carnival processions in the French textile town in 1579–80, carnival took place at a time of high historical tension, of struggles between Huguenots and Catholics, and of peasant revolts and urban unrest in the developing towns of the Renaissance. Peasants and urban craftsmen deeply resented not only paying the high taxes demanded of them; they also resented and continually protested at what they perceived to be the high percentage of land owned by nobles and the clergy that was tax-exempt. In the winter of 1579-80, each side, the upper crust of Romans' merchant-landowner society and the bourgeois patricians on the one hand, the small property-owner sector of crafts-men on the other, began to arm. During carnival, they symbolically mocked and derided each other. The poor in their processions, dis-guised with mud, ashes, and flour to transform them into devils and ghosts, threatened cannibalistic intentions towards the rich. The patrician groups, in their rival procession, derided the capacity of the lower to become higher, and so reaffirmed the hierarchical order that so advantaged them. As it turned out, the patricians attacked first, killing or imprisoning the leaders of the craftsmen's carnival. If anything does, Ladurie's book shatters forever any lingering image of early modern Europe as stable and consensual.[21]

The frighteningly judicious Peter Burke also argues that the safety-valve view is unsatisfactory, and that carnival was polysemous. The ruling classes of early modern Europe, he suggests, well knew their Roman history, and consequently were not averse to trying to use the rituals of carnival like the bread and circuses of old, hoping such rituals would permit a harmless temporary release of the ordinarily repressed. The upper classes were aware that the society that privileged them, with all its inequalities of wealth, status, and power, could not survive without a periodic means for subordinates to purge their resentments and to compensate for their frustrations. But, Burke feels, while protest was expressed in licensed ritual forms, such ritual was not always sufficient to contain the protest, which, disturbingly for those in power, could lead to rebellion and riot. Rebels and rioters in their turn knew what they were doing when they appropriated rituals and symbols to legitimise their actions. Carnival enabled both social stability and social protest and change.[22]

CHAPTER FIFTEEN

Fools: Carnival–Theatre–
Vaudeville–Television

. . . Marcolf crawled into an old oven and lay there in such a posture that when the King found him he could only see his back view, not his eyes. This coarse insult was more than the King could stand, so he ordered his servants to hang him, his only concession being that Marcolf might choose the tree which was to serve as a gallows. 'So Marcolf and the servants travelled through the valley of Josaffat, and over the hill of Olivet, and through all Arabia and over the Grand Desert to the Red Sea, but they never found the tree on which Marcolf chose to be hanged.'

Enid Welsford, The Fool [1]

. . . it wasn't only the poor who went to see him (Roy 'Mo' Rene). One of his greatest admirers was Lord Beauchamp, a former Governor of New South Wales. He thought this fellow Mo the funniest man he had ever seen, and told him so at a backstage meeting . . .. 'The old bloke came to see the show, and he woke up right away that I was the best comic in the world. I was in my dressing room, taking off my jock-strap, when he walked in. He was a real bloody aristocrat. He said he enjoyed my work, that I was a bloody genius, then he put his hand in his kick and pulled out a bunch of fivers. He said, "Mr Rene, sir, I'd like you to accept this money as a slight token of my appreciation for your work." But I shook me head and said, "No, Earl, I don't want any. Your praise is all I need."'

Fred Parsons, A Man Called Mo [2]

In this chapter I challenge the primary modernist myth that there could be no positive continuities between pre-industrial popular culture and the mass culture of the nineteenth and twentieth centuries. One such continuity is surely the irrepressible presence of the 'fool'.

In discussion of Derrida's *Of Grammatology* I've already touched on Bakhtin's argument, explicated in his essay 'Forms of Time and of the Chronotope in the Novel' in *The Dialogic Imagination*, that fools, emerging from deep within the ancestry of the folk, already familiar in classical antiquity and the ancient Orient, were important in cultural history for thousands of years. In story, legend and performance fools are 'figures', not (realist) psychological characters. Their being coincides with their role, their significance is allegorical, entirely on the surface. Fools are life's maskers. They possess the time-honoured privilege to be other in this world, the right not to make common cause with any of life's available categories; the right not to participate, to be in life but not of it, to be life's perpetual spy and reflector; to make public what is usually regarded and guarded, as in the sexual sphere, as private. They have the right not to understand, the right to confuse, to tease, to hyperbolise; the right not to be taken literally; to act life as a comedy and to treat others as actors. They have the right to blunt language and to anger, to rip off masks, to rage at others with a primeval, almost cultic, rage. Furthermore, they don't exempt themselves from parody, mockery, abuse, for not only are such figures laughed at by others, but they also laugh at themselves. Folly mocks itself; nothing is sacred, no one is safe, including the fools themselves.[3]

Bakhtin distinguishes between various types of fools. There are the ridiculous naive 'innocent' fools, who expose or provoke into expression usual attitudes by being so innocent of them, yet themselves never deceive, always revealing an unselfish simplicity. There are the tricksters, who always get out of daily work, who can be renowned for their sexual prowess, who play with masks and disguise, who out-trick every adversary. There are the rogues, social explorers who can move through every part of society, low or high. There are the cranks, impatient of usual conventions, grumping away at them.

The grotesque body of carnival

In *Rabelais and His World* Bakhtin argues that clowns and fools are the representatives of the carnival spirit in everyday life outside of set carnival times. In the Renaissance, in carnival and carnivalesque, the official, the high, the spiritual, everything that claimed authority and absolute truth, was brought into comic relation to the body. To understand carnivalesque fool figures in Bakhtin's terms, we must understand the philosophy and poetics of the grotesque body. Bakhtin argues that in the Renaissance the comic performers of the marketplace, a motley world that included not only clowns but jugglers, acrobats, magicians, vendors of panaceas, trainers of monkeys, were an important source of grotesque bodily images. Clowns and fools, along with figures of story and legend, often giants, represented in their own body the grotesque aesthetic.[4]

Bakhtin evokes in detail those facial and bodily features of clear carnivalesque signature. The nose, often evoked in animal terms as snout or beak, a well-nigh universal comic image, is symbolic of the phallus. The grotesque is also interested in protruding eyes, but the most important of facial features is the mouth, the gaping mouth, a wide-open bodily abyss, through which the world enters to be swallowed up, transformed, and renewed. Bakhtin suggests that the grotesque body is cosmic and universal, merging with the natural world, with mountains, rivers, seas, islands and continents, the sun and stars.[5]

The carnivalesque stress is always on those parts of the body that are open to the world, the parts through which the world enters the body or emerges from it, or by which the body goes out to meet the world. Its convexities and orifices, concavities and protuberances, apertures and offshoots, the nose, open mouth, breasts, potbelly, the genital organs, phallus, bowels, often appear in exaggerated, hyperbolised form. They can detach themselves from the body and, dismembered, lead an independent festive life, floating free or in jumbled fantastic combinations. Bodies and parts unite in androgynous confusion. Bakhtin refers to an emblem on Gargantua's hat portraying a man's body with two heads, four arms, four feet, and a clutch of sexual organs, both female and male.[6]

Bakhtin feels that an important source for such grotesque bodily images, both in the Middle Ages and the Renaissance, was the cycle of legends, literary works and pictorial art (in manuscripts, as well as frescoes and sculptures in churches and cathedrals), related to what were known as the Indian Wonders. The first collector of tales about the wonders of India was Ctesias, a Greek who lived in Persia in the fifth century before Christ, and the legends, in travel stories, bestiaries, cosmography, had grown and spread through medieval times and thence into the Renaissance. The legends would describe India's wondrous wealth and resources, as well as remarkable creatures and topography, of devils spitting fire, magic herbs, enchanted woods, fountains of youth. There were fantastical beasts – harpies, unicorns, phoenixes, griffins, dragons. There were giants, dwarfs and pigmies, or beings half-human, half-animal, constituting an entire gallery of bodies of mixed parts: cyclopes with one eye on the forehead, others with eyes on their shoulders, creatures with six arms. Given such numerous demons, medieval writers wondered if the entrance to the underworld was hidden in India. They also became convinced that the earthly paradise, the first abode of Adam and Eve, was located there, some three days' journey from the Fountain of Youth. It was said that Alexander the Great had found in India the abode of the just, closed until the Day of Judgement; and the legend of Prester John and his kingdom, set in India, tells of the roads leading to the underworld and to the earthly paradise. Rabelais, Bakhtin says, loved such fantasies, with their free play with bodies and organs.[7]

The grotesque body, 'ever unfinished, ever creating', was most frequently represented in immediate proximity to birth or death, to infancy or old age, to the womb or the grave. Many traditional popular comic gestures and tricks are based on a mimicking of the three main acts in the life of the body: sexual intercourse, death throes (presented as hanging tongue, expressionless protruding eyes, suffocation, death rattle), and the act of birth. Frequently these three primal acts are merged together (in spasms, popping eyes, sweat, convulsion of arms and legs). There is a mimicking of death-resurrection, the trick of the clown simulating death and renewal. Again, such bodily topography is interwoven with a cosmic topography, as we can still see in the organisation of the stage for the circus ring: the air (acrobatic feats and stunts), water (swimming), earth, and fire.[8]

During the Renaissance the concept of the grotesque body, Bakhtin argues, challenged and helped destroy the 'medieval hierarchic picture of the world'. The medieval cosmos was constructed according to Aristotle, whereby the four elements, earth, water, air, fire, were subject to a definite, vertical order. The basic principle of all physical phenomena is the transformation of one element into the element nearest it. Above the earthly world, however, there rises the world of celestial bodies, not ruled by this law of the transformation of elements. The higher the element on the cosmic scale the more nearly perfect was it. In Renaissance cosmology, the higher and lower strata became relative, and the elements were transferred from a stable, immovable, unchanging and unchangeable vertical hierarchy of being, to the horizontal line of time, from the past to the future. New concepts were now permitted, the existence of many possibilities, the freedom of choice, as in the becoming of history.[9]

The centre of this new conception was the grotesque body. The entire universe, its elements and forces, its higher and lower stata, its most remote phenomena, could now be pictured within the human body – but a human body that is always exceeding itself, taking in and reaching out to the world.[10]

The aesthetic of the grotesque body also acted in conscious opposition to the aesthetic of perfection, the beauty of the perfect body, finished, complete, enclosed within itself, smooth, impenetrable, that had developed during the Renaissance.[11] Bakhtin feels that the grotesque mode, in images where the body copulates, defecates, overeats, and where speech flows with references to genitals, bellies, excrement, urine, disease, noses, mouths and dismembered parts, prevailed in art and creative forms of speech over thousands of years. By contrast, the bodily canon of art, belles-lettres, and polite conversation of the last four hundred years in the official literature of European peoples, especially from the late sixteenth century, is but a tiny island in this cultural sea.[12]

Theatre

Bakhtin tells us that Rabelais in his travels became acquainted with an important aspect of the fairs of his time, the theatrical spectacle, with theatre scaffoldings being put up in the marketplace square, the people crowding around to enjoy mysteries, moralities and farces. Certain towns were famous for their theatrical productions, and during this time France's dramatic culture in particular was closely related to the marketplace.[13] Curiously, however, in general, Bakhtin minimised the theatre in the cultural history of early modern Europe, preferring to relate carnival and carnivalesque to the novel. It has been theatre critics who have applied Bakhtin's theories to Renaissance drama.[14]

In his *Shakespeare's Clown* (1987), David Wiles argues that the importance of clowns has been underestimated in the cultural history of the Elizabethan playhouse, including Shakespeare's. Criticism this century has focused on texts, plays as unified expressions of the author's vision, and character as psychological; the demands and expectations of audiences have been of little interest. Taking clues from Bakhtin's theory of carnivalesque, as well as from critics like C.L. Barber in his *Shakespeare's Festive Comedy* (1959) who have stressed Shakespeare's relation to popular festive traditions of misrule and world upside-down, Wiles argues that we should start noticing the important role of stage clowns as independent 'authors' in the creation of performances.[15]

So popular were famous clowns of Elizabethan times like Richard Tarlton and Will Kemp that playwrights had to construct parts and segments for them (Wiles argues that Falstaff, as clown and mock-knight, was a role Shakespeare specially created for Kemp). The clowns might wish to establish their independent presence by disrupting the flow and speed of narrative with spectacle and display, and by direct address to and confrontations with the audience. The Elizabethan play was not necessarily, then, a unified whole: it could be fragmented in performance; there could be tensions between clown and playwright; and, indeed, a thrust of neoclassical drama in the seventeenth century was the reigning in of the clown in the interests of dramatic unity and the primacy and control of the 'author'.[16]

Wiles argues that we can see in the professional stage clown of Elizabethan times the meeting of a previous 'amateur' popular tradition (the Lord of Misrule, the Boy Bishop in the feast of fools, Robin Hood and Maid Marian in morris dances), with the theatre as a commercialised venture, a new leisure industry, in a rapidly expanding London. In the 1580s Tarlton became in London a surrogate Lord of Misrule. Tarlton's appeal cut across class, in court, theatre and tavern. He assumed a cover of naivety, representing himself as a plain rustic, poor and drunken. With his flat nose and squint, the very sight of his face set audiences laughing. He invited mockery, telling tales against himself (how he was arrested by the watch, deceived by women, left penniless), and he constantly set up situations where he would be humiliated by the audience. But in the end it was he who would have the last laugh on those taunting and duelling with him. At the conclusion of the play audiences might throw up clever rhymes with the aim of outwitting Tarlton, who would give an instant riposte. His relation to his audience was interactive and competitive.

Will Kemp, Tarlton's successor as dominating clown in the 1590s, when he shared equal status with Shakespeare in their theatre company, also had an 'ill face' and represented himself as a plain man. He was most famous for his jigs, fusing song with mime and dance. Like Robin Hood, lord of the anti-authoritarian, often rebellious summer festivals and by ancient tradition leader of the popular morris dance, Kemp on stage might partner a Maid Marian, played by a man, a burlesque descendant of the May Queen. Kemp was known for his sexual innuendo, and the jigs were also highly sexual, indeed, says Wiles, a kind of 'soft commercial pornography'. Kemp would carry with him a kind of extruding phallus, a staff, truncheon, or broom-handle. In these jigs, confusing gender, Kemp woos the man-woman Maid Marian. He might also himself appear on stage as a country lass, with swinging hips.

The jigs, offered at the end of a play, usually involving four comic characters, two male and two female (played by men), added new meanings to the plays themselves, for example, challenging romantic love in Shakespeare's comedies by mocking and travestying it. In such jigs, married life was usually shown as rife with adultery, thrashings (of husband by wife), seduction of servants, the clown offering throughout a direct commentary on events to the audience. Wiles' general argument is that the clown wasn't merely there for comic relief, but as a key actor in a contestation of ideals and perspectives. Whatever moral order is realised in an Elizabethan play will be in tension with its parody in the closing jig, where, like Kemp, the clown dominates as festive Lord of Misrule, creating for audiences to ponder not a definite conclusion but an anarchy of values.

Roy Rene: Clown of vaudeville and radio

Bakhtin was perhaps unduly pessimistic when he argued in *Rabelais and His World* that with the rise to power in the seventeenth century of rationalism as well as the neoclassical hierarchy of genres, the grotesque could only continue in a reduced way, in the 'low' forms of comedy, satire, fable, in the novel, in burlesque and the popular stage.[17] Bakhtin is offering here a totalising judgement on post-Renaissance popular culture that we might now think is far too harsh. Theatre historians in particular have been revealing for some time the robustness, in colonial Australia, Britain and the US, of nineteenth-century popular stage forms like pantomime, farce, blackface minstrel, music-hall, vaudeville, variety, pointing to the continuities of their comedy with pre-modern forms, with *commedia dell'arte*, carnivalesque, world upside-down.[18] In similar spirit historians of the fool see twentieth-century clowns like Chaplin or Keaton as worthy successors of the fools of old.[19] And popular entertainments were structured in the nineteenth century much like Elizabethan performance as described by Wiles, with the wrenching experience of melodrama followed by a farce, the hope of melodrama that fate can be defeated contested by farce's cosmology that the universe is uncontrollably absurd.[20] Hollywood vigorously continued this tradition of ever confronting seriousness with parodies and burlesques.

I will discuss two Australian fool figures, Roy 'Mo' Rene, the recognised King of Vaudeville and then radio from the 1920s through to the late 1940s, and Graham Kennedy, known as the King of Australian TV from the late 1950s to the present. As with so much in Australian cultural history, Roy Rene and Graham Kennedy continue and develop and distinctively transform features and characteristics from European and American cultural history.[21]

Universally known as Mo, Roy Rene (1892–1954) was considered at the height of his fame during the interwar period and a few years on (commercial) radio after World War Two, comparable to the great overseas clowns like Chaplin and Grock.[22] As Fred Parsons, his longtime scriptwriter, tells in his biography, Mo himself would say there are but 'two real comics in the world today – me and Chaplin'. Then he would cheekily add: 'Yair, me and Chaplin . . . and Chaplin is a bit of a mug, too.' Certainly overseas comics and actors, Fred Allen, W.C. Fields, Jack Benny, Sybil Thorndike, thought him a comic genius.[23]

Roy's father, a Dutch Jew, was in the cigar-making trade, and had come via Britain to Australia, finding himself in Adelaide. In that rather respectable city he married an English woman, a Miss Barnett. Born as Henry Van der Sluys but known as Harry Sluice, Roy was, like many Jewish children in Australia then and since, given a Catholic education, attending a Dominican Convent and a Christian Brothers school. Or rather, not attending, since he spent so much time at Adelaide's variety theatres, one of them near his father's cigar factory. Determining on a show business career, Roy became a boy soprano, getting his break in the immensely popular blackface minstrel shows, where, known as Roy Boy, he supported Ivy Scott, a soubrette; together they would sing 'My Creole Belle'.[24]

The family moved to Melbourne when Roy was thirteen, but he continued to spend more time fascinated by the stage than book learning. He loved to go to the Opera House, managed by Harry Rickards, an important figure in vaudeville in Australia. There Roy could watch imported English music-hall stars like Marie Lloyd, whose reputation for risqué comedy 'Roy Rene' (he took the Rene from a French clown well known in that era) was himself soon to inherit. Meanwhile he learnt his stage craft in minstrel shows touring country areas.[25]

In 1914 Roy teamed up with another Jewish comedian, Nat Phillips, known as Stiffy, in the Stiffy and Mo Revue Company, which for some fifteen years delighted popular audiences and outraged the respectable. From that time through to the 1940s Mo dominated Australia's popular stage, in pantomimes like *The Bunyip*, in vaudeville and variety, and in the stories that circulated about him. Though it was felt by some that his stage comedy was too 'blue', too risqué, for radio, the assumption proved egregiously wrong when he starred as Mo McCackie in the late-1940s Colgate-Palmolive radio show *McCackie Mansion*, which became the highest rating program of its day (beginning in mid-1947, it ran for three years).[26]

I will try and construct my sense of Mo as public clown figure from Fred Parson's generous and moving tribute.[27] Perhaps needless to say, given I was a baby-boom baby, I neither saw nor heard Mo, and my Australian Broadcasting Commission-loyal Communist parents never, to my memory, mentioned him.

In a century when Jews were becoming increasingly important in the new mass entertainment industries, not least Hollywood, and when there were many overseas Jewish comedians, Roy chose to present himself as Mo, a Jewish stage persona, with chalk-white face and surrounding black beard. Roy told Parsons that he got the idea from a World War I American west coast comedian, Will King.[28] But, as Parsons notes, while clearly Jewish in persona, his comedy routines did not usually involve 'Jewish' gags about meanness or shrewd business tactics, and the Mo character was never well heeled enough to be a businessman. On the contrary, Mo was usually the down-trodden employee, the clown as 'low'. But comic tensions could be played out between Mo's obvious Jewish persona and whatever routine he was involved in. There were constant jokes made about his nose, but, again, as Parsons points out, such jokes were also this century made about non-Jewish comedians like Bob Hope and Jimmy Durante.[29]

Mo is clearly recognisable as a clown in carnivalesque terms, the poetics of excess, display, parody and self-parody. He delighted in exaggerating the clown's grotesque body. His accentuated eyes were large, heavy-lidded, sad. Mo himself was proud of the 'lovely pathos' he felt he could achieve, singing songs to make his audience cry. In one vaudeville routine, the theatre manager would come onto the stage and pretend to sack Mo, who would then sing in a quavering voice his most famous sad song, 'Life's a very funny proposition, after all'. His voice was distinctive, high-pitched with a lisp that would develop into a liquid splutter, burst into spray. His long tongue was always threatening to lick the tip of his nose. And he himself would set up jokes about that latter organ.[30]

Recall Goethe's account of carnival in Rome in 1788, when he notices a ritual whereby sons would blow out the candle held by their fathers, an inversion and uncrowning of usual authority, of the phallus.[31] In *McCackie Mansion*, Mo's son Young Harry would insult his father whenever he could, for example, by rhapsodising over a carrot he had picked in the garden, and saying it was even bigger than his dad's nose. Each time he insulted his father, Mo would yell, 'Cop this, Young Harry!', followed by the sound effect of a smack on the head.[32] In another *McCackie Mansion* sketch, 'A Letter from Lana', Mo sends a photo of himself to Lana Turner, who writes back comparing him to a huge-beaked galah. As with Tarlton and Kemp, Mo was continually parodied, mocked, abused.

Mo also revelled in gender ambiguities and cross-dressing. When he stripped to reveal his comedy underwear, the audience would see Mo in a swimsuit of the 1910 era, often with frills below the knees, and little pink bows on the shoulder straps. Parsons says that in performance Mo was 'bisexual'. One moment he would be making a pass at a pretty young woman, who would invariably knock him back. The next minute he would be leering and making insinuating gestures to a 'mincing male'. The army and navy were seen as a prime area of gaydom. In one vaudeville sketch, Mo is conned into volunteering for a dangerous mission at war. There are four characters on stage. Mo says ordinary farewells to the first three, then sidles up to the fourth, lowers his fluttering eyelashes and murmers, 'I won't be able to come to your tent tonight, Eric.' In a Stiffy and Mo routine, 'The Sailors', which Parsons first saw in 1924, the curtain goes up on the deck of a battleship. Mo makes his appearance, in the uniform of a 'Jewish admiral' (I'm not sure I quite follow this), with a cutless drooping obscenely between his legs. Stiffy, the straightman, yells, 'Tell me, Mo – what did our brave sailors do in the North Sea?' Mo simpers, then lisps, 'Don't be dirty, Stiffy, don't be dirty'. As with anti-jingoistic songs in British music-hall, there's no nationalistic celebration of the martial or masculinity here.[33]

In the historical burlesque 'Queen Elizabeth', one of Roy's own favourites, the Tivoli audience would see Bess on stage, in a gold costume, with matching headpiece and fan. Then the fan was withdrawn, to reveal the bearded Mo. The Earl of Essex character, played by a plum-voiced English actor, would then declare his love for Elizabeth in a remarkably convincing way. In another sketch, Mo appears as the glamorous Dutch espionage agent Mata Hari. An army officer under Mata Hari's spell would play the ensuing love scene as if Roy actually were a beautiful woman, his voice throbbing with tenderness and passion, his eyes burning, Mo meanwhile coyly nibbling his ear. Whenever Mo played a female character, Mata Hari or the Virgin Queen, or the Matron of a Baby Health Centre, or the unmarried mother in 'The Strawberry Blonde', he always retained his beard.[34] (We might think here of the 'female' characters in Kemp's Elizabethan jigs, obviously 'male' of face.)

As with Mo, gender blurrings, confusions and inversions were everywhere on the Australian popular stage, from pantomime where the Dame would be a comedian in drag, the Principal Boy a woman, to Stiffy and Mo routines like 'The Sailors'; this would begin with the young ballet women dancing on dressed as sailors, headed by the soubrette (a pert young female character) as a cheeky middy. Following in the famous footsteps of Vesta Tilly in nineteenth- and early twentieth-century British music-hall, male impersonators, like Nellie Kolle or Ella Shields, local or imported, were also popular in vaudeville and variety. Parsons describes Shields, for example, coming on stage, smiling, dapper, in immaculate tails, the dandy. She would leisurely remove her silk topper and white bow-tie and nonchalantly shoot her cuffs. Audiences were fascinated.[35]

Mo's humour, as with so much performance on the popular stage, was highly self-reflexive, was always drawing attention to its own theatricality. Parsons notes that Mo was an expert at moving in and out of character. In a sketch involving the well-known husband-and-wife team Mike Connors and Queenie Paul, Mike's character sees Queenie at a party, turns to Mo, and asks who is that beautiful young woman. Mo suddenly steps out of character and abuses Mike for not recognising his own wife, the mother of his children. Mike turns his back on the audience and shakes with laughter. The technique was apparently known as 'cod break-ups', a standard part of vaudeville/revue. Mo would often at the end of the final call take off his beard, bringing a gasp of surprise from the audience for the contrast between the grotesque Mo and the nattily dressed Roy Rene.[36]

The audience was often invited to participate. There were, for example, regular amateur nights, where the worse the act, most of them, says Parsons, being breathtakingly bad, the more the audience loved it. (This tradition continues in television variety, *Hey Hey It's Saturday* featuring 'Red Faces', one of its most enduring and popular segments.) On radio, despite the frequent modernist myth that the electronic media do not permit audience participation, listeners were also invited to join in the fun, as in a sketch featuring Mo, 'The Barmaid and the Butcher'. The story of their amorous adventures, says Parsons, changed each week and led nowhere, closing just as Mo was about to relate what the barmaid was going to say to the butcher. After a year, the station offered a big prize to any listener who gave the best answer for what the barmaid really did say. Parsons says that about 20 per cent of the entries, most of them from women, were highly obscene.[37] (Unfortunately, he doesn't say what the winning entry was.) It would seem that popular radio was also not necessarily enamoured of narrative closure: it was the audience here who provided the (comic) endings.

The Mo character was known for his complete lack of respect for authority, though Parsons himself finds this audience belief a bit curious, since sometimes Mo would play a cringing sycophant. He quotes Mo as McCackie apologising for coming late to work at Mr Gurkinshaw's emporium – though here Mo, I think, takes sycophancy to such an excessive extreme he's clearly parodying it. At other times Mo would parody the desire to be a social celebrity or be refined. Then there was the radio sketch where Mo played a new-chum dairy farmer who picks up a cow-pat under the impression that it was Field-Marshall Montgomery's beret. Parsons says abusive letters poured into the station, particularly retired army colonel types who informed Roy that he wasn't fit to blacken Monty's boots, and that he was obviously a damned Communist, or at least a Fellow Traveller. Years before, Mo and Stiffy had been appearing at a variety theatre (the Bijou) when the Duke of York (later King George the Sixth) was visiting Melbourne. The more conservative of Melbourne's citizens were outraged when a large banner proclaiming 'Stiffy and Mo Welcome the Duke' appeared across the front of the theatre, with many indignant letters to the papers speedily following in its wake.[38]

How does Mo's comedy relate to discourses of ethnicity, race, nation? His Jewishness interests me personally, given my mother was Jewish (from the East End), my father, born in Australia, of Irish and English descent. Mo, I think, represented himself as Jewish and not-Jewish, never the one, exclusive identity. Mo, indeed, was always playing with race and ethnicity, highlighting it. He'd make dubious racial jokes (for example, in a sketch where he'd say he wanted to become a social celebrity, he'd let slip that his mother 'was a Kanaka tart'). There would also be jokes about Mo's supposed facial resemblance to Haile Selassie. In another skit, on radio, Mo asked a female Greek character for some useful Greek words and phrases. She tells him some, which turn out, as Parsons puts it, to be words not usually used in mixed company. The station's phones rang hot for two days.[39] Mo's 'ethnic' humour spoke to a 'postcolonial' Australia not of single but of mixed, problematic identities.

For over thirty years Mo was for Australian popular audiences their Lord of Misrule, their carnival monarch. He was known as such, the King of Comedy, the King of the Tiv., the Old Maestro, the King of Radio. Though other comedians parodied him, none could take his crown. Sometimes he would deliberately provoke and annoy his audiences – he offended the Deanna Durbin Fan Club by saying that any film with her in it was a 'horror film'. As Parsons says, he would fight with those who watched and listened to him, flatter, coax, cajole, bully and abuse them. As with Tarlton and Kemp, that is, his relationship to his audience was competitive and interactive, a relationship deliberately highlighted on stage by having in the audience heckling him (often planted in a dress circle box) some straight men, with whom he could duel and joust.[40]

People loved Mo, Parsons feels, precisely because he was outrageous, a quality which also endeared him to Sydney's irreverent, iconoclastic journalist and literary Bohemia. Parsons tells the story of Roy being persuaded by gagwriter Alexander Macdonald to meet poet Kenneth Slessor in a bar. Roy gave Slessor a cool nod, turned his back on him and asked Macdonald, 'Who did you say the ginger-headed mug was?' Slessor, hearing this, was delighted. There was also the story of a policeman at an intersection recognising Mo and, leaning on his car, asking him how he was. After telling the officer he was fine, Mo turns to his passenger and, without lowering his voice, says, 'Mug copper'. Because he was King, Mo, says Parsons, could get away with anything. Mo died on 22 November 1954. His funeral procession to Rookwood Cemetery in Sydney went through city and suburban streets lined with mourning crowds. His passing was treated by the media at the time as the death of a national hero, a Don Bradman or a Phar Lap.[41]

Graham Kennedy

We come now to Mo's successor as Australian popular entertainment's King of Comedy, the title transferred to and bestowed on Graham Kennedy during the years of his immense popularity as host of *In Melbourne Tonight*. *IMT* was a long-running variety show that began in 1957, not too long after Australian TV itself had begun, in late 1956, just in time for the Melbourne Olympics. English readers might recall a glimpse of Kennedy on a Clive James program about television in the rest of the world, positioned as the low and the other (feared yet desired) to British television. After showing a bit of Clive Robertson grumping on his news show the week before, James said he was acceding to requests from astonished viewers by showing a similar late news program, *Graham Kennedy Coast to Coast* (1988–89). We see Kennedy making obvious copulating motions while referring to a female colleague (Jana Wendt, Australian TV's highest rating current affairs host, on the same commercial station as Kennedy's show, Network Nine).

I never saw *In Melbourne Tonight*. But I have seen some of Kennedy's major incursions into popular television since. In the middle 1970s he was host of *Blankety Blanks*, a variety quiz show that parodied regular quiz programs. On *Blankety Blanks* contestants would be asked to provide a reply which matched the responses offered by a panel of celebrities; there was no 'true' answer, only answers that matched, as Kennedy would occasionally remind viewers amidst the mayhem and clowning. The program tended to go sideways into nonsense and fooling, rather than go straight ahead as in a quiz 'race'.[42]

Kennedy's humour was and is saturated with self-reflexivity. On *Blankety Blanks* he would make jokes about the props he had to use, or the young lad called Peter behind the set who had to pull something (Peter the Phantom Puller); he would chide the producer, and chaff with the audience.[43] When Kennedy was invited in 1988 to host *Graham Kennedy Coast to Coast* in direct competition with Clive Robertson on Channel Seven (their rivalry and popularity significantly increased later night viewing audiences, in the 10.30–11.30 timeslot), he continued to make comedy out of self-reflexivity. At various times he would show how on the desk in front of him he could beep out words; he would demonstrate the cue system, and reveal the cue words themselves. He might discuss his smoking problem, that he was a chainsmoker, and how he had a lighted cigarette just below his desk, that he wasn't supposed ever to puff on in front of viewers. He would do an ad, making fun of the product, and saying how much the station charged for it. He would show a new tiny camera, and what it could do, and invite the audience to ring in with what he could do with it. Every night he would read out telephone calls resulting from the previous night's show, some registering their disgust with his extremely 'crude' – grotesque bodily – jokes.

Everything about the studio, everything about the situation of sitting in front of cameras and dealing with a producer, everything about the off-screen personalities of his straight men, first Ken Sutcliffe (a sports compere) and then John Mangos (back from the United States where he'd been Network Nine's main reporter), Kennedy would refer to and make into comedy. Once, when it was Ken Sutcliffe's birthday, Graham embarrassed Ken (who was indeed very straightforward in his screen personality) by showing photos of him when he was a baby that Graham had got from Ken's wife; Ken looked at the screen, at his wife, and said 'I'll get you for this'. Graham was always making jokes about Ken as a simple country boy, about Ken's prominent nose, and also took to calling him Two Dogs, after the joke about how Native American families name their children. (A Native American character tells the joke in *Silkwood*.)

It was clear Kennedy went out of his way to be self-reflexive, and always had, given some of the skits from *In Melbourne Tonight* occasionally shown on *Coast to Coast*. (In one routine, 'The Wilsons', with Graham as a dirty old man married to his Joyce, there is, amongst the jokes about water divining with a stick, an obvious 'cod break-up'.)

The similarities between Mo and Graham Kennedy as comic personae are many and intriguing, from the way they both enjoy self-parody and invite mockery by others, down to details as in Graham sporting his own version of comic underwear; occasionally during some foolery Kennedy would stand up to reveal that beneath his shirt, tie, and suit jacket he only had on white jocks. Kennedy also highlighted his face and body as grotesque, with his protruding eyes, open gaping mouth, and long wandering tongue. His comedy was indeed risqué, calling on every aspect of the body to bring down solemnity or pomposity or pretension; his references to any and every orifice and protuberance, from bowels, penis, breasts, to internal organs to any and every bodily fluid, were often such that one laughed and cried out at home, 'that's disgusting'. His relationship with his audience was competitive and interactive, particularly in the segments when he'd read out and respond to phone calls. To one viewer, who must have been demanding them, Graham commented, 'There are no limits, love, there are no limits': the credo of the clown through the ages, the uttering of what others only think, the saying of the unsayable.

When Queen Elizabeth was shown in a news item visiting Hong Kong in 1989 (I think it was Hong Kong), Graham remarked that for a woman her age she didn't have bad breasts, an outrageously sexist comment, that he knew was sexist, that he was directing against a figure traditionally revered by Anglo-Australians. The night following the San Francisco earthquake, Graham and John Mangos staged a mock earthquake in the studio, with the ceiling apparently falling in on them. This piece of comic byplay was discussed in the press for some days, in the 'quality' papers like the *Sydney Morning Herald* in terms of how distasteful it was. (Interviewed about the incident, Kennedy said it was precisely bad taste he was hoping to achieve.) Discussing the quake jokes that week with my TV study students, some thought Kennedy had gone too far this time in being thoughtless and insensitive, given how many people had died, and the world was in a state of shock and sympathy. Others pointed out that disaster jokes were not uncommon, recalling that (apparently) they had erupted in the wake of the Titanic, the Hindenberg, and more recently the Challenger. Other students pointed to the rash of dingo-eating-babies jokes that followed the Lindy Chamberlain inquests and trials (Chamberlain, subject of Meryl Streep's *Evil Angels*, had said that a dingo came into her tent in the Australian outback and took her baby, Azaria). Others pointed out that in the US there are lots of Helen Keller jokes. Kennedy was perhaps calling on an aspect of carnivalesque, the uncrowning by laughter of the monster Death. He was also mining a store of humour, the profaning of the unbearably sacred, that usually remains verbal and underground.[44]

Another area of such profaning lay with news stories about animals around the world. When the Chinese government allowed two giant pandas to be housed for a while in Australian zoos, drawing large crowds, the news item about the pandas was run on Graham's show, with Graham making the same joke he'd made about other revered gentle wild creatures like the Australian koala: 'I wonder what they'd taste like?' The joke was repeated frequently on the show, becoming that feature of comedy of playing with audience expectations.

Graham was always highlighting and playing with gender and gender identity and confusion. As Fred Parsons said of Mo, that his stage persona was 'bisexual', so could we say of Kennedy. Indeed, Kennedy suggested as much himself one night. He might make jokes of heterosexual provenance, as in claiming to want to make love to Jana Wendt. Or he would play up being gay. One night Ken suddenly said to Graham, 'Would you like to take your hand off my knee?' Jokes flowed, and Kennedy later included the performance in his final 1989 *Coast to Coast* program. Graham and John Mangos were very affectionate to each other. One night, responding to a viewer's phone request, they parted each other's hair down the middle to see what it would look like. In his last appearance on the show, Graham kissed John Mangos' hand, and said of Ken and John that 'he loved them both'.

As Mo highlighted ethnicity, so did Graham, particularly with Greek-Australian Mangos. They clearly quickly became firm friends. Graham would mention that he'd been invited home for dinner and met John's mother. He would play up learning about Greek food at restaurants. He made extravagant business of getting John to teach him some Greek words, including terms like 'malacca' (I think it was 'malacca') that John, playing up being embarrassed, said were not for family viewing. (Malacca apparently means masturbator, wanker, stupid, fool, idiot.) With George Donikian, an Armenian-Australian, reading out headlines every half-hour, and with an American-Australian reading out stock exchange reports, Graham set about exploring contemporary cultural and ethnic identities in Australia, making ethnic jokes, probing, provoking, teasing, uncertain, revealing how uncertain he was, challenged.

Watching *Graham Kennedy Coast to Coast* nightly was for me a rare moment in cultural history, a privileged opportunity to observe cultural innovation in action, in the hybridising of genres we would usually think of as incompatible. Kennedy made news, with its conventions of seriousness and its frequent urgency, meet the traditions of carnivalesque and vaudeville. In the nightly clash, each was at once highlighted and transformed.

The popularity of Kennedy since 1957, a popularity almost coterminous with Australian television itself, has been extremely important and influential for contemporary entertainment. Kennedy has licensed, in many princes and lesser courts, parody and self-parody, comic self-reflexivity and direct address, the grotesque body.[45]

I would like to pay tribute to Graham Kennedy here. Since his death Roy Rene has been acknowledged as a master, in a flow of memoirs and reminiscences, as well as a musical tribute, radio shows, a play; the annual awards of the Variety Club of Australia are named after him. But Kennedy, a living master, should also, I think, receive recognition. The quickness of his wit, hallmark of his comedy, is ever celebrating human language itself, in verbal play, double-entendre, sexual suggestion, inverted meanings, festive abuse. He belongs to a long line of great comedians thrown up by popular culture, comparable indeed to legendary names from the past, to Rene, Chaplin, Grock, Grimaldi, Kemp, Tarlton . . .

Australian cultural history

The comedy of Mo and Graham Kennedy destabilises a key trope of historiography in Australia. A persistent interpretation of Australian cultural history is the bush legend, that Australian cultural identity derives from the nomadic bushmen of the late nineteenth century, the outback drovers, shearers, bullockies. Their values, of egalitarianism, sharing, community, anti-authoritarianism, anti-pomposity and anti-pretension, a laconic self-ironic humour, were taken up by, reflected in, and became the preoccupation of, Australian literature and film. This myth has proven peculiarly protean, for even when it has been sharply criticised (as male-centred, as ignoring racism, as exclusively Anglo-Celtic), its basic position has been accepted: the cultural imaginary of Australian history is to be found in a fascination with the rural, the bush, the outback; such has a 'central place in the iconography of the national self-image'.[46]

Yet, from the 1920s to the late 1940s, the most popular and loved character in Australian mass entertainment was Mo, a white-face Jewish comedian, always playing with gender and ethnicity, cross-dressing, 'bisexual', his comedy, in skits about the present or in his historical burlesques, almost invariably urban and cosmopolitan. He would play Mata Hari, the Strawberry Blonde, the Matron of a Baby Health Centre, Good Queen Bess the Virgin Queen, a top-hatted larrikin attending the races at Royal Randwick, the god Apollo, Henry VIII, Hamlet, or a seedy ne'er-do-well slouched on a park bench.[47] Stiffy and Mo routines involved jockeys, the army, aristocrats, waiters, wharfies, a beauty parlour.[48] In *McCackie Mansion* Mo was a suburban householder, and the comic figures around him, relatives and neighbours and Spencer the Garbageman, were similarly of the city. The closest Mo came to portraying the Australian bush legend was in parodying it. Mo recalled that in the Australian pantomime *The Bunyip*, he would descend in the finale as the bushranger Ned Kelly, with a big tin mask on: 'Stiffy would take the mask off, and there I was with my white face and whiskers. And it would bring the house down'.[49]

Similarly, Graham Kennedy, the most popular figure of Australian television history, its acknowledged King, sharply distances himself from any set legendary 'Australian' figure or language. (When John Mangos, for example, would sometimes address him as 'mate', Graham would draw back and mock him.) His comedy is also urban and cosmopolitan. *Coast to Coast* showed a skit from *In Melbourne Tonight* where Graham, desperate to get to a toilet, finds himself stuck in a lift in an office building. *Coast to Coast* jokes wove in news events in the rest of the world as much as in Australia, the bra being one hundred years old in Paris, the tenth birthday of *Penthouse*, sperm donors, condoms (Graham says if they're too tight he cuts the head off), Jimmy Bakker breaking down during his trial, Tammy Bakker, Zsa Zsa Gabor's courtroom performance, Rob Lowe's home video, the Rolling Stones' Bill Wyman and his young bride.

A cultural history that recognised the importance of the popularity of Mo and Kennedy and the largely urban and cosmopolitan vaudeville tradition they develop would surely question the trope of a dominating masculinist bush nationalism.[50] The centrality frequently accorded to the bush legend seriously underestimates how much Australian cultural history has been concerned with multiple, fragmented, uncertain, contradictory national and ethnic identities.[51]

Conclusions

Raymond Williams' claim in his *Television: Technology and Cultural Form* that in most parts of the world, since the spread of television, there has been a scale and intensity of dramatic performance which is without precedent in the history of human culture,[52] might also be argued of the protean presence of the fool on television and popular film.

We can, perhaps, cheekily update Bakhtin's range of fool figures. In terms of the innocent fool, we might think of Woody in *Cheers*, Rose in *The Golden Girls*, Boner in *Growing Pains*. In terms of tricksters, we can think of Ronnie Barker/Fletch in *Porridge*, Paul Hogan's character Mick in *Crocodile Dundee*, Madonna in *Desperately Seeking Susan*, the Fonz in *Happy Days*, Hawkeye in *MASH*.[53] In terms of rogue figures, Rhett Butler in *Gone With the Wind* would perhaps be the most famous example in film history. In terms of crank figures, picture, in the unexpected context of a late night news show, sour Clive Robertson on Australian TV, sniping at his producer, becoming irritated at the news items he has to read out, moralising at the subjects of stories, being pedantic about pronunciation, telling everyone how boring the events that day are, or refusing to put on sporting highlights because he considers sport tiresome.

Fools are fascinating figures. I don't, however, wish to argue that they are necessarily admirable, or even likeable. John Fiske is, we've noted previously, the main champion these days of a reading of popular culture as 'oppositional'.[54]

But the comedy of fools is never usually ideologically 'clear' enough to be declared unequivocally oppositional. Mo's greatest appeal, for example, Parsons notes, was to working-class people, Parsons movingly describing how their tired faces at the end of a day's work would light up at Mo's entrance on the vaudeville stage. But the Bohemian writers and journalists Mo attracted, some of them gathered about *Smith's Weekly* (1919–1950), a journal that was at once iconoclastic and pro-White Australia and frequently racist, were often politically conservative.[55] At the same time, Mo was admired by the Communist actor Hal Lashwood, who, after his stint on *McCackie Mansion* came to an end, tried to get Mo work on the Australian Broadcasting Commission. (The ABC, however, sure of the superiority of its 'public sphere' mode of broadcasting, humiliated Mo by making him audition and then coldly rejecting him; Parsons' account makes chilling reading.)[56]

Historically fools have inspired displeasure and disgust as well as surprise and delight. Clowns can be heroes of their performances and narratives, signifying the friendship, loyalty, trust, and sense of community lacking in the society around them; or they can be extremely individualistic. They could be felt to represent the body of the people, mocking and taking revenge on power, yet also to act only for themselves and their own enjoyment and survival, as in Bakhtin's account in *Rabelais and His World* of the abbot Gaster. Enid Welsford writes, in her classic (if, now, rather quaintly moralistic) study, that clowns were always ambiguous figures, starting with those created over the centuries in myth and legend. Some of these mythical buffoon figures migrated from the East. Welsford tells us that in the fourth century of the Hegira, the Muslim era (tenth century AD), the Arabs possessed collections of stories and jokes, similar to the jest-books popular in the West at a much later date. *The Jests of Si-Djoha*, for example, contained anecdotes concerning an apparent simpleton called by the Arabs Si-Djoha or Joha, and by the Persians Juha or Juhi. According to tradition, Si-Djoha was court-jester to the famous conqueror Timur-leng, and would engage his master in comic dialogues. In these stories, Si-Djoha is sometimes a learned and even saintly buffoon, at other times he is a poor tradesman and perhaps beggar. Sometimes he is so poor he engages in unscrupulous trickery; or he is astonishingly callous. The figure of Si-Djoha travels to Turkey where he becomes the comic character Nasr-ed-Din Hodja or Khoja, his fame still surviving; his legendary doings and sayings also travelled westwards to Sicily, where he became the shrewd booby Guifa, a favourite figure of folklore.

Welsford also writes of that other well-known mythical buffoon emerging from the Orient, the ungainly peasant Morcolf, represented as a bald hunchback, whose resourceful wit would prove more than a match for the wise king Solomon. In their comic dialogues, the King would give voice to some general truth or moral platitude, which Morcolf would counter by a saying embodying the homely commonsense or shrewd cunning necessary for the poor man who would make his way in the world. Sometimes Morcolf would parody, or give a coarse version of, or expose a flaw in the King's wisdom; sometimes they both simply cap one another's proverbs. At other times, the incorrigibly impudent Morcolf would engage in a series of pranks that would always raise a laugh at the King's expense. Morcolf emerged variously in stories as representative of rustic wisdom, a sage, greater in his practical sense than Solomon's theoretical idealism; but also, as wanderer and trickster, surviving on secretive cunning, maddening persistence, and heartlessness.[57]

Of the sixteenth-century Neapolitan clown Pulcinella, Welsford tells us that the most constant traits in his character, beside his power of turning the tables on his would-be oppressors, were cynicism and cruelty.[58]

Nor are clowns themselves necessarily joyful figures. There's that interesting comment of Fred Parsons that Mo's eyes were always sad even when he was being funny. And there is a pathos about Graham Kennedy, a sense of his aloneness and apartness. Here we have the sadness of the clown as outsider, as not part of ordinary society, as having no place, as monster. The clown is indeed kin to all those other outsider figures that are so irrepressible in cultural history, from Frankenstein's disowned 'child', refused a name, to King Kong in New York to Jeff Bridges' character in *Starman* to Darrell Hannah's mermaid in *Splash!*.

Fools, then, disclose no single discursive meaning. The professional clowns of stage, cinema, radio and television exhibit from Renaissance times onwards a dual inheritance. As wise fools they represent in their grotesque body the carnivalesque body of the people, mocking on behalf of humanity those who proclaim authority, rules, binding conventions, received proverbial wisdom. As tricksters, they hold out the irrepressible hope for humanity that life is not necessarily preordained towards loss, failure, and tragedy, that fate is not inconquerable, for can't the trickster always defeat death, the hangman, fate at its most destructive?[59] Just as Morcolf escaped death by hanging, so at the end of a Neapolitan play, *Pulcinella, Brigand-Chief*, Pulcinella is taken to be hanged, but he feigns stupidity and pretends not to be able to find the noose. The hangman, becoming impatient, slips the noose over his own head to show Pulcinella how it is properly done, and the fool then seizes the moment to strangle the hangman.[60]

But the clown can also be perceived as outside of and possibly hostile to humanity, bespeaking a mixed mythological ancestry, of supernatural powers, a magician, devilish, demonic, uncanny, sinister, dangerous. The clown is endearing and disturbing, lovable and inspiring of fear, discomfort, dislike, for no one is safe from the fool's mocking barbs.

Perhaps what we can say, with Bakhtin, is that the carnivalesque comedy of fools relativises all absolute claims to truth. Fools keep alive ambivalence and ambiguity, the destabilising of fixed categories, leaps into uncertainty. It is here that carnivalesque foolery can be distinguished from traditional (and modernist, as in Jameson) notions of satire, comic criticism of others in terms of fixed ideals, values, and maps.

CHAPTER SIXTEEN

Fool, Trickster, Social Explorer:
The Detective

The dreadful condition of these poor beasts, whom I might
soon be brought to resemble, so depressed me that I drooped
my head like them and grieved for the degradation into
which I had fallen since those far-off days when I was Lord
Lucius. My only consolation was the unique opportunity I
had of observing all that was said and done around me;
because nobody showed any reserve in my presence. Homer
was quite right to characterise Odysseus, whom he offered as
an example of the highest wisdom and prudence, as one who
had 'visited many cities and come to know many different
peoples'. I am grateful now whenever I recall those days: my
many adventures in ass-disguise enormously enlarged my
experience, even if they have not taught me wisdom. It was at
this mill that I picked up a story which I hope will amuse you
as much as it amused me.

Apuleius, The Golden Ass [1]

They had Rembrandt on the calendar that year, a rather
smeary self-portrait due to imperfectly registered colour
plates. It showed him holding a smeared palette with a dirty
thumb and wearing a tam-o'-shanter which wasn't any too
clean either. His other hand held a brush poised in the air, as
if he might be going to do a little work after a while, if
somebody made a down payment. His face was ageing, saggy,
full of the disgust of life and the thickening effects of liquor.
But it had a hard cheerfulness that I liked, and the eyes were
as bright as drops of dew.

Raymond Chandler, Farewell, My Lovely [2]

The recent interest of cultural theory in genre has often been marred
by a continuing modernist functionalism: the assumption and insistence
that genres are in themselves ideological, that ideology is inscribed in
their very form. Therefore a genre like the detective novel will reflect

the dominant social values and anxieties of its time. For while a nod is given to the detective figure as having remote ancestors, as in the knight of medieval chivalric romance, the genre is seen as the child of the nineteenth century, a creation of the capitalist era, somehow an inherently bourgeois product. Jerry Palmer argues in his *Thrillers* (1978) that the 'dominant element' is the combination of mystery with 'competitive individualism'. Stephen Knight, the moonlighting medievalist, tells us in the introduction to his well-known *Form and Ideology in Crime Fiction* (1980) that what his book is going to outline is the 'ideological nature and function of crime fiction'. Analysis of such texts will establish their 'social function', which is to provide for their audience – about whom, Knight admits, he knows very little – a 'consoling' resolution for their anxieties. Cultural products like detective fiction may appear to deal with 'real problems', but 'in fact' they are both conceived and resolved in terms of the 'ideology of the culture group dominant in the society'. Not only the 'content' of the text but its very 'form' will accord with the 'audience's belief' in such dominant cultural values, values which interlock with the social structure, hence assisting in economic and political as well as cultural 'hegemony'. Even where crime fiction reveals conflicting values, indicating areas of 'central anxiety' in the society, such conflict will be artificially resolved by the plotting and structure of the novel, so that form and content produce together a 'pleasing, comforting world-view'. A range of phenomena called 'ultimate realities' are hence 'ideologically obscured'.[3]

Form and Ideology in Crime Fiction flows along in the mainstream of modernist mass-culture theory that courses from early in the century, with Q.D. Leavis' *Fiction and the Reading Public* as key source. There is the magisterial assumption of knowledge of audiences and their true psychic needs. There is the ascription of a central meaning to a whole form, a meaning which yet always turns out to be outside the texts, in the way popular fiction serves social conformity (for Q.D. Leavis this is the herd mentality, for Knight, in the language of 1970s Marxism, hegemony). There is the confident possession of factual knowledge about ultimate realities and real problems that popular fiction somehow deliberately intends (in Knight's terms, is 'conceived') to obscure.

We can, however, contrast the comical levels of disdain for detective fiction in Q.D. Leavis with the fondness for the genre evident in Knight's text. But it is a fondness that is *just* evident, that is continuously repressed in the interests of stern ideological judgement of the 'social function' of detective fiction. If we can return the psychoanalytic gaze, we might say that in a Late-Modernist work like *Form and Ideology in Crime Fiction* its narrator feels bound to engage in a strange public ritual of ascetic renunciation of enjoyment of a mass-culture form, enjoyment displaced into severe humourless critique. Affection for popular forms in the last few decades has become a 'dangerous supplement' for modernism, creating anxiety, strain and fissure in its desire to maintain and sustain the hierarchy of genres, where the detective novel, alongside science fiction (though above romance and melodrama), was ever to be kept low. Modernism was on the verge of a crumbling of its culture of consolation, its anti-mass-culture certainties.

The increasing presence in the last decade or so of thrillers featuring detective figures announcing themselves as radical, feminist, gay, was also straining modernist functionalism and certitude.[4] Just as with postmodern architecture, there was a blurring occurring between 'high' and popular cultures. Radical, feminist and gay detective figures were suggesting the clear possibility that aesthetic conventions can be distinguished from the discursive uses a particular text at a particular time might make of those conventions. Ideology does not issue from the detective genre itself, but from the historical character of individual texts. In such a postmodernist critical mode, form cannot be identified with ideology, cultural conventions are not the same as discourse. Genres are open fields of possibility, not closed books of fixed discursive meaning.

Unless we so sharply distinguish between genre in general and particular ideological inflections, it is not possible to work out why genres like detective or romance or melodrama are so historically lively, so durable, flexible, and productive. I will, then, begin with the long view, calling again on the historical poetics of Mikhail Bakhtin, hoping to show that the detective is a considerably more complex, contradictory, and interesting figure, and that the genre has a much longer and more diverse cultural history, than modernist analysis could usually acknowledge.

In *Form and Ideology in Crime Fiction*, Stephen Knight (agreeing with Terry Eagleton in *Criticism and Ideology*) argues of the novel in general that its form as such responds to and ratifies the idea that the individual is the essential seat of knowledge and the real social unit.[5] It was this standard view of the novel, that it was conceived and took its form in the nineteenth century as psychological realism, as concerned with individual formation, that Bakhtin was so concerned to critique, drawing attention to the long history of diverse novelistic genres from antiquity onward, ever differing and contesting, mixing and hybridising.

Updating Bakhtin on genre

In his study in *The Dialogic Imagination* of the chronotope, the way that genres, ancient and recent, are constituted in and by particular organising principles of space and time and character, Bakhtin reveals fascinating insights that we can extend and develop in terms of contemporary culture. Talking of one kind of ancient novel, the 'adventure novel of everyday life', like Apuleius' *The Golden Ass*, Bakhtin argues that the problem of how to reveal private, personal everyday life was not tackled directly in classical ancient literature, which was a literature of 'public life and public men'. If private life were closed to public view (and so to 'public' genres), how could it be discovered and exposed in narratives? One way is the insertion of crime into private lives, for it is by crime that private passions erupt involuntarily into the public arena. And crime, the criminal trial, and criminal-legal categories, Bakhtin suggests, are of enormous organisational significance in the history of the novel – as, we can add, they are in popular theatre, film, radio, and television.[6]

Another method of making the private realm public is through the narrative use of a character who can legitimately 'spy and eavesdrop'. In *The Golden Ass* the young nobleman Lucius is transformed by the magic of Fotis the slavegirl not into a bird as he hoped, but into an ass. Even though he then has to suffer many humiliating adventures and experiences, his position in various households and situations as an ass is of great help to him. Everyone talks freely in front of him, as if, lowest of the low, he doesn't exist; and his big ears can catch the most distant conversation. As an ass Lucius is an ideal 'third person', one who enters into a social (or family or psychological) situation, usually in crisis, and reveals it to us.

Bakhtin suggests that the later history of the novel is witness to a multitude of variations on Lucius as ass. The servant, for example, can go from one master to another. He is the eternal 'third man' in the private life of his lord: 'People are as little embarrassed in a servant's presence', Bakhtin says, 'as they are in the presence of an ass, and at the same time the servant is called upon to participate in all intimate aspects of personal life.' Other witnesses to the secrets and intimacies of private life, Bakhtin feels, are the courtesan, the prostitute, the rogue, the adventurer, the parvenu. Such characters do not occupy any definite fixed place in everyday life, yet they can move between or be privy to all levels and layers of society. They are privileged observers of social heterogeneity. The fictional 'third person' is in but not of private everyday life, and therefore can see it in sharp focus, as a whole, in all its nakedness, playing out its roles but not fusing his or her identity with any of them.[7]

An obvious example from twentieth-century popular culture is the rogue and adventurer figure of Rhett Butler in *Gone With the Wind*. Other modern 'third persons' are journalists, doctors, forensic scientists, vets, nannies, and – detectives.

Later in this wonderfully fertile essay, 'Forms of Time and of the Chronotope in the Novel', Bakhtin relates the 'third person' of ancient narratives to the cultural history of fool, clown, crank and rogue figures.[8] He points to their robust presence in late medieval times in the folkloric and semi-folkloric forms that tended towards satire and parody. Such figures carried with them into literature a vital connection with the theatrical trappings of the public square and the folk use of festive masks. The rogue, he notes, still has some ties that bind him to 'real life'. The clown and fool, however, are not of this life, and therefore possess their own special rights and privileges, including the 'right to betray to the public a personal life, down to its most private and prurient little secrets'. For the novel the masks of the clown and fool are invaluable. For example, the novel can use the device of not understanding, where a fool's unselfish simplicity is opposed to greedy falsehood and hypocrisy; conventions, of everyday life, mores, politics, art and suchlike, are portrayed through and exposed by a character who neither participates in nor comprehends them.

Bakhtin notes the importance of the device of character as outsider or foreigner in *Gulliver's Travels*; Pierre, a civilian staring at war at the Battle of Borodino in *War and Peace,* is an outsider; and we could mention examples from film and television like *Splash!, Greystoke, Starman, Crocodile Dundee, Mork and Mindy.* The novel can utilise the level-headed, cheery, and clever wit of the rogue, or the parodic taunts of the clown. As outsiders, these characters are analogous in their narrative position to the 'third person'. But they also add a carnivalesque dimension, what Bakhtin refers to as the 'exposure of the entire existing social structure', in that clowns, fools, cranks, tricksters have the right to mock and parody; they have the 'right to rip off masks' and to 'rage at others with a primeval (almost cultic) rage'.

Certainly the fool's time-honoured use of blunt language can be observed in the detective figures of the American crime fiction tradition, in Chandler's Philip Marlowe, Dashiell Hammett's Sam Spade, Gregory McDonald's Fletch; in TV and film it's there in the *Rockford Files'* Jimmy Rockford, and in Eddie Murphy's character Axel Foley in *Beverly Hills Cop* (Foley is a rogue cop, a festive figure of wise folly, within the force). Indeed, the ancient festive licence to be rude, now applied to the police, the wealthy, psychiatrists, the pretentious, all those who try to conceal the secrets of power and control and influence, is one of the most enjoyable features of the genre. Certainly in Chandler's *Farewell, My Lovely* (1940) Marlowe will say anything to anyone. When Nulty the incompetent, lazy cop says he might go and search for a clue, Marlowe says, 'That's a good idea . . . If you can get somebody to lift you out of your chair.' When another cop, Randall, cool, competent, sharp, says of Nulty that he should be a brakeman on a wheelless box-car in the hills, Marlowe says, 'That's not nice . . . A fellow officer'. If the fool of old was licensed to mock the king, the detective confronts the law, challenging its monopoly of force. For the law might always have to compromise with power and wealth. In some ways Marlowe's arguments and confrontations with representatives of the law (there's also Bernie Ohls in *The Long Goodbye*) might recall the dialogues and exchanges popular for centuries in early modern Europe between Solomon and Morcolf, between ruler and fool, platitude and puncturing wit, official wisdom and carnivalesque suspicion.

Marlowe in this sense is very much a trickster figure, cheating fate in always escaping death as it closes in on him (as Morcolf or Pulcinella would always escape the hangman), parodying the solemnity and official attitudes of the state, unmasking the rich and powerful, playing with language with great daring (the famous jokes and similes and snappy conflict-dialogue, as with the remarkable Anne Riordan), and, in parodying himself, disestablishing any claims to absolute truth. The grotesque humour of *Farewell, My Lovely* embodies seriousness, pathos, sadness – for example, in Marlowe's perception of the criminal Moose Malloy, hopelessly in love with Mrs Grayle (his Velma of old), as a giant with gentle, vulnerable moments. Throughout the novel Marlowe feels affinity with Malloy, in some ways a fellow permanent outsider figure, a monster to ordinary humanity. It is perhaps because of such affinity that Marlowe produces such bluntness of language towards Mrs Grayle, the figure of the dangerous woman that we recognise from film noir (here about how she killed her associate Lindsay Marriott):

> . . . But some day a tough guy named Moose Malloy was going to get out of jail and start finding things out about his former sweetie. Because the big sap loved her – and still does. That's what makes it funny, tragic-funny. And about that time a private dick starts nosing in also. So the weak link in the chain, Marriott, is no longer a luxury. He has become a menace. They'll get to him and they'll take him apart. He's that kind of lad. He melts under heat. So he was murdered before he could melt. With a blackjack. By you.

There's another dimension to Marlowe, where he is indeed like a medieval knight, on a crusade to save the world. Anne Riordan says:

> You're so marvellous. So brave, so determined, and you work for so little money. Everybody bats you over the head and chokes you and smacks your jaw and fills you with morphine, but you just keep right on hitting between tackle and end until they're all worn out. What makes you so wonderful?

Here is the detective as hero, even superhero, through whose wondrous deeds crises are confronted and people selflessly helped.

Bakhtin comments of the miraculous world of the chivalric romance that in its 'adventure-time' the 'unexpected, and only the unexpected, is what is expected', a time where 'suddenly' rules. The heroes enjoy adventure as their natural element. Through their heroic deeds they glorify themselves and others (their liege lord, their lady), highlighting the similarity of chivalric romance and the epic.[9] The detective (Anne Riordan's 'marvellous' and 'wonderful' assessments of Marlowe are partly ironic, given all the mistakes Marlowe makes, and partly affectionate serious tribute) is also a performer of heroic deeds, manifesting endurance, recovery, fast thinking and swift action, all in a compressed, headlong 'adventure-time'. And while opposing the incompetence or compromises of the Law, the detective stands for another liege lord, or rather lady, Justice.

Here the detective genre joins another literature, the trial and testing of the hero in the novel of ordeal (*Prüfungsroman*). Bakhtin writes that in ancient Greek adventure-romance what is tested are the hero and heroine's qualities like chastity and mutual fidelity as well as 'nobility, courage, strength, fearlessness, and – more rarely – their intelligence'. Such characters experience dangers and tribulations through which their initial virtues are proved. This chronotope of the unchanging or fixed character, however, Bakhtin suggests, is unlike that of narratives like *The Golden Ass*, where Lucius goes through a transformation, a sequence of moral weakness, error, guilt, then punishment, then redemption and blessedness: a chronotope related to the meta-morphoses of folklore, to Christian hagiography (sinner, suffering and inner struggle, rebirth as holy), and, we can add, to the realist novel of moral development and awareness (*Bildungsroman*). Detectives, however, in general don't change. At the end of a narrative their basic qualities are re-affirmed. Each time they (just) pass the test. As Bakhtin says, the trial of the hero as a compositional idea has proved extremely productive in the history of the novel.[10]

Contemporary contexts

The daring play with language in *Farewell, My Lovely* is in tension throughout the novel with an extreme precision of social observation. This precision brings in another context, particular developments in the nineteenth century of the idea of social exploration: I'm not denying the importance of the nineteenth century in the development of crime fiction, only disputing its being regarded as fount, source, origin, essence. The literary sociologist Peter Keating argues in his *Into Unknown England* that there is barely an area of nineteenth-century fictional and non-fictional prose where the attitudes and terminology of social exploration do not appear. Of all the dilemmas faced by the Victorians, the perception that society was becoming rapidly divided into two classes, rich and poor, capital and labour, was felt to be the most fundamental. So separate, so hostile to each other, were these classes becoming, that they were like two nations, even two different races or species, or like inhabitants of different planets. If this division continued, society must be rent apart, and it was therefore imperative for the social order that the vast new unknown zones of lower-class life be penetrated and reported on, so that ways of healing such a breach could be found. It was a situation ready made for Victorian social explorers like Mayhew, Greenwood, Sims, who, often with the aid of disguise, would spend a night in a workhouse or tramping streets: the social explorer sharing the use of disguise with the detective, from Sherlock Holmes in a dosshouse to Eddie Murphy in *Beverly Hills Cop* masking himself as a journalist in order to stay at a high-class hotel. The social explorer offers the story of one person's journey into an alien culture, within one's own society. Another mode of investigation was by Royal Commission, and later in the century, particularly with the work of Charles Booth, individual observation of suffering, poverty and social difference is supplemented by surveys and statistics. Passionate vignettes contend with notions of the scientific and objective, in the context of the rise of sociology and anthropology, the human sciences, as professions. Yet, says Keating, as modern society is always creating new kinds of divisions, fresh impetus is always being given to explorers to penetrate a suddenly 'new' and 'unknown' social group. The vividness, the immediacy, the first-handedness, of ethnography remains indispensable.[11]

The late nineteenth-century perception of London's East End as an 'abyss' of slums, overcrowding, incest, homelessness, swearing and general jungle-like brutishness and desperation, in part replaced a mid-century perception of capital and labour, or the chill winds of utilitarianism, as rending forces, as shown in 'industrial novels' like Disraeli's *Coningsby* (1844) and *Sybil* (1845), Mrs Gaskell's *Mary Barton* (1848) and *North and South* (1855), and Dickens' *Hard Times* (1854). The social explorer would descend into the abyss and report on it, frequently with revulsion and disgust, as did James Greenwood after a night spent in the Lambeth workhouse. 'Towzled, dirty, villanous,' Greenwood commented of his wakeful companions, 'they squatted up in their beds, and smoked foul pipes, and sang snatches of horrible songs, and bandied jokes so obscene as to be absolutely appalling'. When serialised in the *Pall Mall Gazette*, 'A Night in a Workhouse' created a sensation, and there is throughout a tension between a general rhetoric of repulsion and an evident pleasure in listening to and trying to inventory for his readers the cockney dialect as well as relishing not being able to 'even hint' at the 'most infamous things to be heard'.[12]

Towards and by the end of the century, however, Greenwood's touch of on-the-job enjoyment and entertaining of his readers had become alien to the social explorer's task, so overwhelming was the threat of anarchy and destruction posed in the East End rookeries. Jack London's grim *The People of the Abyss* (1903) was the result of the American socialist's wandering about the East End for seven weeks in 1902 (trailed by a detective he hired), dressed as a penniless American sailor, doing participant observation: as in *Gulliver's Travels*, a cultural outsider discovering an unknown society, this time, ironically, in the faltering heart of the British Empire itself. His reports were originally published in a small American socialist journal, but it is American chauvinism, rather than socialist internationalism, that more than occasionally surfaces in the narrator's observations. Not only is he worried about the way the 'overstrung Manchester factory operative hankers after excessive quantities of pickles and similar weird foods', but the Americans he meets in London, compared to the local cockneys, are taller, prouder, less subservient to authority, more cheerful, of greater pluck, and swear in a way that is more 'luminous and varied'. The narrative is a journey of 'descent', past the respectable working class trying to live a decent life, into the 'infernal regions' of the ghetto, where the poor live on the streets and sleep on park benches and in dosshouses and workhouses. Yet because of disease or industrial accidents or age, the respectable can soon slip over the edge into the mire of pauperism, the enveloping abyss, a vast and malodorous sea. Then they are people, human beings worthy of the (American) name, no longer. Now 'helpless, hopeless, unrelieved, and dirty', they can only be described as 'indecent and bestial'.[13]

By 'right of race', says the narrator, with a quick input of a familiar nineteenth-century discourse (London once declared, 'I am first of all a white man, and only then a Socialist'), the English working classes should be efficient, imaginative, inventive, and quick. But their oppressed condition forces them to excessive drink. Women almost as much as men frequent the ubiquitous public house; children go there as well, sipping from their elders' glasses and listening to the 'coarse language and degrading conversation', the 'licentiousness and debauchery'. Such creatures, sodden and forlorn, have no culture left of their own, only a 'vacancy'.[14]

As Keating points out, however, in his *The Working Classes in Victorian Fiction*, by no means all social explorers belonged to the 'industrial' tradition of fear, crisis, and abyss. There was throughout the nineteenth century another active and influential mode of perceiving the city, the 'urban'. Located supremely in London, it builds on age-old images in English literature of London low-life scenes, as well as on the art of Hogarth and his successors as caricaturists in the nineteenth century like the Cruikshanks. Fiction in this 'urban tradition' stresses the variety and mystery of street life. It focuses on what distinguishes social groups from each other rather than what unifies them, on the idea of contrast rather than monolithic unity; it highlights individual rather than composite 'class' types, especially the bizarre and grotesque; it moves towards farce rather than in the direction of unrelieved solemnity; it foregrounds, often in the midst of appalling poverty, a milling vitality and vigour, a sense of continual movement and life. Keating argues that Pierce Egan's comic *Life in London* (1821), graphically illustrated by the Cruikshanks, is the archetypal 'urban' novel of the early nineteenth century, establishing a contrast between upper-class life in the West End and lower-class in the East End. Real life and enjoyment exist not in the sameness of fashionable life, but in the fascinating bewildering contrasts and happenings of its opposite. ('It is,' says LOGIC to TOM, 'I am quite satisfied in my mind, the LOWER ORDERS of society who really ENJOY themselves.')   The urban tradition is not, however, indifferent to poverty or suffering. Dickens' London novels, the great successors to Egan's *Life in London*, are, for example, continually infused with loathing for all kinds of social grievances, injustice, inequality, oppression.[15]

Keating's reference to Tom and Jerry, the fashionable heroes of *Life in London*, as they stroll through London, journeying into diversity, as slim and elegantly tailored, might remind us of the cultural figure that so interested Walter Benjamin. In Paris, that other great nineteenth-century metropolis, could be observed the *flâneur*, the purposeful male stroller, perhaps by profession a journalist, writer, poet, illustrator, caricaturist or Impressionist painter. From the 1830s on, the *flâneur*, in impeccable dress and of exquisite manners, always detached and unruffled, never directly involved, was clearly interested not in the natural world or in the exotic, but in the theatre of daily life of Paris and its suburbs. The *flâneur* promenaded the boulevards, moved coolly through the excitement of the crowds, displayed himself as he tried to observe everything about him, from the race-track, riverside bathing, pleasure boating, to the café-concert and theatre. The *flâneur*'s strolling was absorbed, reflective, contemplative, and his acute powers of observation were readily likened, in a culture already intrigued by Edgar Allen Poe, to those of the detective.[16]

The modern detective

The twentieth-century detective figure and genre are heir to all such narrative and discursive positions and opportunities. The genre for a start is always negotiating the competing 'urban' and 'industrial' traditions evoked by Keating, often entwined in the same text. In his essay on Baudelaire in *Illuminations* Benjamin suggests that Baudelaire was highly ambivalent about the big-city crowd. As a *flâneur* Baudelaire was drawn to the crowd and made one of them; but at the same time he was unable to rid himself of a sense that the spectacle of the crowd was menacing, inhuman. Baudelaire, Benjamin writes, becomes the accomplice of city crowds even while he is always dissociating himself from them, relegating them to oblivion with a glance of contempt. We can perceive such ambivalence in this century's detective writing, in Chandler's *Farewell, My Lovely*, where with Marlowe we see the city as variegated and exciting in its ever surprising, bizarre difference, or in the Dickensian scenes involving huge Moose Malloy at the beginning of the novel. Malloy is evoked in famous phrases as a 'big man but not more than six feet five inches tall and not wider than a beer truck', and the outlandishly colourful clothes are drawn with a precision worthy of early twentieth-century Imagist poetry. When Marlowe, however, in search of the previous owners of the night-club where Malloy's Velma once sang, visits the alcoholic Mrs Florian, the writing moves in and out of comic Hogarthian grotesquerie and a generalised language of blanket disgust. Mrs Florian gives Marlowe a package of old photos of entertainers:

> I leafed through the bunch of shiny photographs of men and women in professional poses. The men had sharp foxy faces and racetrack clothes or eccentric clown-like make-up. Hoofers and comics from the filling station circuit . . . You would find them in tank town vaudeville acts, cleaned up, or down in the cheap burlesque houses, as dirty as the law allowed and once in a while just enough dirtier for a raid and a noisy police court trial, and then back in their shows again, grinning, sadistically filthy and as rank as the smell of stale sweat. The women had good legs and displayed their inside curves more than Will Hays would have liked. But their faces were as threadbare as a book-keeper's office cat. Blondes, brunettes, large cow-like eyes with a peasant dullness in them. Small sharp eyes with urchin greed in them. One or two of the faces obviously vicious.[17]

Later in the novel Marlowe notes his disgust while he moves about at night in Bay City. Older social explorers like Greenwood or Jack London would have been proud of such moralising as they registered dismay at the abyss of London's East End: the 'industrial tradition' was not merely English and nineteenth century, but international and strongly continuing worldwide. Throughout *Farewell, My Lovely*, the anti-urban and pro-urban war is left unresolved.

Also unresolved is the detective as a liminal figure, ever poised between conflicting, contradictory attitudes and categories. With a complex ancestry and just as complex a set of contemporary affiliations, the detective can never be categorised as any one fictional thing, and certainly not as an ideological essence. The detective is poised between magic and science, between on the one hand hunch and intuition and wondrous feat, on the other rational deduction and logical puzzle (a potentiality taken to an extreme in English crime fiction, where the detective's journey of social exploration frequently comes to a terminus, the subjects of investigation all being assembled in one place). The detective is poised between ethnography, the actuality of observation, and 'social science', the detached reporting style of the sociologist, urban anthropologist, investigative journalist.

The detective moves between faith in ultimate justice and cynicism that it can ever be realised in a world corrupted by wealth and power; between belief in humanity (otherwise detectives would never help people), and sure knowledge that people rarely tell the truth and will always conceal motives; between law and outlaw (Jim Rockford has been in prison, as has Terry, a detective figure, in *Minder*).

The detective can be a hero like the knight of medieval chivalric romance, yet also fool, trickster, rogue, crank. If tricksters in early modern Europe were often feared as well as admired, unable finally to be trusted, possibly only using those they saw as the humbler simpler souls around them for their own upstaging ends, so too has there been in cultural history a continuing ambivalence about the admired outlaw figure. Peter Burke writes of popular heroes like Robin Hood, Rob Roy, Dick Turpin, that while such heroic outlaws, often credited with supernatural powers, were held in legend to right wrongs and help ordinary people, they could also be perceived as cruel; popular attitudes to them were always ambivalent.[18]

The detective is poised between explorer and voyeur. In P.B. Yuill's *Hazell Plays Solomon*, James Hazell goes to see Toni Abrey, a housewife and young mother who lives in a block of flats in 'tatty old Bethnal Green' in the East End of London. He pretends he's doing research about a hospital's maternity section for a TV documentary. As it happens, he has to reveal to Toni that he's all along been a private detective working on a case about switched babies. The developing relationship, where Hazell finds himself deeply drawn to Toni, is stopped by the detective's tricksterish use of disguise, the suspicion of creating ties and attachments only for information-gathering.

The detective has to penetrate social and family life, to uncover the answers to mysteries, finding out why crimes were perpetrated in terms of a specific family history of motivations, conflicts, tensions, and repressions. The contemporary detective here has a psychoanalytic dimension, but the Freudian uncoverer and hunter of knowledge can easily become like a bird of prey, a threat, descending on people and ripping open their secrets.

We might think of Harrison Ford in Peter Weir's *Witness*, where in relation to the tranquillity of the Amish rural life giving him shelter, he appears at moments like a dark dangerous hawk. An interesting aspect of the controversial thriller *Basic Instinct* is its playful inversion of Hitchcock's *Vertigo*. Sharon Stone as key character Katherine Trammel is made up to look like Kim Novack, and the film has a soundtrack very similar to that of Hitchcock's haunting classic. But whereas in *Vertigo* the Kim Novack character is followed round and constructed by the gaze and fantasy of the James Stewart detective character, in *Basic Instinct* the relationship of detective and woman, gaze and object of gaze, is reversed. Katherine, a powerful female figure, a 'woman on top' in Natalie Davis' term, is a writer working on a thriller about a detective, and it is she who becomes the hunter of Michael Douglas' character Nick. (Appropriately, when they make love, she is indeed on top.) It is he who as the narrative unfolds feels psychoanalytically explored, pursued, investigated and constructed by Katherine's active, sharp, pondering, voyeuristic 'writerly' gaze for the purposes of her research: an affinity between writer and detective that Nick comes to recognise and is part of his growing affection for her, in a movie of complex, uncertain, enigmatic, unresolved meanings.

The detective can be at once free of conventional social relations, and also cut off from them. In an episode of *Minder*, for example, a young woman from up north sends her child down to stay with Terry while she escapes from her violent man. It turns out that Terry is (perhaps) the father, the result of a casual encounter. Terry enjoys being with the boy, playing soccer with him, expressing affection, becoming involved in the developing bond between them. But Arthur derides what's happening. How could Terry, shadowed by danger, including danger to those nearest to him, keeping no regular hours, ever be involved in ordinary human relationships? The inevitable answer is that he can't be. Yet the story movingly registers Terry's sadness at the loss. In *Farewell, My Lovely*, Marlowe is also afraid, after he's escaped from the asylum, to be with and commit himself to Anne Riordan because of a danger that he is being followed.

Similar dilemmas face the superhero. In *Superman II*, for example, Superman loses his magic powers when he permits himself to fall in love with Lois Lane, and only recovers them at the cost of losing Lois as lover. In *Monkey* the irrepressible Monkey, 'great sage, equal of heaven', loses his magical powers when he falls in love with a young village woman. Like Superman, he becomes a weakling and laughing stock; he can no longer oppose evil figures, and has to recover his powers at the expense of his love. This may appear obviously sexist: women impair men's powers. But television superheroes like Bionic Woman, Wonderwoman, and Isis face similar situations with men, ordinary mortals; they love, but they can't act on that love. All such figures, female and male, are in effect immortal beings with a universal quest to find or maintain justice in the world. Detectives, too, we know, are god-like in their indestructibility. Whatever dire troubles they get into, however much they're sapped or captured, they'll survive to fight on. What is clear is the ambiguous relationships to ordinary mortals detectives and superheroes have: they're their ultimate defenders, yet are rarely able to enjoy relations with them except in ephemeral, threatened ways. The detective as superhero, that is, can be enviably free and independent, yet also a sad and tragic figure, the permanent lonely outsider: we return to Marlowe's empathy with Moose Malloy, figure of the grotesque giant rejected, like Frankenstein's monster, by ordinary humanity.

CHAPTER SEVENTEEN

Crime Fiction as Changing Genre

... the theme of the mask, the most complex theme of folk culture. The mask is connected with the joy of change and reincarnation, with gay relativity and with the merry negation of uniformity and similarity; it rejects conformity to oneself. The mask is related to transition, metamorphoses, the violation of natural boundaries .... It contains the playful element of life; it is based on a peculiar interrelation of reality and image, characteristic of the most ancient rituals and spectacles. Of course it would be impossible to exhaust the intricate multiform symbolism of the mask.

Bakhtin, Rabelais and His World [1]

'Janet', he [Jim Chee] said, 'Spare me all that lawyer talk ... '
... That had touched a nerve. Janet's voice turned chilly.
'I'll spare you the lawyer talk. You spare me the "I'm more Indian than you are" crap. Okay?'

Tony Hillerman, Coyote Waits [2]

Like the trickster, the detective is not necessarily or always admirable or likeable. Nor are the narratives through which this cultural figure moves. For some of the worst of the genre, we have only to pause over the character of Mickey Spillane's Mike Hammer. Spillane's novels are violently Cold War in their hatred and destruction of any Reds that Hammer might come across. But the gender politics of the novels can also be hair-raising.

In *I, the Jury* (1947) Mike meets psychiatrist Charlotte Manning in the course of investigating the murder of his friend Jack Williams, an old army buddy. Jack had been shot in the stomach, and Mike vows to shoot his murderer in exactly the same place. It turns out it is Charlotte who has killed Jack. Strong, lithe, with big shoulders, she also kills everyone else. Driven by desire for wealth and power, she gets her clients hooked on heroin. Yet she seems so caring, intelligent, understanding, warm, even maternal as well. Charlotte appears to reciprocate Mike's love for her, they agree to marry and have kids, and Charlotte will give up working upon marriage. Mike keeps on refusing to make love with Charlotte, despite her invitations; he'll wait until they're married. He does make love with Mary Bellemy the nymphomaniac: but with Mary what you get is what you see. Charlotte, however, is evilly duplicitous. Mike comes to realise that as a psychiatrist she is in a position to see men's 'frailty', and take advantage of it to further her secret criminal career. In the showdown Mike comments, as Charlotte undresses in front of him, that she 'no longer has the social instinct of a woman – that of being dependent upon a man'. And indeed he does shoot her where she'd shot Jack. The male criminals and their antics in *I, the Jury* hold very little interest for Mike. What drives him excitedly on is desire for revenge against the dangerous woman, Charlotte and her manly independence. When, shot by Mike, Charlotte gasps 'how c-could you?' he offers her the final notorious words of the novel: 'It was easy.'

In *Vengeance is Mine* (1951) Mike wakes up drunk in a hotel room, a friend of his, another old army buddy from out of town, next to him, dead. The publicity-seeking DA and the dumb police (except for his friend Pat Chambers) believe it was suicide, and take Mike's licence away from him, because it was a bullet from Mike's gun that shot his friend. Mike follows clues to a high-class modelling agency, run by Juno Reeves, so beautiful she's like a goddess, wearing her looks 'proudly and arrogantly'. But something is wrong. The models are used to attract businessmen (like Mike's friend) and assorted big shots and politicians, who are photographed for blackmailing purposes. Hammer goes over various possibilities concerning who might be the ultimate organiser and brains of the operation. It turns out not to be recognisable criminals, as he thinks for most of the time, but – Juno. Juno starts to seduce Mike, and Mike is near to giving in and being possessed: 'Her eyes were a fathomless depth that tried to draw me down into them.' Yet something steadies him, makes him want to 'reach out across the table and smack her right in the teeth'. There is the anguish of a memory, of a woman whom he once had had to kill (this is a reference to the remarkable conclusion of *I, the Jury*). 'She was the most gorgeous thing that ever lived,' Mike confides to Juno of Charlotte Manning,

> 'and I was in love with her. But she did something and I played God; I was the judge and I the jury and the sentence was death. I shot her right in the gut and when she died I died too.'

Indeed, Mike bleeds internally because he's killed two women by this method in the past, Charlotte and Lola. By the end of the narrative

Mike works out that Juno is the New York strangler and has killed almost everyone in and out of sight, including his army buddy. He tells her he won't kill her, he'll take her in (shades of Sam Spade and Brigit O'Shaughnessy in Hammett's *The Maltese Falcon*, Brigit also having killed Sam's partner at the beginning of the novel). But then the enormously strong Juno attacks him. In the ensuing struggle her gown is ripped away, 'falsies' and all, to reveal Juno for what he is. Mike allows a shooting match in which he gets to his gun first and pumps bullets into the 'queen': 'I forgot all my reservations about shooting a woman then.'

Mike can now work out that the vague resentment he'd all along felt towards Juno was really revulsion. He realises he should have suspected something when Juno had taken him for drinks to a 'fag joint' in the Village. Spellbound then, he had thought Juno was all woman in contrast to the bar's usual clients. There had even been a 'lesbian' there. When Juno went to the powder room a 'kid who had artist written all over her in splotches of paint', followed, apparently 'another one of those mannish things that breed in the half-light of the so-called aesthetical world'. But the artist came back scowling, having noticed what Mike is only privileged to witness right at the end.

Certainly no one could accuse Mike Hammer of being the sophisti-cated Nick Charles of Dashiell Hammett's *The Thin Man*. In comparison to most private eyes, Mike has no wit, no composure, no cool. He hides nothing, wearing his psychopathologies on his sleeve. He's always getting 'hopping mad', he's always shouting, always snarling at cops and the DA. He can't seem to become sexually excited without also becom-ing violent. He's driven by vengeance against people who think that he's a chump or that they're tougher than he is. He spends his waking hours punching, kicking, shooting and generally out-toughing tough guys. He leaves a trail of fear, broken teeth, gunshot wounds, dismemberment, blood and vomit.

Spillane's novels trail an air of absurdity, of the more than faintly ridiculous. They indicate the extreme ideological uses the conventions of genre, any genre, can be put to. But, just as we wouldn't leave the story of high literary modernism with the spectacle of Ezra Pound broadcasting for Mussolini, it might be refreshing to glance at detective writing of a less repugnant kind.

Some of the best of the genre

The detective of course has never been confined to the city. The mystery novels of Tony Hillerman feature two Navajo heroes, Lieutenant Joe Leaphorn and Officer Jim Chee, members of a fictional Navajo Tribal Police on the big reservation, on the Four Corners of Utah, Arizona,

Colorado and New Mexico. While part of a police force, Leaphorn and Chee are continually detective-like in their independence from conventional plodding or inept police methods, especially those of the FBI, who have jurisdiction over homicides on the reservation.

Crime fiction is a much-loved form worldwide. Reading Hillerman novels like *The Ghostway, Skinwalkers, A Thief of Time, People of Darkness, Listening Woman, Talking God, Coyote Waits,* has been for me an intense, moving, enjoyable and wrenching experience. The novels are exciting and Chandleresque in their wit and play with language. Comic moments often turn on Chee's waywardness as loose cannon, inevitably disobeying any instruction to steer clear of mysteries that also involve the FBI. In *The Ghostway* Chee is firmly told by his Captain to find someone on the reservation for the feds, but not to pursue his own inquiries: 'Chee finds. Chee calls in. Chee leaves it at that. Chee does not do any freelance screwing around.'[3] I was intrigued to know whether Hillerman was Navajo, but on reading *Talking Mysteries,* a volume of autobiographical sketches and interviews with Hillerman by his friend Ernie Bulow (bookdealer and author of *Navajo Taboos*), quickly learned that Hillerman was Anglo-American. As Hillerman whimsically tells the story, he was raised in a rural area of Oklahoma, in a pre-television culture which was often too poor to buy batteries to operate the radio. He grew up feeling that, along with his Seminole and Pottawatomie Indian neighbours, his people were mere country boys compared to the nearest town-boy Greeks. The crossroads he came from, Sacred Heart, had no library, and the young Hillerman had to order books from the mimeographed catalogue of the state library. The librarian, however, would send books like the *History of the Masonic Order in Oklahoma,* or *Modern Dairy Management.* Once, however, came a 'novel about a half-breed Australian aborigine policeman who could solve crimes in the desert Outback because he knew the country and understood the culture'. Hillerman says that the memory lingered on of this strange ethnology and the plot of a novel where the grotesque, empty landscape was as important as any character. Hillerman forgot the name of the book and its author until reminded by a reviewer some thirty years later that it was Arthur Upfield.

In July 1945, just back from World War II, with a patch over a damaged eye and a gimpy leg, Hillerman found a job driving a truckload of pipe from Oklahoma City to an oil drilling site on the Navajo reservation. Suddenly a party of about twenty Navajo horsemen and women emerged from the piñons and crossed the dirt road in front of him, wearing ceremonial regalia, performing a part of the Enemy Way, a curing ceremonial The People conduct to bring themselves back into harmony with their universe (it was being held for a returned serviceman like himself). Hillerman records that at that moment he was fascinated and, forty years later, is still fascinated by Navajo culture.

Hillerman became a journalist, editor of *The New Mexican* in Santa Fe for eleven years. Then he moved with his family to Albuquerque, enrolled as a graduate student in English at the University of New Mexico, and finally became a professor of journalism. When he decided to write a mystery, *The Blessing Way*, he chose at first to have the novel turn on the observations of an anthropologist engaged in a study of Navajo witchcraft beliefs. But another character he had sketched in, Lieutenant Joe Leaphorn of the Navajo Tribal Police, was, Hillerman realised, clamouring for a bigger part. Leaphorn, and Jim Chee who was created later, became central to his novels.

Lieutenant Joe Leaphorn and Officer Jim Chee are very different characters. Leaphorn is of retirement age, upset and to some degree lost because of the death of his wife; he is wily, clever, legendary for his persistence and capacity to unravel the most difficult of cases, comfortable with white ways, with a local FBI agent, Kennedy, as a longstanding friend, and also sceptical and pragmatic, so much so that other Navajo, including Chee (and Navajo readers of the novels) suspect him of a rationalism that opposes all religion, including the Navajo belief in witches ('skinwalkers'). Chee, a much younger man but more traditional, has received training in Navajo curing rituals, and wishes to practise healing ceremonies; unfortunately, he is rarely asked to do so. He does, however, perform a curing ritual for Leaphorn after Leaphorn's wife Emma dies. The two men were, initially, not friends, though they have come more and more to respect each other, if warily. Leaphorn and Chee often begin an investigation separately and unaware of the other's involvement; when they find out the other is working on the case, they are frequently irritated. Their relationship is a difficult one, rather like father and son, with Chee the heir-apparent to Leaphorn as the Navajo Tribal Police's 'Sherlock Holmes', as Hillerman puts it in *Talking Mysteries*.[4]

Hillerman doesn't like the Agatha Christie tradition of crime fiction that focuses on the element of puzzle, wishing to locate his writing within a primarily though not exclusively American tradition, following names like Chandler, Graham Greene, Ross Macdonald. As Hillerman says, he is interested not so much in who did it as why.[5] His novels feature exploration of Navajo society, customs and beliefs as they entwine with and are keys to the mystery narrative. The novels also frequently powerfully evoke the desert and mountain landscapes and the cloud formations of the Utah–Arizona–New Mexico region.

It was not long before Hillerman's reputation as mystery writer grew and flourished. In his introduction Ernie Bulow points out that there

are no actual Navajo policemen of the sort Hillerman writes about; on
the reservation Navajo police are used primarily as traffic cops and for
crowd control at functions and little else. Hillerman has been honoured
as a Friend of the Navajos because of his respectful attitude toward
cultural matters and the dignity with which he invests his Navajo police
characters. Bulow says that Hillerman's novels are used in English
classes in reservation schools and are so popular with the Navajo people
that they are passed from hand to hand until they fall apart. Often there
is argument amongst Navajo readers about details of customs
mentioned in the novels, which, Bulow notes, is not surprising as hardly
any two Navajos will agree on much of anything, and in any case
individual variation by Navajos of customs is traditionally encouraged.
Hillerman himself talks of his delight that he has been voted as most
popular author by the students of St Catherine Indian School, and that
middle-aged Navajos tell him how reading his work has revived their
children's interest in the Navajo Way. The best review he feels he
received was by a Navajo librarian who said the novels, with Leaphorn
and Chee winning in the narratives, make Navajos feel good about
being Navajos.[6] In Hillerman's mysteries, the Navajos are not victims,
are not defeated.

I won't, however, be discussing the novels set on the reservation, but
will glance at *Talking God* (1989), located largely in Washington DC and
perhaps the most avowedly 'political' of Hillerman's novels, turning on
concern for Native American remains held by the Smithsonian Natural
History Museum. *Talking God* here has a particular resonance with an
Australian issue: Australian Aborigines have been agitating for several
years for return of ancestral skeletal remains, particularly from
museums in Britain. (There is, for example, the terrible story of the
robbing of the grave of the Tasmanian Aboriginal William Lanne in
1869, the dismemberment and stealing by various European men of
science, including Fellows of the Royal Society, of different parts of his
body.)[7] Aboriginal people have campaigned in Britain against museums
holding large collections of skeletal remains, and the issue has been
highly controversial amongst archaeologists, anthropologists, historians,
museum directors.[8]

In *Talking Mysteries* Hillerman notes that he has a lot of readers
amongst anthropologists and archaeologists, that he is invited to talk to
them, and that they 'never seem to resent the fact that archaeologists
are treated rather roughly in my books'. Some of his novels have turned
on dramas to do with excavations of pottery of the Anasazi, the famous
cliff-dwellers who mysteriously walked away from their canyon homes.
Hillerman comments that well into the twentieth century, archaeologists

were hauling off to museums wagon loads of artifacts without proper field notes or documentation of the digs. During the Depression years the anthropology department of the University of Utah distinguished itself by putting out word that it would pay $5 for a pot from the Four Corners area. At least up until the recent past archaeologists were world-champion ruin looters, grave robbers, and many ex-academics are prominent in the antique Indian trade.[9]

Talking God

Talking God's complicated strands of narrative involve not only North American but Chilean politics, all converging in the final scenes of crisis and desperate action on the Smithsonian Museum. The novel opens with a dramatic prologue. An administrator, a lawyer, someone with a high WASP New England name, Catherine Morris Perry, finds on her desk one Monday morning a parcel. Mrs Perry had been in the news recently, interviewed as a spokesperson for museum policy on the return of ancestral bones. A colleague of hers, Henry Highhawk, a curator, had been making a splash in the media, saying that he was a Navajo, and that the museum's entire collection of some 18,000 Native American skeletons, dating from the nineteenth century to immediate ancestors, should be returned to their relatives and owners, with the museum making plaster casts. The museum had unsuccessfully tried to get rid of Highhawk. To media enquiries, Mrs Perry had said that Mr Highhawk's suggestion of plaster casts was not practical both because of the needs of scientific research and because of the public's right to expect 'authenticity'. When she opens the parcel on her desk she finds to her horror that it contains the bones of her own ancestors – her grandparents. Accompanying this find is a note from her colleague Henry Highhawk, saying he hoped the enclosed were authentic enough for her. Mrs Perry cries out in fright to Mrs Bailey, her African-American secretary, introducing a motif of racial and ethnic hierarchy that continues through the novel.

In the media hubbub featuring Highhawk that follows, a Chilean opposition group in exile, living in Washington DC, determines to make contact with the Smithsonian curator, in order, as it turns out, to put into operation a plan to gain revenge on the Pinochet regime, which is still surveilling and repressing them in Washington from its embassy. When the intelligence operatives from the embassy had some time back killed a member of the exiled group with a car bomb, the publicity the action generated had stirred the State Department to declare various embassy personnel persona *non grata*. The embassy, worried about what might happen during a forthcoming visit to an exhibition at the Smithsonian by Chile's chief of secret police, General Ramon Huerta Cordona, hires a professional assassin, Leroy Fleck, to tail the opposition group. Fleck kills one of the Chilean dissidents, but they send another of their number, Santero, who makes contact with and befriends the ingenuous Highhawk.

Highhawk wants to become initiated as a Navajo. He says his grandmother is Navajo, of the Bitter Water Clan, and he contacts old Agnes Tsosi, who, seriously ill with cancer, is to have a major week-long winter ceremony performed for her, the Yeibichai, named after Talking God, the maternal grandfather of all the spirits. Also known as the Night Chant, the Yeibichai involves masked dancers as well as sand paintings, prayers, songs and rites.[10] Highhawk is arrested at the reservation by Jim Chee, given the task because of Highhawk's curious parcel to Mrs Perry. Highhawk has been making the point in the media that the digging up of the graves of grandparents of Native Americans is considered an act of science, with the bones being displayed in museums, but digging up white bones of similar age is considered a shocking crime. He insists on being defended by a Navajo lawyer, which brings into the narrative a friend of Jim Chee's, Janet Pete, who lives in Washington, working for a law firm which also includes her white lover, an ex-university professor of law, John McDermott. Janet had left her job as a lawyer with the Navajo Tribe to follow John McDermott to Washington. But, wheels within wheels within wheels, John's law firm wants her to take the case, in order to manipulate Highhawk to return a Tano Twin War God fetish that will help them in a business case they're involved in where they're acting for a white corporation on Tano Pueblo land.

Leroy Fleck, son of poor white trash, racist, raped in prison, now a professional killer, his only concern how to look after his aged Mama in a rest home, murders the first Chilean opposition leader sent to make contact with Highhawk on a train near the Navajo reservation. Fleck dumps his body beside the tracks, having removed all signs of identity – the Chilean embassy now trying to be more indirect and discreet in their methods. This murder brings in Joe Leaphorn, who with great skill follows various difficult clues and establishes that the murdered man was indeed a Chilean dissident from Washington: that Leaphorn can discover his identity shows up the ineptitude of the Law, here the Washington FBI. Leaphorn goes to Washington to continue the hunt. Unknown to Leaphorn, so does Chee, called there by Janet Pete who feels in danger because of her association with her new client, Mr Henry Highhawk.

The exhibition of pre-Columbian masks at the Smithsonian is to open soon. Highhawk wishes to plant in a mask of Talking God, the chief god of the Yeibichai, a recorded speech protesting against the imperial display of colonised cultures. Highhawk's trust in the Chilean dissidents turns out, however, to be fatally misplaced, for they substitute in the mask a bomb intended for the general. With some help from an African-American cop in Washington, the Navajo detectives unravel multiple mysteries, producing as they do so multiple inversions: of country over city, Native American and African-American over white, and detective figure over official police. Chee also resumes ownership of the mask of Talking God, to take back to its Navajo owners (he leaves behind a replica expertly made by Highhawk).

Yet if Chee is carrying out Highhawk's desires at the end, there is nevertheless a complex play of attitudes to Henry Highhawk and to dilemmas of identity more generally. In the Americas, it would appear, North and South, with their centuries-long history of invasion, dispossession, colonising and slavery, identity always has dimensions of race and ethnicity. Identity always carries that history, the urgent presentness of history, and so always is unstable, uncertain, contradictory, in process, in conflict, never realised, never realisable.

The Navajos are initially unimpressed, indeed amused, by Highhawk's desire to be considered Navajo. Leaphorn sees a photo of the curator, sent to Mrs Tsosi, showing his long, slender face, large blue eyes, and long blond hair woven into two tight braids. Leaphorn thinks Highhawk certainly 'doesn't look like a Navajo'. When Captain Largo calls in Chee to tell him to arrest Highhawk, Largo is scornful of people who 'decide to turn Indian', saying they usually call themselves Whitecloud or Squatting Bear and declare themselves Cherokee or some other 'dignified tribe that everybody knows about'. But, says the tough Captain, 'this jerk had to pick Navajo'. Both Largo and Chee think it's ironic that 'this Highhawk nut' would excavate graves as he did with Mrs Perry's relatives, since Navajos traditionally have a fierce religious aversion to corpses and everything associated with death. When Chee sees Highhawk at the Yeibichai ceremony the Smithsonian curator is wearing clothes Navajos might have worn in the 1920s, including a leather jacket with fringes, reminding Chee of a Hollywood Indian. Chee observes other whites at the ceremony, known to the Navajos as Lone Rangers, part of the 'liberal/intellectual covey' that had flocked into the Navajo Mountain territory and declared themselves spokesmen for, and guardians of, Navajo families facing eviction from their lands in what had become the Hopi part of the old Joint Use Reservation. The Lone Rangers come in the invariable guise of ragged jeans, jean jacket, and horse-blanket, the 'uniform of their clique'. Is Henry Highhawk a Lone Ranger?

Yet Chee's attitude to Highhawk is marked, as the narrative goes on, by ambivalence, by continuing scepticism, doubt and scorn mixed with interest, respect, admiration. Even at the Yeibichai on the reservation Chee notices that Highhawk's expression, as he watches the Night Chant ceremony, is 'reverent', and that Highhawk also seems to know the words of the songs. In Washington Chee again finds himself impressed by Highhawk's knowledge of Navajo traditions and his curatorial skill with and respect for the Talking God mask. Chee even finds himself at one point contrasting the way 'this crazy white man' *believed* with Leaphorn's agnosticism about the Navajo Way. Janet Pete also finds herself respecting Highhawk, even while acknowledging his hunger for media attention. Neither Chee nor Pete can decide quite what they think about Highhawk, nor do they totally dismiss his desire and claim to be a Navajo.

The Navajo characters in the novel reject being essentialised as a single known identity, and indeed Chee at one point returns the traditional anthropological gaze when he looks down on the urban subway crowd in Washington as a species that had evolved to survive overcrowding and endure aggression. Chee, Leaphorn and Pete dislike being granted by curious whites in Washington an enclosing identity as 'Indians'. Janet Pete tells Chee that her law firm regards her as their 'Indian', as if one Indian is supposed to know about all Indians. When Leaphorn comes across Leroy Fleck at one point, Fleck asks are you an Indian, and Leaphorn replies that he's a Navajo. (In *The Ghostway* the narrator tells us that the 'isolation, the sense of space' of remote areas of the reservation is 'treasured' by the Navajos, but called 'loneliness' by both whites *and* Pueblo Indians.)[11]

But is Highhawk, with blue eyes, blond hair, at home with corpses, a Navajo? Can they accept Highhawk as a fellow Navajo? What does it mean to be Navajo, or any identity?

Hillerman's novels break with much crime fiction tradition in being interested in transformation and metamorphosis of characters. We can enjoy a serial dimension from one novel to the next of changing attitudes and relationships, as in Chee's relations with Leaphorn or his friendship with Janet Pete. Chee in particular is not a 'fixed character'. Chee is caught between his liking for Mary Landon, an Anglo-American teacher who had taught on the reservation, and a growing attraction to fellow-Navajo Janet Pete, though Chee is wary of Janet Pete because of her affair with the Anglo-American lawyer, John, and because she doesn't live within the area of the four Sacred Mountains that maintains the Navajo traditional way. Janet Pete in turn is irritated by Chee's assumption of being somehow more truly Navajo than she is.

Talking God does play with a traditional modernist literary and sociological contrast between tradition and modernity, community and mere association, the rural society of the reservation, where people know each other, and Washington DC as an abyss of impersonality and uniformity, atomised, anomic, alienating. When Chee arrives in the national capital the day is 'gray, chilly, drizzling', and in general the Washington scenes draw on film noir traditions registering the contemporary city in a chronotope of dimness, darkness, mist, rain. Also, the assassin, Leroy Fleck, is like other professional assassins in Hillerman mysteries, at one end of a continuum of humanity, extreme in his aloneness, with only one affective tie in the world, to his Mama (who no longer recognises him), in contrast to the Navajos, where everyone is involved with deep and wide ties of kinship and community.

Yet Navajo society is not idealised in the Hillerman novels, especially in relation to witchcraft beliefs, engendering suspicion, violence, and murder (as in *Skinwalkers*), the suspicion that fellow-Navajos might turn out to be witches, malevolent beings who can transform themselves from human form into dog or wolf or werewolf.[12] Who are what they seem?

Navajo customs themselves always (always-already) involved a play with identity. Trickster figures are important in Navajo mythology, as in the feared Coyote spirit, bringing ill-fate. In *Talking God* one of the exhibits for the Smithsonian's 'Masked Gods of the Americas' display is of Watersprinkler, a Navajo spirit based on Kokopelli, the humpbacked flute player, a mythological figure widespread in pre-Columbian folklore, rock art depictions of him ranging from Alaska to the tip of South America. Kokopelli is associated with fertility, music, agriculture, sometimes portrayed with horns, perhaps with a staff of some kind, often with a flute or playing a flute, usually with a large hunchback, and oftentimes with a large erection.[13] In some ways we can see Leaphorn and Chee themselves in *Talking God* as tricksters, wise fools (from the country) exposing the unbending unflinching conventionality and stupidity of the FBI (which hasn't got a clue what's happening).

Tricksters are masters of masking, and masking is very important in Hillerman novels. As in Bakhtin, with his evocation in *Rabelais and His World* of folk- and carnival-masking as a tribute to the openness of identity, to the possibilities of change, transformation, metamorphosis, so masking is everpresent in *Talking God*, masking as mystery, uncertainty, difficulty, opportunity, pain, masking as endless and always imbricated in colonial and post-colonial histories and contexts. Being part of kinship-structured communities doesn't guarantee secure identity in a Navajo world that can never be isolated from a history of dispossession, marginalisation, racial and ethnic hierarchy.

Attitudes in *Talking God* to the Spanish-speaking Chilean dissidents in Washington are varied and complex. The Pinochet regime's representatives in the Washington embassy are upper-class, arrogant, brutal and murderous, and the novel records the grief of the dissidents when they find out from Leaphorn that one of their number, the old man Santillanes, has been murdered. Leaphorn had realised, when he'd examined Santillanes' body in New Mexico near the reservation, that the old man had been tortured, as had Santero (most of his fingers are missing), the next dissident who befriended Highhawk.

Observing Santillanes' body, Leaphorn speculates that here was an aristocratic face, with fine bones, high forehead, and 'narrow, arrogant nose'. When Jim Chee observes Santero at the Yeibichai, he notes the contrast between Highhawk's intensity of attention and reverence for the Navajo ceremony and the Chilean's total lack of interest: his only concern is to meet Highhawk. We might say that the Chilean regime and the dissidents, while so bitterly divided politically, share a cultural arrogance. The dissidents wish to kill General Huerta as revenge for how they, 'victims of Chilean terror', have been tortured, maimed and murdered by the military. But the explosion would have killed not only General Huerta (who was campaigning to have a jewel-encrusted gold Incan mask returned to Chile, presumably so he could keep it for himself), but many innocent bystanders at the exhibition as well. It would also have destroyed the display of Native American artifacts: the heirs of the Spanish conquest held no interest, sympathy or empathy for the pre-Columbian culture of the Americas. The proposed bombing of the masked gods by the dissidents mimicked the original Spanish desecration.

Talking God doesn't, that is, construct a simple binary proposition of a unified Anglo ascendancy opposed to a unitary ensemble of non-Anglo groups. As in other Hillerman mysteries, the novel doesn't construct anything but dilemma, complexity, perplexity, yet in a recognisable carnivalesque spirit, a narrative ever challenging the harshness and finality of fate.

CHAPTER EIGHTEEN

Melodrama, Farce, Soap Opera

Melodrama is one of the most ubiquitous of modern aesthetic forms. Heir to nineteenth-century stage melodrama, it flourished and flourishes in the cinematic language of Hollywood. In serial form it flourished on radio and then television as 'soap opera' or 'the soaps', increasingly so all over the world.

As a living, expanding, vibrant form, melodrama needs no defending.[1] Yet since it began its march from Paris in the late eighteenth century, soon after the Revolution, taking shape in the aesthetic maelstrom in which also swirled Gothic and Romanticism, melodrama, in terms of 'high culture', has proved valuable only as a critical swear-word, a ready term of disparagement – 'it's melodramatic', 'it's verging on melodrama', 'by the end it became indistinguishable from a soap'. Such scorning was applied not only to stage melodrama but also to the fiction it influenced, particularly as the nineteenth century went on and the melodrama aesthetic hybridised with other forms and genres, with serial fiction, the novel of sensation, romance-melodrama (with 'romance' an abundant presence both in its 'female' form of dilemmas of love and its 'male' direction of adventure stories). Comparing something cultural to melodrama has provided a nearly two-centuries-old yardstick for measuring aesthetic weakness, a critical standard of what not to do compared to what should be done in terms of the hierarchy of forms and genres by which 'high culture' ordered its preferences, conferred value and awarded prestige.

In the nineteenth century, melodrama became very firmly associated with 'sensation' and 'popular' fiction as not culture, not literature, not art. Dickens' friend and writer of melodramatic mystery novels Wilkie Collins had suffered from this inviolable rule in the middle decades of the century, the *Pall Mall Gazette* observing of his *The Moonstone* (1868)

245

that a 'conjuror at a country fair has as much right to prate about his art'. Arthur Conan Doyle's Dr Watson also felt such a binary opposition to be common wisdom when he came to contemplate the state of general knowledge of a new and eccentric friend. In *A Study in Scarlet* (1887), Watson, invalided from the British Army in Afghanistan, returns to London to live on a small pension. He is introduced by a mutual friend to someone who can help share the cost of lodgings, and at their rooms at Number 221B Baker Street the underemployed doctor has plenty of time to study his mysterious companion. Under a heading of 'Sherlock Holmes – his limits', Watson methodically tabulates his observations, for example, 'Politics – Feeble' and 'Anatomy – Accurate but unsystematic'. He also decides that whereas Holmes' knowledge of 'Literature' is 'Nil', his acquaintance with 'Sensational Literature' is 'Immense'. Holmes apparently knows 'every detail of every horror perpetrated in the century'. 'Literature' and 'Sensational Literature', Proper Literature and Popular Literature – Watson was but applying a century's high culture knowledge to his task.[2]

Modernism did not take it upon itself to disturb this inherited 'high culture' hierarchy of genres, the neoclassical hierarchy that Bakhtin saw as settling in during the seventeenth century and working to marginalise carnival and carnivalesque genres. I agree with Andreas Huyssen's argument that modernism is a relational term, a reaction formation. The modernist aesthetic defined itself by its opposition not only to what it saw as bourgeois culture, but to mass culture and entertainment. In its formative period from the late nineteenth century, modernism constituted itself in relation to an apparently ever-expanding realm of pulp, romances, serialised *feuilleton* novels, popular and family magazines, the stuff of lending libraries, fictional bestsellers, and the like. Mass culture became, Huyssen feels, modernism's other, the spectre that haunts it, the threat against which it has to shore up its terrain. The modernist aesthetic must work by permanent contrast, it must never be contaminated by mass culture, it must abstain from trying to please a wider (or, theoretically, any) audience, it must be autonomous, self-referential, separate, pure.[3]

I think Huyssen goes too far in unifying modernism as a single mode. Yet I agree with him that in this century, as modernism triumphed aesthetically, an associated criticism exalting terms like controlled, restrained, spare, taut, tough-minded, hard-edged, gritty, became frequent common coin in much academic criticism, newspaper commentary, and 'bourgeois public sphere' conversation. These terms were assumed to be aesthetic absolutes, and melodrama, wherever it rose its head, whenever it moved, in fiction, Hollywood film, television, could be scorned as disgustingly lush, extravagant, overblown, inflated, uncontrolled, theatrical, extreme: rather like the lush mixture of styles and the extravagance of ornament and decoration of Victorian building, that modernist architecture reacted so strongly against in its insistence on geometric purity. Further, for modernist criticism, again inheriting a centuries-old high-culture hierarchy, the tragic was a superior effect, its presence an almost necessary sign of true art.[4] In these terms, melodrama was easily convicted of a fatal lack of the cosmology of tragedy, where the universe, the nature of life, being, is fundamentally sombre and bleak, with fate as ever destructive.

What luminously stares out at us in the two centuries of melodrama's existence is its continuing and now worldwide popularity, yet a popularity always accompanied by hostility from those, not least modernists amongst them, who saw and see themselves as fostering and guarding serious, quality art, whether it be in the theatre, in fiction, or on television.

Stage melodrama

Yet, as Peter Brooks argues in *The Melodramatic Imagination*, here was a form that never did have to be embarrassed by its cultural history. If Bakhtin has given us ample ground for evoking the strengths of popular genres in general, Brooks offers a sophisticated complex theory of melodrama as a specific mode, a 'total and coherent aesthetic'. Brooks tells us that he came to feel that important aspects of a long list of novelists, from Balzac and Dickens through to Henry James, Gogol, Dostoevsky, Conrad, Proust, Lawrence and Faulkner, were clearly melodramatic: melodrama itself must therefore have continuities with the highest achievements of the modern imagination. Brooks studies it in terms of its history and historical contexts, its dramaturgy, its narrative structures, its notions of representation and character, the way it constructs the moral and ethical, its cosmology, its manner of presenting itself to audiences, and its audiences.[5]

Brooks identifies melodrama's beginnings as French, and while it quickly spread to England and later the United States, and while later still it was transformed as a pervasive popular form by cinema and then television, he prefers to look to the originary period, from 1800 to 1830, as melodrama burst onto the Parisian stage in the heady days of the French Revolution when an old world was turned upside-down. The pre-Revolutionary legitimate theatre was dominated by what had been the illustrious forms of neoclassical French theatre, tragedy and high social comedy, *comédie de caractère*. Yet such glory had long faded. Tragedy as a vital form was exhausted a century before because, Brooks believes, since the end of the seventeenth century the Sacred as a unifying idea in society was lost, and so no longer could tragedy act as a communal ritual of sacrifice. The comedy of manners survived better, but its necessary basis in a unified audience committed to identical social and moral values was gradually undermined by liberal political thinking and then exploded by the Revolution.[6]

The official theatre was essentially verbal, its meanings generated almost exclusively from word, intonation and diction. Brooks refers to the mid-eighteenth-century attack on it mounted by Diderot, vainly attempting to reform 'high theatre' from within. Diderot criticised the performing style of the Comediens-Français, for example, as cold, rigid, and formalised, the Comediens tending to arrange themselves in semicircles and speak formally to the audience, with a minimum repertory of restrained and conventional gestures.[7]

The secondary theatres, however, made the most of their legally enforced muteness, developing indeed what Brooks calls an aesthetic of muteness, particularly in all sorts of pantomimes: *dialogées, heroiques, historiques,* and *féeriques.* Pantomime developed for the stage, as it settled in the Boulevard du Temple (or Boulevard du Crime as it was to become known, from the high rate of murder and abduction in its spectacles), a whole range of non-verbal expressionistic effects, which directly influenced the rising bourgeois and domestic novel as well as melodrama. In 1791 the Revolution liberated theatres in Paris to show anything they wished, and there followed, Brooks says, a rich flowering of spectacles of all sorts: dramas, topical vaudevilles, fantasies, pantomimes, *mimodrames;* and, in 1800, *Coelina,* usually recognised as inaugurating the period of 'classic' French melodrama. It was such popular theatre, along with the Gothic novel, that would help renew 'high theatre' in the Romantic drama of the 1830s and so greatly influence the novel, particularly since the novel in the nineteenth century, including for Henry James, enjoyed an unembarrassed relationship with popular entertainment. With the French Revolution as its intense context, melodrama was born as a democratic art, its representations intended to be understood by all. The bourgeoisie as well as the working class flocked to the Boulevard du Crime for their entertainment, realising that here was a theatre offering much more than the bloodless official houses.[8]

For Brooks, then, there are direct lines of influence and descent in terms of expressionistic effects from pantomime and melodrama to later culture, proper and popular. The very name 'melodrama' indicates what in part helped make it a new and distinct genre, the pervasive use of background music, a convention which cinema directly inherits. Music in melodrama marks entrances, announcing by its theme which characters are coming on stage and what emotional tone they are introducing. In every classic melodrama there is a ballet and frequently a song or two. There is further recourse to music at climactic moments and in scenes of rapid physical action, to strike particular emotional pitches, to lead the audience into a change or heightening of mood. The soliloquy of classic melodrama is clearly on its way to becoming operatic aria, and melodrama indeed finds one possible logical outcome in grand opera.[9]

The acting style of what Brooks at one point refers to as melodramatic pantomime is clearly 'non-naturalistic and irreal'. The aesthetic of muteness has in store a rich rhetoric of the non-verbal – for example, at the end of scenes and acts there is frequently a temporary resolution of meaning, a visual summary of the emotional situation, in a tableau where the characters' attitudes and gestures are compositionally arranged and frozen for a moment, like an illustrative painting. In climactic moments and in extreme situations melodrama has recourse to a dramaturgy of inarticulate cry and gesture, and indeed there is a gallery of mute roles proper, characters who can't speak but only gesture. There are blind men, paralytics, invalids of various sorts, and also non-human characters, dogs and so on, who bodily indicate extremes of attitude in the drama. Acting takes on a kind of 'plastic figurability', of bodily and facial posture, which tries to give visible shape to emotions so powerful and charged that they are almost impossible to express, that are near ineffable.

This plastic figurability derived from pantomime has its nearest equivalent, Brooks feels, in silent cinema, in the kind of modern theatre urged by Antonin Artaud, and in the importance given to bodily posture and facial grimace in the painting styles of Mannerism and Expressionism. There is also a possible connection between the aesthetic of muteness and Freud's psychoanalysis. The rhetoric of gesture and posture are attempts to render visible signs of what are usually felt to be irrecoverable, the potent 'primal' feelings of the unconscious. In this way the text of muteness is like a 'dream script'. It suggests a world of dream and nightmare, of repression, recognition of what is being repressed and release from repression – the movement of psychoanalysis, and psychoanalysis in turn can be read as a systematic realisation of the melodrama aesthetic.[10]

Melodrama is like psychoanalysis in its structures of narrative: 'The dynamics of repression and the return of the repressed figure the plot of melodrama.' Virtue, almost inevitably represented by a young heroine (unlike in later American melodrama, she need not be a virgin), stands opposed to what will seek to discredit it, to misrepresent, silence, expel, imprison or bury it alive. In one narrative structure the play opens with virtue intact and apparently happy, the heroine enjoying her state in an enclosed garden. But mystery, ambiguity and menace hover, and soon, down the road leading to the garden, the space of innocence, comes the villain, often in the guise of friendship or courtship. Even if rejected at first, the villain returns, producing the topos of the interrupted fête, the violated banquet. Then follows the triumph, for most of the action, of evil, and the fall, eclipse and often expulsion of virtue. The villains will have a number of fellow damned souls to call on for assistance, but success often comes because of errors of perception and judgement by those who should rightfully be the protectors of virtue, especially an older generation of fathers, guardians, uncles or sovereigns.

The heroine will not so much struggle against evil (the villain as seemingly all-powerful destructive fate), as simply resist. But she will be aided by a handmaiden, a fiancé, a faithful (often comic) peasant, and very often by a child, a bearer of the sign of innocence, a perceiver and bringer of truth and knowledge in a deceptive and deceived world where the villain's activities appear legitimate. As representatives of innocence and purity children can guide virtue through various perils and upset the machinations of evil in ways denied to the more worldly.[11]

We might at this point think of Wilkie Collins' *The Woman in White*, a work not discussed by Brooks, where the heroine is betrayed by her father into a promise of marriage to the villain, who is helped by another villain, Count Fosco; she is let down by her guardian, is expelled from her enclosed garden of happiness, loses her identity and name in the world, and is in effect buried alive in an asylum. But she is helped after many perils by her sister as handmaiden and by her fiancé, whose paths of assistance are illuminated by the child-like woman in white.

An important alternative to this structure, revealing close affinities to its probable source, the Gothic novel, particularly M.G. Lewis' *The Monk* (1796), is that of thwarted escape. The play might begin in a Gothic castle, and soon the virtuous prisoner appears able to escape the villain-tyrant. But, discovered, she is then imprisoned in a more frightful and subterranean chamber, and might then be granted a sentence of death. The Gothic castle itself, with its pinnacles and dungeons, crenellations, moats, drawbridges, spiralling staircases and concealed doors, realises an architectural approximation of the Freudian model of the mind, especially of the traps laid for consciousness by the unconscious and the repressed. In the topos of the castle as mind, the dungeon becomes the realm of uncontrollable id forces, and *The Monk* can be seen as close to the Romantic critique of repression, as in Blake's feeling that organised religion suppresses the 'natural' until it turns monstrous.

Brooks is surely right to point to affinities and exchanges between the Romantic, the Gothic, melodrama, and the melodramatic novel. In particular Gothic and melodrama share a preoccupation with nightmare states, with claustration and thwarted escape, with virtue and innocence buried alive and unable to voice their claim to recognition (both Agnes in *The Monk* and Laura in *The Woman in White* are believed dead). In Gothic and melodrama, evil is perceived as a major, irreducible force in the world, constantly menacing, triumphing, destroying, controlling events for long periods, appearing always frighteningly close to complete victory. Along with the heroine, we, the spectators, enter a nightmare world where those who should listen don't, and those who want to help can't. Because the heroine is passive, we must also accede to the nightmare. It carries us along so that with her we have to endure almost unbearable extremes of pain and anguish. We are paralysed to all possible threats to the self, and the moment of evil's triumph, when innocence is driven out or imprisoned, is like a 'primal scene', a moment of intense, originary trauma. But in virtue's eventual success and its public recognition is enacted a liberation from the primal scene of repression: by the end of the drama desire, the desire of good to be recognised as good, will have achieved its satisfaction, its fulfilment. And Brooks suggests another historical connection, not only to Gothic in literature but to the French Revolution as an opening-up of and liberation from the 'claustral', democracy as virtue released from its depths of imprisonment.

Melodrama is a release of the repressed in another sense, in the way it reverses ordinary social codes of behaviour. If melodrama possesses a rich dramaturgy of the non-verbal, words are still extremely important. Words are used in non-naturalistic and non-realist ways, just as 'character' in melodrama is constructed along lines that have nothing to do with any ideal of psychological realism. In melodrama the use of word and character has much more in common with the ambition of early Romantics like Rousseau and Sade, that they must say all, *tout dire,* that nothing of the possible human response must be left unexpressed, that writing must be a continual overstatement. As Brooks says, one of the most immediately noticeable things about melodrama is the way characters utter the unspeakable, give notice of their deepest feelings, dramatise through their heightened and polarised words and gestures the whole lesson of their relationship. What stands out is the explicitness and directness of the characters, the way they tell us and each other their moral judgements of the world and their opinions of each other. Conversations become confrontations.[12]

It is for this reason that theorists of drama like Eric Bentley have said that melodrama is a childish form,[13] a form that doesn't observe the necessary reticences and hidings-of-true-opinions of adults in ordinary social life, the surface of good manners that children indeed find puzzling given that they might already have heard their parents' 'true' opinions. To Bentley we can reply that it is the right and privilege of 'culture' precisely to be different from ordinary life. We can also say that if children love melodrama, as I very much suspect they do, it is because, like the adults, they love seeing rules of politeness in adult conversation broken. They are, as we are, fascinated by and delight in an imaginary world where characters can say anything, where manners, the fear of self-betrayal, and accommodation to the conventional, no longer confine and control.[14]

Melodrama exteriorises conflict. It makes visible psychic structures at work in relationships and situations. Characters represent extremes and they undergo extremes, passing through 'peripaties', changes of fortune, from heights to depths or the reverse, almost simultaneously. In the 'aesthetics of astonishment' of melodrama, usual life, the ordinary and humble and quotidian (including family life), is always brought to the pitch of crisis to reveal itself as full of excitement and suspense, charged with inner meaning. Melodrama attempts to break through the repression of daily life by reaching towards and bringing to the surface the most basic, the most primary roles and relationships, of Father, Daughter, Protector, Persecutor, Judge, Duty, Obedience, Justice, exteriorised in particular characters and in their conflicts and confrontations. It becomes a 'drama of pure psychic signs'.[15]

Melodrama's mode, says Brooks, is Manichaean, the conflict and confrontation of characters offering polarised moral values, of good and evil, light and darkness. The villain represents the force of evil in the universe, and one clear sign of this is that the necessary motives for such villainy are often never adequately presented. Evil is because evil is. The villain violates a fête or banquet at the beginning, and so betrays and undoes the moral order. The fête or banquet is resumed at the play's end, signifying melodrama's cosmology, the victory of the basic forces of good in the universe over the destructiveness of fate, the near-irresistible force of harsh destiny.[16]

Melodrama believes in the reality of moral forces in the world and a central plenitude of the good, even if those forces are so elusive that they have to be drawn out from below consciousness, from behind usual daily life. While the melodramatic in this sense influences novelists like Dostoevsky, Conrad, Balzac, James, Lawrence and Faulkner, it is opposed by another important strand of modern writing, as in Flaubert, Maupassant, Beckett, Robbe-Grillet, possibly Joyce and Kafka. Flaubert in particular inaugurates a modern tradition that most consciously holds out an alternative to melodrama, an attitude of deconstructive and stoic materialism, a language of deflationary suspicion. This tradition refuses to believe in signifieds. It stays with the void as regulatory principle of life and fiction. It sees the task of the novelist as setting in motion the play of the signifier, enjoyment of the narrative itself, the novel celebrating its status as pure fiction. But, Brooks says, melodrama recognises the provisionality of its 'created centres', the constant threat that its plenitude may be a void, the need – almost ritualistic – with each new text and performance to find the centre again. Melodrama thereby does not betray 'modern consciousness'.[17]

Brooks and Bakhtin: Compare and contrast

Let us conclude our summary of Brooks and relate him back to Bakhtin's cultural theory and forward to later forms of melodrama. In Brooks' reprise of history, melodrama is an appropriate dramatic form for a 'post-sacred era', which was no longer 'organic and hierarchically cohesive'. (I think the degree of cohesiveness is perhaps exaggerated.) With the French Revolution as context, melodrama sprang into the world as a democratic form, for all to 'read'. It was also democratic in another sense. Among the repressions broken through is class domination. Melodrama characteristically suggests that a poor persecuted girl can confront her powerful oppressor with the truth about his moral condition. Villains are frequently tyrants and oppressors, an attribute developed in the 'romantic socialism' of Romantic drama where they are often aristocrats, squires, landlords, factory owners. The victims of evil are egalitarian in their basic attitudes, for whatever their class origin they believe or come to believe in merit rather than privilege, and in the community of the good.[18]

Brooks is like Bakhtin in supporting what he refers to in connection with Diderot as a 'more libertarian aesthetic', a critical pluralism. As Brooks points out, there is a range from high to low examples in any literary field. The aesthetic coherence of a genre – any genre – is not disproved by a 'bad' example of it. Like Bakhtin, then, Brooks opposes the hierarchy of genres. He gets irritated at the kind of criticism that uses 'melodramatic' as a pejorative term, and that mourns in writers like Balzac, Dostoevsky and Henry James lapses from serious social realism into lurid romance.

Like Bakhtin, Brooks separates ideology from literary convention. He observes that while melodrama presents itself democratically, its social implications may be variously revolutionary or conservative.[19] Being ideologically radical, or liberal, or conservative, is not intrinsic to the genre, nor to any genre. This is the kind of insight that also illuminates Bakhtin's wonderful writing in *The Dialogic Imagination,* in 'Forms of Time and of the Chronotope in the Novel', on ancient narrative genres like Greek Romance or the adventure novel of everyday life. Like

Bakhtin, Brooks is trying to move criticism away from a preoccupation with value judgements within 'high literature' towards a more anthropological view of culture. Just as Bakhtin sees the carnivalesque as a mode where totalising definitions of reality and truth can be challenged so that alternative visions of life and history can be created, so we can say that Brooks sees melodrama as a 'liminal' activity (to call once again on Victor Turner's term), a state of between and betwixt where the usual forms and rules and modes of interaction of daily life are suspended, and where anything can be expressed: an 'anti-structure' to society's 'structure'. To call on another anthropologist, melodrama is in Clifford Geertz's phrase a form of 'deep play' where attitudes, conflicts, tensions, traumas, fears, anxieties, resentments, passions, desires and dreams not usually permitted expression can be represented, played and experimented with.

Peter Brooks – His limits

There is in *The Melodramatic Imagination* a kind of nostalgia for the past, a nostalgia that allows elements of the hierarchical and even the snobbish to violate its analysis. Part of the reason, we learn, that Brooks studies the heroic or classic period of French melodrama in its first three decades is that it was 'written for a public that extended from the lower classes, especially artisans and shopkeepers, through all sectors of the middle class, and even embraced members of the aristocracy – including the Empress Josephine'. In England, by contrast, melodrama quickly became entertainment exclusively for the populace – for the 'lower orders, indeed, in the Surreyside houses, for the mob'.[20] Good society in England stayed away from the theatre, until later in the century when smaller, more élite houses began providing drawing-room melodrama.

In France, however, the audience in class terms was more 'encompassing'. This explains, says Brooks, why French melodrama, while so radically democratic in style and pitched to a popular audience, strove towards more coherence as an entertainment, towards greater aesthetic self-consciousness in regard to its effects and their means. I don't see why being more 'encompassing' suggests that. You could surely argue, for example, that when British music-hall became more encompassing in class terms it lost its coherence as an entertainment and as an aesthetic, becoming too bland, too respectable, too 'legitimate'.

Brooks also suggests that a historical decadence of the genre begins to set in from the late 1830s. It begins to have a less cosmic ambition, and to be concerned more with plot, suspense, excitement, the search for new categories of thrills. He does, however, say that melodrama, continuing into cinema and television (though he sees TV soap opera as 'cheap and banal'), is by no means finished, though he himself will do no more than mention its later manifestions.[21]

Why do some people always interpret change, transformation and diversification as loss? This is an important question for the later history of melodrama, since one of these transformations is towards something very much played down in Brooks' account – the mix of the melodramatic and the comic. This is not to suggest that the melodrama and theatre of Brooks' classic period were without comedy. At one point in talking of 1800–30 as a time of prodigious theatrical efflorescence and creativity, Brooks says such work, 'if we exclude the comic productions', was principally pantomime, melodrama, and *drames*.[22] But why so exclude? He does mention the comic peasant figure as a heroine-helper, but he doesn't in *The Melodramatic Imagination* theorise the comic in relation to the melodrama aesthetic, perhaps because he has allowed to return a repressed concern for genre purity that was such a feature of French cultural history in the neoclassical period. But if Brooks doesn't want to, we can try.

In his *English Melodrama* Michael Booth points out that one of the trademarks of melodrama is that farcical scenes and scenes of violence and pathos follow each other in rapid alternation.[23] Comic genres and productions flourished on the nineteenth-century stage, and melodramas were often quickly parodied in burlesque and farce. Booth argues that nineteenth-century farce presented a lunatic world where the individual pitted the 'ingenuity of his own insanity against the massive blows of hostile coincidence and a seemingly remorseless fate'. Indeed, farce's guiding philosophical concept was that the individual was the 'chosen victim of the Fates'. Farce was frankly 'absurdist'.[24]

How, then, might we theorise the relationship of melodrama and comedy? One way is to refer to Bakhtin's notion of carnivalesque humour as challenging the harshness of fate and history: in the most dire, tense, near-unbearable moments of melodrama, when all must be lost, humour or a humorous scene can keep alive this challenge, this cosmological hope. Yet comedy also perhaps has a reverse implication. Farce, presenting humanity and life as governed by incomprehensible inexplicable absurd forces, was parodying melodrama's final refusal of tragedy. The cosmology of melodrama, of fate as open, was ever being challenged by the cosmology of farce, of fate as closed: melodrama was not permitted to put itself forward as an absolute, its reaching for an ultimate goodness in the universe was ever under comic notice. We can remember Bakhtin's argument that philosophically carnivalesque always involved self-parody, its own relativising.

We might think here too of David Wiles' *Shakespeare's Clown*, where he argues of Elizabethan theatre that the jigs that were offered at the end of a play by famous clowns of the day added new meanings to the play itself. If Shakespeare's comedies might re-affirm romantic love, such an ideal was mocked and travestied in the jigs, showing married life as rife with adultery, seduction of servants, and thrashings. The audience was presented not with a definite conclusion but with a contestation of ideals and perspectives, for whatever moral order was realised in an Elizabethan play was always in tension with its parody in the closing jig.[25]

In similar terms we might say that whatever moral order is realised in melodrama is, in nineteenth-century stage farce or parodies on television, like *Soap*, or 'Blooper' programs showing actors making mistakes in melodrama scenes, or situation comedies like *Married . . . With Children*, always in tension with an anarchy of values. *Married . . . With Children* parodies both American sitcoms that have been strongly influenced by the traumas, pathos yet hope of melodrama, and daytime soap opera shows themselves. *Married . . . With Children* presents a family and neighbourhood world that violates every ideal of romantic love, kinship, friendship, community, where life emerges as outrageously routine, uncaring, with manipulation, distrust, treachery, betrayal, and the comically violent equivalent of the thrashings of Elizabethan jigs. *Cheers*, too, the wonderful *Cheers*, increasingly offered a comically bleak world of failure and loss, of disillusioned hopes, cynical motives, fading ideals, disloyalty, treachery, undermining, the reverse of any utopian ethos of sharing and *communitas*.

It is a strength of melodrama that historically it has frequently included such elements of farce, burlesque and parody within itself, in an ever-fertile production and range of comic characters and narratives. In the famous, or, as usually perceived in modernist cultural criticism, infamous American daytime soap *Days of Our Lives*, prominent comic character Calliope is played by New York comedian Arlene Sorkin, her farcical romances parodying the intensity of romance in the other narratives, suggesting that all romance might end in absurdity.

Serial melodrama

Serial melodrama, soap opera, the soaps, would appear to be the result of the fateful meeting in the early and middle decades of the nineteenth century of stage melodrama and serial fiction, with serial fiction beginning its spectacular career of popular success in the 1830s with *The Pickwick Papers*. Increasingly through the century serial fiction expanded its range, in Dickens and Wilkie Collins, and, from the mid-century on, amongst the 'railway novelists' such as G.W.M. Reynolds, a leading

Chartist, whose immensely popular *Mysteries of London*, sensational tales of love and crime, poverty and riches, sympathised with democratic and republican causes. Critics like John Ruskin despised the 'lower middle orders' who read such material, but such 'orders', spreading lower and lower, nonetheless continued to read it more and more, in particular enjoying its serial aspect, the mystery and suspense generated by the instalment form. When Collins' *The Woman in White* began its serialisation in late 1859 in *All the Year Round*, queues would form outside the magazine office to buy the next instalment, and cloaks, bonnets, perfumes, waltzes and quadrilles were called by the book's title.[26]

Serial fiction, in print, on radio in the 1930s and 1940s, and then translated into TV soap opera, is always calling attention to its own storytelling, its own delight and resourcefulness not in presenting reality but in making culture, inventing narratives, creating suspense and endless mysteries that beget not solutions but more suspense and new mysteries. I agree with Tania Modleski in 'The Search for Tomorrow in Today's Soap Opera' that soap opera differs from traditional stage melodrama in refusing an ending and in the way the characters retain secrets, thus complicating the narrative until it can never be resolved. Soap opera narratives constantly present viewers with the many-sidedness of any question, never reaching a permanent conclusion, breaking identification with a single controlling character, providing multiple points of contradictory, ever-shifting viewpoints and perspectives. I also agree with her argument that the desire of characters to say all in melodrama, to reveal desire, dream, nightmare, trauma, fear, terror, is in tension with the serial form of the narrative which is always trying to maintain suspense and mystery and deflect resolution and knowledge by concealing and deferring.[27] In this sense we might say with Bakhtin that the soaps reveal heteroglossia, a space where the centripetal forces of melodrama (as revelation) and the centrifugal forces of serial narrative (fleeing from revelation into mystery) ever, deliciously and teasingly, collide.

Soap opera's chronotope, the way it organises its time and space, is as unlike everyday reality as possible, being always one of crisis or temporary quietness and retreat from crisis, and then crisis and cliff-hanger again. Its rhythms are sensuous, erotic. Serial melodrama is also a kind of meta-genre, is multi-genre, freely including and mixing comedy, romance, detective, adventure, mystery, horror, even, on occasion, the naturalistic and tragic.

Often its villains are businesspeople; soap opera explores the way the desire for wealth and power threatens relations of love, family, kinship, friendship, community. Here soap opera speaks to the history of stage

melodrama, which Michael Booth has argued was the chief social
protest drama of the nineteenth century, predating the industrial novel
of the 1840s and 1850s in its contemporary concerns, its interest in
drink, homelessness, poverty, the poor laws, the game laws, naval
discipline and press-gangs, slavery, attitudes to ex-convicts. It was
interested in the two-nations theme of rich and poor, and in the
morality of the strike and industrial discontent, coming down on the
side of man more often than master (he cites the remarkable 1832 play
The Factory Lad). It was also fascinated by business life, commercial
ambition, and financial intrigue.[28] Serial melodrama too is continuously
exploring social and psychological issues, issues which are never easily
or simply resolved or resolved at all; and because of the serial form
itself, issues and dilemmas can be explored at length, over many
episodes.

Soap opera's characters are not realist, are not well rounded and
believable and explicable in an everyday psychological sense, but are
more 'figures', like the masked figures of carnival; and as with carnival
masking, playing with identity, characters are not 'fixed' but struggle to
find their way through transformation and metamorphosis. Sometimes
characters are explicit social explorer figures, Lucius the Ass in modern
form, as doctors, nurses, vets, detectives, police, forensic scientists,
lawyers. But such figures are not put forward as ideal, as if beyond the
mistakes and sufferings and dilemmas experienced by every melodrama
character.

Serial melodrama continues stage melodrama's dramaturgy of
excess, a dramaturgy that is always highlighting its own theatricality. It
frequently brings such dramaturgy to new levels, very close to the point
of self-parody. Serial melodrama, we can say, parodies its own intensities,
its own commitment to utopian ideals of love and friendship and
community, just as farce did with nineteenth-century stage melodrama.
In its theatricality and teasing closeness to self-parody it perhaps joins a
postmodern aesthetic, also evident in architecture, of excess,
extravagance, flamboyance, extremes. The way characters continually
confront each other might also remind us of Lyotard's evocation in *The
Postmodern Condition* of the agon, communication and conversation as
jousting, contest, language-games, duelling. Such jousting assumes
equality between characters, however young or old, whatever their class
or gender position: there is no guaranteed wisdom, no figures of
authority. Such might also remind us of Bakhtin in *Rabelais and His
World* suggesting that in the 'world of carnival all hierarchies are
canceled', all 'castes and ages are equal'.[29] The villain, source of fate as
destructive, figure of evil as indestructible, is usually also granted
eloquence, persuasive argument, and wit as deliverer of the sarcastic

and cynical (sometimes villains are played by ex-comedians, most famously with Larry Hagman as JR in *Dallas*), thereby often becoming, especially when female, popular figures in themselves.

Melodrama, stage and serial – a great and fertile form, spreading since the late eighteenth century across the globe, but in no master mode, different and distinctive in Britain, the US, Australia, Latin America, the Middle East, its future unlimited.

CHAPTER NINETEEN

Melodrama in Action:
Prisoner, or Cell Block H
(with Ann Curthoys)

When Ann Curthoys and I gave our paper on *Prisoner*, one of Australia's most popular and long-running television serials, to a communication conference in 1983, the program still had some three years to run. It ceased production in September 1986, after almost eight years, during which it maintained consistently good ratings and won over twenty major industry awards. It has since become widely known in many other countries, sometimes under the title of *Cell Block H*, frequently attracting 'cult' audiences, particularly amongst gays. When we gave our paper, *Prisoner* had attracted little 'serious' critical praise or attention. More than ever, however, are we convinced that *Prisoner* represents not only an outstanding achievement of the Australian commercial television industry, but that in terms of television history worldwide, it is something very special indeed.[1]

Prisoner, set in 'Wentworth', a female prison, strikes us as remarkably distinctive. There's certainly no overseas serial or series from which one can see it as deriving directly. Yet every cultural product has a history, antecedents, contexts, speaks to other texts. We will begin with the political, cultural, and production contexts of *Prisoner*, move on to some textual analysis, and conclude with a discussion of its critical reception and some speculation about its audiences.

Prisoner's mixed conception

Prisoner was devised in 1978, by the Grundy Organisation for the Ten network, at a specific historical moment. Australia had had television for a little over twenty years, locally produced serials for eleven. Grundys had already in the middle 1970s started successful serials, with an emphasis on youth, like *The Young Doctors* and *The Restless Years*. The inspiration for both had come from Reg Watson, in the senior ranks of Grundys, an Australian who had returned from England where he had worked for many years for ITV. Watson had been one of the originators of the long-running British serial *Crossroads*. In the early 1960s there was no daily television serial in Britain, and Watson began discussing with Lew Grade the possibility of establishing one. It was Watson who thought of locating the projected serial in a Midlands motel and who, as its producer for ten years, had a great impact on its style and development. Watson had long had a philosophy of attempting to attract audiences, not please the critics (which *Crossroads* notoriously didn't – nor, as it turned out, Britain's draconian TV regulators). Of *The Young Doctors* (it could have been any of his projects) he commented, 'Are you trying to please the critics? The answer is no.'[2]

In 1978 Watson set out to devise his third serial in three years. But why set it in a women's prison? There was through the latter 1970s considerable public attention, especially in New South Wales and Victoria, to prison issues generally and the position of female prisoners in particular. Key events around this time were the Bathurst gaol riots, the Nagle Royal Commission into New South Wales' Prisons in 1976 and 1977, and the founding of Women Behind Bars in 1975, with its very sustained and eventually successful public campaign for the release of Australia's longest-serving female prisoner, Sandra Willson. In 1978 *St Theresa*, a low-budget discussion film about women in prison, was made in Sydney by independent filmmaker Dany Torsch, with a script by feminist historian and journalist Anne Summers and music by folk-singer Margaret Roadknight.[3] An active women's movement, prisoner action groups, and an atmosphere of public inquiry and media attention, together laid a basis for an interest in the lives of women in prison.

Watson and his team at Grundys began nine months of research for the new serial. Women in New South Wales and Victorian prisons were interviewed, as were prison officers and others associated with women's prisons. The Nagle Report was studied closely, and later some of the actors visited women's prisons. Watson was proud of the program's attention to detail. Even the prison bars, he told *TV Week*, were the same size as those inside: 'We've gone for realism.' The interviews with women prisoners formed the basis of many of the stories. Wentworth Gaol was to be based on a combination of Silverwater (Mulawa) in Sydney and Fairlea in Melbourne, and the rules and regulations depicted in the program were an amalgam of those operating in New South Wales and Victoria. Watson urged the depiction of unpleasant prison officers and also lesbian relationships, on the grounds that everyone interviewed agreed these were part of the reality of prison life.[4] Ian Holmes, who took over from Reg Grundy as President of the organisation in 1979, also insisted that research for the program was important and that notice be taken of suggestions by prison reform groups.[5] Sandra Willson commented that the depiction in *Prisoner* of a halfway house for women related more to the plans of prison reformers than to actual provisions in New South Wales at that time (1981).[6]

When production began in late 1978, *Prisoner* was to show for one hour per week, but an early decision was made to increase the production schedule from one hour to two. Some key actors subsequently quit after the first six months, but the program survived and gathered strength.[7]

If *Prisoner* talks to very contemporary, historically specific concerns, it also draws on much wider, longer, older cultural histories. Mass-culture interest in crime has often been attributed to the voracious appetite for the sensational and morbid amongst popular audiences and readerships. We would rather (naturally) follow Bakhtin who notes the 'enormous organisational significance' that crime, the criminal trial, and legal-criminal categories have in cultural history. For Bakhtin crime is that intersection where the personal and private become social and public: where private passions erupt into public knowledge, debate, contestation, judgement.[8] Hence its enduring cultural fascination, hence why it is a staple of twentieth-century tabloid newspapers and radio and TV news, just as it was of the forerunners of the tabloids, in broadsheets and chap-books. Hence its enduring prominence in so much popular culture generally, in detective novels, westerns, police shows, courtroom dramas. We can perhaps also see contemporary American discussion shows, like those hosted by Oprah Winfrey, Sally Jessy Raphael, Phil Donahue, as reprising the charivari of old, public trial and discussion of usually hidden, private experiences, sufferings, dilemmas, choices, an exposing and exploration of 'moral crimes', of difference.

Prisoner can be located in a long female tradition of inversion and inversionary figures in popular culture, from the 'unruly' or 'disorderly' woman of early modern Europe evoked by Natalie Davis in 'Women on Top', to the rebellious Maid Marians important in Robin Hood ballads and associated festive activities of the May-games, with their plays, pageants, and morris dances, to the witches of seventeenth-century English stage comedy.[9] In such 'wise witch' figures we perhaps approach the female equivalent of the male tradition of Robin Hood, Dick Turpin, Rob Roy – figures who, as discussed before in relation to the trickster and outlaw, could inspire fear as well as admiration.

Here is part, a strong part, of *Prisoner*'s carnivalesque ancestry, carried through into Australian cultural history and developed and transformed in terms of a robust mythology, literature, and drama of inversion involving prisoners and authority, convict and officer, bush worker and squatter, bushranger and police. In this mythos, looking to white Australia's beginnings as a convict colony, 'Australians', or at least 'true' Australians, are recounted as different from other Western peoples in supporting prisoners rather than their keepers, outlaws rather than the police. Australians are to be seen as anti-authority, anti-police, pro-prisoner, a tradition deriving from images of ill-treated convicts, sadistic convict overseers, and 'Ned Kelly', bushranger extraordinaire, Irish, small selector, his family and friends and class oppressed and hounded by corrupt cowardly police and an Anglo-Scottish political establishment, a man of great dignity, a rebel, a noble bandit, tragically hanged. This mythos can take many forms, and become bound in with other historical discourses, of tensions between Irish and English, as in television series like *Ben Hall* and *Against the Wind*, or between Australians and English as in the World War I Anzac legend and films like *Breaker Morant* and *Gallipoli*.

But attitudes to law and crime in Australia have been much more complex and ambivalent than such mythologising suggests, as has been argued of the public response to the police incapacity to capture the Ben Hall bushranger gang in the early 1860s.[10] In terms of modern Australia, we only have to think of the difficulties facing prison reform movements to realise that Australians are by no means universally or consistently pro-prisoner. There are indeed both pro- and anti-prisoner popular conceptions, often negotiated, both in public discussions and cultural representations, in terms of a division between two kinds of prisoners – those who are 'hardened criminals' as against social victims, prisoners whose circumstances have driven them into conflict with the law.[11]

If a modern audience inherits conflicting images of prisons and prisoners generally, so too does it construct conflicting images of female criminals and prisoners. While an influential image of women is that they are less violent than men, less a danger to society, another common one is that women who transgress, who end up in prison, are somehow more foul, more corrupt. They have, after all, broken social codes even more thoroughly than have their male counterparts. For a long time an image of the women convicts of the early nineteenth century was indeed that they were worse than the men – more abandoned, profligate, degenerate.[12] They were slatternly, lazy, foul-mouthed, wandering around in a drunken stupor with their dresses half falling off. But just as there has been a conflict in popular consciousness between images of the early convicts as hardened criminals and as the starving stealers of handkerchiefs, so too Australian female convicts have been seen as victims as well as exemplars of viciousness. Anne Summers' version of female convicts as pressed into prostitution to provide sexual services

for the males – a narrative in which convicts and convict overseers are
not very clearly distinguished – has had considerable impact on cultural
depictions of female convicts in recent years, for example in *Journey
Among Women* and *The Timeless Land*. In some ways it's as if an earlier
historiography, whereby all convicts were the victims rather than perpe-
trators of a vicious social order, has now been reserved for female
convicts only.[13]

Australian audiences don't, of course, receive only these kinds of
contradictory images. There is also the whole Hollywood tradition, a
heritage which includes a strong strand of representations of women
prisoners as brutishly lesbian: suggestions of lesbian rape or seduction
of young girls, of leather and chains, of a deep viciousness of character,
and of an extraordinary capacity for violence, all tolerated by the
sadistic screws. Prisoners are irremediable and unchangeable. In an
episode of *Charlie's Angels* the main difficulty for the Angel concerned,
who had to pose as a prisoner, was how to escape the terrifying lesbians
in the gaol, and save the one good prisoner, young and confused, from a
life of crime. Whereas in historical dramas and representations it's the
issue of prostitution which is central, in modern dramas and representations that of lesbianism tends to be more important.

Prisoner, however, speaks to this Hollywood tradition as a strongly
dissident voice. Overturns it.

A grainy text

In the following discussion we focus on and use the ethnographic
present for *Prisoner* in its 'middle' or 'classic' period, in the early 1980s,
and especially 1983. We believe that the structuring relationships and
conflicts evident then persisted through later changes in the cast of
characters.

We can begin by noting that in *Prisoner* many of the ambiguities so far
touched upon appear. There is an ambiguity about the 'law' and the
breaking of it, a concern with the relation of the moral to the legal, and
a distinction between 'hardened criminals' and the other prisoners.
And there is an ambiguity surrounding the issue of lesbianism. The
'hardened criminals' are usually few in number. There might at any
time be only one, like the evil doctor Kate, or later, Nola MacKenzie. But
dramatically they are very important. They help establish a counterfoil
to the troubled, confused, sometimes silly, but basically ordinary and
sympathetically drawn majority of prisoners. Most of the inmates are in
for things like petty theft, soliciting, involvement in the drug trade, and
various kinds of fraud or non-payment of debts. Few are inside for
crimes of violence, and even those who are may fall into the social victim
category. At times the drama shows how they came to be in prison, and

the forces leading to recidivism. There's a strong element of seeing them as victims of social inequalities and misfortune, as people who never really had a chance. Once in prison their sentences are often made longer because of their resistance to the repression by the harsh screws. Some characters, especially the wayward granddaughter figures like Maxie or Bobby, are often in prison or return to prison because of their 'good', their selfless and loyal, actions. (Maxie, for example, out of prison and living with her mother, covers up for her respectability-seeking sister, when brother-in-law robs the bank he works in.)

Prisoner established plenty of room for dramatic conflict and tension. There is the pathos of the lives of many of the women. From time to time, various characters such as the long-term prisoners Bea Smith and Judy Bryant express with painful clarity the experience of being locked up. On one occasion Judy was asked by another prisoner what she'd like to do if she were outside and Judy replied something like 'I don't know, just move around . . . just, you know, be *free*.' Bea at times contemplates the terrifying prospect of spending the rest of her life in prison, never able to have a sexual relationship, never really able to do anything, her enormous talents and energies doomed to remain wasted. At times we see old Lizzie Birdsworth contemplating dying in prison. Particularly important here is Hazel Kent. Hazel is not very clever, has got into trouble really through weakness and stupidity, and feels the loss of her children acutely. Hazel represents more than anyone else the plight of the ordinary woman who can't get her life together, can't take charge of her own destiny. Hazel is you and me, except that she's been unlucky and a bit silly. In terms of melodrama as meta-genre, the strand of narrative involving Hazel is in a naturalistic mode, harsh and relentless.

Another source of dramatic conflict arises from relations between the women. Since they are now away from their families, or have no family, or have through being in prison lost their family, they are outside the usual context of women's lives. To a certain extent family-type relationships are formed between most of them. Lizzie, whom we presume is in her seventies and looks as old as or older than anyone else regularly seen on television, is clearly a grandmother figure. But although Lizzie has a certain wisdom about human relationships, and is loving, concerned and kind, she's also a mischievous old lag rather like a child, liable to get herself into trouble. Bea Smith is in a certain sense her daughter, and a mother to the rest of the women.

Bea has been a key character in the program since it began, and is in many ways a moral centre for the other prisoners. She is inside for the murder of her husband in an act of revenge, for supplying and thereby killing her daughter with drugs. Bea's main problem is a propensity to solve problems through violence: this is what got her into prison and what keeps her there. Although Bea generally mothers the women, she gets tired of this role at times, and wants to look after herself for a change, though never at their expense. And in this surrogate family, characters like Maxine and Doreen and Bobby are the granddaughters, with Judy as 'aunt' figure. These 'kinship' relationships, often remembered rather wistfully by ex-prisoners who are having a hard time of it alone on the outside, offer the possibility of close friendship, fierce loyalty, co-operation, genuine concern for each other: an image of *communitas*, inversionary since it is this community of 'good' prisoners, not those in authority, that the text continually invites us to sympathise and empathise with.

But the relationships between the women are by no means all of this supportive kind. Conflict and violence often erupt, and indeed the advertising for *Prisoner* tends to accentuate this side of it. A key struggle is between Bea and other dominant personalities, like the remarkable Nola MacKenzie, trying to topple Bea from her position as 'top dog'. The drama of *Prisoner* provides for continuous contrast between 'figures' like Nola and Bea. Despite her propensity to use violence to get her own way or for purposes of revenge – she kills Nola for trying to drive her insane over the memory of her dead daughter Debbie – Bea acts on moral principles that are the reverse of Nola's extreme individualism and selfishness. Bea possesses considerable wisdom about people and human relations which she uses for the benefit of the prisoners as a whole. Where 'hardened' criminals like Nola or Kate would lag to the screws, Bea practically never does; she dislikes and tries to counter and perhaps punish actions that are self-seeking and competitive at the expense of what she perceives as a family group. But if Bea is a moral centre in *Prisoner*, she's an unusual and complex one, drawn as she is to exerting her control through violence or the threat of it: she brands K for Killer on Nola's chest with a soldering iron. Even within her own 'family' Bea is to some extent always feared as well as admired.

Prisoner is complex in its treatment of the warders, the screws. These are a mixed lot, and from time to time we see aspects of their personal lives. They include Joan Ferguson (the Freak), who is hard, corrupt and extremely clever at avoiding detection though not suspicion from her colleagues. At the other end of the spectrum is Meg Morris, who is more of a social worker, and indeed for a while became a parole officer but later returned to her original role. Meg, unlike Ferguson, or Vera Bennett (known as Vinegar Tits), or on most occasions Colleen Powell, is aware that the women could make good with a bit of assistance such as skills, jobs, a place to live, caring family and friends. Meg's position is a little confused, for after all she is still a screw, as Bea and some of the other prisoners continually remind each other. Amongst the warders

Meg is a counterpart to Bea, a force for morality and commonsense. But whereas Bea is able most of the time to exert some kind of moral authority and crafty strategical leadership over the women, Meg is only able to have her point of view prevail in the administration when extreme authoritarian measures are seen to fail.

Another source of dramatic tension lies in relations between the prisoners and the screws, and beyond the screws, the department. The screws know Bea has more direct control of the women than they do, and both use and resent this. Bea, on the other hand, knows that the screws and the department really control everything that goes on, have the final sanction of lock and key and gun and solitary confinement. The screws – for the prisoners – are always 'them', an alien force that controls, exploits, hurts and confines them. But *Prisoner* also explores differences between formal authority and actual power. The screws, if they are to maintain order within the prison, have constantly to rework their strategies, and to take cognisance of Bea. Also, the struggle between the advocates of rigid discipline and of a more permissive, helping approach goes on and on, never really resolved, as each approach is alternately seen to result in further tension, restlessness, and disorder.

Prisoner seems to rely very little on conventional definitions of masculinity and femininity, beyond the basic point that sympathy generated for most of the women rests on the perception that women are not usually violent or physically dangerous. Many of the women are very strong characters indeed, active and independent. The Freak, Bea, Nola and the evil Marie Winters are most unusual in the gallery of characters of television drama. They are not substitute men, but active strong women. There have also been several gentle male characters, like Doreen's husband, or old Syd, the handyman who marries Lizzie, and several young shy boys who enter the story via the halfway house. On the other hand there have been some hard violent male characters as well, such as the corrupt rapist screw Jock Stewart. Strength and gentleness are not distributed in *Prisoner* on male–female lines. The binary image of the powerful man and the weak or decorative woman is simply not there. Images of female strength are not uncommon in television drama; indeed they have proved extremely popular in *The Bionic Woman*, *Wonderwoman*, Steed's offsiders in *The Avengers*. But in all these cases strength and capability are intertwined with an emphasis on female beauty.

The women in *Prisoner* are not in the least glamourised. They are usually dressed in crummy prison uniforms, or for those on remand usually in fairly ordinary clothes. Their faces suggest no make-up, and they range in bodily shape from skinny wizened old Lizzie to the big girls like Bea, Doreen, and Judy. Their faces, luminously featured as in so much serial melodrama, are shown as interesting, faces full of character, of signs of hardship and suffering, alternately soft and hard, happy and depressed, angry or bored. The sets more often than not are brick walls, a rudimentary laundry, a dull recreation room, a boring office or entry lobby. The appearance of *Prisoner* is occasionally varied by indoor and outdoor scenes set outside the prison but overall its 'look' is spare, hard, yet dynamic.

An objection to *Prisoner* we've heard is that it is voyeuristic, relying on images of caged and uniformed women, with a sexual suggestion of bondage. Further, it is felt to rely on images of violence between women, with soldering irons, knives, bashings and so on, which are something of a pornographic turn-on. The program encourages the male viewer to enjoy seeing women controlled and confined, while positioning the female viewer as masochistically seeking to be caged.

Certainly the early advertising for *Prisoner* could at times be seen to display these elements. We ourselves did not watch it at all in its first year, for just this kind of reason, a suspicion that the whole thing was somehow anti-lesbian, and exploiting images of women in bondage. But *Prisoner*, we quickly realised (also quickly very much regretted the year of viewing lost), regards lesbianism in complex ambiguous ways. Both Judy Bryant, ex-prisoner and manager of the halfway house, and Joan Ferguson have been established as lesbians. Judy is an extremely sympathetic character, whose lesbianism has been stressed less and less as time goes on. Ferguson's lesbianism, however, seems to be signified by her sinister black gloves, providing her with an extra dimension for threatening and controlling the women. *Prisoner* seems to suggest that lesbianism is OK among the women (though mainly in terms of an expressed identity than actual sex in prison) but not OK among the officers, for it introduces the possibility of sexual harassment.

But apart from this, is *Prisoner* voyeuristic? We don't think so. The prisoners are on the whole portrayed as fairly ordinary women, not violent sexual monsters in a cage. Their strong pro-children and anti-childbasher morality clearly establishes them outside this image. They are located in their society. *Prisoner can* be read voyeuristically, but we are not convinced that it has to be. The women are not held up as sexual objects, but as human, female, subjects.

Contemporary responses to *Prisoner*

Prisoner was undoubtedly very popular in Australia, only in its eighth year showing signs of falling ratings. Right from the beginning, on Monday 26 February 1979, in Sydney and Melbourne, *Prisoner* achieved good solid ratings in its 8.30–9.30 pm timeslot. Its popularity is measurable not only in the ratings but also in the continuing attention given to *Prisoner*'s stars like Val Lehman (Bea), Sheila Florance (Lizzie), Maggie Kirkpatrick (Joan Ferguson), Elspeth Ballantyne (Meg Morris), in *TV Week* stories and Logie awards, in the participation of *Prisoner* actors in telethons or in their well-publicised appearance in a performance in Melbourne's Pentridge Gaol.[14] As with all successful serials with long-running parts the stars of *Prisoner* became popular favourites, and things they did that affected the show – like Lizzie leaving – earned headlines in the tabloid press.

Popularity, however, is not necessarily accompanied by critical acclaim, instant or eventual. It might indeed be the fact of popularity itself which, either from a need to assert their independence and toughness or from the application of high-culture criteria, or both, gives critics the irrits, as Bea might have said. Dorothy Hobson remarked of *Crossroads* that it was at the same time enormously popular and yet devastatingly criticised, and a similar comment could be applied to *Prisoner*'s history of reception.[15]

It wasn't so much the academics as the journalists who led the criticism. *TV Week*'s John Michael Howson responded soon after *Prisoner* began with a hostile sneer, saying it wasn't a drama at all, and it was so bad it was funny. Peter Dean of *TV Times* was only a little less disapproving. *Prisoner* was, he felt, a 'slickly made tear-jerker that succeeds in showing a little of the torment endured by unhardened unfortunates thrust among harridans'. An American critic in the US *TV Guide*, with a weekly circulation of six million, was typical of those who opposed *Prisoner* for showing too seamy a side of life:

> Violence, homosexuality, humiliation and tough-talking female convicts. It's hard enough to believe that adult viewers really want a series that panders to the shabbiest, most sadistic tastes. It's much harder – in fact it's sickening – to think that in several large cities some stations don't mind if the kids watch too.[16]

The television reviewers for the 'quality' *Sydney Morning Herald* were rarely if ever kind to *Prisoner* either. Rayleene Harrison described it in the *Herald*'s TV and Radio Guide, widely read on Monday mornings by the middle class and professionally trained, as lost in a 'myriad of second-class plots and truly unbelievable characters'. Then there was restaurateur Peter Simpson's judgement, offered in the *Herald* Guide's 'My Choice' column: 'It's an insult to the intelligence – nothing but nasty people behaving nastily in a nasty situation'.[17]

In all this we can discern the operation of a double standard common to much cultural criticism: what is 'good' in 'high' culture becomes 'bad' in popular culture. What might be hailed in 'high' culture as admirable realism or touching pathos or tragedy that questions the very depths and bases of human existence, is dismissed in popular culture as *too* realistic. Popular culture can't win: it's either regarded as mere light entertainment, or it's viewed with alarm and distaste as overly grim. In comments like those of Peter Simpson, restaurateur, we hear the double standard speaking loud and clear. How different must *Macbeth* and *King Lear* and *Hamlet* be – nothing but nice people behaving nicely in nice situations.

Double standards are also evident in the comments of journalist Sandra Hall in her book on Australian television of the 1980s. That *Prisoner* depicts lesbianism earns it a hostile attack, in a way unlikely in criticism of 'high' culture:

> Sex is plainly an important part of its appeal, although it's sex of a kind which has nothing to do with sensuality . . . *Prisoner* is helped immeasurably by the fact that a large proportion of its cast is lesbian at least some of the time. The presentation of life in a women's prison is a mixture of a lesbian lonely hearts' club and *Tom Browne's Schooldays* gone ocker.[18]

Hall's is a type of television criticism, as was Marion Macdonald's in the *Sydney Morning Herald* and Nancy Banks-Smith's in the English *Guardian*, which likes to reveal the critic's wit and verbal play at the expense of contemptible popular offerings – and at the expense, often, of even the remotest accuracy of what actually happens in a program.[19] It wasn't just the lesbianism that annoyed Sandra Hall, to the point where a very few characters' lesbianism could become 'a large proportion of its cast'. It was also its general grimness. As Hall put it, there is

> no light and shade, no humour, no time for anything but belligerence. Consequently its characters are not so much characters as laboratory animals, and the actors are called on to produce just two emotions. They are only ever dour or hysterical.[20]

An exception to this hysterical chorus of dislike, disapproval and contempt was an essay by Lesley Stern. Writing from within a post-structuralist approach that drew on Modleski's 'The Search for Tomorrow in Today's Soap Operas' and owing much to Roland Barthes' *S/Z*, Stern delighted in the very raggedness of *Prisoner*, its narrative discontinuities, its play of contending and contradictory discourses, of identity and difference, of unreconciled and unreconcilable oppositions, of resolutions that only beget new dramas requiring new solutions, all without end; and in this view there is no single place, and so no secure ideological stance, in which viewers can be confined and inscribed.[21]

Let's return to *Prisoner*'s indubitable popularity. The ratings varied considerably according to city and age group, proving most popular in Melbourne (where it was made) and with 13–17 year-olds irrespective of city. Clearly, then, in attempting to ponder why *Prisoner* gained popularity, we need to look for reasons for popularity within specific groups.

Prisoner might have been popular with children because it was perceived as portraying a situation not so very different from that of school: the ethic about not dobbing, or lagging, the ingenious strategies for circumventing formal authority, the informal networks of knowledge and relationships, the getting of things in and out of the institution that are not supposed to be there, the use of humour, cheek and wit to resist authority and rules.[22] Do the 13–17 year-olds enjoy *Prisoner* because they respond to a portrayal of confinement and resistance not unrelated to their own experience? Do they recognise their teachers as similar to *Prisoner*'s screws, especially when those screws tell the women, in the mornings on the way to the shower or later in the laundry, to get a move on, hurry it up, no talking, why isn't everyone working in here, or when they confiscate various possessions of the prisoners or withdraw privileges? Do kids see in the differences between officers like Vera Bennett and Joan Ferguson and Mrs Powell and Meg Morris recognisable differences between their own teachers? Do they sense that the teachers are not unified or undivided or free of conflict amongst themselves, like *Prisoner*'s screws – but yet all have a final power and authority and possible recourse to discipline and punishment, even the kindest and 'softest' of them? Do children see in the efforts of Bea to maintain her position as 'top dog' against various contenders dramas of attempted leadership and conflict amongst themselves?

Christine Curry and Christine O'Sullivan wrote in 1980 about the results of their research into the responses to certain programs, including *Prisoner*, of thirteen-year-old working-class school children in Sydney. They argued that children are not passive receivers of television but 'seek out aspects of commercial television as a consolidation and confirmation of their everyday lives'. The kids spent some part of each day at school talking about the TV they watched the night before, and using it subversively against the rule-bound culture and institutions of the school. Aggressive female teachers are nicknamed Vinegar Tits, after former tough screw Vera Bennett. As Curry and O'Sullivan put it, the 'similarity between gaol and school had not escaped the notice of the students and these generated a number of possibilities for simulations of both a narrative and a visual kind'.[23]

Ethnographic research in Melbourne schools revealed similar appropriations of *Prisoner* amongst 'unruly [young] women'. For working-class girls, school can be perceived as a hostile and repressive institution, likened to prison:

This school is like Wentworth Detention Centre. It is!
It's like *Prisoner* on Telly! (T, 15)
It's poxed! (unknown)
The teacher don't even care about us. (S, 14)
Yeah, 'cos they're screws! (Chorus)[24]

We also felt it was clear, from personal observation, and from several interviews with children printed in the *Sydney Morning Herald* TV and Radio Guide, that *Prisoner*'s appeal was not confined to children of high school age. Could younger as well as older children have seen in the tricks and unrestrained language of old Lizzie, or the waywardness and mistakes of 'children' to Bea like Doreen or Maxie, the mistakes they make and the negotiations they attempt with parental as well as school authority?

If *Prisoner* could invoke school life, it also could perhaps refer to other kinds of institutional experience, as in the highly undemocratic, authoritarian workplace, in factory or office. *Prisoner* here suggests contradictory images. Work in the laundry is revealed as tedious, unendingly repetitive, and the screws regularly visit to complain if work appears to be slackening. Yet the women often resist the oppression of a labour process that the prison 'management' forces on them by taking smokes, having fun, chatting, planning rituals like birthday celebrations, or being involved in dramas of various kinds that distract them from the boredom of work. In offices, too, we might think, workers try to negotiate and resist petty rules and the 'panoptic' discipline of managerial-level eyes always on them by creating their own social relations – of friendship, conversation, jokes, and rituals like the birthday celebrations that might be held in the pub at lunch-time or with cakes and presents at afternoon tea. But, as in *Prisoner*, such social relations are intersected and threatened by tensions and drama arising from conflicts of personalities and values. Did adults as well as children, then, see in *Prisoner* the drama of power in different contexts, in the family, the school, the workplace – of how power is exercised, desired, embraced, negotiated, resisted, disdained?

Prisoner – there is and has been nothing else quite like it.

CONCLUSION

Carnival and Contemporary Popular Culture

> In so concluding my Ash Wednesday meditation, I trust that
> I have not saddened my readers. Such was very far from
> my intention. On the contrary, knowing that life, taken as
> a whole, is like the Roman Carnival, unpredictable,
> unsatisfactory and problematic, I hope that this carefree
> crowd of maskers will make them remember how valuable is
> every moment of joy, however fleeting and trivial it may seem
> to be.[1]

When, in the early 1980s, I began venturing the thought that twentieth-century popular culture, especially television, might be comparable somehow to carnival in early modern Europe, people I talked to mostly said the project was odd, interesting, even quixotic, but it had some insurmountable obstacles, in the very differences between the societies of modernity and early modern Europe. These obstacles can be indicated by Goethe's observations in *Italian Journey* about the Roman Carnival of 1788, that it is 'not really a festival given *for* the people but one the people give themselves'. The Romans leave their houses to enter the Corso, which becomes like a 'salon full of acquaintances'. There in the street, amidst the revelry created by their own and others' masking and performances, a person participates as 'both actor and spectator'. As Bakhtin would say in *Rabelais and His World*, 'carnival does not know footlights, in the sense that it does not acknowledge any distinction between actors and spectators'. Footlights would 'destroy a carnival', for it is 'not a spectacle seen by the people; they live in it'.[2] Carnival, my interlocutors would observe, took place in the streets, squares, marketplaces of a past era, it was made by the people them-selves for themselves, whereas television, I surely didn't need reminding, was made for people by large media companies, and was received by people in their private homes, a feature of twentieth-century society,

273

where they could be spectators only, with no possibility of participating, and where they were obviously cut off from their fellow viewers. They could not be part of the sensuous body of carnival, of a collective festive experience, with, as Bakhtin would have it, out and inflowing relationships with the cosmos. Carnival and TV could not be more different.

Yet I foolishly soldiered on. I never of course intended to argue that carnival and TV, the most popular mass medium of the latter part of our century, are directly comparable. Of course I recognise there are immense and obvious differences between the two eras. In early modern Europe peasants and craftsmen constituted, so Peter Burke tells us, 80 to 90 per cent of the population.[3] Modernity is implicated in the industrialisation and urbanisation of the last two centuries. In early modern Europe the mass of people had few opportunities to express political dissent outside carnival, whereas modernity has witnessed a growth of liberal freedoms, suffrage, political parties, trade unions, the media.

There are, nevertheless, similarities and continuities, otherwise we wouldn't think of the period from 1500 to 1800 as 'early modern'. It's true that carnival happened in the street and marketplace, and that in Catholic Europe the carnival period was followed by the stringencies of Lent; at the end of carnival there was frequently a contest between giant figures of carnival and Lent, with carnival ritually losing. But early modern Europe also experienced the disintegration of Catholic Europe as monolithic, with the carnival spirit of dissidence and scepticism more and more refusing to be confined to set periods, becoming part of everyday life, a continuous all-year-round challenge to authority and official views: the fable of Falstaff.

In modernity, with music-hall in the second half of the nineteenth century and then spectacularly with Hollywood, mass culture was increasingly commercialised and made by large companies and networks (though television also relies on the energies and ideas of many relatively small independent production companies). Yet early modern Europe also witnessed the commercialisation of popular culture, in professional clowns, singers, chapbook sellers, storytellers – whose narratives might continue over several days through various instalments, much as would happen later with serial fiction – and in the theatre as a new mass leisure industry. It's interesting how much Bakhtin, given the perils of the political situation he was in, could conceal neither his affection for the marketplace as a setting for carnival activities, nor for the advertising that accompanied it, the cries and songs of the sellers.[4]

We cannot totalise the popular culture of early modern Europe in any ideal terms as culture made by the people for themselves. Popular culture then was not coterminous with carnival, rather there were continuous interactions between carnival and its activities, cosmology, philosophy, and professionalised entertainment.

It's undoubtedly true that in the twentieth century a great deal of popular culture has left the public street and marketplace, where it enjoyed itself for centuries, well into the nineteenth century, and proceeded indoors, into the cinema and then the living room featuring the TV set. Such change can be exaggerated: there is still a remarkable amount of public life, of street processions, commemorations of all kinds, celebrations, political demonstrations, attendance at myriad sporting activities, though many processions and commemorations are of an official or semi-official kind. There has also been a continuance and even growth of carnival, not only in Latin America but in Australia, with, for example, the Sydney Gay and Lesbian Mardi Gras. We can remember too Walter Benjamin's argument in 'The Work of Art in the Age of Mechanical Reproduction' that popular audiences in the twentieth century liked cinema because, unlike in the salon, the gallery, the art museum, they could organise their enjoyment in their own way, as simultaneous collective experience.

The modernist myth of the passive spectator is already moving towards becoming an historical curiosity. Even with television there is enormous participation by mass audiences, directly as contestants in game shows, and as studio audiences, for situation comedies as well as variety and infotainment programs. Audiences participate in serial melodrama, in terms of popularity, public interest in soap opera stars, fan clubs, magazines catching readers up with stories as well as an informal culture of information-sharing about stories past and present. There is pressure by audiences to retain characters that are threatened by storyliners with death and disappearance; or to bring back 'dead' characters with either the return of the original actor or a replacement. As one example, when Emilio, an Hispanic character in *Days of Our Lives*, was written out of the show, 45,000 angry letters from fans helped convince the producers that he should be brought back.[5] Peter Burke says that in early modern Europe singers and storytellers were under pressure to modify or transform their offerings in responding to what their audiences wanted.[6] Surely there is a long continuity here.

There are also the massive implications of popularity itself. I would argue that the majority public does exercise great power in the broadcasting process. Popularity is the very key to commercial broadcasting. It's precisely what the different networks compete for, fight over.

The networks have to put on programs that majority audiences will find popular; unless such programs are popular, the advertisers will not wish to advertise as much with them. And to be popular in a majority sense, programs and the 'collective drama', the overall tone and feel of the commercial networks, have to appeal to popular traditions. Such traditions are always open to the new, in technology and form, and at the same time go back deep into the history of centuries and even millennia of popular culture, back through Hollywood and radio, back through nineteenth-century melodrama, vaudeville, music-hall, pantomime, farce, magic shows, back to early modern Europe with its carnival *and* its new leisure industries in the theatre and professional clowning, back to thousands of years of folk cultures. If networks, those networks owned by the media barons so obsessively, myopically, demonised in modernist mass-culture theory, didn't put on programs that answered to such popularity and popular traditions, they would financially ail and die.[7]

Carnivalesque

What I thought was clear, from my TV watching and watching TV with my child, was that a great deal of popular television, for children as well as adults, included a great deal of inversion, and that such inversion could be compared not directly to carnival but to carnivalesque as a cultural, philosophical and cosmological mode, present obviously in carnival but also in associated activities in early modern Europe. I was particularly struck, for example, when I came to read David Kunzle's essay on World Upside Down in European broadsheets, the forerunner of today's comic books, how much the inversions he was pointing to are still strongly present not only in television but in twentieth-century popular culture generally.

Take that persistent inversion he describes of small turning the tables on large, a category of broadsheets where a fox is chased by hens, a large bird of prey by small birds, a cat by mice.[8] Now compare this last broadsheet image to that most famous of comics and animated cartoons, *Tom and Jerry*. Let's take an example. The lead strip, 'A Dog's Life' (dated 1960) of a Tom and Jerry comic book, begins with Tom in bed, looking large and threatening, holding Jerry and his mouse friend Tuff, both tied to a leash. The mice have to call Tom sir and master, and they complain to him that he treats them like dogs, though they also continually cheek him. He orders them to make and bring him his breakfast and the morning paper. But in the paper Tom reads that all cats must have licences, and that licence men would be around that day. Then follows a journey of humiliation for Tom, as he tries to evade the licence man, who is helped by Jerry and Tuff at every turn. Tom tries to hide as a pig in mud. Discovered, he races to a local pond and attempts a trick he says he 'saw once in a comic book'. He hides under water, breathing through a reed; but Jerry puts his hand over it. The mice persuade a cringing Tom, now hiding in an alley, to put on a dog collar and impersonate a pooch, but the dog licence is out of date, and Tom is caught by a dog catcher. The mice deliver Tom from the fearsome dog pound by producing a new licence, and Tom is released into their care. They proceed home with a leashed cat. In the final frame we see the mice in the foreground looking out the window at Tom, in the backyard, in the dog house, chained to a spike, looking small: the topos of world upside-down, *mundus inversus*, topsy-turvy.

We can speculate that the fascination for children of such spectacles, not only in Tom and Jerry comics but in animated cartoons like the aardvaark trying to kill the clever, wise, humorous ant, or the coyote trying to slow to a final halt the roadrunner, lies in enjoying the overturning of the usual relations of power found in their own lives, ruled by adults of various kinds, from parent to teacher. Small invariably triumphs over big. Take another example, *I Dream of Jeannie*, endlessly repeated as were the old World Upside Down broadsheets, and now a classic of children's TV. Kids love watching the fun of Jeannie and astronaut Major Tony Nelson and his friend Roger (the only humans who know she's an Oriental genie), cast adrift in situations usually involving Tony's superior Dr Bellows and the military top brass, who are ever made to look silly. The popular tradition of mockery of military hierarchy is indeed long.

I Dream of Jeannie, like almost anything else in popular culture – indeed, in culture of any kind – is a bundle of contradictory ideological and discursive elements.[9] Feminists might object to the program (as to that other classic of children's television, *Bewitched*) because it appears clearly to reinforce notions of women being tied to the house as homecarers. Jeannie, released from eternal confinement in her bottle on a tiny island by the major, now serves him as a maid in his house and calls him master all the time; she does the cooking and cleaning for him, presumably using her magic powers. Feminists might also object to the touch of Orientalism in the way Jeannie is dressed in skirt and bikini top, the identification of the Orient with female sensuousness, inviting male viewers to position themselves as voyeurs ('ogling and all that', as the narrator says in Pope's *The Rape of the Lock*). Jeannie is also shown as the faithful monogamous wife, unlike her amoral and sensual genie sister.

We can observe some of these contradictory discourses at work in a particular episode, in a series when Jeannie has married the major. A committee of officers' wives, bossily conducted by the admiral's wife, and including Mrs Bellows and Jeannie, have a competition to find the best husband-around-the-house, the prize being a vacation in Hawaii. Jeannie uses all her magic powers to spirit Tony from a capsule, in which he's locked, to their home for the committee of ladies to see him cooking and cleaning. Tony is asleep, and Jeannie has to make him walk and talk like a robot, but he falls over in front of the admiral's wife. Later he tries to escape in a dress and scarf, looking like a charlady. Jeannie spirits him back to his capsule, from which he emerges in the dress, to Dr Bellows' astonishment. The prize goes to Tony, but Mrs Bellows protests that he couldn't have got out of the capsule to be in the competition at all; Dr Bellows demands an explanation of the dress Tony was wearing. Tony whispers to Jeannie, 'take away all the clothes'. She gets him wrong, does her blink, and manages to undress all the ladies, including the admiral's wife, who run off wearing only petticoats. The episode ends in mayhem, chaos, anarchy.

It is Jeannie who has fantastic power. Dr Bellows' science is ridiculed by her magic. She helps create situations where social status is mocked. Her husband is like a ventriloquist's dummy in her hands. With a blink of the eye she can render him helpless, silly, powerless.

Kunzle points out that male–female inversions were the most ubiquitous of all in the old World Upside Down prints.[10] The frequent mockery of the husband in early modern Europe, not only in broadsheets but in festivities, theatre, pictorial representation, stories, can be compared to the way in sitcom after sitcom in television, in Britain, the United States, Australia, there is a comic quizzing of the notion of the husband and father as source of moral authority, wisdom, and guidance. What is so often mocked is his blustering attempts to claim patriarchal control over his household and its opinions and attitudes. We can think, for example, of the cultural history of programs in Britain like *Till Death Do Us Part*, *Bless This House*, *Robin's Nest*, *George and Mildred*, George in *Man About the House*.

In *Robin's Nest* the father Mr Nichols had financial control over the restaurant run by his daughter Vicki and Robin. Mr Nichols is Robin's father-in-law and also his employer, as well as employer of Albert the funny Irishman (a figure descending from nineteenth-century theatre). Given widespread English attitudes towards the Irish, it is interesting that Mr Nichols, rich, successful, well-fed, ex-army officer, comes off worst in every verbal exchange with Albert, the one-armed waiter and kitchen-hand. Mr Nichols openly derides Robin's right to possess his daughter – he is, after all, working-class and lacking in style, only an employee and in effect only a son. But Nichols also comes off worse in every verbal exchange with Robin. Estranged from his wife, Mr Nichols openly desires his daughter, presumably because she looks like his wife when he was young and in the prime of his masculinity: the father's desire to recover his masculinity via an incestuous attraction to his daughter is explicitly mocked. Robin continually tells Mr Nichols that he's long lost his masculinity, he's an old woman, and in one episode Mr Nichols is manoeuvred into doing the washing-up, in a pink apron with breasts painted on it.

Mockery and disestablishing of the husband, the man, is also a feature of American sitcoms. We only have to think of the plight of Al Bundy, and the comedy of his ritual defeat in *Married . . . With Children.* In the series when Peggy is pregnant, and insists on household meetings to prepare for the baby, there is an episode where Al, disagreeing with a family decision inevitably going against him, says to Peggy that he has the right of veto, he is the husband and the man and his word is law. Al of course is defeated once again, the defeat of the male Bundys past, present and for ever.

The image of the disorderly or unruly woman evoked by Natalie Davis also, I think, clearly lives strongly on in popular culture now, just as ambivalently or 'multivalently', and in just as many diverse manifestations. The powerful female figures Davis mentions, Rabelais' Gargamelle, Chaucer's Wife of Bath, *As You Like It*'s Rosalind (her tongue loosened by her male apparel and holiday humour), Maid Marian presiding with Robin Hood over the May games, have comparable twentieth-century characters in Hollywood, from Mae West, Jane Russell, Rita Hayworth, even Marilyn Monroe (as powerful 'innocent fool' in her screen presence), to Cher and Madonna. To see the luminous power of Madonna in a film like *Desperately Seeking Susan* or on video and in concert, playing with gender reversals and transvestism (in one stage performance the male dancers make love to her with large phallus-like breasts), is to recall a centuries-long cultural history of women on top.

Interestingly, Madonna figures in arguments within contemporary feminism. In a British collection of essays on *The Female Gaze,* on the power, complexities and contradictions of female cultural figures and spectatorship in film and television, essays that challenge Laura Mulvey's older Screen Theory view that twentieth-century visual culture is dominated by the male gaze, Shelah Young argues that Madonna poses an acute problem for those older feminists, white and middle class, who throughout the 1970s and early 1980s set the agenda for the liberation of women. Not only did such Western feminists, in presuming a single feminist project, ignore the forces that divide women, as in age, race, ethnicity, sexuality, class. They also tried to impose a kind of alternative puritanism, stressing an authentic natural look and disdainful of women who dared to dress up.

Madonna, says Young, outraged such puritanical politics. Madonna's image in 'Material Girl' encapsulates a wanton celebration of consumer capitalism. Numberless teenage girls have been influenced by 1970s feminism to be strong and independent. Yet they also admire Madonna for her playful irreverence and the way she confidently returns the fetishist's gaze while wearing his favourite sexual accessories, parodying the classic pornographic peepshow. For a new generation of women, Madonna both outrages conventional images of a passive femininity, and scorns the power of 1970s feminism itself to define and restrict their lives. The older feminism, proclaiming a pure liberatory position, has itself become a power to be resisted.[11] It turned out, for the rest of feminism, to be certain Western Women on Top.[12]

Carnivalesque and the bourgeois public sphere

I also wished to explore a thought that popular television was carnivalesque in a cosmological way, particularly in conceptions of fate and destiny. In a beautiful passage in *Rabelais and His World* Bakhtin evokes the philosophy of carnival games of luck and chance in the marketplace, in sports, children's games, cards, dice, chess, as well as in various forms of fortune-telling, wishing, and predictions.

Bakhtin argues that the carnivalesque genre of parodic prophecies is opposed to another genre, the serious prophecies which were of a gloomy and eschatological character, incorporating the medieval concept of history. Parodic prophecies try to approach the world, time and the future not as a sombre mystery play but as a satyric drama. Prognostics and prophecies now concern not only the fate of kings, popes and nobles, and the great events of the official world, but the life and destinies of the lower classes. In opposing the jocular and merry to the serious and gloomy, the eschatology of the Middle Ages is uncrowned, is turned into a 'gay monster'. Instead of accepting the future as fixed and unalterable, as sad and terrifying, time and destiny can appear carefree and open; the universe can be seen as not necessarily tragic.

So too with carnival games and sports:

> The images of games were seen as a condensed formula of life and of the historic process: fortune, misfortune, gain and loss, crowning and uncrowning. Life was presented as a miniature play ... a play without footlights. At the same time games drew the players out of the bounds of everyday life, liberated them from usual laws and regulations, and replaced established conventions by other lighter conventionalities.[13]

In their modern form as TV game, quiz and dating shows such genres are usually viewed with modernist dismay because of the large amount of internal advertising of prizes and holidays; therefore they must be constructing people as subjects of consumerism, the systematic production of false needs. I would rather explain their irrepressible persistence into the modern era as a result both of the undoubted attraction of various prizes (the reward of luck and skill), and of a carnivalesque cosmology challenging the notion that the stringencies and deprivations of everyday life are inevitable.[14]

Popular television culture is everywhere suffused with such carnivalesque cosmology, in its overall tone, its 'collective drama'. Popular commercial television offers its collective drama as a sprawl of composite 'life': as the permanent mixed irruption of excitement, spectacle, happiness, joy, tragedy, sadness, loss, conflict, dilemma, terror, horror and death. It is such cosmology that informs commercial TV news, as well as its melodrama, the long-running, going-anywhere (sprawling with life and death) serial. Because time and destiny are conceived as open, or at least as not finally tragic, history is not predetermined to failure and loss, history might be open to change and transformation, to utopian glimmers of abundance and equality in the reversal of usual relations of order and power. Hence the impetus, the irrepressible energy, for mockery and parody: carnivalesque as social critique, none the less serious for being theatrical, extravagant and playful.[15]

Modernist mass-culture theory could not entertain the thought that mass culture might be a form of critical reason; to the contrary, mass culture tried to destroy critical distance, was an absence of negation. Here modernism owed a strong debt to that which it so often tried to distance itself from, the Enlightenment and its 'bourgeois public sphere'. Stallybrass and White argue that the development of the 'public sphere' in England in the late seventeenth and early eighteenth centuries permitted the emerging bourgeois and professional classes a space of rationality, equality in discussion, democracy in action. There they could exercise true judgement, wit and discrimination, in an atmosphere of refinement, propriety, decorum, restraint, politeness, civility. Its sites and media of discourse were the coffee-house, the clubroom, the salon, the assembly rooms of the spas and resorts, the pleasure and tea gardens, the periodical, the journal. This public space was forged not only in opposition to the aristocratic presumption that rank confers intellectual authority, but also in active opposition to the carnivalesque, to the grotesque activities and enjoyments and entertainments of the lower classes in their cultural geography, in pubs, inns, fairs, theatres, shows, circuses, forests. In carnival in early modern Europe everyone had participated, upper and lower estates, if often with contrary and frequently hostile purposes. But with the rise of the 'bourgeois public sphere' the bourgeois and professional classes would break their link with carnivalesque, which became submerged in the unconscious, as a repressed desire for the low and the other.[16]

There has been disagreement with Stallybrass and White's assertion that the new spaces of the 'bourgeois public sphere' excluded women. E.J. Clery argues that the coffee-house, introduced to Europe from the Middle East in the mid-seventeenth century, might have physically excluded bourgeois and aristocratic women, but their spirit nevertheless presided, a spirit of 'gentle' manners, temperance (the stress on coffee or tea, not alcohol), purity of language, conversational skill, moral guardianship: men in coffee-houses had to behave as if ladies were present. Such feminisation was occurring at the same time as literate, leisured urban women were being addressed as consumers by an emergent print culture as well as becoming active cultural producers in their own right.[17]

Gender and class, that unholy imbrication, that unsettling of any simple binary opposition of men and women. The 'bourgeois public sphere', feminised and supported by middle- and upper-class ladies, was forged not only as different from carnivalesque – a carnivalesque mode itself highly gendered in terms of the unruly or disorderly woman – but as superior, and so charged with a historical mission to instruct, supervise, enlighten. Such attitudes and activity would continue in the differentiated print culture of the nineteenth century, perhaps attaining its apotheosis early in this century in the invincibly confident, 'superior', moralising of Q.D. Leavis in her *Fiction and the Reading Public*. The Leavisite movement certainly did not exclude female voices and participation, yet at the same time the mass culture it despised, Q.D. Leavis made clear, was frequently perceived as 'female', in genres such as romance and melodrama, and in its readership, the silent sorry women who, under Q.D.L.'s pitiless gaze, lined up in circulating libraries to borrow contemptible bestsellers.

In the history of broadcasting, the 'bourgeois public sphere' can be related to the development of state-funded or public radio and television this century. Raymond Williams in his *Television: Technology as Cultural Form* refers to such 'public sphere' broadcasting as Type A television, centred on news and public affairs, features and documentaries, education, arts and music, children's programs, plays. We can see Type A broadcasting in the historical formation and development in Britain of the BBC, in Australia of the ABC and SBS (a multicultural TV network), in the United States in public television. Its 'collective drama' has been predominantly restrained, formal, impersonal and instructive, likely to present life under the sign of the tragic, where the individual is shaped by an environment and is ultimately locked in a final hopelessness; characters drag themselves about the screen to an inevitable predestined end.[18]

The adherents of Type A television have regarded what Williams refers to as Type B broadcasting, popular commercial TV, as mere entertainment, the merely sensational, without seriousness and aesthetic quality, not art, not knowledge, a mess down there that has to be regulated, cleaned up, if possible removed. For the 'bourgeois public sphere' and its allies, the modernist mass-culture theorists, there could be only one broadcasting mode, one kind of broadcasting 'reason', and other, popular, manifestations should be compelled to adopt that singular mode. Modernist mass-culture theorists have either not actively protested against the establishment of state regulatory apparatuses in Britain and Australia that have turned their panoptic disciplinary gaze on popular carnivalesque television, or (at least in the antipodes) have enthusiastically joined in, even initiated and given theoretical force, to such surveillance and attempted disciplining. Modernists, supposedly alienated from a ghastly world, have looked to and participated in the power of the modern state. They have come in from the cold of alienation that is also opportunity, to be intellectually free, detached, independent, and have enfolded themselves in Power. They have been thoroughly conventional.[19]

I am not here wishing to argue against Enlightenment reason as such, as a major discursive basis of modern intellectual life, the life of discussion and rational argument that daily takes place in universities, journals, newspapers. I am certainly not opposed to the strengths of 'public sphere' broadcasting, to its modes of documentary, information, debate, or its particular conceptions of drama (most often the one-off self-contained well-made rounded-off play, drawing on middle-class theatre). I am not opposed to tragedy as genre or cosmology. But I agree with the critique, performed in the name of postmodernism (as in Lyotard), of the Enlightenment when it puts itself forward in an imperial way as the unfinished project of modernity, a meta-discourse that can include and guide all other discourses; which assumes that if 'reason' does not appear in recognisable 'Enlightened' form then it is not reason at all, but its enemy.

Rather would I argue for a history of different forms of 'reason', a history where, in relation to entertainment, carnivalesque as social critique doesn't have to be considered inferior to 'public sphere' reason; where playfulness, juxtaposition, heterogeneity, parody, inversion, grotesque humour, self-parody, are not inferior to more formal modes of argument and analysis, reflection and contemplation. I'm suggesting a reading of cultural history and contemporary culture where wildly divergent sources of reason and critique at the same time contest, contradict, interact, parody and, sometimes, learn from each other.[20]

Carnivalesque, then, offers an ongoing challenge, to the narrowly conceived forms of reason of the 'public sphere', as well as to modernism desiring to legislate, in an equally imperial way, single standards for all culture: what's good for the modernist avant-garde is good for the world. In relation to both, carnivalesque remains an always dangerous supplement, challenging, destabilising, relativising, pluralising single notions of true culture, true reason, true broadcasting, true art.

Notes

Preface

1. Jan Bruck and John Docker, 'Puritanic Rationalism: John Berger's *Ways of Seeing* and Media and Culture Studies', *Continuum*, vol.2, no.2, 1989; a version of this essay also appeared in *Theory Culture and Society*, vol.8, no.4, 1991.
2. Roland Barthes, *Image–Music–Text* (Fontana/Collins, Glasgow, 1979), p.146.
3. Cf. John Docker, *Australian Cultural Elites: Intellectual Traditions in Sydney and Melbourne* (Angus and Robertson, Sydney, 1974).
4. John Tulloch and Graeme Turner (eds), *Australian Television: Programs, Pleasures and Politics* (Allen and Unwin, Sydney, 1989); see also my 'The Sydney Connection: A Reflection on *Arena*', *Arena* 99/100, 1992.

Introduction

1. See also John Docker, 'Walter Benjamin, Postmodernism and the Frenzy of Gender', in Gerhard Fischer (ed.), *Walter Benjamin: New Perspectives* (Berg, forthcoming).
2. Stuart Hall, introduction to Allon White, *Carnival, Hysteria, and Writing* (Clarendon Press, Oxford, 1993).
3. Ibid., p.2.

Chapter 1
Architectural Modernism: Le Corbusier

1. Le Corbusier (Charles Jeanneret), *Towards a New Architecture* (The Architectural Press, London, 1965), pp.31, 89.
2. Richard Ellmann, *James Joyce* (OUP, New York, 1983), p.515.
3. *Towards a New Architecture*, pp.7, 9 (in order of quotation).
4. Ibid., pp.18, 33, 88, 37, 22–3, 114, 94, 107–9, 111–12, 15.
5. Ibid., pp.46, 69, 71, 84–5.
6. Ibid., pp.49, 14, 250, 55–6.
7. Ibid., p.269.
8. Ibid., pp.23–4, 26.
9. Ibid., pp.18–19, 7–8, 33, 20, 105.
10. Ibid., pp.33, 23, 68, 31, 71, 52, 47–8, 189.
11. Ibid., pp. 68, 33, 156–7, 160–1, 141–2.

12. *The Works of John Ruskin,* ed. E.T. Cook and Alexander Wedderburn (George Allen, London, 1904), vol.II, *The Stones of Venice,* pp.180–269.
13. The preface is reprinted in May Morris, *William Morris, Artist, Writer, Socialist* (Basil Blackwell, Oxford, 1936), vol.I, pp.292–5.
14. See Terence Lane and Jessie Serle, *Australians at Home. A Documentary History of Australian Domestic Interiors from 1788 to 1914* (Oxford University Press, Melbourne, 1990), pp.36–7, 41, 44.
15. Frank Whitford, *Bauhaus* (Thames and Hudson, London, 1986), pp.23, 132, 198.
16. *Towards a New Architecture,* pp.22, 32.
17. Ibid., pp.32, 37, 33, 214.
18. Ibid., pp.31–3, 47, 195, 10, 202, 123, 134, 204.
19. Ibid., pp.205, 135, 40, 123, 128.
20. Ibid., pp.17, 201, 61, 214, 41, 10, 23.
21. Ibid., pp.86–97, 246.
22. Ibid., pp.100, 61, 218, 108–115, 230, 216–9, 246, 123.
23. Ibid., pp.9, 52, 55–62, 49.
24. Ibid., pp.28–33, 40–1, 55, 252–4.
25. Ibid., pp. 62, 128–9, 27–8, 210, 94–7, 101, 119, 135, 188.
26. Le Corbusier, *The City of Tomorrow* (The Architectural Press, London, 1971), p.231n.
27. Ibid., pp.25–9, 66, 68.
28. Ibid., pp.66, 178, 280, 240, 281.
29. Ibid., pp.202, 82, 186–7.
30. Ibid., pp.187, 190, 282–3, 177, 238–9.
31. Ibid., pp.31, 232, 214, 217.
32. Ibid., pp.220, 217, 220, 216, 76, 216.
33. Ibid., pp.203, 225, 232, 80–1, 236–7, 82, 174–5, 199, 202, 205–6.
34. Ibid., p.287.
35. Ibid., pp.233, 7, 16–17, 51, 78, 177, 64, 82, 184–5, 240, 282, 64, 169, 288.
36. Ibid., 23, 11–18, 66, 68.
37. This moment is discussed in Marshall Berman, *All That is Solid Melts into Air* (Penguin, Harmondsworth, 1988), pp.166–7.
38. *The City of Tomorrow,* pp.63, 80–1, 65, 3, 179, 191, 187.
39. Ibid., pp.191, 197, 2–3, 300–1.
40. Ibid., pp.6, 231, 296.

Chapter 2
Literary Modernism

1. F.R. Leavis, *Mass Civilisation and Minority Culture* (Minority Press, Cambridge, 1930), reprinted in Leavis, *For Continuity* (Minority Press, Cambridge, 1933), pp.16–17.
2. Le Corbusier, *The City of Tomorrow* (The Architectural Press, London, 1971), pp.30, 302,13. Re Le Corbusier's élitism, see Charles Jencks, *Le Corbusier and the Tragic View of Architecture* (Penguin, Harmondsworth, 1987), pp.18, 35, 66–7, 71.
3. John Docker, *In a Critical Condition* (Penguin, Ringwood, 1984), Prologue.
4. *New Bearings in English Poetry* (Penguin, Harmondsworth, 1963), pp.90–1, 86, 79, 93, 115.
5. *Mass Civilisation and Minority Culture,* pp.13–14, 19, 32.
6. Ibid., pp.14, 20, 15, 44.
7. Ibid., pp.24, 32.
8. Ibid., pp.38–9.
9. Ibid., p.39.
10. Ibid., pp.26, 29–30.
11. Ibid., p.19.
12. Ibid., pp.18–20.
13. Ibid., pp.20–1.
14. Ibid., p.21.

15. Ibid., pp.32–8.
16. Ibid., pp.22–4, 28.
17. Ibid., p.40.
18. Ibid., p.30.
19. Le Corbusier, *The City of Tomorrow*, pp.190–1.
20. *Mass Civilisation and Minority Culture*, pp.16, 45, 17.
21. Ibid., pp.30–2.
22. Ibid., p.21.
23. Ibid., pp.44–6.
24. *New Bearings in English Poetry*, pp.162, 163, 167, 170.
25. Cf. A.L.French, '"Olympian Apathein": Pound's *Hugh Selwyn Mauberley* and Modern Poetry', *Essays in Criticism*, vol.VX, no.4, 1965, p.430.
26. *The Great Tradition* (Penguin, Harmondsworth, 1962), p.33.
27. *For Continuity*, p.2. See also *D.H.Lawrence: Novelist* (Penguin, Harmondsworth, 1964), p.10.
28. *The Great Tradition*, p.29.
29. *Anna Karenina and Other Essays* (Chatto and Windus, London, 1967), p.145.

Chapter 3
Modernism versus Popular Literature

1. Q.D.Leavis, *Fiction and the Reading Public* (first published by Chatto and Windus, London, reprinted by Folcroft Library Editions, New York, 1974), p.209.
2. Ibid., pp.40–1.
3. See Peter Keating (ed.), *Into Unknown England 1866–1913. Selections from the Social Explorers* (Manchester University Press, Manchester, 1976).
4. As pointed out by Iain Wright in his excellent 'F.R. Leavis, the *Scrutiny* Movement and the Crisis', in J. Clark, M. Heinemann, D. Margolies, and C. Snee (eds), *Culture and Crisis in Britain in the Thirties* (Lawrence and Wishart, London, 1979), p.49.
5. *Fiction and the Reading Public*, pp.15, 4–5, 7, 18, 44, 54, 11–12, 50.
6. Ibid., pp.202, 245, 38, 74, 62.
7. Ibid., pp.67, 70, 64, 23, 76, 28, 115, 134, 137, 168, 164, 179, 245.
8. Ibid., pp.85, 98.
9. Ibid., pp.86, 89, 92, 33–4, 118–19, 35, 120, 143, 149–50.
10. Ibid., pp.122–5, 157, 127, 129, 132.
11. Ibid., pp.48–9, 284–5 (note 32), 95.
12. Ibid., pp.83–4, 86, 193, 210, 187.
13. Ibid., pp.97–100, 206, 112–17.
14. Ibid., pp.129–30, 237–8.
15. Ibid., pp.154–7.
16. Ibid., pp.154–9.
17. Ibid., pp.117, 164, 171, 176–185.
18. Cf. Iain Wright, 'F.R. Leavis, the *Scrutiny* Movement and the Crisis', pp.51–2, and Francis Mulhern, 'English Reading', in Homi K. Bhabha (ed.), *Nation and Narration* (Routledge, London, 1990), pp.252–3.
19. *Fiction and the Reading Public*, pp.57–8.
20. Ibid., pp.57, 60, 69.
21. Ibid., pp.55, 182, 6–8, 19.
22. Ibid., pp.51, 53–4, 138, 88.
23. Ibid., pp.164, 308 (note 91), 64, 88–9, 119, 92, 165, 236.
24. Ibid., pp.74, 114, 146, 177.
25. Ibid., pp.85, 143, 177–8, 191.
26. Ibid., pp.35, 64, 74, 224.
27. Ibid., pp.224, 67, 35.
28. Ibid., p.225.
29. Ibid., p.209.

30. Ibid., pp.60, 27, 61, 77, 25, 74, 178, 185, 31, 27, 193–4, 28.
31. Ibid., pp.92, 101.
32. Ibid., p.83.
33. Ibid., p.183.
34. Ibid., p.138.
35. Ibid., pp.270–1.
36. Ibid., pp.168–9, 67.
37. Ibid., p.271.
38. Ibid., pp.272, 191.
39. Ibid., p.208.
40. Ibid., pp.132, 144, 189.
41. Ibid., pp.79, 102, 115.
42. Cf. Eugene Lunn, *Marxism and Modernism* (University of California Press, Berkeley, 1984), p.49.

Chapter 4
The Frankfurt School versus Walter Benjamin

1. Theodor Adorno and Max Horkheimer, *Dialectic of Enlightenment* (Verso, London, 1979), p.144.
2. F.R. Leavis, *For Continuity* (Minority Press, Cambridge, 1933), pp.184–9. See also the opening chapter, 'Prefatory: Marxism and Cultural Continuity'.
3. The similarities between Q.D. Leavis' *Fiction and the Reading Public* and Frankfurt School positions were commented on by Alan Swingewood, *The Myth of Mass Culture* (Macmillan, London, 1977), pp.114–15.
4. Cf. Ernst Bloch, Georg Lukács, Bertort Brecht, Walter Benjamin, Theodor Adorno, *Aesthetics and Politics* (New Left Books, London, 1977), and Pauline Johnson, *Marxist Aesthetics* (Routledge and Kegan Paul, London, 1984).
5. Cf. Swingewood, *The Myth of Mass Culture*, pp.114–5.
6. Adorno and Horkheimer, *Dialectic of Enlightenment*, pp.120–1.
7. Ibid., pp.123–4, 152.
8. Ibid., pp.120, 122, 126–7.
9. Ibid., pp.127–8.
10. Ibid., pp.130–1.
11. Ibid., pp.161–7.
12. Ibid., pp.167, 133, 150.
13. Ibid., pp.152–4, 141.
14. Ibid., p.134.
15. Ibid., pp.165–6, 138, 145.
16. Ibid., p.167.
17. Peter Burger, *Theory of the Avant-Garde* (University of Minnesota Press, Minneapolis, 1984), p.30, in refutation of Walter Benjamin's 'The Work of Art in the Age of Mechanical Reproduction', says that there has been a fading of any alleged critical potential of cinema in favour of a training in consumer attitudes, which extends to the most intimate interhuman relations. When we look up the endnote for this assertion, stated as if it's a self-evident truth, we find its source is – Adorno. Like Adorno, Burger omits to tell us how he gained such privileged access.
18. *Dialectic of Enlightenment*, p.126.
19. Cf. Thomas Schatz, *Hollywood Genres* (Random House, New York, 1981). See p.221 for Schatz' linking of Hollywood in general to melodrama.
20. *Dialectic of Enlightenment*, p.150.
21. Ibid., p.149. In 'In Defence of Popular Culture', *Arena* 60, 1982, my opening shot across the bows of the Frankfurt School, I accused it of functionalism and mechanical social control theory.

22. *Dialectic of Enlightenment*, p.139.
23. T.W. Adorno, 'Television and the Patterns of Mass Culture', in Bernard Rosenberg and David Manning White (eds), *Mass Culture. The Popular Arts in America* (Free Press, New York, 1975).
24. Cf. Hannah Arendt's introduction to Walter Benjamin, *Illuminations* (Schocken, New York, 1969), p.18, and Eugene Lunn, *Marxism and Modernism. An Historical Study of Lukács, Brecht, Benjamin, and Adorno* (University of California Press, Berkeley, 1982), p.194.
25. Lunn, *Marxism and Modernism*, pp.169–72, 179, 190–2.
26. Andreas Huyssen, *After the Great Divide: Modernism, Mass Culture and Postmodernism* (Macmillan, London, 1986), pp.152–3.
27. Walter Benjamin, *Illuminations*.
28. Andreas Huyssen, 'Mass Culture as Woman: Modernism's Other', in Tania Modleski (ed.), *Studies in Entertainment* (Indiana University Press, Bloomington, 1986), and Patrice Petro, *Joyless Streets: Women and Melodramatic Representation in Weimar Germany* (Princeton University Press, Princeton, 1989).
29. John Docker, 'In Defence of Popular Culture'.
30. Walter Benjmain, *Charles Baudelaire: A Lyric Poet in the Era of High Capitalism* (Verso, London, 1989), pp.38–9, 121.
31. Ibid., pp.151–2.
32. Ibid., pp.128, 131, 58.
33. Ibid., pp.129, 131, 47–8, 52, 54–6.
34. Ibid., pp.58, 55, 122, 49–50.
35. See the replies to my 'In Defence of Popular Culture' by Anthony Ashbolt, 'Against Left Optimism: a Reply to John Docker', and Ingrid Hagstrom, 'Popular Culture Undefined', *Arena* 61, 1982. See my reply, 'Popular Culture and its Marxist Critics', *Arena* 65, 1983.

Chapter 5
Flowering of an Orthodoxy

1. Richard Hoggart, *The Uses of Literacy* (Penguin, Harmondsworth, 1963), p.340.
2. Angela McRobbie and Jenny Garber, 'Girls and Subcultures: An exploration', in Stuart Hall and Tony Jefferson (eds), *Resistance through Rituals* (Hutchinson, London, 1977), p.222, note 3.
3. Roland Barthes, *Mythologies* (Paladin, London, 1979), p.21.
4. Ibid., p.23.
5. Cf. Jan Bruck and John Docker, 'Puritanic Rationalism: John Berger's *Ways of Seeing* and Media and Culture Studies', *Continuum*, vol.2, no.2, 1989. In his 1971 essay 'Change the Object Itself', his own revisiting of *Mythologies*, Barthes writes that the approach of *Mythologies* has itself become conventional, a 'mythological doxa': 'any student can and does denounce the bourgeois or petit-bourgeois character of such and such a form (of life, of thought, of consumption)'. See Barthes, *Image-Music-Text* (Fontana/Collins, Glasgow, 1979), p.166.
6. *The Uses of Literacy*, p.72.
7. Ibid., pp.84–8, 94.
8. Ibid., pp.102–7, 110.
9. Ibid., pp.103, 105, 137–9.
10. Ibid., pp.140–1, 143–4.
11. Ibid., pp.197, 178, 183–4, 188.
12. Ibid., pp.191–3, 202–3.
13. Ibid., pp.201, 369.
14. For a most thorough analysis of Wertham's *Seduction of the Innocent*, see Martin Barker, *A Haunt of Fears* (Pluto, London, 1984); see also John Docker, 'Culture, Society and the Communist Party', in Ann Curthoys and John Merritt (eds), *Australia's First Cold War* (Allen and Unwin, Sydney, 1984).

15. *The Uses of Literacy*, pp.247–9, 251, 258, 264.
16. Ibid., pp.330–1, 340, 328, 324–5, 327–8.
17. See Graeme Turner, *British Cultural Studies: An Introduction* (Unwin Hyman, London, 1990).
18. *The Uses of Literacy*, p.326.
19. Stuart Hall, 'Culture, Media and the "Ideological Effect"', in James Curran, Michael Gurevitch and Janet Woollacott (eds), *Mass Communication and Society* (1977; Edward Arnold, London, 1979).
20. On Gramsci, see also Richard Johnson, 'Histories of Culture/Theories of Ideology: Notes on an Impasse', in Michèle Barrett, Philip Corrigan, Annette Kuhn and Janet Wolf (eds), *Ideology and Cultural Production* (Croom Helm, London, 1979), pp.73–4.
21. 'Culture, Media and "Ideological Effect"', p.342.
22. Hall in Raphael Samuel (ed.), *People's History and Socialist Theory* (Routledge and Kegan Paul, London, 1980), p.239.
23. Cf.my essay 'Popular Culture and its Marxist Critics', *Arena* 65, 1983, pp.114–15, where I criticise Hall on this point.
24. 'Culture, Media and the "Ideological Effect"', pp.320, 344.
25. See Angela McRobbie and Jenny Garber, 'Girls and Subcultures', in Women's Study Group, Centre for Contemporary Cultural Studies (eds), *Women Take Issue* (Hutchinson, London, 1978).
26. For a critique of Angela McRobbie's work, see Martin Barker, *Comics: Ideology, Power and the Critics* (Manchester University Press, Manchester, 1989), pp.154–9.
27. For an earlier assessment of the Birmingham Centre and cultural studies, see the introduction to Susan Dermody, John Docker and Drusilla Modjeska (eds), *Nellie Melba, Ginger Meggs and Friends. Essays in Australian Cultural History* (Kibble, Malmsbury, 1982), pp.2–7.

Chapter 6
Myths of Origin:
1970s Screen Theory and Literary History

1. *Screen*, vol.15, no.2, 1974, partially reprinted in Tony Bennett, Susan Boyd-Bowman, Colin Mercer and Janet Woolacoot (eds), *Popular Television and Film* (BFI and Open University Press, London, 1981), p.217.
2. *Screen*, vol.16, no.3, 1975, partially reprinted in *Popular Television and Film*, p.206.
3. *Arena* 60, 1982, p.99.
4. John Docker, 'In Defence of Popular Culture', *Arena* 60, 1982.
5. See Iain Wright, '"What Matter Who's Speaking": Beckett, the Authorial Subject, and Contemporary Critical Theory', *Southern Review*, vol.16, no.1, 1983, pp.11–12.
6. McCabe, 'Realism and the Cinema . . .', pp.218–19.
7. Charlotte Brontë, *Jane Eyre* (Penguin, Harmondsworth, 1983), p.474 (ch.38).
8. Peter Brooks, *The Melodramatic Imagination: Balzac, Henry James, Melodrama, and the Mode of Excess* (Yale University Press, New Haven, 1976).
9. Wilkie Collins, *The Woman in White* (Penguin, Harmondsworth, 1983), p.33.
10. Ibid., pp.358–9.
11. Ibid., pp.360, 426.
12. 'In Defence of Popular Culture', p.83.
13. Henry James, *The Turn of the Screw* (Penguin, Harmondsworth, 1983), pp.7–8, 28, 10.
14. Tom Gunning, 'An Aesthetic of Astonishment. Early Film and the (In)Credulous Spectator', *Art and Text* 34, 1989, pp.31–45. The film medium was introduced to Australia in 1896, at the Melbourne Opera House, by magician Carl Hertz, advertising it as the most startling scientific marvel of the age; moving pictures were usually included as a part of varied vaudeville offerings, and often associated with the world of dream and the unconscious by being likened to the seance. Hertz's display in 1896 was followed by vaudeville performances, a burlesque showing the death of Svengali, and 'Beautiful Jessica', a new slack wire artist. Despite the popularity of the cinematograph, other visual entertainments continued to be popular, lantern slides,

panoramas, cycloramas, and the mutoscope enjoyed at fun fairs and carnivals. See Ina Bertrand (ed.), *Cinema in Australia. A Documentary History* (University of New South Wales Press, Sydney, 1989), pp.16–20.

15. McCabe, 'Realism and the Cinema . . .', p.221.
16. Ibid., pp.232–4.
17. Mikhail Bakhtin, *Problems of Dostoevsky's Poetics* (Manchester University Press, Manchester, 1984), pp.67–73; *The Dialogic Imagination* (University of Texas Press, Austin, 1981), p.46.
18. John Docker, 'Orientalism and Zionism: Images of the Arab', *Arena* 75, 1986, pp.83–6.
19. See Lorraine Mortimer, 'Godard and Reflexivity . . . ivity . . . ivity', pp.99–118.
20. Martin Barker, *Comics: Ideology, Power and the Critics* (Manchester University Press, Manchester, 1989), p.222.
21. Cf. Patrice Petro, *Joyless Streets: Women and Melodramatic Representation in Weimar Germany* (Princeton University Press, Princeton, 1989).
22. Mulvey, 'Visual Pleasure and Narrative Cinema', pp.211–13.
23. Ibid., pp.214–15.

Chapter 7
Architectural Postmodernism:
Learning from Las Vegas

1. Robert Venturi, Denise Scott Brown, Steven Izenour, *Learning from Las Vegas* (MIT Press, Cambridge, Mass., 1988), Revised Edition, pp.3, 161, 155, 114.
2. Ibid., pp.3, 6.
3. Ibid., pp.6–7, 102–3, 53, 103.
4. Ibid., pp.115, 143, 135–7, 148, 102, 104.
5. Ibid., pp.6, 152–3.
6. Ibid., pp.8, 34, 115–16.
7. Ibid., pp.130, 105, 6, 91, 72.
8. Ibid., pp.161–2.
9. Ibid., pp.116–17.
10. Ibid., pp.8–9, 104, 13.
11. Ibid., pp.13, 34–5, 108, 105–6, 52, 163.
12. Ibid., pp.9, 13, 106.
13. Ibid., pp.105, 34, 51.
14. Ibid., pp.52–3, 87.
15. Ibid., pp.161, 51, 49, 53. For ethnographic research that supports the argument here of *Learning from Las Vegas*, see Mark Neumann and David Eason, 'Casino World: Bringing It All Back Home', *Cultural Studies*, vol.4, no.1, 1990.
16. *Learning from Las Vegas*, pp.34, 92, 153 (note 18), 6, 162.
17. Ibid., pp.129, 154, 118, 53, 155.

Chapter 8
From Las Vegas to Sydney

1. Norman Lindsay, *My Mask: An Autobiography* (Angus and Robertson, Sydney, 1970), pp.159–60.
2. John Haskell, 'A search for power to stir the blood', *Sydney Morning Herald*, 16 Jan. 1988.(Haskell is Professor of Architecture at UNSW). See also *SMH*, advertisement for opening of Darling Harbour, 16 Jan. 1988.
3. *SMH*, 'Brereton launches west's first beach "wonderland"', 23 Nov. 1987; Mark Coulton, 'Tough flyer who didn't fit in', *SMH*, 26 Nov. 1987. When the Museum of Contemporary Art was opened in Sydney in November 1991, it was revealed that it was Laurie Brereton who in the early 1980s had promised the Maritime Services Board building at the Quay, a startling golden Art Deco palace opposite the Opera

House, to the future museum (Wanda Jamrozik, 'The Transformation', *SMH*, 12 Nov. 1991)

4. Richard Coleman, 'How Tony's City of Sydney left Laurie whingeing in the wind', *SMH*, 17 Oct. 1987; Jim McClelland, 'How Sydney can still be saved, despite the mayhem of developers', *SMH*, 6 Sept. 1989.

5. McClelland, 'The monorail and the edifice complex', *SMH*, 16 Oct. 1987; 'If I ruled Sydney for a day', *SMH*, 3 Dec. 1987; Don Anderson, 'Behind the Lines', *SMH*, 19 Dec. 1987.

6. When Brereton chose to defend himself he argued that more than one poll indicated majority public support in New South Wales, city and country, for the monorail: Brereton, letter, *SMH*, 4 Nov. 1987; report on *Bulletin* Morgan Gallup poll, *SMH*, 19 Nov. 1987.

7. *SMH*, 29 June, 1991.

8. Ibid.

9. Robert Venturi, Denise Scott Brown, Steven Izenour, *Learning from Las Vegas* (MIT Press, Cambridge, Mass., 1988), Revised Edition, p.53.

10. Information in this and succeeding paragraphs was provided by Bob Perry.

11. Robyn Tudor, 'Decorative Terrazzo', *craft arts international*, September/November 1988, pp.55–60.

12. For Lucien Henry see Terence Lane and Jessie Serle, *Australians at Home: A Documentary History of Australian Domestic Interiors from 1788 to 1914* (Oxford University Press, Melbourne, 1990), pp.42, 48, 228–9. For Henry's interest in Australian flora, see 'The Waratah in Applied Art', *The Technical Gazette*, August 1911 and May 1912. Concerning his Centennial Hall windows in the Sydney Town Hall, see *The AustralianBuilder and Contractors' News*, 21 December 1889.

13. Joseph Conrad, *The Mirror of the Sea* (1906; Methuen, London, 1919), pp.147–8.

Chapter 9
Are We Living in a Postmodern Age?

1. Hillel Schwartz, *Century's End. A Cultural History of the Fin de Siècle from the 990s through the 1990s* (Doubleday, New York, 1990). See also John Docker, *The Nervous Nineties: Australian Cultural Life in the 1890s* (Oxford University Press, Melbourne, 1991).

2. Bruce Sterling (ed.), *Mirrorshades: The Cyberpunk Anthology* (Paladin, London, 1988), introduction, p.xi, quoted in David M.Bausor and Simon Cooper, 'Cyberpunk: Writing the Present into the Future', *Arena* 97, 1991.

3. In Hal Foster (ed.), *The Anti-Aesthetic. Essays on Postmodern Culture* (Bay Press, Seattle, 1983), p.128.

4. Bram Stoker, *Dracula* (Oxford University Press, Oxford, 1983), p.38.

5. Cf. John Docker, 'In Defence of Popular TV: Carnivalesque V. Left Pessimism', *Continuum*, vol.1, no.2, 1988, pp.95–6.

6. Jean Baudrillard, *America* (Verso, London, 1988), p.5.

7. Ibid., pp.7, 5, 3, 10–11 (in order of quotation).

8. Ibid., pp.14–16, 3. Cf. Bernard Gendron, 'Fetishes and Motorcars: Negrophilia in French Modernism' *Cultural Studies*, vol.4, no.2, 1990.

9. *America*, pp.18–19, 22–3.

10. Ibid., pp.15, 17, 7.

11. Ibid., pp.10, 9, 20–1, 23.

12. Ibid., pp.1, 16, 15, 18, 19, 22.

13. See Julian Pefanis, *Heterology and the Postmodern. Bataille, Baudrillard, and Lyotard* (Allen and Unwin, Sydney, 1991), pp.99–100.

14. J-F. Lyotard, *The Postmodern Condition: A Report on Knowledge*, translated by Geoff Bennington and Brian Massumi (Manchester University Press, Manchester, 1987), pp.15, 17, 90, note 55.

15. See, however, Katherine Hayles, *Chaos Bound. Orderly Disorder in Contemporary Literature and Science* (Cornell University Press, Ithaca, 1990), pp.27, 215, 288, who

questions Lyotard's claim that Chaos Theory scientists have jettisoned positivistic and universalist ambitions to describe the truth of the natural world.

16. *The Postmodern Condition*, p.11.
17. Ibid., pp.65–6.
18. Pefanis, *Heterology and the Postmodern*, pp.87–90. See also J.G.Merquior, *Western Marxism* (Paladin, London, 1986), pp.195–6.
19. Cf. John Docker, '"Those Halcyon Days": The Moment of the New Left', in Brian Head and James Walter (eds), *Intellectual Movements and Australian Society* (Oxford University Press, Melbourne, 1988).
20. Pefanis, *Heterology and the Postmodern*, pp.84–5. See also Margaret A. Rose, *The post-modern and the post-industrial* (Cambridge University Press, Cambridge, 1991), pp.59–60, 65, 229 note 112.
21. *The Postmodern Condition*, appendix, pp.71–82.
22. Cf. Andreas Huyssen, *After the Great Divide: Modernism, Mass Culture and Postmodernism* (Macmillan, London, 1986), pp.214–15. Huyssen argues that Lyotard's 'turn to Kant's sublime forgets that the 18th-century fascination with the sublime of the universe, the cosmos, expresses precisely that very desire of totality and representation which Lyotard so abhors and persistently criticises in Habermas' work'.
23. Cornell West, 'Black Culture and Postmodernism', in Barbara Kruger and Phil Mariani (eds), *Remaking History* (Bay Press, Seattle, 1989).
24. Ibid., p.92.
25. Lyotard, 'Le Postmoderne expliqué aux enfants', quoted in Pefanis, *Heterology and the Postmodern*, p.83.

Chapter 10
Mapping Frederic Jameson's grand Narrative

1. Frederic Jameson, 'Postmodernism, or The Cultural Logic of Late Capitalism', *New Left Review* 146, 1984, pp.53–92. For examples of the debate, see Douglas Kellner (ed.), *Postmodernism/Jameson/Critique* (Maisonneuve Press, Washington DC, 1989), and Mike Featherstone, *Consumer Culture and Postmodernism* (Sage Publications, London, 1991). In his *Postmodernism: or, The Cultural Logic of Late Capitalism* (Verso, London, 1991), ch.1, Jameson reprints, in somewhat revised form, the *New Left Review* essay.
2. 'Postmodernism, or The Cultural Logic of Late Capitalism', pp.91, 55, 78 (in order of quotation).
3. Ibid., pp.78, 55–7, 66, 89.
4. Ibid., pp.61, 58–9, 78–9, 89.
5. Ibid., pp.78, 54, 66, 76.
6. Ibid., pp.57, 61.
7. Ibid., p.60.
8. Ibid., pp.84, 81–2.
9. Ibid., p.83.
10. Ibid., pp.87, 85, 61.
11. Ibid., pp.65–6.
12. Ibid., pp.66–7.
13. Ibid., pp.56, 54, 64, 79.
14. Ibid., pp.80, 54, 81.
15. Margaret A. Rose, *The post-modern and the post-industrial* (Cambridge University Press, Cambridge, 1991), pp.76–80; Charles Jencks, *The Language of Post-Modern Architecture*, 5th edn (Academy Editions, London, 1987), pp.34–5.
16. *Sydney Morning Herald*, 4 March, 1992.
17. 'Postmodernism, or The Cultural Logic of Late Capitalism', p.83.
18. Ibid., pp.65, 71–2, 63, 66, 83.
19. Ibid., pp.90–2.

20. Ibid., pp.63–5.
21. George J.Zytaruk and James T.Boulton (eds), *The Letters of D.H.Lawrence* (Cambridge University Press, Cambridge, 1981), vol.II, pp.182–4.
22. T.S. Eliot, *The Sacred Wood* (Methuen, London, 1957), pp.47–59.
23. 'Postmodernism, or The Cultural Logic of Late Capitalism', pp.60, 57.
24. Mikhail Bakhtin, *Problems of Dostoevsky's Poetics* (Manchester University Press, Manchester, 1984), pp.5–7, 14–17, 69–73, 111–37.
25. Cf. Robert Young, *White Mythologies: Writing History and the West* (Routledge, London, 1990), pp.112–18.
26. *The post-modern and the post-industrial*, pp.236–7, note 172.
27. Cf. John O'Neill, 'Religion and Postmodernism: The Durkheimian Bond in Bell and Jameson', and Georg Stauth and Bryan S.Turner, 'Nostalgia, Postmodernism and the Critique of Mass Culture', *Theory Culture and Society*, vol.5, nos 2–3, 1988; Mike Featherstone, *Consumer Culture and Postmodernism*, pp.61–2. See also Dominick LaCapra, *Rethinking Intellectual History: Texts, Contexts, Language* (Cornell University Press, Ithaca, 1983), ch.7.
28. 'Postmodernism, or The Cultural Logic of Late Capitalism', pp.66, 84.

Chapter 11
From Structuralism to Poststructuralism

1. Jacques Derrida, *Writing and Difference* (University of Chicago Press, Chicago, 1978), pp.278–9.
2. Edward Said, *The World, The Text, and the Critic* (1983; Vintage, London, 1991), p.211; see also p.196.
3. James Clifford, *The Predicament of Culture: Twentieth-Century Ethnography, Literature, and Art* (Harvard University Press, Cambridge, Mass., 1988), p.272.
4. Imre Salusinszky (ed.), *Criticism in Society* (Methuen, New York and London, 1987), p.185.
5. Interview with Derrida in ibid., p.23.
6. The reference to the Yale Mafia is in Lentricchia, *After the New Criticism* (Athlone Press, London, 1980), p.283.
7. The New Historicists, however, have been criticised, not least by Frank Lentricchia, for following the unfortunate side of Foucault in *Discipline and Punish*, a totalising conception of power as all-controlling, a paranoid and totalitarian narrative. See Lentricchia, 'Foucault's Legacy – A New Historicism?', in H. Aram Veeser (ed.), *The New Historicism* (Routledge, London, 1989), pp.234–5.
8. See, for example, James Clifford and George Marcus (eds), *Writing Culture* (University of California Press, Berkeley, 1986), and James Clifford, *The Predicament of Culture*.
9. Dominick LaCapra, *Rethinking Intellectual History: Texts, Contexts, Language* (Cornell University Press, Ithaca, 1983), chapter on 'Reading Marx: The Case of The Eighteenth Brumaire', pp.284, 288–90. For the suggestion of Derrida and Marx as carnivalesque figures in intellectual life, see LaCapra, *History and Criticism* (Cornell University Press, Ithaca, 1985), p.107. See also Peter Stallybrass and Allon White, *The Politics and Poetics of Transgression* (Methuen, London, 1986), p.129, and Edward Said, *The World, The Text, and the Critic*, pp.121–5.
10. Salusinszky, *Criticism in Society*, p.10.
11. *Writing and Difference*, ch.10. In chapter two of *Writing and Difference*, 'Cogito and the History of Madness', Derrida argued against the view in Foucault's early book *Madness and Civilization* that there can be a preferred space of madness, of otherness, figured in writing, that is beyond repressive reason. Foucault replied in 'My Body, This Paper, This Fire', *Oxford Literary Review*, vol.4, no.1, 1979, pp.9–28. See also Robert Young, *White Mythologies: Writing History and the West* (Routledge, London, 1990), pp.71–2. Young, however, perhaps too easily prefers Derrida to Foucault. For discussion of the Foucault–Derrida conflict, though this time perhaps too kind to

Foucault, see Said's essay 'Criticism Between Culture and System' in *The World, The Text, and the Critic.*

12. Jacques Derrida, *Margins of Philosophy* (University of Chicago Press, Chicago, 1986), chapter on 'White Mythology: Metaphor in the Text of Philosophy', p.213.
13. Jacques Derrida, *Of Grammatology* (The John Hopkins University Press, Baltimore and London, 1980), pp.3, 10, 70, 102, 10–12, 112, 13, 20, 97, 16 (in order of quotation).
14. Ibid., pp.134–9, 110, 18, 86, 83.
15. Ibid., pp.3, 68, 129, 89, 9, 87.
16. Ibid., pp.7–8, 89, 106, 109–12, 128.
17. Ibid., pp.68, 112, 127–8.
18. See Foucault, 'My Body, This Paper, This Fire', pp.24, 27.
19. *Of Grammatology*, pp.60–2, 73, 65–6, 128.
20. Ibid., p.158.
21. Ibid., pp.69, 166, 150, 147, 143.
22. Ibid., pp.159, 179, 152–3, 156–7, 163.
23. Ibid., pp.158, 195, 120, 131.
24. *Writing and Difference*, p.279.
25. *Of Grammatology*, pp.6–7, 124.
26. Ibid., p.98.
27. Cf. Said, 'Criticism Between Culture and System', p.189; Lentricchia, *After the New Criticism*, pp.176–7.
28. *Of Grammatology*, pp.3, 5, 8, 98–9, 115, 13–14, 161, 71, 86, 72, 301.
29. Ibid., pp.69, 8, 11, 70, 86, 72, 87.
30. Ibid., pp.5, 8, 14, 23, 86–7, 92–3. Robert Young's *White Mythologies* also presents a teleological narrative of theoretical progress, where the admired destination is to be mapped by measuring greater and greater closeness of various theorists to 'Derrida'. Indeed, we might say that in Young's book 'Derrida' is the centre that is not there, the origin of the book's method and valuations, yet beyond any play of interpretation.
31. Said, 'Criticism Between Culture and System', p.191.
32. *Of Grammatology*, pp.97, 17–18, 138, 162, 167, 298, 301, 98.
33. Ibid., p.99; see also p.149.
34. 'Criticism Between Culture and System', pp.192–201.
35. *Of Grammatology*, pp.113–15, 125, 163, 180, 262.
36. Mikhail Bakhtin, *The Dialogic Imagination* (University of Texas Press, Austin, 1981), pp.158–66.
37. See in particular Derrida's essay 'White Mythology: Metaphor in the Text of Philosophy'.
38. Andreas Huyssen, *After the Great Divide: Modernism, Mass Culture and Postmodernism* (Macmillan, London, 1986), pp.206–16; Cornell West, 'Black Culture and Postmodernism', in Barbara Kruger and Phil Mariani (eds), *Remaking History* (Bay Press, Seattle, 1989), p.88.
39. *Of Grammatology*, p.92.
40. Cf. J. Claude Evans, *Strategies of Deconstruction: Derrida and the Myth of the Voice* (University of Minnesota Press, Minneapolis, 1991).
41. *Of Grammatology*, pp.114, 90.

Chapter 12
Cultural Studies: Transitional Moments from
Modernism to Postmodernism

1. Gerard de Nerval, *Journey to the Orient* (1851; Panther, London, 1973), pp.159–60.
2. Dorothy Hobson, *Crossroads: The Drama of a Soap Opera* (Methuen, London, 1982), p.135.
3. See John Docker, 'Williams' Challenge to Screen Studies', *Southern Review*, vol.22, no.2, 1989.

4. Theodor Adorno and Max Horkheimer, 'The Culture Industry as Mass Deception', *Dialectic of Enlightenment* (Verso, London, 1979), pp.121, 128.
5. *Television: Technology and Cultural Form* (Fontana, London, 1974), pp.84, 86.
6. Cf. John Docker, 'Unprecedented in history: drama and the dramatic in television', *Australasian Drama Studies*, vol.1, no.2, 1983, p.61.
7. *Televison: Technology and Cultural Form*, pp.77, 59, 62, 38–9.
8. Cf. John Docker, 'Popular Culture versus the State: An Argument against Australian Content Regulations for Television', *Media Information Australia* 59, 1991.
9. See Michael Booth, *English Melodrama* (Herbert Jenkins, London, 1965) and 'Early Victorian Farce: Dionysius Domesticated', in Kenneth Richards and Peter Thomson (eds), *Essays on Nineteenth-Century British Theatre* (Methuen, London, 1971); Veronica Kelly, introduction to Garnet Walch's pantomime, *Australia Felix, or Harlequin Laughing Jackass and the Magic Bat* (University of Queensland Press, St Lucia, 1988), pp.6–7.
10. See Jan Bruck and John Docker, 'Puritanic Rationalism: John Berger's *Ways of Seeing* and Media and Culture Studies, *Continuum*, vol.2, no.2, 1989, reprinted in somewhat revised form in *Theory Culture and Society*, vol.8, no.4, 1991.
11. Tania Modleski, *Loving with a Vengeance: Mass-produced fantasies for women* (Methuen, New York, 1982), chapter 4.
12. Ibid., pp.86, 108.
13. Ibid., pp.87, 103, 92, 88.
14. Ibid., pp.87, 93, 107.
15. Ibid., pp.91, 94, 97.
16. Ibid., pp.98, 100, 102.
17. A saying attributed to Collins by Kenneth Robinson, *Wilkie Collins: A Biography* (London, 1951), p.160, quoted in Virginia Blain, 'Copy-Text and Compromise: Wilkie Collins in the Nineteenth Century and Now', in J.C. Eade (ed.), *Editing Texts: Papers from a Conference at the Humanities Research Centre May 1984* (Humanities Research Centre, Australian National University, 1985), pp.63, 67.
18. *Loving with a Vengeance*, p.94.
19. Ibid., p.93.
20. Ibid., pp.108–9.
21. Robert C. Allen, 'On Reading Soaps: A Semiotic Primer', in E. Ann Kaplan (ed.), *Regarding Television* (AFI, Los Angeles, 1983), and his *Speaking of Soap Operas* (University of North Carolina Press, Chapel Hill, 1985), pp.93–5. See also John Docker, 'In Defence of Popular TV: Carnivalesque v. Left Pessimism', *Continuum*, vol.1, no.2, 1988.
22. Hobson, *Crossroads*, p.11.
23. Ibid., pp.14, 141, 138, 162–3, 109. For *Crossroads'* post-Meg Mortimer years, see Christine Geraghty, *Women and Soap Opera: A Study of Prime Time Soaps* (Polity Press, Cambridge, 1991), pp.189–94.
24. Hobson, *Crossroads*, pp.150–1.
25. Ibid., pp.162, 169, 164.
26. Ibid., pp.113, 109.
27. Ibid., pp.105, 119, 136.
28. Ibid., pp.118, 124–5.
29. Ibid., pp.108–10.
30. Ibid., pp.120, 136.
31. See James Clifford and George Markus (eds), *The Poetics and Politics of Ethnography* (University of California Press, Los Angeles, 1986).
32. Cf. Elspeth Probyn, 'Bodies and anti-bodies: feminism and the postmodern', *Cultural Studies*, vol.1, no.3, 1987, p.354. See also Tania Modleski, 'Some Functions of Feminist Criticism, or The Scandal of the Mute Body', *October* 49, 1989: 'the viewer's unconscious, an area which is unfortunately neglected by most ethnographers - *Screen's* psychoanalytic emphasis having been the first victim of ethnographic criticism' (p.6). Modleski singles out Janice Radway's 1984 *Reading the Romance* for harsh criticism in this essay.

33. John Fiske, 'TV Quiz Shows and the Purchase of Cultural Capital', *The Australian Journal of Screen Theory* 13 & 14, 1983, pp.5–20.

34. The paper was eventually published in revised form as 'In Praise of *Prisoner*', in John Tulloch and Graeme Turner (eds), *Australian Television. Programs, Pleasures and Politics* (Allen and Unwin, Sydney, 1989). I also discuss *Prisoner* in 'Unprecedented in history: drama and the dramatic in television'.

35. John Fiske, *Understanding Popular Culture* (Unwin Hyman, Boston, 1989), Preface.

36. Ibid., pp.20–1, 24.

37. Ibid., pp.10–11, 19, 23, 27. Cf. John Fiske, 'TV: Re-situating the Popular in the People', and Tim Rowse, 'Reply to John Fiske's Paper', *Continuum*, vol.1, no.2, 1988.

38. *Understanding Popular Culture*, pp.11, 23, 27, 47, ix, 4–5, 18, 19, 25, 28, 45, 35, 44, 54, 46, 49, 64, 24–5, 30.

39. Ibid., pp.24, 47, 4, 18–19, 25, 34, 28–31, 34, 47, 64.

40. Ibid., pp.4–5, 19, 43–5.

41. Ibid., pp.1, 23, 27, 45, 56, 69–90.

42. Ibid., pp.100–102.

43. Ibid., pp.11, 27.

44. Ibid., pp.47, 64.

45. Cf. Terry Lovell, 'Ideology and *Coronation Street*', in Richard Dyer et al., *Coronation Street* (BFI, London, 1981), p.43, and John Docker, 'Popular Culture and its Marxist Critics', *Arena* 65, 1983, p.110.

46. *Understanding Popular Culture*, p.29.

47. Ibid., pp.30–1.

48. Ibid., p.6.

49. Meaghan Morris, 'Banality in Cultural Studies', in Patricia Mellencamp (ed.), *Logics of Television* (Indiana University Press, Bloomington, 1990).

50. I analyse shows like *New Price is Right, Sale of the Century*, and *Mastermind* in 'In Defence of Popular Culture', *Arena* 60, 1982, pp.82–3, and 'Unprecedented in history: drama and the dramatic in television', pp.51–5. I apply Bakhtin to cultural theory in 'Antipodean Literature: A World Upside Down?', *Overland* 103, July 1986, and 'In defence of melodrama: towards a libertarian aesthetic', *Australasian Drama Studies* 9, 1986. I relate Bakhtin's notions of carnivalesque to TV game shows, including the dating show *Perfect Match*, in 'In Defence of Popular TV: Carnivalesque v. Left Pessimism', pp.89–91.

Chapter 13
Bakhtin's Carnival

1. Mikhail Bakhtin, *Speech Genres and Other Late Essays*, translated by Vern W. McGee, edited by Caryl Emerson and Michael Holquist (University of Texas Press, Austin, 1987), p.162.

2. J.W. Goethe, *Italian Journey*, translated by W.H. Auden and Elizabeth Mayer (Penguin Books, Harmondsworth, 1982), pp.451–2.

3. Quoted in Jeffrey Moussaieff Masson, *The Assault on Truth: Freud's Suppression of the Seduction Theory* (Harper Perennial, New York, 1992), p.57. This is part of a chapter concerning Freud and Fliess' treatment of Emma Eckstein.

4. Katerina Clark and Michael Holquist, *Mikhail Bakhtin* (Belknap Press, Cambridge, Mass., 1984), pp.142–3, 139, 238, 321, 323–5, vii.

5. Ibid., pp.238, 332–5.

6. Ibid., pp.240, 242; Mikhail Bakhtin, *Problems of Dostoevsky's Poetics*, edited and translated by Caryl Emerson (Manchester University Press, Manchester, 1984), p.6.

7. *Mikhail Bakhtin*, pp.240, 242, 276–7; *Problems of Dostoevsky's Poetics*, p.7.

8. *Mikhail Bakhtin*, pp.242, 13, 7–8, 10, 120, 260; see also Michael Holquist, 'Bakhtin and Rabelais: Theory as Praxis', *boundary 2*, September 1983, p.12.

9. *Mikhail Bakhtin*, pp.307–16; 'Bakhtin and Rabelais', pp.9–17.

10. Mikhail Bakhtin, *Rabelais and His World*, translated by Hélène Iswolsky (Indiana University Press, Bloomington, 1984), pp.72, 76.
11. Ibid., pp.74, 78–9, 81.
12. Ibid., pp.82–7. My perhaps odd epigraph from Freud's friend Fliess can now be explained. Rabelais would surely have enjoyed the sight of a modern physician taking seriously a joke descending from thousands of years of folk humour about the connection of the nose with the sexual organ. The results of such solemnity for Freud's patient Emma Eckstein were, however, as Masson tells the story in *The Assault on Truth*, horrific. Called in by Freud, Fliess the physician indeed operated on her nose in order to cure her of her perverse interest in masturbation, leaving a length of gauze behind in the wound, with Emma almost bleeding to death and suffering permanent disfiguration. It was Fliess' first major operation, his other interventions in this line of surgery being confined to cauterisation and cocainisation of the nose.
13. *Rabelais and His World*, pp.72–4.
14. Ibid., pp.81, 96, 73, 75.
15. Ibid., pp.94–6.
16. Ibid., pp.13, 72, 97.
17. Ibid., pp.96–7. C.L. Barber, *Shakespeare's Festive Comedy* (Princeton University Press, Princeton, New Jersey, 1959), pp.213–21, argues that whereas in a static, monolithic society the carnival spirit, as embodied in a Lord of Misrule, can be put back in its place after the revel with relative ease, in Shakespeare's time culture was not monolithic and scepticism, especially in and around London, was becoming part of everyday consciousness, dangerous to official sanctities. In part two of *Henry IV*, Falstaff as Lord of Misrule hopes to extend his festive licence to all-year-round everyday licence. Hal, however, become king, wishes to kill off the temporary Lord of Misrule, to confine festive scepticism to carnival times only. Hence his notoriously cold, priggish rejection of his erstwhile friend ('I know thee not, old man. Fall to thy prayers . . .').
18. *Rabelais and His World*, p.96.
19. Ibid., p.245.
20. *Italian Journey*, pp.446–70.
21. Goethe's account of the carnival in Rome is discussed in *Rabelais and His World*, pp.244–56.
22. Ibid., pp.282, 286, 297–302.
23. Ibid., pp.10, 296–7, 302, 286.
24. Ibid., pp.278–9, 291, 281, 283.
25. Ibid., pp.283, 286.
26. Ibid., pp.154, 187–8, 165–6.
27. Ibid., pp. 283–6, 296.
28. Ibid., pp.181–3.
29. Ibid., pp.189, 147–8.
30. Ibid., pp.148, 151.
31. Ibid., pp.370, 297, 81, 251.
32. Ibid., pp.240–3.
33. Ibid., pp.243, 251; *Italian Journey*, p.468.
34. *Rabelais and His World*, pp.39–40.
35. Ibid., pp.255–7.
36. Ibid., pp.12, 160, 162, 256.
37. Ibid., pp.64–6.
38. Ibid., pp.33, 101–3.
39. Ibid., pp.124, 116–19, 34.
40. Ibid., pp.252, 36–43, 120n.
41. Ibid., pp.34, 101–2.
42. Ibid., p.33.
43. Ibid., pp.33–4.
44. Ibid., p.44.
45. Ibid., pp.28–30.

46. Ibid., p.116.
47. Bakhtin, *Speech Genres and Other Late Essays*, chapter on 'The *Bildungsroman* and Its Significance in the History of Realism (Toward a Historical Typology of the Novel)', pp. 42–7; Holquist, introduction, pp.xiv–xv.
48. Ibid., pp.26–32, 36, 38.
49. Cf. Jan Bruck and John Docker, 'Puritanic Rationalism: John Berger's *Ways of Seeing* and Media and Culture Studies', *Theory Culture and Society*, vol.8, no.4, 1991, pp.89–93.
50. *Rabelais and His World*, pp.6, 20–1.

Chapter 14
Dilemmas of World Upside Down

1. Robert Collison, *The Story of Street Literature. Forerunner of the Popular Press* (J.M. Dent, London, 1973), p.16.
2. Katerina Clark and Michael Holquist, *Mikhail Bakhtin* (Belknap Press, Cambridge, Mass., 1984), pp.310–11.
3. Peter Stallybrass and Allon White, *The Politics and Poetics of Transgression* (Methuen, London, 1986), pp.26, 7, 28–9, 30, 35, 38.
4. Mikhail Bakhtin, *Rabelais and His World*, translated by Hélène Iswolsky (Indiana University Press, Bloomington, 1984), pp.72–3, 96–7.
5. *Rabelais and His World*, pp.82, 154–6.
6. Ibid., pp.465–72.
7. J.W. Goethe, *Italian Journey*, translated by W.H. Auden and Elizabeth Mayer (Penguin, Harmondsworth, 1982), pp.448–9, 455–6, 458–9.
8. *Rabelais and His World*, pp.291–4, 300–1.
9. *Italian Journey*, pp.454–5.
10. *The Politics and Poetics of Transgression*, p.19.
11. Enid Welsford, *The Fool. His Social and Literary History* (Faber and Faber, London, 1935), p.234; Peter Burke, *Popular Culture in Early Modern Europe* (Temple Smith, London, 1979), pp.177, 187, 184, 198, 200, 204; Michael D. Bristol, *Carnival and Theater. Plebean Culture and the Structure of Authority in Renaissance England* (Methuen, New York, 1985), p.51; Stallybrass and White, *The Politics and Poetics of Transgression*, pp.53–70.
12. Mikhail Bakhtin, *Speech Genres and Other Late Essays*, translated by Vern W. McGee (University of Texas Press, Austin, 1987), pp.45–7.
13. *The Politics and Poetics of Transgression*, pp.40–2. See also Richard D. Altick, *The Shows of London* (Harvard University Press, Cambridge, Mass., 1978).
14. *Rabelais and His World*, pp.33–4; Holquist, 'Bakhtin and Rabelais: Theory as Praxis', *boundary 2*, September 1983, p.14.
15. Max Gluckman, *Custom and Conflict in Africa* (Basil Blackwell, Oxford, 1970), p.109.
16. Ian Donaldson, *The World Upside-Down* (Oxford University Press, London, 1970), pp.14–15.
17. Cf. Michael D. Bristol, *Carnival and Theatre*, pp.6–7, 25–30.
18. See Barbara A. Babcock (ed.), *The Reversible World. Symbolic Inversion in Art and Society* (Cornell University Press, Ithaca, 1978).
19. Natalie Davis, 'Women on Top: Symbolic Sexual Inversion and Political Disorder in Early Modern Europe', in ibid. The essay is printed as 'Women on Top' in Natalie Davis, *Society and Culture in Early Modern France* (Stanford University Press, Stanford, 1975), ch.5. Concerning parodies of Aristotle, see also Enid Welsford, *The Fool*, p.234.
20. David Kunzle, 'World Upside Down: The Iconography of a European Broadsheet Type', in Babcock (ed.), *The Reversible World*.
21. Emmanuel Le Roy Ladurie, *Carnival in Romans* (Penguin, Harmondsworth, 1981), ch.7 and pp.273, 292, 295, 329.
22. Burke, *Popular Culture in Early Modern Europe*, pp.191, 199–204.

Chapter 15
Fools: Carnival–Theatre–Vaudeville–Television

1. Enid Welsford, *The Fool: His Social and Literary History* (Faber and Faber, London, 1935), p.37.
2. Fred Parsons, *A Man Called Mo* (Heinemann, Melbourne, 1973), p.34.
3. Mikhail Bakhtin, *The Dialogic Imagination* (University of Texas Press, Austin, 1981), pp.158–66.
4. Mikhail Bakhtin, *Rabelais and His World* (Indiana University Press, Bloomington, 1984), pp.4, 8, 352–3.
5. Ibid., pp.316–18, 344–7.
6. Ibid., pp. 27, 318, 323.
7. Ibid., pp.344–7.
8. Ibid., pp.353–4.
9. Ibid., pp.363–5.
10. Ibid., pp.365–7.
11. Ibid., pp.18–29.
12. Ibid., pp.318–320.
13. Ibid., p.155.
14. See, for example, Michael D. Bristol, *Carnival and Theater* (Methuen, New York, 1985).
15. David Wiles, *Shakespeare's Clown. Actor and Text in the Elizabethan Playhouse* (Cambridge University Press, Cambridge, 1987). See also C.L. Barber, *Shakespeare's Festive Comedy: A Study of Dramatic Form and its Relation to Social Custom* (Princeton University Press, Princeton, 1959); Bristol, *Carnival and Theater*.
16. See also the argument of Peter Stallybrass and Allon White, *The Politics and Poetics of Transgression* (Methuen, London, 1986), pp.66–79, concerning Ben Jonson.
17. *Rabelais and His World*, pp.101–2, 120.
18. In the Australian context, see *Australia Felix, or Harlequin Laughing Jackass and the Magic Bat*, a Pantomime by Garnet Walch, edited by Veronica Kelly (1873; University of Queensland Press, St Lucia, 1988).
19. Enid Welsford, *The Fool: His Social and Literary History*; William Willeford, *The Fool and his Sceptre* (Edward Arnold, London, 1969).
20. See Michael Booth, 'Early Victorian Farce: Dionysus Domesticated', in Kenneth Richards and Peter Thomson (ed.), *Essays on Nineteenth-Century British Theatre* (Methuen, London, 1971), pp.96–101.
21. Cf. John Docker, 'Antipodean Literature: A World Upside Down?', *Overland* 103, 1986, and *The Nervous Nineties* (Oxford University Press, Melbourne, 1991).
22. Alexander Macdonald, *The Ukulele Player Under the Red Lamp* (Angus and Robertson, Sydney, 1972), p.220.
23. Fred Parsons, *A Man Called Mo*, pp.2, 9, and foreword by Graham Kennedy.
24. Ibid., pp.12–15.
25. Ibid., p.15. See also Roy Rene (with Elizabeth Lambert and Max Harris), *Mo's Memoirs* (Reed and Harris, Melbourne, 1945), p.32. For the popularity of minstrel shows in Australia, see Richard Waterhouse, 'Blackface and the beginnings of bifurcation: the minstrel show and the emergence of an Australian popular stage', *Australasian Drama Studies* 14, 1989.
26. *A Man Called Mo*, p.109.
27. See also John Thompson, *Five to Remember* (Lansdowne, Melbourne, 1964), pp.1–24; Jacqueline Kent, *Out of the Bakelite Box* (Angus and Robertson, Sydney, 1983), pp.12–21; Nancye Bridges, *Wonderful Wireless* (Methuen, Australia, 1983), pp.81–7; Celestine McDermott, 'National Vaudeville', in Harold Love (ed.), *The Australian Stage* (New South Wales University Press, Sydney, 1984), pp.135–43 (also pp.178–81).
28. *A Man Called Mo*, pp.3, 107. In *Mo's Memoirs*, Mo mentions quite a few Jewish comedians – Jordan and Harvey (a 'Jewish team'), Julian Rose, Bert Le Blanc, Henry Green (pp.45–6, 74, 89).
29. *A Man Called Mo*, p.4.
30. Ibid., pp.1–3, 83.

31. J.W. Goethe, *Italian Journey* (Penguin, Harmondsworth, 1982), p.468.
32. *A Man Called Mo*, p.112.
33. Ibid., pp.2, 5, 11. Cf. Peter Davison, *Songs of the British Music Hall* (OAK, New York, 1971),p.66.
34. *A Man Called Mo*, pp.5, 61–2, 88, 105–6, 114.
35. Ibid., pp.11, 20, 35, 76. Cf. Sara Maitland, *Vesta Tilley* (Virago, London, 1986), pp.114–15.
36. *A Man Called Mo*, pp.76–7, 59.
37. Ibid., pp.43, 103.
38. Ibid., pp.4, 85–6, 128, 156.
39. Ibid., pp.85–6, 105, 122.
40. Ibid., pp.55, 61, 83–4, 99, 103, 107, 118, 123, 127, 139, 151.
41. Ibid., pp.147, 160; Nancye Bridges, *Wonderful Wireless*, p.87.
42. Cf. Graeme Turner, 'Transgressive TV: From *In Melbourne Tonight* to *Perfect Match*', in John Tulloch and Graeme Turner (eds), *Australian Television* (Allen and Unwin, Sydney, 1989).
43. Cf. John Docker, 'In Defence of Popular TV: Carnivalesque v. Left Pessimism', *Continuum*, vol.1, no.2, 1988, p.92.
44. Cf. Mary Klages, 'What to Do with Helen Keller Jokes: A Feminist Act', in Regina Barreca (ed.), *New Perspectives on Women and Comedy* (Gordon and Breach, Philadelphia, 1992).
45. I have analysed *Hey Hey It's Saturday* in these terms – see John Docker 'In Defence of Popular TV: Carnivalesque v. Left Pessimism', pp.91–3.
46. Susan Dermody and Elizabeth Jacka, *The Screening of Australia*, vol.2, *Anatomy of a National Cinema* (Currency Press, Sydney, 1988), p.62. See also John Tulloch, *Legends on the Screen. The Narrative Film in Australia 1919–1929* (Currency Press, Sydney, 1981); Graeme Turner, *National Fictions: Literature, Film and the Construction of Australian Narrative* (Allen and Unwin, Sydney, 1986); Kay Schaffer, *Women and the Bush: Forces of Desire in the Australian Cultural Tradition* (Cambridge University Press, Cambridge, 1988).
47. *The Ukulele Player Under the Red Lamp*, p.221.
48. *Mo's Memoirs*, p.64.
49. Ibid., p.83. Cf. *A Man Called Mo*, p.20.
50. For the urban preoccupations of vaudeville, see Richard Waterhouse, 'Minstrel Show and Vaudeville House: The Australian Popular Stage, 1838–1914', *Australian Historical Studies*, no. 93, 1989, pp.366–85.
51. Cf. John Docker, *Dilemmas of Identity: The Desire for the Other in Colonial and Post Colonial Cultural History*, Working Papers in Australian Studies, Sir Robert Menzies Centre for Australian Studies, University of London, 1992. See also John Docker, 'The Feminist Legend: A new historicism?' in Susan Magarey, Sue Rowley and Susan Sheridan (eds), *Debutante Nation: Feminism Contests the 1890s* (Allen and Unwin, Sydney, 1993).
52. Raymond Williams, *Television: Technology and Cultural Form* (1974; Fontana, Glasgow, 1979), p.59.
53. For Ronnie Barker/Fletch, see Terry Lovell, 'A Genre of Social Disruption?', in Jim Cook (ed.), *Television Sitcom* (British Film Institute Dossier No.17, London, 1982). Lovell here relates comic reversal to carnival and its possibly vertiginous effects (p.29).
54. See, for but one example, Fiske, 'Everyday Quizzes, Everyday Life', in John Tulloch and Graeme Turner (eds), *Australian Television*, p.85.
55. Macdonald, *The Ukulele Player Under the Red Lamp*, p.223, mentions Kenneth Slessor, Cyril Pearl, King Watson (the editor of the *Daily Telegraph*), and Edgar Holt (editor of *Smith's Weekly*).
56. *A Man Called Mo*, pp.133–5, 147.
57. Welsford, *The Fool*, pp.29–52.
58. Ibid., pp.300–2.
59. Ibid., p.315.
60. Ibid. pp.300–2.

Chapter 16
Fool, Trickster, Social Explorer: The Detective

1. Apuleius, *The Golden Ass* (Penguin, Harmondsworth, 1980), p.180.
2. Raymond Chandler, *Farewell, My Lovely* (1940; Penguin, Harmondsworth, 1984), p.39.
3. Jerry Palmer, *Thrillers* (Edward Arnold, London, 1978), p.144; Stephen Knight, *Form and Ideology in Crime Fiction* (Macmillan, London, 1980), introduction.
4. Cf. Stephen Knight, 'Radical Thrillers', *Leftwright Intervention*, 1986, and Bronwyn Levy, 'The Victim Fights Back: Women, Politics, Fiction, Crime', *Hecate*, vol.9, 1983, p.179.
5. *Form and Ideology in Crime Fiction*, p.5.
6. Cf. Ann Curthoys and John Docker, 'In Praise of *Prisoner*', in John Tulloch and Graeme Turner (eds), *Australian Television* (Allen and Unwin, Sydney, 1989).
7. Mikhail Bakhtin, *The Dialogic Imagination* (University of Texas Press, Austin, 1981), pp.122–9.
8. Ibid., pp.158–65.
9. Ibid., pp.152–4.
10. Ibid., pp.106–7, 111–21.
11. Peter Keating (ed.), *Into Unknown England 1866–1913: Selections from the Social Explorers* (Manchester University Press, Manchester, 1976). See also Graeme Davison and David Dunstan, '"This Moral Pandemonium": images of low life', in Graeme Davison, David Dunstan and Chris McConville (eds), *The Outcasts of Melbourne* (Allen and Unwin, Sydney, 1985).
12. Greenwood, 'A Night in a Workhouse', in *Into Unknown England*, p.38.
13. Jack London, *The People of the Abyss* (1903; The Journeyman Press, London, 1978), pp.121, 43, 92, 94.
14. Ibid., pp.120–2, 94, and Introduction by Jack Lindsay, p.4. Cf. John Docker, *The Nervous Nineties* (Oxford University Press, Melbourne, 1991), pp.159–62.
15. Peter Keating, *The Working Classes in Victorian Fiction* (Routledge and Kegan Paul, London, 1971), chapter 1. Egan's *Life in London* was also extremely influential on the English and colonial stage, as Richard Fotheringham points out in *Sport in Australian Drama* (Cambridge University Press, Cambridge, 1992).
16. Keating, *The Working Classes in Victorian Fiction*, p.14; Robert L. Herbert, *Impressionism: Art, Leisure, and Parisian Society* (Yale University Press, New Haven, 1988), pp.33–43. Dana Brand, 'From the *flâneur* to the detective: interpreting the city of Poe', in Tony Bennett (ed.), *Popular Fiction: Technology, Ideology, Production, Reading* (Routledge, London, 1990), p.233, essentialises, finalises, reduces and manages the meaning of the *flâneur* as one who seeks to 'reduce the city to a set of manageable and predictable types' and is 'always looking for what he has already seen and defined'.
17. *Farewell, My Lovely*, p.31.
18. Peter Burke, *Popular Culture in Early Modern Europe* (Temple Smith, London, 1978), pp.165–7, 172.

Chapter 17
Crime Fiction as Changing Genre

1. Mikhail Bakhtin, *Rabelais and His World* (Indiana University Press, Bloomington, 1984), pp.39–40.
2. Tony Hillerman, *Coyote Waits* (Sphere Books, London, 1991), pp.159–60.
3. *The Ghostway* (Sphere Books, London, 1989), p.13.
4. Tony Hillerman and Ernie Bulow, *Talking Mysteries* (University of New Mexico Press, Albuquerque, 1991), pp.83, 25 (in order of quotation).
5. Ibid., pp.27, 67.
6. Ibid., pp.14–15, 17, 43.

7. See Cassandra Pybus, 'Oyster Cove 1988', in Jenny Lee, Philip Mead and Gerald Murnane (eds), *The Temperament of Generations. Fifty Years of Writing in Meanjin* (Melbourne University Press, Melbourne, 1990).
8. See for example John Mulvaney, 'Reflections on the Murray Black Collection', *Australian Natural History*, vol.23, no.1, 1989; Colin Pardoe, 'Sharing the past: Aboriginal influence on archaeological practice, a case study from New South Wales', *Aboriginal History*, vol.14, part two, 1990; Des Griffin, 'Time to talk about human dignity', *Sydney Morning Herald*, 5 May 1990.
9. *Talking Mysteries*, pp.75–7, 62–3.
10. Cf. ibid., p.79.
11. *The Ghostway*, p.19.
12. Cf. *Talking Mysteries*, pp.42, 54, 82–3.
13. Ibid., pp.74–5.

Chapter 18
Melodrama, Farce, Soap Opera

1. Much of this chapter draws on my 'In defence of melodrama: towards a libertarian aesthetic', *Australasian Drama Studies* 9, 1986, pp.63–81, and 'In Defence of Popular TV: Carnivalesque v. Left Pessimism', *Continuum*, vol.1, no.2, 1988, pp.86–8.
2. Julian Symons, introduction to Wilkie Collins, *The Woman in White* (Penguin, Harmondsworth, 1983), p.16; Arthur Conan Doyle, *The Celebrated Cases of Sherlock Holmes* (Octopus Books, London, 1985), p.556.
3. Andreas Huyssen, 'Mass Culture as Woman: Modernism's Other', in Tania Modleski (ed.), *Studies in Entertainment: Critical Approaches to Mass Culture* (Indiana University Press, Bloomington, 1986).
4. On the neoclassical hierarchy of genres, see Ian Watt, *The Rise of the Novel: Studies in Defoe, Richardson and Fielding* (Penguin, Harmondsworth, 1968), pp.81–2.
5. Peter Brooks, *The Melodramatic Imagination: Balzac, Henry James, Melodrama, and the Mode of Excess* (Yale University Press, New Haven, 1976), pp.ix, 22, 81, 92, 198.
6. Ibid., pp.65, 82.
7. Ibid., pp.64–6, 83–4.
8. Ibid., pp.x, 15, 43–4, 50, 64, 75, 84–6, 89–90.
9. Ibid., pp.48–9.
10. Ibid., pp.48, 63, 67, 79–80.
11. Ibid., pp.29–33, 201.
12. Ibid., pp.4, 20, 34–6, 42, 67.
13. Eric Bentley, *The Life of Drama* (Methuen, London, 1969), pp.216–17.
14. *The Melodramatic Imagination*, pp.41–2.
15. Ibid., pp.4, 35, 54.
16. Ibid., pp.28, 33, 48, 50.
17. Ibid., pp.198–200.
18. Ibid., pp.15, 44, 87–8.
19. Ibid., pp.12, 15, 55, 83.
20. Michael Booth, *English Melodrama* (Herbert Jenkins, London, 1965), writes that the Surrey Theatre was the headquarters of nautical melodrama, and drew a considerable portion of its patrons from sailors, Thames watermen, shipwrights, dock workers, and all those who worked and lived near the river or sailed on it to the open sea (pp.102–3). Such people, in Brooks' view, constitute the mob.
21. *The Melodramatic Imagination*, pp.xii, xiv, 12, 88–9.
22. Ibid., pp.85–6.
23. *English Melodrama*, p.35.
24. Michael Booth, 'Early Victorian Farce: Dionysius Domesticated', in Kenneth Richards and Peter Thomson (eds), *Nineteenth-Century British Theatre* (Methuen, London, 1971), pp.95–103, and Booth (ed.), *The Magistrate and Other Nineteenth-Century Plays* (Oxford University Press, London, 1974), introduction.

25. David Wiles, *Shakespeare's Clown: Actor and Text in the Elizabethan Playhouse* (Cambridge University Press, Cambridge, 1987).
26. Tony Davies, 'Transports of Pleasure: Fiction and its Audiences in the Later Nineteenth Century', in Tony Bennett et al., *Formations of Pleasure* (Routledge and Kegan Paul, London, 1983); Margaret Dalziel, *Popular Fiction 100 Years Ago* (Cohen and West, London, 1957); Julian Symons, introduction to *The Woman in White*, p.15.
27. Tania Modleski, *Loving with a Vengeance* (Methuen, New York, 1984).
28. Booth, *The Magistrate and Other Nineteenth-Century Plays*, introduction.
29. Mikhail Bakhtin, *Rabelais and His World* (Indiana University Press, Bloomington, 1984), p.251.

Chapter 19
Melodrama in Action: *Prisoner*, or *Cell Block H*

1. The following is based on Ann Curthoys and John Docker, 'In Praise of *Prisoner*', in John Tulloch and Graeme Turner (eds), *Australian Television: Programs, Pleasures and Politics* (Allen and Unwin, Sydney, 1989).
2. Albert Moran, *Images and Industry: Television Drama Production* (Currency, Sydney, 1985), p.153; *TV Week*, 24 February 1979, p.8; Albert Moran, *Making a TV Series: The Bellamy Project* (Currency, Sydney, 1982), pp.23–4; Dorothy Hobson, *Crossroads: The Drama of a Soap Opera* (Methuen, London, 1982), p.39.
3. *Womanspeak*, vol.4, no.5, June–July 1979, p.24.
4. *TV Week*, 24 February 1979, p.8.
5. Interview with Ian Holmes, *Cinema Papers*, no.24, December-January 1979–80, pp.613–15.
6. Sandra Willson, 'Prison, Prisoners and the Community', in S.K. Mukherjee and J. Scutt (eds), *Women and Crime* (Allen and Unwin, Sydney, 1981), pp.196, 199–200.
7. *TV Week*, 17 March 1979.
8. Mikhail Bakhtin, *The Dialogic Imagination* (University of Texas Press, Austin, 1981), 'Forms of Time and of the Chronotope in the Novel', pp.111–29.
9. Natalie Davis, *Society and Culture in Early Modern France* (Stanford University Press, Stanford, 1975); Peter Stallybrass, ' "Drunk with the cup of liberty": Robin Hood, the carnivalesque, and the rhetoric of violence in Early Modern England', *Semiotica*, vol.54 – 1/2, 1985, pp.113–45; Ian Donaldson, *The World Upside-Down* (Oxford University Press, Oxford, 1970).
10. See Robin Walker, 'Bushranging in Fact and Legend', *Historical Studies*, no.42, April 1964, pp. 206–210.
11. For sympathy for escapees, as in the famous Simmonds and Newcombe case, see Les Newcombe, *Inside Out* (Angus and Robertson, Sydney, 1979), and Jan Simmonds, *For Simmo* (Cassell, Melbourne, 1979).
12. Cf. Elizabeth Windschuttle, 'Women, Crime and Punishment', in Mukherjee and Scutt, *Women and Crime*, pp.31–50.
13. Anne Summers, *Damned Whores and God's Police* (Penguin, Ringwood, 1975).
14. *TV Week*, 9 May 1981. This performance resulted in a one-hour special entitled '*Prisoner* in Concert', shown on 7 May 1981 at 7.30 pm in Melbourne.
15. Hobson, *Crossroads*, p.36.
16. Quoted in *TV Week*, 14 June 1980.
17. *TV Week*, 3 March, 7 April 1979, 14 June 1980; *Sydney Morning Herald* TV and Radio Guide, 30 May and 6 June 1983.
18. Sandra Hall, *Turning On, Turning Off: Australian Television in the Eighties* (Cassell, Melbourne, 1981), p.41.
19. See Michael Poole, 'The State of TV Criticism', *The Listener*, 22 March 1984, on the tone that from early on dominated British TV reviewing: 'playful, top-heavy with "personality", aggressively non-specialist. Clive James inherited this tone and became its most accomplished exponent . . . Here is a man who knows full well that his real

subject is not television but himself.' See also John Docker, 'The Culture Police: TV Criticism in Australia', *Hermes* (Sydney University), 1987.

20. Hall, *Turning On, Turning Off*, p.42.
21. Lesley Stern, 'The Australian Cereal: Home Grown Television', in Susan Dermody, John Docker, and Drusilla Modjeska (eds), *Nellie Melba, Ginger Meggs and Friends* (Kibble Books, Melbourne, 1982). Stern's argument largely concerns the early *Prisoner*. See also Diane Powell, 'Soap', *Third Degree*, no.1, 1985 (Faculty of Humanities and Social Sciences, New South Wales Institute of Technology), drawing on the work of Tania Modleski.
22. Cf. John Docker, 'Unprecedented in history: drama and the dramatic in television', *Australasian Drama Studies*, vol.1, no.2, 1983, p.59.
23. Christine Curry and Christine O'Sullivan, *Teaching Television in Secondary Schools* (New South Wales Institute of Technology Media Papers, no.9, 1980).
24. Claire Thomas, 'Girls and Counter-School Culture', in David McCallum and Uldis Ozolins (eds), *Melbourne Working Papers 1980* (Department of Education, University of Melbourne, 1980), p.143. See also Patricia Palmer, *The Lively Audience: A Study of Children Around the TV Set* (Allen and Unwin, Sydney, 1986), and *Girls and Television* (New South Wales Ministry of Education, Sydney, 1986).

Conclusion
Carnival and Contemporary Popular Culture

1. J.W. Goethe, *Italian Journey* (Penguin, Harmondsworth, 1982), p.470.
2. *Italian Journey*, pp.446, 450–1, 469; Mikhail Bakhtin, *Rabelais and His World* (Indiana University Press, Bloomington, 1984), p.7; also p.249.
3. Peter Burke, *Popular Culture in Early Modern Europe* (Temple Smith, London, 1978), p.29.
4. Ibid., pp.119–20, 253; David Wiles, *Shakespeare's Clown: Actor and Text in the Elizabethan Playhouse* (Cambridge University Press, Cambridge, 1987); Bakhtin, *Rabelais and His World*, pp.181–5.
5. *TV Week*, 11 July 1992, p.52.
6. *Popular Culture in Early Modern Europe*, p.115.
7. Cf. John Docker, 'Popular Culture versus the State: An Argument against Australian Content Regulations for Television', *Media Information Australia*, no.59, 1991, pp.23–4.
8. David Kunzle, 'World Upside Down: The Iconography of a European Broadsheet Type', in Barbara A. Babcock (ed.), *The Reversible World. Symbolic Inversion in Art and Society* (Cornell University Press, Ithaca, 1978).
9. Cf. John Docker, 'Give them Facts – The Modern Gradgrinds', *Media Information Australia* 30, 1983, pp.6–7.
10. Kunzle, 'World Upside Down', p.42.
11. Shelah Young, 'Feminism and the Politics of Power. Whose Gaze is it Anyway?', in Lorraine Gamman and Margaret Marshmen (eds), *The Female Gaze* (The Women's Press, London, 1988).
12. Cf. Vron Ware, *Beyond the Pale: White Women, Racism and History* (Verso, London, 1992).
13. Mikhail Bakhtin, *Rabelais and His World*, p.235.
14. Cf. John Docker, 'In Defence of Popular TV: Carnivalesque v. Left Pessimism', *Continuum*, vol.1, no.2, 1988, pp.89–91.
15. Cf. Jan Bruck and John Docker, 'Puritanic Rationalism: John Berger's *Ways of Seeing* and Media and Culture Studies', *Theory Culture and Society*, vol.8, no.4, 1991, p.95.
16. Peter Stallybrass and Allon White, *The Politics and Poetics of Transgression* (Methuen, London, 1986). See also John Docker, 'In Defence of Popular TV: Carnivalesque v. Left Pessimism', pp.97–8 and, with Jan Bruck, 'Puritanic Rationalism: John Berger's *Ways of Seeing* and Media and Culture Studies', pp.87–9.

17. E.J. Clery, 'Women, Publicity and the Coffee-House Myth', *Women: A Cultural Review*, vol.2, no.2, 1991.
18. Cf. John Docker, 'Unprecedented in history: drama and the dramatic in television', *Australasian Drama Studies*, vol.1, no.2, 1983, pp.59–60.
19. Cf. John Docker, 'Popular Culture versus the State: An Argument against Australian Content Regulations for Television'.
20. Cf. Jan Bruck and John Docker, 'Puritanic Rationalism: John Berger's *Ways of Seeing* and Media and Culture Studies', p.95.

Index